The Turkish Language Explained for English Speakers

A Treatise on the Turkish Language and its Grammar for English Speakers.

John Guise

One of the problems when learning Turkish, especially when reading, is that only the root words are found in dictionaries. So the student has to learn the meanings of the suffices and their extended forms to be able to translate anything. This is far more difficult in speech, both in listening and conversing, and it is why learning Turkish to an acceptable level is difficult for English Speakers. However, practice makes perfect and this is the reason that Turkish grammar has to be learned in the first place. Without any knowledge of it them we are defeated from the start. Reading and analysing Turkish text is a must in the learning process. In the following chapters we show examples of the suffices you may come across in reading; they have to learned in order for ultimate success. Be patient, eventually the "light-bulb" will switch on.....

- *Manisa Turkish.*

Manisa Turkish Website
http://www.turkishlanguage.co.uk *Hosted in NZ*

Printed by CreateSpace, An Amazon.com Company
Available from Amazon.com and other book stores

DEDICATION

Thanks to the helpers along my own learning curve...
I would like to thank some of the many people who have made suggestions, corrections and other contribution to these notes over the last 30 years.

Especially my friends Ergun and Jale Kirkağaçlı, Nejati and Ayşe Sarıkut, the Biçer Family of Manisa and my old friend and colleague Ergun Karaca, who has now sadly left us.

Finally I thank my dear wife, Dorothy, for her help and support in this venture.

John Guise
Kawerau, New Zealand March 2012

ACKNOWLEDGMENTS

Along the way there have been many other contributors and I thank them all:

Bahaddin Çankut, Oytun Arslan, Uğur Görgülü, John Rees, Jim Masters, Kim Sanders, Andrew Wroblewski, Princeton University, USA, Ulas Kayusu, Emrah Ayar, Nurcan Akaltun Çiftçi, Gülçin K., Dan Kneezel, Necati Türe, akyaka.org, Carl Boswell, A.E.R.Taylor, wikipedia.com, Onur Üstünel, Ebru Salıç, K. Murat Aras, audioenglish.net, Fırat Özgül, Stan Sutherland, Tuğba Demireli, Kadir Demirel, Nilda Ginn, Özer Kaan, Kıvılcım Günbattı, Alex Taurus, Dicle Düzgün, Ergin Asyalı, Umut Odabaşı, Nicholas Ragheb, Volker Bodegom, and many others.

And the book which I originally learned from many years ago, *"Colloquial Turkish"* by Yusuf Mardin which was published in 1976 by RKP.

Cover Picure: *Islamic Tiles*
Dick Osseman http://www.pbase.com/dosseman/

INTRODUCTION

This Treatise on the Turkish Language and its Grammar explains and answers some of the difficulties that the learner of Turkish may encounter along their way. This book focuses on understanding Turkish grammar and logic. Those who are interested in the whys and wherefores of Turkish will find amongst these pages the key to their particular problem of Turkish grammar and syntax. The book covers the basics of Turkish and further expands knowledge and understanding of Turkish by using many examples with explanations. It does not contain any practice exercises or sound files as many of these type of basic Turkish grammar lessons can be found in other text books or on the world wide web.

It is a book that will be used over the whole of the learning process from basic beginner through to intermediate and advanced stages of learning.

The contents of the 45 chapters range over:

Turkish Basic Grammar: Alphabet, Vowel Harmony, Agglutination, Consonant Mutation, Lack of Gender.

Intermediate: Nouns and Pronouns, Adjectives, Verbs and Tenses, Possessive Relationship and Possession.

Advanced: Verb Moods, Participles, Clauses, Spatials and Spatial Relationships, Word Formation in Turkish

Conversational Items: Time, Seasons, Numbers, Colours, Saying "Thank you", About "*buyurun*", Expressing need, Daily Interjections, Modes of Address, Turkish Sign Language, How to say "too much, too many", Daily Talk, Common Door Signs.

Glossaries: List of Daily Locutions, Daily Word List, Irregular Tense List, Turkish Single Syllable Verb List, Intensified Adjectives List.

Full Conjugation: of the verb **etmek** *to do, perform*.

****

A Nutshell Overview Turkish

In Turkish words are changed by suffixing other words on to them. These other little important words show motion towards, location and motion from. These added words change their spelling according to set rules and they must follow the same vowel pattern (Vowel Harmony) as the word they are being affixed to. Sometimes they also have a consonant change for ease of pronunciation. Thus little words (suffixes) added to the stem of a verb may indicate its positive or negative form. Suffixes are then added for tense and person.

Further meaning to verbs such as *may, might, can, can't* are also supplied by a suffix to the original verb, thus producing a new word.

Nouns are also suffixed with possessor and the motion or location words are then added. There is no word for *"the"* (the Definite Article) and also there is no gender forms (no "le" or "la" as in French).

Adjectives (describing words) precede their noun as in English and always remain in their basic form. There being a lack of gender, thus no agreement is required.

The sentence form is SOV Subject, Object, Verb.

****

Table of Contents

7 TURKISH NOUNS   **74**

8 TURKISH ADJECTIVES   **86**

9 PERSONAL PRONOUNS   **103**

10 POSSESSIVE ADJECTIVES   **114**

11 THE POSSESSIVE RELATIONSHIP   **121**

12 POSSESSIVE CONSTUCTIONS   **127**

13 POSSESSION VAR AND YOK   **130**

39 TIME, SEASONS , NUMBERS **380**

43 THE GLOSSARIES   **427**

44 THE VERB "ETMEK" FULLY CONJUGATED   **455**

45 ABOUT THE AUTHOR AND THE BOOK   **473**

1 ABOUT THE TURKISH LANGUAGE.

The Turkish Language and its Grammar

"Turkish is a real pleasure; the ingenious grammar, the regularity, the transparency and intelligibility of the whole structure show the wonderful power of the human mind displaying itself in language."

The Origins of Turkish.

The Turkish Language originated in The Altay Mountain Range in Northern Siberia centuries ago. For this reason it is called an Altaic Language. As nomads expanded further into Asia Minor, they brought their language with them to Turkmenistan, Kazakhstan, Uzbekistan, Azerbaijan and other countries. Many of these languages are mutually intelligible although local usage and vocabulary, spelling and alphabet may differ. However they all exhibit the same grammatical structure of agglutination and vowel harmony.

Turkish is spoken from the borders of Greece to the hinterland of Western China. While the Ottoman Empire flourished Turkish was spoken from Vienna to Arabia, Egypt and Northern Africa. The Turkish vocabulary contains many words from Arabic, Persian and European languages. These imported words mostly follow the basic grammar and vowel harmony of native Turkish.

The Structure of Turkish.

Turkish is not a Classical Structured Language.
The Turkish grammar is not looked on by the Turks themselves as a Classical Structured Language. They have their own grammar rules which are not based on the Classical System as those in Latin or Greek. Most Turkish grammars for foreigners are written by linguists and grammarians, usually in consort with a Turkish

national, and they tend to use a classical language framework. Consequently these grammars are peppered with "classical terms" such as "*accusative, dative, locative and ablative*" together with such tenses and moods as "*aorist, subjunctive etc.*" This book uses Turkish grammar nomenclature and many classical grammar terms have been discarded.

Suffixation, Vowel Harmony and Consonant Mutation

So Turkish is characterized by agglutination (word suffixation) and has the concept of Vowel Harmony where the vowels of the suffixes must mirror the final vowel of the root word being suffixed. Also there is Consonant Mutation, where spelling changes are made to preserve phonetic euphony with actual pronunciation. English has some consonant change but not for the same reasons.

The Possessor and The Possessed

There is also a "Reflexive Genitive" in Turkish where both the "owner" and "owned" are suffixed. This construction does not occur in classical grammar so many teachers have resorted to using a Persian name "*izafet*". However in this book, Turkish grammar rules are followed and it is called the "Possessive Relationship".

Buffer Letters

The letter **-Y-** is considered as a consonant in Turkish, and it is widely used as a **buffer consonant** to keep vowels apart during word building. The alphabet consists of twenty-one consonants and eight vowels. It is phonetic as each letter retains its individual pronunciation at all times. There are no diphthongs, except in a few foreign loan words, and no letters "W", "X" or "Q".

Summary of the Structure of Turkish

Post positions are used instead of prepositions. Thus suffixes added to the stem of the verb may indicate positive or negative forms of the passive, reflexive, causative, potential, "wish/desire" moods plus further additions for tense and person.

Nouns are also suffixed with possessor ("*my, your, etc*") and condition ("*to, from, in, etc.*"). Both the subject definite article and grammatical gender are lacking. Adjectives precede their noun and do not have to agree in number or case.

The Turkish Alphabet.

The Turkish Alphabet was changed in 1928 from the Ottoman script to Latin characters soon after the Turkish Republic was declared.

Turkish does not as a rule allow two vowels to occur together. There are exceptions, but mostly in foreign imported words. As there are no diphthongs then whenever vowels do occur together they are each pronounced as a separate sound.

**A B C Ç D E F G Ğ H I İ J K
L M N O Ö P R S Ş T U Ü V Y Z**

Letter Pairs
There are six pairs of similar but different letters. Each letter of the pair has a different pronunciation.

C-Ç G-Ğ I-İ O-Ö S-Ş U-Ü

Turkish Vowel Pronunciation.

The Eight Vowels are divided into two groups for Vowel Harmony purposes. All pronunciation examples shown are given in British English.

The A-UnDotted Vowel Group.
A is as **u** in English lucky or mutter.
I (UnDotted I) is the **er** sound in *porter* or *water* without any **r** sound.
O is as the **o** sound in *lottery* or *bottom*.
U is as the **oo** sound in *loot* or *boot*.

The E-Dotted Vowel Group.
E is as **e** in *letter* or *set* or *met*.
İ (Dotted İ) is as **ee** in *meet* or **ea** in *seat*.
Ö is as **ir** in *bird* or *shirt* without any **r** sound.
Ü is as **ew** sound *few* or *stew*.

Turkish vowels are pronounced shorter than English vowels. This is one of the difficulties for Turkish learners as they are sometimes difficult to distinguish in normal paced conversation.

3

Turkish Consonant Pronunciation.

The Pronunciation of these Consonants differs from English
Pronunciation:
C is always a **j** sound as in *jam jar.*
Ç is the **ch** sound as in *church.*
G is always hard as in *gate.* It is never soft as in "**general.**"
Ğ (soft G) lengthens the preceding vowel. It has no sound and never
begins a word. The Turkish **soft ğ** can be likened to the **silent**
"**gh**" sound in the English words *weight, light, fought.*
H is always aspirated as in *Henry.* It is never silent as in "Heir".
R is always strongly rolled even on the end of words.
S is always hissed as in *safe.* It is never a **z** sound as in "the**se**" or
"those".
Ş is the **sh** sound as in *sharp* or *bash.*

Sound Names used in Wireless and Telegraphy.
A-Adana, B-Bolu, C-Ceyhan, Ç-Çanakkale, D-Denizli, E-Edirne, F-
Fatsa, G-Giresun, Ğ-Yumuşak ge, H-Hatay, I-Isparta, İ-İzmir, J-
Jandarma, K-Kars, L-Lüleburgaz, M-Muş, N-Niğde, O-Ordu, Ö-
Ödemiş, P-Polatlı, R-Rize, S-Sinop, Ş-Şirnak, T-Tokat, U-Uşak, Ü-
Ünye, V-Van, Y- Yozgat, Z-Zonguldak

The Features of Turkish Grammar.

The Adjectives
Adjectives and adjectival phrases precede their noun and do not
agree in number or gender. Some adjectives have an "intensified"
version. A list of these is shown in the Word Glossary (Chapter 43)

Vowel Harmony
Turkish has eight vowels consisting of four pairs:

A-E I-İ O-Ö U-Ü

having corresponding front/back, and rounded/un-rounded sounds.
This difference in pronunciation forms the basis for Vowel Harmony
Rules. According to these rules, vowels of suffixes must have the
same properties as the vowel in the last syllable of the word being
suffixed: either front/back or rounded/un-rounded.

4

Agglutination (addition of suffixes)

Agglutination in Turkish takes the form of suffixes attached to the end of nouns and verbs. These suffixes add to the word's meaning and/or mark its grammatical function. Words may have chains of different suffixes added to them.

The Absence of Gender

Turkish does not have a definite article, nor does it have gender pronouns. A single word signifies *he, she, it.*

Verbs

Always come at the end of the sentence. Sentence construction follows the subject-object-verb (SOV) pattern.

The Structure of Turkish

It differs in both grammatical structure and vocabulary from the Indo-European and Romance languages, English, Spanish, French etc. It is also a phonetic language as each letter always retains it own sound. In English the sound of the letters can change, as the letter *a* does in *"fat, fate, fare"* etc. In Turkish there is no such pronunciation change to letters of the alphabet.

Consonant Mutation

In certain circumstances changes are made to the spelling of consonants. If the pronunciation of a consonant changes the spelling also changes to reflect this.

Turkish Noun Conditions.

These six conditions are suffixed to the root word according to Vowel Harmony Rules. The vowels of the suffix match the final vowel of the root word.

Subject Condition (Nominative):

The root word which carries no suffix. The Subject Condition is regarded as already substantive in Turkish. There is no separate subject definite article.
el *hand, the hand.*

Ownership Condition (Genitive): -in/-ın/-un/-ün

This is the condition of "belonging to" meaning *of, 's* in English.
elin [el-in] *the hand's, of the hand.*

Specific Object Condition (Accusative): -i/-ı/-u/-ü
This is the direct object of a verb meaning specific *the* in English.
eli [el-i] *the hand (obj.)*

Movement Towards Condition (Dative): -a/-e
This is the condition of movement towards meaning *to, towards* in English.
ele [el-e] *to/towards the hand.*

Static Position Condition (Locative): -da/-de or -ta/-te according to Consonant Mutation rules.
This is the condition of place and position meaning *in, on, at* in English.
elde [el-de] *in/on/at the hand.*

Movement Away Condition (Ablative): -dan/-den or -tan/-ten according to Consonant Mutation rules.
This is the condition of movement away meaning *from, by, via* in English.
elden [el-den] *from/by/via the hand.*

Turkish Grammar is Regular.
Turkish Pronunciation is Phonetic, In Turkish each letter of the alphabet always retains its basic pronunciation. Turkish grammar is regular but differs in that it consists of post-positions which are suffixed directly to nouns or other parts of speech to modify their meaning. This use of suffixes is called **agglutination**, literally meaning "a gluing on". This is in contrast to English which uses individual prepositions for the same reasons.

Agglutination *(a sticking on to).*

The putting together of language particles where each expresses a single definite meaning, thus forming a new word.

In English there are many words which agglutinate (extend) to form other words. The word **argue** can be agglutinated to **argument** by sticking on a **-ment** suffix. This word can take additions of further suffixes: **-ative** giving **argumentative** and even further to **argumentatively** by adding a the **-ly** suffix. This then, is the way of Turkish.

*Another peculiarity of Turkish is **Vowel Harmony** where vowels can change in pronunciation and spelling to mirror the previous vowel in a word. Most suffixes follow the **Rule of Vowel Harmony**. There is an **A-UnDotted Vowel Form A I O U** and an **E-Dotted Vowel Form E İ Ö Ü** for the each suffix.*

Even the little words like *in, from, at* are suffixed to their noun, thus producing an extended word. As examples, adding the suffix **-de** *in, on, at* and the suffix **-dan** *from*

ev *house*
evde [ev-de] *in the house.*
evden [ev-den] *from the house.*
These suffixes harmonize with the vowel in the word **ev**.

Similarly adding suffix **-da** *in, on, at* and **-dan** *from*
oda *room*
odada [oda-da] *in the room*
odadan [oda-dan] *from the room*
These suffixes harmonize with the final vowel of the word **oda**.

Consonant Mutation.

Changes in pronunciation and spelling of consonants to preserve phonetics and euphony.

About Voicing of Consonants.
A Voiced Consonant is one where the voice box is used to produce the sound **d, b** are in this category. An Unvoiced Consonant is where the voice is silent and only air is expelled to produce the sound such as **t, p.**

The Main Consonants with Two Forms in Turkish.

There is some consonant mutation in English. The terminal -y of lady changes to an -ie- in its plural ladies, and the terminal -f of knife changes to a -v- in its plural knives. Turkish has consonant change, but it is on a larger scale than English.

The changes: *k to ğ* and *d to t.*

7

The main changes that occur in Turkish words is that a terminal -**k** may change to a -**ğ (soft g)** when a suffix with a vowel is added. The first letter -**d** of a suffix may change to a -**t** when the suffix is added to a word ending in an unvoiced consonant **ç f h k p s ş t**. There are also some other minor consonant changes.

Vowel Harmony Basics.

Vowel Harmony A grammatical rule where subsequent vowels in a word or suffix follow the vowel properties (rounded/un-rounded, front produced/back produced) of the previous vowel

The Eight Vowels of Turkish.
In Turkish the voice sounds are separated into two main groups, consonants and vowels. When there is no obstacle to a voice then the sound is called a vowel. There are eight vowels in Turkish: **a e ı i o ö u ü.**

The eight vowels are divided into two groups, the A-UnDotted Vowels and the E-Dotted vowels.

The four A-UnDotted Vowels **a ı o u.**
The four E-Dotted Vowels **e i ö ü.**

E-Dotted vowels are pronounced at the front of the mouth, as the French Language. The A-UnDotted vowels are pronounced at the back of the mouth more like English.

Vowel Classification.
Here is a description of how the Turkish vowels are classified by linguists. This book does not use this system, it is only added for completeness. This book divides the eight vowels into two groups only, the A-UnDotted Group and E-Dotted Group, to ease the explanation of Vowel Harmony rules.

(A) According to the position of tongue and exit.
Thick vowels: **a ı o u.**
Thin vowels: **e i ö ü.**

(B) According to the lips positioning.
Straight vowels: **a e ı i.**

8

Rounded vowels: **o ö u ü.**

(C) According to the mouth opening.
Wide Vowels: **a e o ö.**
Narrow vowels: **ı i u ü**.

In this book Turkish vowels are classified into two groups as follows:
The **E-Dotted Group** of four vowels are **e i ö ü.**
The **A-UnDotted Group** of four vowels are **a ı o u.**

The harmony lies in the fact that all Turkish words of Altaic Turkic Origin are pronounced either entirely containing A-UnDotted Vowels, as **kapılardan** [kapı-lar-dan] *from the doors* and **bulmacalarında** [bulmaca-ları-nda] *in their crosswords*, or entirely containing E-Dotted Vowels, as **evlerinden** [ev-leri-nden] *from their house* or **köylülerin** [köy-lü-ler-in] *of the villagers.*

Grammatical and verb suffixes also follow vowel harmony, being divided into two groups for A-UnDotted words and E-Dotted words. For example, the A-UnDotted plural suffix **-lar** would be added to **kapı** to form the word for *doors* **kapılar**, whereas the E-Dotted plural suffix **-ler** would be added to **köylü** to produce *villagers* **köylüler.**

Turkish has imported many words from French, such as **televizyon** *télévision* and **müzisyen** *musician*, **kuaför** *coiffure* which have been modified phonetically to the Turkish Alphabet and incorporated into the language. These are spelled according to Turkish phonetics and often have both A-UnDotted and E-Dotted vowels within one word which is unnatural for Turkish. Such is true for the numerous Turkish words of Arabic origin, such as **mektup** *letter* and **merhaba** *hello*, and of Persian origin as **hane** *office* where vowel harmony does not occur in the word itself. In these cases, consistent with the general rule for vowel harmony in Turkish, the final vowel of the word determines the vowel harmony for suffixation.

UnDotted Vowels follow each other.
Dotted Vowels follow each other.

Turkish Verbs.

There are no irregular verbs in Turkish. One single conjugation is used for all verbs. Turkish Verbs also obey Vowel Harmony rules when adding tense and person suffixes. All verbs belong to one of two groups determined by their infinitive forms; those ending in **-mak** (The A-UnDotted Vowel Group) and those ending in **-mek** (The E-Dotted Vowel Group). In consequence there is more than one form for the tense sign suffix. For illustration the Future Tense suffix may be **-acak** or **-ecek** to follow Vowel Harmony Rules. The suffixes for all **-mak** verbs have only A-UnDotted Back Vowels. **bakmak** *to look* is **bakacak** [bak-acak] *he will look.* Only E-Dotted Front Vowels are found in the suffixes of -**mek** verbs. **gelmek** *to come* is **gelecek** [gel-ecek] *He will come.*

Turkish Gender and Articles.

English uses the same Definite Article "THE" for both subjects and objects. "**THE dog** bit **THE man.**" Turkish does not have separate definite articles. This is a problem for English speakers when learning Turkish.

Turkish does not have a Subject Definite Article *"THE"*, also there is no gender distinction, so there is no *"le"* and *"la"* problems as in French. This borne out by the fact that Turkish only has one word for *he, she and it*, namely "**O".**

Turkish makes an object definitive by adding an object suffix which equates to the English Object Definite Article *"THE"*. This is the objective *" THE"* in Turkish. This is one of the difficulties for those learning Turkish as English does not distinguish between subject *"the"* and object *"the"* as it uses the definite article *"the"* for both.

An illustration of the Objective Definite Article   (accusative):
Fincan masada.*The cup is on the table.*
[The subject: *"The cup"* is already considered as a specific subject in Turkish.]
Masadaki fincanı bana verin. *Give me the cup which is on the table.* [object: *"The cup"*].   Here the object *the cup* **fincan** has been made definitive (specific) by the addition of the objective suffix **-ı** to produce **fincanı** [fincan-ı], the way of saying *"the cup"* as a specific object.

10

Turkish Adjectives

Turkish is a descriptive language, adjectives abound. If Turkish can make something into an adjective then it will do so.

Being an descriptive language basically the adjective or adjectival phrase always preceded its noun: **kara kedi** *a black cat* as in English. However Turkish makes great use of adjectival phrases and clauses to describes nouns, actions and thoughts.

In English:
The black cat with the long tail which is sitting on the mat looks hungry.
Using a reduced relative clause:
The long-tailed black cat sitting on the mat looks hungry.

The Turkish Way
Describes the cat not only as "black and long-tailed" but also "where and upon what it is sitting" together with any other attributes, such as "its long tail":
Minderin üstünde oturan uzun kuyruklu kara kedi aç görünüyor.
On the mat which is sitting long tailed black cat hungry looks.

In Turkish the subject and object are described adjectivally with regards to place and disposition. Once all the describing is done, the verb is placed last in the sentence.

Structure of Turkish Words.

In the structure of Turkish words a vowel always follows a consonant and a consonant always follows a vowel. There are no diphthongs (two vowels occurring together) in Turkish words, other than imported foreign exceptions. In order to preserve this rule certain consonants are inserted as "buffers" between vowels. These buffers are always **Y, N** or **S**. (**Y** is considered as a consonant in Turkish.)

The majority of Turkish Vowels are always pronounced quite short, there is no lengthening of vowels. For Turkish learners this sometimes makes understanding difficult as there is little and light stress in Turkish pronunciation.

Turkish Word Order.

Word order is regular, but differs from English.
Adjectival Descriptions of Subject.
The Subject.
Time Clauses.
Adjectival Descriptions of Object.
The Object.
The Verb. *The verb is always last in a sentence.*

Turkish punctuation normally puts a comma after the subject of a sentence. It is good practice to do this especially if the subject is extended by a long adjectival description.

An English Example:
The man with the fishing rods in his hands, (a long described subject) *will be* (the verb) *at your friend's 50th birthday party* (a long described object) *tomorrow night* (time phrase).

The Turkish Structure:
Ellerinde oltası olan adam, yarın gece arkadaşının 50'ci doğum günü partisinde bulunacak.
Hands-his-in-which-are fishing-rods-the-with man, (a described and suffixed subject) *tomorrow night* (time phrase) *friend-your-of 50th birthday party-his-at* (a described and suffixed object) *will be* (and at last, the verb).

The Turkish Language Summarized

• Turkish is characterized by vowel harmony, consonant mutation and agglutination.

• Post positions are used instead of prepositions. Thus suffixes added to the stem of the verb may indicate positive or negative forms of the passive, reflexive, causative, potential, subjunctive (Tur: "Wish/Desire") moods plus further additions for tense and person.

• • Nouns are also suffixed with possessor and aspect (movement toward, movement away suffixes etc.). Both the subject definite

article and grammatical gender are lacking.

- Adjectives precede their noun and do not have to agree in number or case. The sentence form is **S.O.V** Subject, Object Verb.

* You can easily spell the words phonetically.
* There are no irregular verbs.
* There is only one irregular noun. [**su** *water*].
* There is no gender: *He, she, it* are represented by one single pronoun namely **"o".**
* There is no distinction between adjectives and adverbs.
* You can convey the meaning without using verbs when you are referring to existence of something by using **var** *it exists* and **yok** *it does not exist.*

2 VOWEL HARMONY

The Eight Vowels of Turkish

There are eight vowels in Turkish which are divided into two groups as follows:
The A-UnDotted Vowels **A I O U.**
The E-Dotted Vowels **E İ Ö Ü.**

The Vowels A and E.

Forming the Plural.
Either the Plural Suffix **-ler** or **-lar** is chosen to mirror the final vowel of its noun. All other suffixes will follow these Vowel Harmony rules. To form the plural we have a choice to add either **-lar** or **-ler** to the word:

Plural of the A-UnDotted Vowel Group.

Add **-lar** to words whose final vowel is any of the **A-UnDotted Vowels.**

balta final vowel **-a** *axe*
baltalar [balta-lar] *axes*
kapı final vowel **-ı** *door*
kapılar [kapı-lar] *doors*
palto final vowel **-o** *overcoat*
paltolar [palto-lar] *overcoats*
boncuk final vowel **-u** *bead*
boncuklar [boncuk-lar] *beads*

The vowels in these Turkish words are all of the **A-UnDotted Group** so the added Plural suffix **-lar** must also contain an **A-UnDotted Vowel.**

Plural of the E-Dotted Vowel Group.

Add **-ler** to words whose final vowel is one of the **E-Dotted Vowels.**

ev final vowel **-e** *house*
evler [ev-ler] *houses*
kedi final vowel **-i** *cat*
kediler [kedi-ler] *cats*
göz final vowel **-ö** *eye*
gözler [göz-ler] *eyes*
ödül final vowel **-ü** *present (gift)*
ödüller [ödül-ler] *presents*

The vowels in these Turkish words are all of the **E-Dotted Group** so the added Plural suffix **-ler** must also contain an **E-Dotted Vowel.** This echoing of the final vowel by the suffix is called Vowel Harmony.

Some Exceptions In Formation of Words.

There are a very few exceptions to this rule where the suffix does not vowel harmonize:

saat *hour, clock*
saatler *hours, clocks*
harf *letter* (of alphabet)
harfler *letters*

To form the word **rol** *rôle* in Turkish the suffix **-ler** is added to form its plural **roller** *rôles*. This is contrary to the general rule. Normally -**lar** would be added to **rol**, as it contains the Undotted Vowel **O.**

Words like **rol** also constitute exceptions when other suffixes are attached :

Bu rolü almak istiyorum. [rol-ü NOT rol-u]
I want to take (on) the this rôle.

Bu rolden çok bıktım. [rol-den NOT rol-dan]
I am really fed up with this rôle. ["-den bıkmak" *to get fed up with*]

Bu rolde bir sürü aksaklık var. [rol-de NOT rol-da]
There is something wrong in this rôle.

Bu role hiç alışamadım. [rol-e NOT rol-a]

15

I could not get used to this rôle at all. ["-e alışmak" *to get used to*]

Some Other Exceptions.

Vaat *Promise*
Vaatler *Promises*
Vaadi *Promise* (obj.)
Vaadin *of the promise*
Vaade *to the promise*
Vaatten *from the promise*

Kalp *Heart*
Kalpler *Hearts*
Kalbi *Heart* (obj.)
Kalbin *of the heart*
Kalbe *to the heart*
Kalpten *from the heart*

Harf *Letter* (alpha.)
Harfler *Letters*
Harfi *Letter* (obj.)
Harfin *of the letter*
Harfe *to the letter*
Harften *from the letter*

There are imports from Arabic and other foreign languages which exhibit this irregularity.

Vowel Harmony of Suffixes

Words with their last vowel in the **A-UnDotted Group** take **-lar** as their plural. This rule applies for all suffixes which contain **-a.**

Those words with an **E-Dotted Group Vowel** take **-ler** as their plural. This rule applies for all suffixes which contain **-e.**

Common but important words in constant use: These little words *in, on, at, from, to, with, etc.* are suffixes in Turkish and are affixed to the word they modify. The Principle of Vowel Harmony must be taken into account.

16

The Static Position (Locative) Suffix -da/-de /-ta/-te *-in, on, at.*

If the word ends in an **Unvoiced Consonant [p ç t k f h s ş]** When adding a suffix beginning with a consonant then the suffix consonant **"-d"** changes to its Unvoiced Form **"-t"**. *See Chapter 3 Consonant Mutation*

This suffix shows concrete place (static location):

Odadayım. [oda-da-yım] *I am in the room.*
Ali bey, evdeymiş. [ev-de-ymiş] *Ali bey is at home.*

kedide [kedi-de] *on the cat*
kedilerde [kedi-ler-de] *on the cats*

girişte [giriş-te] *in/at the entrance*
girişlerde [giriş-ler-de] *in/at the entrances*

evde [ev-de] *at the house, at home*
evlerde [ev-ler-de] *at the houses*

köprüde [köprü-de] *on the bridge*
köprülerde [köprü-ler-de] *on the bridges*

adamda [adam-da] *on the man*
adamlarda [adam-lar-da] *on the men*

kapıda [kapı-da] *at the door*
kapılarda [kapı-lar-da] *at/by the doors*

çıkışta [çıkış-ta] *in/at the exit*
çıkışlarda [çıkış-lar-da] *in/at the exits*

odada [oda-da] *in the room*
odalarda [oda-lar-da] *in the rooms*

Two suffixes have been used, **-ler** and **-de** or **-lar** and **-da**. They are tagged together to make a single word in Turkish.

The suffix -dan/-den or -tan/-ten *from, by, via, through.*

If the word ends in an **Unvoiced Consonant [p ç t k f h s ş]** When

17

adding a suffix beginning with a consonant then the suffix consonant **"-d"** changes to its Unvoiced Form **"-t"**. *See Chapter 3 Consonant Mutation*

This is the Motion Away suffix:

kediden [kedi-den] *from the cat*
kedilerden [kediler-den] *from the cats*

girişten [giriş-ten] *from/via the entrance*
girişlerden [giriş-ler-den] *from/via the entrances*

evden [ev-den] *from home*
evlerden [evler-den] *from the houses*

köprüden [köprü-den] *from the bridge*
köprülerden [köprüler-den] *from the bridges*

adamdan [adam-dan] *from the man*
adamlardan [adamlar-dan] *from the men*

kapıdan [kapı-dan] *from the door*
kapılardan [kapılar-dan] *from the doors*

odadan [oda-dan] *from the room*
odalardan [odalar-dan] *from the rooms*

çıkıştan [çıkış-tan] *from/via the exit*
çıkışlardan [çıkış-lar-dan] *from/via the exits*

Two suffixes **-ler** and **-den** or **-lar** and **-dan** have been used and tagged together to make a single word in Turkish.

The suffix -(ya)/-(y)e *to, towards*

If the root word ends in a vowel then the buffer letter -y- is used to separate the suffix -e or -a

This is the Motion Towards suffix:

adama [adam-a] *to the man*
adamlara [adamlar-a] *to the men*

kediye [kedi-ye] *to the cat*
kedi *cat* ends in a vowel so "kedi-y-e" is used [kedi-e] is incorrect.
kedilere [kediler-e] *to the cats*

eve [ev-e] *to home*
evlere [evler-e] *to the houses*

kapıya [kapı-ya] *to the door*
kapı *door* ends in a vowel so "kapı-y-a" is used [kapı-a] is incorrect.
kapılara [kapılar-a] *to the doors*

**Some more words which end in vowels which show the buffer -y-
inserted.**

köprüye [köprü-ye] *to the bridge*
köprülere [köprü-ler-e] *to the bridges*

odaya [oda-ya] *to the room*
odalara [oda-lar-a] *to the rooms*

The Buffer Letter **-y-** is used when the word ends in a vowel.
Turkish does not like two vowels to be together.

The Vowels I, İ and U, Ü.

Explanation about Dotted and Undotted Vowels.

*The Front Produced (Dotted) Vowels are formed at the front of the
mouth similar to the French Language. The Back Produced
(Undotted) Vowels are produced nearer the throat as in English.*

The Four Forms of the Suffix -I-

There are two different forms of **I İ** and two different forms of **U
Ü** in Turkish.

(1) The Undotted Forms of **I** or **U** must follow the **A-UnDotted
group A I O U.**

(2) The Dotted Forms of **İ** or **Ü** must follow the **E-Dotted group E İ
Ö Ü.**

The Principle of Vowel Harmony states that a suffix containing the letter **a** can have two forms either **a** or **e**. The suffix **-den** *from* which is used with the E-Dotted vowels and **-dan**, which is used with the A-UnDotted vowels.

Suffixes which contain a (generic) letter **-i** can have four forms. These are **-i -ı -u -ü**. For example the suffix **-im** *my*. Its own vowel, basically the **-i-** changes to any of **-i -ı -u -ü** to mirror the last vowel of the word to which it is suffixed. Similarly all other suffixes with an internal **-i-** vowel will follow these Vowel Harmony Rules.

Some Examples.

ev *house*
evim [ev-im] *my house*
evlerim [ev-ler-im] *my houses*

raf *shelf*
rafın [raf-ın] *your shelf*
rafların [raf-lar-ın] *your shelves*

çit *hedge*
çiti [çit-i] *his hedge*
çitleri [çit-ler-i] *his hedges*

kız *girl/daughter*
kızım [kız-ım] *my girl*
kızlarım [kız-lar-ım] *my girls*

göz *eye*
gözüm [göz-üm] *my eye*
gözlerim [göz-ler-im] *my eyes*

yol *road*
yolunuz [yol-unuz] *your road*
yollarınız [yol-lar-ınız] *your roads*

gün *day*
günümüz [gün-ümüz] *our day*
günlerimiz [gün-ler-imiz] *our days*

okul *school*
okulları [okul-ları] *their school(s)*

okulları [okul-lar-ı] *his schools*

Choosing the correct vowel i ı u ü.

The suffix form **-im** follows words whose last vowel is **e** or **-i**:
Harmonizing with final E-Dotted Group Vowel **-e** in the root word:

bilet *ticket*
biletim [bilet-im] *my ticket*

Harmonising with final Dotted **-i** in the root word:

diş *tooth*
dişim [diş-im] *my tooth*
dişlerim [dişler-im] *my teeth*

The suffix **-im** must contain a dotted **-i-** as it follows a vowel from the *E-Dotted Group*. This is also true of the plural form **-ler.**

The suffix **-ım** follows words whose last vowel is **-a** or **-ı**
Harmonizing with final A-Undotted Group Vowel **-a** in the root word:

at *horse*
atım [at-ım] *my horse*
atlarım [atlar-ım] *my horses*

Harmonizing with final Undotted **-ı** in the root word:

kız *girl*
kızım [kız-ım] *my girl*
kızlarım [kızlar-ım] *my girls*

The suffix **-ım** must contain an undotted **-ı-** as it follows a vowel from the *A-dotted Group*. This is also true of the plural form **-lar.**

Suffix **-üm** follows words whose last vowel is **-ö** or **-ü**
Harmonizing with final Dotted **-ö** in the root word:
göz *eye*
gözüm [göz-üm] *my eye*
gözlerim [gözler-im] *my eyes*

Harmonizing with final Dotted **-ü** in the root word:

gül *rose*
gülüm [gül-üm] *my rose*
güllerim [güller-im] *my roses*

The plurals **gözlerim** and **güllerim** take the -im suffix (not the -üm suffix as in the singular) as they immediately follow the final vowel -e of the plural -ler.

Suffix-**um** follows words whose last vowel is -o or -u
Harmonizing with final Undotted -o in the root word:

jeton *token, jeton*
jetonum [jeton-um] *my token, my jeton*
jetonlarım [jetonlar-ım] *my tokens, my jetons*

Harmonizing with final Undotted -u in the root word:

oyun *game*
oyunum [oyun-um] *my game*
oyunlarım [oyunlar-ım] *my games*

The plurals **jetonlarım** and **oyunlarım** take the -ım suffix (not the -um suffix as in the singular) as they immediately follow the final vowel -a of the plural -lar.

The Complete Rules of Vowel Harmony.

UnDotted A I O U are followed by A-UnDotted suffix.
Dotted E İ Ö Ü are followed by E-Dotted suffix.

Undotted A or I are followed by I-UnDotted suffix.
Dotted E or İ are followed by İ-Dotted suffix.

Undotted O or U are followed by U-UnDotted suffix.
Dotted Ö or Ü are followed by Ü-Dotted suffix.

3   CONSONANT MUTATION

Variation of Consonants.

Changes in Spelling to reflect Changes in Pronunciation.

In Turkish the spelling of the words is changed when the pronunciation changes. Generally this does not happen in English. When the pronunciation changes the spelling does not usually change. In fact the spelling is often changed when the pronunciation is the same so that we can recognize the correct meaning.

A number of words can easily show this: *"meet vs meat, feet vs feat, right vs write, main vs mane, sea vs see"*, and many more. If English were written phonetically, the word "does" would be spelt "duz". Turkish however, being a phonetically written language will make changes in spelling due to pronunciation changes. This is for ease of speaking and is concerned with consonants which have voiced and unvoiced equivalents.

About Voicing of Consonants.

A voiced consonant is one where the voice is used to produce the sound, as Letter D. An unvoiced consonant is where the voice is silent and only air is expelled to produce the sound, as the corresponding (unvoiced) Letter T.

In Turkish when a word ends in a consonant it is usually the Un-Voiced Form. The word for *letter* is **mektup**, but *my letter* is **mektubum**. The terminal -**p** has changed to -**b**- when it appears between two vowels. This is simply because it is easier to pronounce in its Voiced form "b". In Turkish the spelling must reflect this change for the rules of phonetics to operate.

Unvoiced and Voiced Equivalents.
Unvoiced **p** equivalent to Voiced **b.**
Unvoiced **ç** equivalent to Voiced **c.**
Unvoiced **t** equivalent to Voiced **d.**

23

Unvoiced **k** equivalent to Voiced **ğ**.
Unvoiced **f** no equivalent.
Unvoiced **s** no equivalent.
Unvoiced **ş** no equivalent.
Unvoiced **h** no equivalent.
The last four **f, s, ş, h** do not have a voiced form, but they do affect the added suffix as they are considered as unvoiced consonants:

raf *shelf*
raftan *from the shelf* [not "rafdan"]

nefis *delicious*
nefistir *it is (certainly) delicious* [not "nefisdir"]

sabah *morning*
sabahtan *from morning* [not "sabahdan"]

güneş *sun*
güneşten *from the sun* [not "güneşden"]

Words ending in an unvoiced consonant change to the voiced equivalent when a vowel is added:

bilek *wrist*
bileği *his wrist*

kitap *book*
kitaba *to the book*

kağıt *paper*
kağıdın *your paper*

Examples of Changes.

Words ending in unvoiced **-K** change to voiced **-Ğ-** when a suffixed vowel is added:

köpek *dog*
köpeğim [köpek + im] *my dog*

bacak *leg*
bacağın [bacak + ım] *your leg*

24

topuk *ankle*
topuğu [topuk + u] *his ankle*

bilek *wrist*
bileğimiz *our wrists*

gözlük *spectacles*
gözlüğünüz *your spectacles*

durak *bus stop*
durağa *to the bus stop*

görecek *will see*
göreceğim *I shall see*

yaptık *we did*
yaptığımız *that which we did*

bardak *glass (tumbler)*
bardağı *his glass*

The consonant change from unvoiced **-k** to voiced **-ğ-** when adding suffixes is the most widespread mainly because so many Turkish words end in a terminal **-k.**

A Special Case Exception.

Examples where terminal **-nk** changes to **-ng** when adding a vowel. If the word ends in **-nk** the terminal **-k** changes to a voiced **-g** as it is totally impossible to utter the letter cluster **-nğ** plus an added vowel.

denk *bale, equation*
dengim *my bale*

ahenk *harmony, accord*
ahengi *its harmony*

kepenk *shutter*
kepenginiz *your shutter*

renk *color*
rengimiz *our colour*

Other Consonant Changes.

25

Some of the other unvoiced consonants which change to their voiced form in similar fashion are as follows :

-p changes to -b in front of suffixed vowels.
-ç changes to -c in front of suffixed vowels.
-t changes to -d in front of suffixed vowels, mainly in verb and tense suffixes.

kitap *book*
kitabın *your book*

öğüt *advice*
öğüdüm *my advice*

tat *taste*
tadı *its taste*

ilaç *medicine*
ilacı *his medicine*

ağaç *tree*
ağacın *the tree's*

Consonants Single Syllable Word Roots.

The general rule is that single syllable words usually do not change their final vowel to be voiced . There are a few exceptions as shown below.

Unvoiced Roots Single Syllable Words.

ak *egg white*
akı *the egg white/his egg white*

at *horse*
atı *the horse/his horse*

ek *addition*
eki *the addition/its addition*

et *meat*
eti *the meat/his, her, its meat*

göç *migration*
göçü *the migration*

ip *rope*
ipi *the rope*

kaç? *how many?*
kaçıncı? *which one?*

kök *root*
kökü *the root/its root*

ok *arrow*
oku *the arrow/his arrow*

ot *grass*
otu *the grass/its grass*

saç *hair*
saçı *the hair/his, her hair*

sap *handle*
sapı *the handle/its handle*

suç *fault*
suçu *the fault/his, her, its fault*

süt *milk*
sütü *the milk/his, her its milk*

üç *three*
üçü *the three/trio*

Exceptions to the rule.

There are some exceptions to this rule where a single syllable word does take on its voiced form when adding a vowel suffix:

Voiced Roots (the exceptions) Single Syllable Words.

but *thigh*
budu *the thigh/his, her, its thigh*

dip *bottom/base*

27

dibi *the bottom/the base/its bottom*

çok *a lot/much/very*
çoğu *the lot/his, her, its lot*

gök *sky*
göğü *the sky/its sky*

kap *vessel* (utensil)
kabı *the vessel/his vessel*

kurt *worm/wolf*
kurdu *the worm, the wolf/his wolf*

uç *point/tip/end*
ucu *the point/his, her, its point*

yok *none*
yoğu *nıl*

yurt *tent, village*
yurdu *the tent, the village*

Terminal Consonant Rules.

Words cannot end with the **voiced** consonants **b c d g**. Words must end in the equivalent **unvoiced** forms **p ç t k** in order to finish the pronunciation without continuity thus helping the listener to determine word breaks in conversation.

An Actual Example.

This is a Public House sign in Altınkum:

SAHİL PUP

In the picture the English import of the word **Pub** (public house) has been changed into a Turkish version of the word **"Pup"** which ends in the equivalent unvoiced consonant **-p**. So **Sahil Pup** has been written for "Sahil Pub" *The Seaside Pub.*

Similarly the spelling **kebab** is wrong. **kebap** is correct.
The name **Mehmed** is wrong. **Mehmet** is correct.

There are a few words which do end in voiced consonants such
as **ad, od, sac.** This simply to make their meaning recognizable from
similar word that have a unvoiced consonant at the end. This little
group of words is an exception to the general rule that words always
end in a unvoiced Consonant.

ad *name* and **at** *horse*
od *fire* and **ot** *grass*
sac *sheet iron* and **saç** *hair*

Proper Names:

Proper Names do not change in writing **Memed'in** *Mehmet's* is only
valid in spoken language. It should be written as **Mehmet'in** but
should be pronounced **Memedin**. Although the letter **-h-** is always
articulated and pronounced in Turkish (it being a phonetic language).
The name "Mehmet" is an exception it is always pronounced as
"Memed" through constant usage. Another example is **Burak'ın** (as
written) should be pronounced as **Burağın**

Suffix Mutation.

Mutation of Word ending in Unvoiced Consonants.

The suffix reverts to its unvoiced form when added to words ending
in an unvoiced consonant.

Suffixes change to agree with the word they are added to:

The suffix *in, on, at* **-de/-da** [voiced form] changes to **-te/-ta**
[unvoiced form].

ayak *foot*
ayakta *on the foot.*
(The suffix must agree with the word's terminal consonant.)

parmak *finger*
parmakta *on the finger*

29

sabah *morning*
sabahtı *it was morning*

The suffix *from* **-den/-dan** changes to **-ten/-tan.**

ağaç *tree*
ağaçtan *from the tree*

bilet *ticket*
biletten *from the ticket*

kitap *book*
kitapta *in the book* [not *kitap-da*]

otobüs *bus*
otobüstü *it was a bus* [not otobüs-dü]

dolmuş *dolmush* (small bus)
dolmuşta *in the dolmush* [not dolmuş-da]

ilaç *medicine*
ilaçta *in the medicine* [not ilaç-da]

sabah *morning*
sabahtan *from morning* [not sabah-dan]

kibrit *match*
kibritten *from the match* [not kibrit-den]

The last example **kibrit** preserves a double letter *-tt-* when adding the suffix **-ten** to produce **kibritten**. Turkish generally abhors two consonants arising together but here are two separate words *match* and *from* being joined together, so each word must retain its full form.

A Very few Exceptions:

There are a few words that historically end in a voiced consonant but for these words that do end in a voiced consonant the suffix retains its voiced form.

Mutation of words ending in Unvoiced Consonants:

Here is an example of the effect of adding a suffix which begins with a consonant.

kitaptı *it was a book*. The word ends in unvoiced **-p** thus kitap-**tı**. The suffix **-tı** takes it unvoiced form from the noun ending.

The same example when adding a Suffix which begins with a Vowel:

kitabınız *your book* suffix **-ınız** begins with a vowel so **kitap** becomes kitab**-ınız**.
kitabınızda *in your book*. Extended word ends in voiced **-z** thus kitabınız**-da**.

The plural -ler/-lar which ends in an voiced letter -r.

Adding suffixes terminal vowels and the Plural Suffix **-lar/-ler** which ends in voiced **-r**.

köpekten *from the dog*
köpeklerden *from the dogs*
köpeğinden (köpeğ-in-den) *from his dog*

ilaçta *in the medicine*
ilaçlarda *in the medicines*
ilacında (ilac-ın-da) *in his medicine*

otobüsten *from the bus*
otobüslerden (otobüs-ler-den) *from the buses*

sokaktan *from the street*
sokaklardan (sokak-lar-dan) *from the streets*

The examples above show where the voiced **-r** ending of the plural suffix **-ler/-lar** forces the subsequent suffix to take its voiced form.

Consonant Mutation Rules.

1. If the word ends in any of these **Unvoiced Consonants [p ç t k]** When adding a suffix beginning with a vowel then the last letter of the root word changes to its voiced form:

p > b   ç > c   t > d   k > ğ

kitap *book*
kitabı *his book*

kazanç *profit*
kazancı *his profit*

kilit *lock*
kilidi *his lock*

köpek *dog*
köpeğiniz *your dog*

2. If the word ends in an **Unvoiced Consonants [p ç t k f h s ş]**
When adding a suffix beginning with a consonant then the suffix consonant **"-d"** changes to its Unvoiced Form **"-t"**.

tıkaç *plug, stopper*
tıkaçtan *from the plug*

kitap *book*
kitaptan *from the book*

kilit *lock*
kilitte *in the lock*

köpek *dog*
köpekten *from the dog*

sabah *morning*
sabahtan *from the morning*

domates *tomato*
domatesten *from the tomato(es)*

giriş *exit*
girişte *at the exit*

raf *shelf*
raftan *from the shelf*

4 BUFFER LETTERS

Buffer Letter Rules

Turkish uses three buffer letters -n-, -y-, -s- to keep vowels apart and to separate suffixes. There are rules for the use of each one.

A few examples of buffer letters being used when suffixes are added to modify a word's meaning :

Babası [Baba-s-ı] *his father*
Sırası [Sıra-s-ı] *his/her/its turn*
Kuzusu [Kuzu-s-u] *his sheep*
Kapısını [Kapı-s-ı-n-ı] *its door (obj.)*
Bundan [Bu-n-dan] *from this*
Onu [O-n-u] *that/him/her/it (obj.)*
Onun [O-n-un] *his/her/its*
Ondan [O-n-dan] *from him/from that*
Şunda [Şu-n-da] *in/on/at that*
Şundan [Şu-n-dan] *from that*
Nereye? [Nere-y-e] *Where to?*
Oraya [Ora-y-a] *To there*
Sobaya [Soba-y-a] *To the stove*
Parayı [Para-y-ı] *the money (obj.)*
Suyu [Su-y-u] *the water (obj.)*
Kapısını [Kapı-s-ı-n-ı] *its door (obj.)*
Arabanın [Araba-n-ın] *of the car*
Yanından [Yan-ı-n-dan] *from his/her/its side*
İkişer [İki-ş-er] *two each*

The buffer letter -S-

Buffer Letter **-S-** is only used with the third person suffix **-i -ı -u -ü** meaning *his, her, its* thus taking the form **-si -sı -sü -su** when added to a root word which ends in a vowel.

şapka *hat*
şapkası [şapka-sı not şapka-ı] *his/her hat.*

As the third person singular suffix is a single vowel **-i**, then it becomes **-si** by using buffer letter **-s-** in order to keep two vowels apart and preserve the original root word. Vowel Harmony Rules are observed when adding the suffix thus producing **şapkası**.

Simple Noun with Extended Meaning:

kedi *cat*
kedisi [kedi-s-i] *his/her cat*

şemsiye *umbrella*
şemsiyesi [şemsiye-s-i] *his/her umbrella*

kapı *door*
kapısı [kapı-s-ı] *his/her/its door*

palto *overcoat*
paltosu [palto-s-u] *his overcoat*

ütü *flatiron*
ütüsü [ütü-s-ü] *his/her iron*

araba *car*
arabası [araba-s-ı] *his/her car*

kuzu *sheep*
kuzusu [kuzu-s-u] *his/her sheep*

The buffer letter **-s-** is only used for the third person singular possessive suffix. It is not used in any other instance.

The buffer letter -Y-

Buffer Letter **-Y** is used **on plain simple un-suffixed nouns only** when suffixed with the Direct Object Condition **-i** *the* and the Motion Towards Condition **-a/-e** *to, towards.*

The Direct Object Condition suffix (Accusative) **-i -ı -ü -u** *the [obj.]* takes buffer letter **-Y-** to become **-yi -yı -yu -yü** when added to a root word which ends in a vowel.

kedi *cat*
kediyi [kedi-y-i] *the cat* (object)

banka *bank*
bankayı [banka-y-ı] *the bank* (object)

kuzu *sheep*
kuzuyu [kuzu-y-u] *the sheep* (object)

To reiterate: The buffer letter **-y-** is only used with simple nouns ending in a vowel which have not already been suffixed. However it takes buffer letter **-n-** to become **-ni -nı -nu -nü** when added as a second suffix to an already extended noun.

kuzusunu [kuzu-su-nu] *his sheep* (object)
bankasını [banka-sı-nı] *his bank* (object)

The Motion Towards Condition -a, -e *to, towards* (Dative) takes buffer letter **-Y-** to become **-ya/-ye** when added to a root word which ends in a vowel.

kedi *cat*
kediye [kedi-y-e] *to the cat*

banka *bank*
bankaya [banka-y-a] *to the bank*

baba *father*
babaya [baba-y-a] *to the father*

The buffer letter **-Y-** is only used with simple nouns which have not already been suffixed. But it takes buffer letter **-n-** to become **-ne/-na** when added as a second suffix to an already extended noun. This shift of buffer letter **-y-** to **-n-** enables the listener to discern that the word is already agglutinated (extended) by previous suffixes.

babasına [baba-sı-na] *to his father*
kedisine [kedi-si-ne] *to her cat*

Buffer Letter "N" Ownership Condition (Genitive possessor).

The Ownership condition uses Buffer Letter **-N-** for both root words and already extended words. It does not use Buffer Letter **-Y.**

The Ownership Condition **-in -ın -ün -un** *of,* *'s* (Genitive) takes buffer letter **-N-** to become **-nin -nın -nün -nun** when added to a root word which ends in a vowel.

kedi *cat*
kedinin [kedi-n-in] *of the cat, the cats*

banka *bank*
bankanın [banka-n-ın] *of the bank, the bank's*

The Ownership Condition also takes buffer letter **-N-** when added to an already extended word which ends in a vowel.

bankası [banka-sı] *his bank*
bankasının [banka-sı-n-ın] *of his bank, his bank's*

gözü [göz-ü] *his eye*
gözünün [gözü-n-ün] *of his eye, his eye's*

mutfağı [mutfağ-ı] *his/her kitchen*
mutfağının [mutfağ-ı-n-ın] *of his kitchen, her kitchen's*

Buffer Letter "N" Object and Motion Toward Conditions.

Buffer Letter **-N** is used on **nouns already suffixed** with the 3rd Person suffixes **-(s)i -(s)ı -(s)ü -(s)u** *his, her, its* and **-lari -leri** *their.*

This shift of buffer letter **-Y-** to **-N-** enables the listener to discern that the word is already agglutinated (extended) by previous suffixes.

Examples Nouns in the Object Condition suffix -i -ı -ü -u.

Extended Noun Examples.

kedisi [kedi-s-i] *his/her cat*
kedisini [kedi-s-i-n-i] *his/her cat* (object)
kedisine [kedi-s-i-n-e] *to his/her cat* (motion toward)

bankası [banka-s-ı] *his/her bank*
bankasını [banka-s-ı-n-ı] *his/her bank* (object)
bankasına [banka-sı-n-a] *to his/her bank*

36

gözleri [göz-leri] *their eye(s)*
gözlerinin [gözü-leri-nin] *of their eye, their eye's*

mutfakları [mutfak-ları] *their kitchen(s)*
mutfaklarının [mutfak-ları-n-ın] *of their kitchen(s), their kitchen's,
their kitchens'*

To reiterate: The buffer letter **-N-** is used on nouns which have
already been extended by the addition of a suffix.

Buffer Letter "N" Motion Toward Condition "-(n)a/-(n)e".

Buffer letter **-N-** is used with nouns that have already been suffixed.

kedisi [kedi-si] *his/her cat*
kedisine [kedi-si-n-e] *to his/her cat*

babaları [baba-ları] *their father*
babalarına [baba-ları-n-a] *to their father*

**Motion Away "-dan/-den" and Static Position "-da/-de"
Conditions.**

The suffixes **-de** and **-dan** are added directly to basic nouns:

kedi *cat*
kedide [kedi-de] *on the cat*
kediden [kedi-den] *from the cat*

kapı *door*
kapıda [kapı-da] *on/at the door*
kapıdan [kapı-dan] *from the door*

Both the suffixes **-da/-de** and **-dan/-den** require a buffer **-N-** when
added to an extended word. Buffer letter **-N-** used with **-da/-de** *in,
on, at* and **-dan/-den** *from, via, by, through* when adding these
suffixes to already extended nouns. They become **-nda/-nde** and -
ndan/-nden to keep the suffix apart from the noun it modifies.

kedisi [kedi-si] *his cat*
kedisinde [kedi-si-nde] *on his cat*
kedisinden [kedi-si-nden] *from his/her cat*
kediden [kedi-den] *from the cat*

kedilerinden [kedi-leri-nden] *from their cat(s)*
kedilerinden [kedi-ler-i-nden] *from his/her cats*

kapı *door*
kapısında [kapı-sı-n-da] *on/at his/her door*
kapısından [kapı-sı-ndan] *from his/her door*

bankadan [banka-dan] *from the bank*
bankada [banka-da] *in/at the bank*
bankası [banka-s-ı] *his/her bank*
bankasında [banka-sı-nda] *in/at his bank*
bankasından [banka-s-ı-n-dan] *from his/her bank*
bankalardan [banka-lar-dan] *from the banks*
onların bankalarından [onlar-ın banka-ları-ndan] *from their bank(s)*
bankalarında [banka-ları-nda] *in their bank*

evi [ev-i] *his/her house*
evinde [ev-i-n-de] *in his/her house*
evden [ev-den] *from the house/from home*
evinden [ev-i-nden] *from his house/home*
evlerde [evler-de] *in the houses*
evlerinde [ev-leri-nde] *in their house(s)*
evlerinden [ev-leri-nden] *from their house*

5 THE SUFFIXES

The Main Suffixes.

In English prepositions "in, on, of, by, etc." are placed separately in front of the word they modify. In Turkish, they are postpositions suffixed directly to the noun that they modify thus forming new complete words.

Suffixes and Vowel Harmony.

In English we have many words which agglutinate (extend) to form other words. Taking the simple word **argue**. It can be modified to **argument** by the addition of a **-ment** suffix. We can further extend this word with other suffixes **-ative** producing **argumentative**, and even more to **argumentatively** by adding **-ly** suffix. This then is the way of Turkish. Even the little words like *in, on, at, from* are suffixed to their noun thus producing extended words with different meanings.

Most suffixes follow the Vowel Harmony Rules:

Adding the suffixes **-de** *in, on, at* and **-den** *from* to an E-Dotted Vowel Form **E İ Ö Ü.**

ev *house*
evde [ev-de] *in the house*
evden [ev-den] *from the house*

Adding the suffixes **-da** and **-dan** to an A-UnDotted Vowel Form **A I O U.**

oda *room*
odada [oda-da] *in the room*
odadan [oda-dan] *from the room*

The Six Noun Conditions.

Turkish has a Subject Condition (nominative) which carries no suffix and five conditions each with a typical ending.

The vowels of the suffix must match final vowel of the root word according to Vowel Harmony Rules and the initial consonant of the suffix may change according to Consonant Mutation Rules.

The suffixes of the Noun Conditions are:

(1) Subject Condition (Nominative):
The noun in its root form without a suffix. The Subject Condition is the subject of a sentence.

(2) Object Condition (Accusative):
Suffix **-i -ı -u -ü** or **-yi -yı -yu -yü** when suffixed to words ending in a vowel or **-ni -nı -nu -nü** when suffixed to already extended words ending in a vowel. The Objective is the direct object of a verb, it equates to *the* in English.

(3) Movement Towards Condition (Dative):
Suffix **-a/-e** or **-ya/-ye** when suffixed direct to word ending in a vowel or **-ne/-na** when suffixed to already extended words ending in a vowel. Movement Towards equates to *to, towards* in English.

(4) Static Position Condition (Locative):
Suffix **-da/-de** any suffix appended to a soft word ending must begin with a soft consonant **-d** according to Consonant Mutation rules.

Or **-ta/-te** any suffix appended to a hard word ending in (**p ç t k s ş h f**) must begin with a hard consonant **-t** according to Consonant Mutation rules.

Or **-nde/-nda** when suffixed to extended words which end in a vowel.
The Static is the condition of place equates to *in, on, at* in English.

(5) Movement Away Condition (Ablative):
Suffix **-dan/-den** any suffix appended to a soft word ending must begin with a soft consonant **-d** according to Consonant Mutation rules.

Or **-tan/-ten** as any suffix appended to a hard word ending in **p ç t k s ş h f** must begin with a hard consonant **-t** according to Consonant Mutation rules.

Or **-nden/-ndan** when suffixed to extended words which end in a vowel.

The Movement Away suffix equates to *from, by, via* in English.

(6) Ownership Condition (Genitive):
Suffix **-in -ın -un -ün** or **-nin -nın -nun -nün** when suffixed plain or extended words ending in a vowel. The Ownership suffix signifies that the noun "owns" something. This suffix equates to *of, -'s* [of Mehmet, Mehmet's].

There are three other suffixes which can be applied to nouns:

(7) The With Condition:
Suffix **-le/-la** or **-yle/-yla** after vowels. It can also stand alone as a separate word **ile**. This suffix means *together with, and, also,*

(8) The Without Condition (lacking):
Suffix **-siz -sız -suz -süz**. This suffix gives the sense of lacking. This suffix equates to *without* ["without sugar"] and the various negating prefixes and suffixes of English *un-, dis-, non-, -less* ["unfair, dishonest, nonsense, hopeless"].

(9) The Containing Condition (Furnished with, Containing, Belonging to, Place of):
Suffix **-li -lı -lu -lü** gives the sense of belonging to somewhere or being contained in something. It equates to *with* [with sugar, sugary, sugared] and various "additional and augmenting" suffixes and prefixes in English. [leafy, salty, coloured, numbered].

The Subject Condition

There is no Turkish word for the Subject Definite Article, only the context tells us when to insert *THE* in English:

Singular Nouns.

Un-suffixed nouns are in the Subject Condition. They can be specific or non-specific in Turkish. English uses the specifier *"the"*. Turkish has no Subject Condition specifier. This can cause translation difficulties both ways.

okul *school, the school*

41

bulut *cloud, the cloud*
gazete *newspaper, the newspaper*
hafta *week, the week*
ödül *present, the gift*

Plural Nouns.

Noun form used for two or more items of an object. The plural suffix is **-ler** or **-lar** which is added to the root word according to Vowel Harmony Rules.

okullar [okul-lar] *school, the schools*
bulutlar [bulut-lar] *clouds, the clouds*
gazeteler [gazete-ler] *newspapers, the newspapers*
haftalar [hafta-lar] *weeks, the weeks*
ödüller [ödül-ler] *presents, the gifts*

The subject can be non-specific or made specific in English with insertion of the Definite Article *"the"*.

The Object Condition.

The English Object Definite Article *"the"* appears as the suffix **-i -ı -ü -u** according to vowel harmony in Turkish. It has the forms:
Suffixed to Plain Nouns: **-i -ı -u -ü.**
Suffixed to Plain Nouns (which end in vowel): **-yi -yı -yu -yü.**
Suffixed to Extended Nouns (which end in vowel): **-ni -nı -nu -nü.**

Formation of the Objective Condition.

The object specifier has the form of a suffix governed by vowel harmony rules:

-i -ı -u -ü is used with root nouns which end in a consonant or used with extended (already suffixed) nouns which end in a consonant.

-yi -yı -yu -yü [buffer letter **-y**] is only used with root nouns which end in a vowel.

-ni -nı -nu -nü [buffer letter **-n**] is only used with extended (already suffixed) nouns ending in a vowel.

The Direct Object Pointer suffix **-i -ı -u -ü** is suffixed directly to all root words which end in a consonant:

ev *house, the house*
evi [ev-i] *the house (obj.)*

sokak *street, the street*
sokağı [sokağ-ı] *the street (obj.)*
(**sokak** shows **-k** to **-ğ** consonant mutation here.)

gül *rose, the rose*
gülü [gül-ü] *the rose (obj.)*

It takes buffer letter **-y** to become **-yi -yı -yu -yü** when added to a root word which ends in a vowel:

kedi *cat, the cat*
kediyi [kedi-y-i] *the cat* (obj.)

banka *bank, the bank*
bankayı [banka-y-ı] *the bank (obj.)*

kutu *box, the box*
kutuyu [kutu-y-u] *the box (obj.)*

The buffer letter **-y-** is only used with simple nouns ending in a vowel which have not already been suffixed.

It is also suffixed to extended (already suffixed) nouns which end in a consonant:

evim *my house*
evimi [ev-im-i] *my house (obj.)*

sokağın *your street*
sokağını [sokağ-ın-ı] *your street (obj.)*

güller *roses*
gülleri [gül-ler-i] *the roses (obj.)*

But it takes buffer letter **-n-** to become **-ni -nı -nu -nü** when added as a second suffix to an already extended noun.

kedisi [kedi-si] *his/her cat*
kedisini [kedi-si-n-i] *his/her cat* (obj.)
bankası [banka-sı] *his/her bank*
bankasını [banka-sı-n-ı] *his/her bank* (obj.)

This shift of buffer letter **y** to **n** enables the listener to discern that the word is already agglutinated (extended) by previous suffixes. To reiterate: The buffer letter **-n-** is only used on extended nouns.

Nouns both bare and extended ending in a consonant.

Adam kilidi (kilid-i) **kapattı. The** *man locked* **the** *lock.*

The **-i** suffix makes the bare noun *the lock* substantive as a **Direct Object.**

Adam kilidimi (kilid-im-i) **kapattı. The** *man locked* **my** *lock.*

The **-i** suffix makes the extended noun *my lock* substantive as a **Direct Object.**

Nouns both bare and extended ending in a vowel.

Adam kapıyı [kapı-y-ı] **kapattı. *The** man closed* **the** *door.*

The **-yı** suffix makes the bare noun ***the*** *door* substantive as a Direct Object.

Adam kapısını (kapı-sı-n-ı) **kapattı. *The** man closed* **his** *door.*

The **-nı** suffix makes the extended (already suffixed) noun ***his*** *door* substantive as a Direct Object.

The Direct Object Suffix is difficult to use naturally for English speakers. It requires observation and practice.

Motion Towards Condition "-e/-ye, -a/-ya, -ne/-na".

Formation of the Motion Towards Condition. This takes the form of a suffix governed by vowel harmony. **-e/-a** is used with root nouns which end in a consonant or used with extended (already suffixed) nouns which end in a consonant. **-ye/-ya** [buffer letter **-y**] is only used with root nouns which end in a vowel. **-ne/-na** [buffer letter **-n**] is only used with extended (already suffixed) nouns ending in a vowel.

The Motion Towards suffix **-a** or **-e** to, towards is suffixed directly to all root words which end in a consonant:

ev *house, the house*

eve [ev-e] *to the house*

sokak *street, the street*
sokağa [sokağ-a] *to the street*

gül *rose, the rose*
güle [gül-e] *to the rose*

It takes buffer letter **-y-** when added directly as the first suffix to a root word which ends in a vowel, thus taking the form **-ye, -ya.**

kedi *cat, the cat*
kediye [kedi-y-e] *to the cat*

banka *bank, the bank*
bankaya [banka-y-a] *to the bank*

It is also suffixed to extended (already suffixed) nouns which end in a consonant:

evim *my house*
evime [ev-im-e] *to my house*

sokağın *your street*
sokağına [sokağ-ın-a] *to your street*

güller *roses*
güllere [gül-ler-e] *to the roses*

But it takes buffer letter **-n-** when added as a second suffix to an already extended noun, thus taking the form **-ne, -na.**

kedi *cat, the cat*
kedisi [kedi-si] *his cat*
kedisine [kedi-si-ne] *to his cat*

baba *father, the father*
babaları [baba-ları] *their father*
babalarına [baba-ları-n-a] *to their father*

This shift of Buffer Letter **-y** to **-n** helps the listener to discern that that noun has already been extended by a previous suffix.

Examples of Motion Toward Suffix.

adama [adam-a] *to the man*

45

adamlara [adamlar-a] *to the men*

kediye [kedi-y-e] *to the cat*
kedi *cat* ends in a vowel so "kedi-y-e" is used ["kedi-e"] is incorrect.
kedilere [kedi-ler-e] *to the cats*

eve [ev-e] *to home*
evlere [ev-ler-e] *to the houses*

kapıya [kapı-y-a] *to the door*
kapı *door* ends in a vowel so "kapı-y-a" is used ["kapı-a"] is incorrect.
kapılara [kapı-lar-a] *to the doors*

Static Position Condition "-de/-da/-te/-ta, -nde/-nda".

The Static Position (Locative) Suffix **de** or **da** *in, on, at*. This suffix shows concrete place (location):

Any suffix appended to a soft word ending must begin with a soft consonant **-d** .

Odadayım. [oda-da-yım] *I am in the room.*
Ali bey, evdeymiş. [ev-de-ymiş] *Probably Ali bey is at home.*

adamda [adam-da] *on the man*
adamlarda [adam-lar-da] *on the men*

kedide [kedi-de] *on the cat*
kedilerde [kedi-ler-de] *on the cats*

evde [ev-de] *at home*
evlerde [ev-ler-de] *at the houses*

kapıda [kapı-da] *at the door*
kapılarda [kapı-lar-da] *at/by the doors*

köprüde [köprü-de] *on the bridge*
köprülerde [köprü-ler-de] *on the bridges*

odada [oda-da] *in the room*
odalarda [oda-lar-da] *in the rooms*

For the plural we have added two suffixes **-ler** (Plural Suffix) and -

de (Static Location Suffix) or **-lar** and **-da** and tagged them together to make one word in Turkish.

*The **-de/-da** suffix appended to a hard word ending in p ç t k s ş h f must begin with a hard consonant **-te/-ta**.*

kitap *book.*
kitapta [kitap-ta] *in the book* but in the plural **kitaplarda** [kitap-lar-da] *in the books.*
kitabımda [kitab-ım-da] *in my book* but in the plural **kitaplarımda** [kitap-lar ım-da] *in my books.*

raf *shelf.*
rafta [raf-ta] *on the shelf* plural **raflarda** [raf-lar-da] *on the shelves.*
(onun) **rafında** [onun raf-ı-nda] *on his shelves* plural (onun) **raflarında** [onun raf-lar-ı-nda] *on his shelves.*

günah *sin.*
günahta [günah-ta] *in the sin* plural **günahlarda** [günah-lar-da] *in the sins.*
(benim) **günahımda** [günah-ım-da] *in my sin* plural **günahlarımda** [günah-lar-ım-da] *in my sins.*

giriş *entrance.*
girişte [giriş-te] *in the entrance* plural **girişlerde** [giriş-ler-de] *in the entrances.*
(onların) **girişlerinde** [giriş-leri-nde] *in their entrance* plural **girişlerinde** [giriş-leri-nde] *in their entrances.* (no change as **-ler** suffix is not reduplicated in Turkish, so the meaning has to be understood from the sentence context.)

domates *tomato.*
domateste [domates-te] *on the tomato* plural **domateslerde** [domates-ler-de] *on the tomatoes.*
(senin) **domatesinde** [domates-in-de] *on your tomato* plural **domateslerinde** [domates-ler-in-de] *in your tomatoes.*

kaşık *spoon.*
kaşıkta [kaşık-ta] *in the spoon* plural **kaşıklarda** [kaşık-lar-da] *in the spoons.*
(bizim) **kaşığımızda** [kaşığ-ımız-da] *on our spoon.*

kaşıklarımızda [kaşık-lar-ımız-da] *in our spoons.*
Hard **-k** softens to soft **-ğ** when followed by a vowel. Consonant Mutation Rules.

bilet *ticket.*
bilette [bilet-te] *on the ticket* plural **biletlerde** [bilet-ler-de] *on the tickets.*
(sizin) **biletinizde** [bilet-iniz-de] *on your* (formal) *ticket* plural **biletlerinizde** [bilet-ler-iniz-de] *on your* (formal) *tickets.*

kazanç *profit, gain.*
kazançta [kazanç-ta] *in the profit* plural **kazançlarda** [kazanç-lar-da] *in the profits.*
(onun) **kazancında** [kazanc-ı-nda] *in its profit* plural (onun) **kazançlarında** [kazanç-lar-ı-nda] *in its profits.*
Hard **-ç** softens to soft **-cında** when followed by a vowel. Consonant Mutation Rules.

Movement Away Suffix -den/-dan, -ten/-tan, -nden/-ndan.

The suffix **-den** or **-dan** *from, by, via, through.* This suffix show movement from a location.

adamdan [adam-dan] *from the man*
adamlardan [adam-lar-dan] *from the men*

kediden [kedi-den] *from the cat*
kedilerden [kedi-ler-den] *from the cats*

evden [ev-den] *from home*
evlerden [ev-ler-den] *from the houses*

kapıdan [kapı-dan] *from the door*
kapılardan [kapı-lar-dan] *from the doors*

köprüden [köprü-den] *from the bridge*
köprülerden [köprü-ler-den] *from the bridges*

odadan [oda-dan] *from the room*
odalardan [oda-lar-dan] *from the rooms*

For the plural we have added two suffixes **-ler** (Plural Suffix) and **-den** (Movement Away Suffix) or **-lar** and **-dan** and tagged them altogether to make one word in Turkish.

The -den/-dan suffix appended to a hard word ending in p ç t k s ş h f must begin with a hard consonant -ten/-tan.

kitap *book.*
kitaptan [kitap-tan] *-from the book* but in the plural **kitaplardan** [kitap-lar-dan] *from the books.*
kitabımdan [kitab-ım-dan] *from my book* but in the plural **kitaplarımdan** [kitap-lar ım-dan] *from my books.*

raf *shelf.*
raftan [raf-tan] *from the shelf* plural **raflardan** [raf-lar-dan] *from the shelves.*
(onun) **rafından** [(onun) raf-ı-ndan] *from his shelves* plural (onun) **raflarından** [(onun) raf-lar-ı-ndan] *from his shelves* .

günah *sin.*
günahtan [günah-tan] *from the sin* plural **günahlardan** [günah-lar-dan] *from the sins.*
(benim) **günahımdan** [günah-ım-dan] *from my sin* plural (benim) **günahlarımdan** [günah-lar-ım-dan] *from my sins.*

giriş *entrance.*
girişten [giriş-ten] *from/via the entrance* plural **girişlerden** [giriş-ler-den] *from/via the entrances.*
(onların) **girişlerinden** [giriş-leri-nden] *from/via their entrance* plural **girişlerinden** [giriş-leri-nden] *from/via their entrances.*
(no change as **-ler** suffix is not reduplicated in Turkish, so the meaning has to be understood from the sentence context.)

domates *tomato.*
domatesten [domates-ten] *from the tomato* plural **domateslerden** [domates-ler-den] *from the tomatoes.*
(senin) **domatesinden** [domates-in-den] *from your tomato* plural **domateslerinden** [domates-ler-in-den] *from your tomatoes.*

Note: "Domates" (from Greek) is a single "tomato" in Turkish. The plural is "domatesler" "tomatoes"! Do not get mixed up!!

kaşık *spoon.*
kaşıktan [kaşık-tan] *from the spoon* plural **kaşıklardan** [kaşık-lar-

dan] *from the spoons.*
(bizim) **kaşığımızdan** [kaşığ-ımız-dan] *from our spoon* plural
kaşıklarımızdan [kaşık-lar-ımız-dan] *from our spoons.*
Hard **-k** softens to soft **-ğ** when followed by a vowel *Consonant Mutation Rules. Chapter: 3.*

bilet *ticket.*
biletten [bilet-ten] *from the ticket* plural **biletlerden** [bilet-ler-den] *from the tickets.*
(sizin) **biletinizden** [bilet-iniz-den] *from your* (formal) *ticket* plural
biletlerinizden [bilet-ler-iniz-den] *from your* (formal) *tickets.*

kazanç *profit, gain.*
kazançtan [kazanç-tan] *from the profit* plural **kazançlardan**
[kazanç-lar-dan] *from the profits.*
(onun) **kazancından** [kazanc-ı-ndan] *from its profit* plural (onun)
kazançlarından [kazanç-lar-ı-ndan] *from its profits.*
Hard **-ç** softens to soft **-cında** when followed by a vowel. Consonant Mutation Rules.

The Suffix of Ownership (Genitive Case).

The form of the ownership suffix is: **-in** or **-nin** (using buffer letter -**n-** when added to words which already end in a vowel) meaning *of, belonging to.* This suffix is used for ownership. It is also used as part of the Possessive Relationship which is dealt with in *Chapter 11.* The sign of the Ownership Condition suffix is **-in** which is added to the noun, singular, plural or extended forms. It is subject to Vowel Harmony, the Vowel Harmonized forms become **-in -ın -ün -un** *of, belonging to.*

A sole exception **su** *water.*
The translation for *of the water* is not "sunun", but **suyun** with the exceptional buffer letter **-y** which is always used with the word **su** *water.* This exception also applies to the Possessed Case you cannot say for *Fruit Juice* "Meyve Susu" as the buffer letter **-y-** is always used with the word **su** *water* consequently **Meyve Suyu.**

Formation of the Ownership Suffix.

The suffix **-in -ın -un -ün** is added to the noun.

ev, evler *house, houses*
evin [ev-in] *the house's, of the house*
evlerin [ev-ler-in] *the houses', of the houses*

evimin [ev-im-in] *my house's, of my house*
evlerimin [ev-ler-im-in] *my houses', of my houses*

evinin [ev-in-in] *your house's, of your house*
evlerinin [ev-ler-in-in] *your houses', of your houses*

memurun [memur-un] *the official's, of the official*
memurların [memur-lar-ın] *the officials', of the officials*

gözün [göz-ün] *the eye's, of the eye*
gözlerimin [göz-ler-im-in] *my eyes', of my eyes*

akşamın [akşam-ın] *the evening's, of the evening*
akşamların [akşam-lar-ın] *the evenings', of the evenings*

tavuğun [tavuğ-un] *the chicken's, of the chicken*
tavukların [tavuk-lar-ın] *the chickens', of the chickens*

bakkalın [bakkal-ın] *the grocer's, of the grocer*
bakkalların [bakkal-lar-ın] *the grocers', of the grocers*

The Plural Suffix is added as first suffix. The Possessive Adjective is added secondly, and finally the Ownership indicating Possession.

The Ownership Suffix Nouns ending in Vowels.

The Suffix changes to **-nin/-nın/-nun/-nün** *of* or *belonging to* using buffer **-n-** in order to keep two vowels apart.

kedinin [kedi-n-in] *of the cat, the cat's*
kedisinin [kedi-si-n-in] *of his cat, his cat's*
onun kedilerinin [kedi-ler-in-in] *of his cats, his cats'*
onların kedilerinin [kedi-leri-n-in] *of their cat/of their cats, their cat's/cats'*

bankanın [banka-n-ın] *the bank's, of the bank*
bankasının [banka-sı-n-ın] *his bank's, of his bank*
köprünün [köprü-n-ün] *the bridge's, of the bridge*

Ali 'nin [Ali-'n-in] *Ali's, of Ali*
Londra 'nın [Londra-'n-ın] *London's, of London*
All suffixes, except the **-li** *containing* suffix, are written apart from

51

any Proper Name which begins with a capital letter. The last two examples above show this.

The Ownership Suffix with already suffixed words.

The suffix **-in -ın -ün -un** *of, belonging to* always takes buffer letter **-n-** to become **-nin -nın -nün -nun** when added either to a root word or to an extended word which ends in a vowel.

kedinin [kedi-nin] *the cat's*
kedisinin [kedi-si-nin] *his cat's, of his cat*

bankanın *of the bank*
bankasının *of his bank*

arabanın *the car's*
arabasının *his car's, of his car*

Ali 'nin *Ali's, of Ali*
Ayşe 'nin *Ayshe's, of Ayshe*

köprünün *of the bridge*
köprülerinin *of their bridge(s)*

The suffix **-in** always becomes **-nin** whether suffixed to a Simple Noun or to an already suffixed noun.

The With Condition ile, -le/-la, -yle/-yla.

The Suffix -le -la *with, and, also.*
The word for *with* in Turkish is **ile**. This is one word which can stand on its own after the word it modifies. In which case it does not follow vowel harmony rules but is always written and spoken **ile**.

Mehmed ile [Mehmed ile] *with Mehmet* or
Mehmet'le [Mehmet-'le] *with Mehmet*

gözlerim ile [gözler-im ile] *with my eyes* or
gözlerimle [gözler-im-le] *with my eyes*

domuzla [domuz-la] *with the pig* or
domuz ile [domuz ile] *with a (any) pig*

domuzuyla [domuz-u-yla] *with the/his pig* or
domuzu ile [domuz-u ile] *with the/his pig*

arkadaşınla [arkadaş-ın-la] *with your friend* or
arkadaşın ile [arkadaş-ın ile] *with your friend*

Using "ile" with words which end in a vowel.

When adding **ile** to words that end in a vowel the initial letter **-i** of **ile** changes to a buffer letter **-y** in order to keep two vowels apart, thus the forms **-yla** and **-yle** are used.

paltosuyla [palto-su-yla] *with his overcoat*
bir arabayla [bir araba-yla] *with a car*

kediyle [kedi-yle] *with the cat*
kedisiyle [kedi-si-yle] *with his cat*

iskemleyle [iskemle-yle] *with the chair*
eliyle [el-i-yle] *with his hand*

elleriyle [eller-i-yle] *with his hands*
babasıyla [baba-sı-yla] *with his father*

If the suffixed form is used then it changes to **-yle -yla** after vowels. As previously stated, whether to use **ile** as *stand alone* or as a *suffix* is a free choice of the speaker or writer, but there is no change in the meaning:

The Containing Condition "-li -lı -lü -lu".

The Suffix -li -lı -lü -lu *originating from, furnished with, place of.*

This suffix gives the sense of belonging to something or somewhere. It is used with place names, especially to say where one is from. The **-li** suffix is not separated from a Proper Noun by an apostrophe as other suffixes generally are "Londra'lı" would be incorrect **Londralı** is correct.

Londralı [Londra-lı] *a Londoner*
Londralılar [Londra-lı-lar] *Londoners*

İstanbullu [İstanbul-lu] *an Istanbuli*
İstanbullular [İstanbul-lu-lar] *Istanbulis*

İngiltereliyim [İngiltere-li-yim] *I am English*

Bolulu [Bolu-lu] *a person from Bolu*
Çinli [Çin-li] *a Chinese Man (Chinaman)*

This suffix also gives the sense of belonging to something or somewhere, it is widely used with place names, especially to say where one is from:

İngiltereliyim *I am from England*
Mançesterliyim *I come from Manchester*
Nerelisiniz? *Where (exactly) are you from?*

An Acutal Example of the -li suffix.

Here is a picture of a sandwich bar's billboard showing the type of sandwiches available.
kaşarlı [kaşar-lı] *containing hard cheese*
karışıklı [karışıklı] *mixed*
sucuklu [sucuk-lu] *containing Turkish type sausage*
salamlı [salam-lı] *containing salami*
sosisli [sosis-li] *containing sausage*
Vowel harmony is operating on the suffix **-li** as it has three of it four forms in this picture.

KAŞARLI
KARIŞIKLI
SUCUKLU
SALAMLI
SOSİSİLİ

The meaning of *"furnished with"* is used to make attributive adjectives, **tuz** *salt* becomes **tuzlu** *salty* is an example. Should you use sugar in your tea then you might ask for **şekerli çay** which can mean *sweet tea, sugared tea, sugary tea,* according to context.

sabır *patience*
sabırlı [sabır-lı] *patient*

kuvvet *strength*
kuvvetli [kuvvet-li] *strong*

yaprak *leaf*
yapraklı [yaprak-lı] *leafy*

çimen *lawn*
çimenli *having a lawn*

yaş *age*
yaşlı *old (aged)*

renk *colour*
renkli *coloured*

ses *noise*
sesli *noisy*

yatak *bed*
yataklı *furnished with a bed*

biber *pepper*
biberli *peppery, peppered*

Mehmet sabırlı bir adamdır. *Mehmet is a patient man.*
Ali kuvvetli bir genç. *Ali is a strong youth.*
Bir yapraklı ağaç. *A leafy tree.*
Çimenli bir ev. *It is a house with a lawn.*
Yaşlı bir at. *It is an old horse.*

İçkili bir lokantaya gittik. *We went to an alcohol serving bistro.*
içkili means *furnished with alcoholic drinks* [i.e. Alcoholic drinks are served.]

We can form plural nouns by adding the **-ler** or **-lar** plural suffix to an adjective:

sabırlılar [sabır-lı-lar] *the patient ones*
kuvvetliler [kuvvet-li-ler] *the strong ones*
yaşlılar [yaş-lı-lar] *the aged*

The Lacking Condition.

The Suffix -siz -sız -süz -suz *without, un-, non-, -less, dis-*

This suffix gives the sense of lacking. In English it can be translated as *un-* as in *unavailable* or *-less* as in *worthless* or *dis-* as in *distaste*.

ehliyet *licence*
ehliyetsiz [ehliyet-siz] *unlicensed*
ehliyetli [ehliyet-li] *licensed*

renk *colour*
renksiz [renk-siz] *colourless*
renkli [renk-li] *coloured*

sabır *patience*
sabırsız *impatient*
sabırlı *patient*

işaret *sign*
işaretsiz *unsigned*
işaretli *signed*

ses *noise*
sessiz *noiseless*
sesli *noisy*

şeker *sugar*
şekersiz *unsugared*
şekerli *sugared, sweetened*

namus *honesty*
namussuz *dishonest*
namuslu *honest*

Bir çay, şekersiz olsun, lütfen. *A tea, no sugar, please.*
Sonsuz bir yolculuk gibiydi. *It was like an endless journey.*
Sensiz gidiyorum *I'm going without you.*
Değersiz bir saat aldım. *I bought a worthless watch.*
İçkisiz bir aile gazinosuna gittik. *We went to a non-alcoholic family restaurant.*
içkisiz means *without alcoholic drinks* [i.e. Alcohol is not served] is seen on many Public Signs.

We can form plural nouns by adding the **-ler** or **-lar** plural suffix to an adjective.

sabırsızlar [sabır-sız-lar] *the impatient ones*
şekersizler [şeker-siz-ler] *the unsugared ones*
renksizler [renk-siz-ler] *the uncoloured/colourless ones*

Dependent Adverbs.

These adverbs require that the preceding noun have the Motion
Towards **-e/-ye, -a/-ya** *to/toward* suffix:

-e nazaran *compared with/to.*

buna nazaran *compared to this*
bunlara nazaran *compared to these*
şuna nazaran *compared to that*
şunlara nazaran *compared to those*
ona nazaran *compared to that*
onlara nazaran *compared to those*

Düne nazaran bugün hava daha güzel.
Compared to yesterday, the weather is better today.

Rakiplerine nazaran ücretsizdir.
Compared to the competitors it is price free.

 FlashFilm'e nazaran "ISO dosyalarını" indirme sürecinde
bozmaz. *Compared to FlashFilm it does not spoil "ISO files" while*
downloading.

-e kadar *up to, until, as far as.*

şimdiye kadar [şimdi-ye kadar] *up to now*
Ankara'ya kadar *as far as Ankara*

Gelecek pazara kadar bekleyelim. *Let us wait until next Sunday.*
Çarşıya kadar gidiyorum. *I am going as far as the shops.*

-e doğru *straight toward.*

bankaya doğru [banka-ya doğru] *straight to the bank*
Eve doğru git! *Go straight home!*
Evden okula doğru gidin. *Go straight to school from home.*

-e göre *according to, compared to.*

bana göre *according to me*
sana göre *according to you*
Memed'e göre *according to Mehmet*

This has both or either the *comparing to* and *according to* meanings in a sentence.

Yeni plâna göre, evimizin arka bahçesi küçültülecekmiş. [plân-a göre]
According to the new plan our back garden will be made smaller.

Okuduğun kitap benimkine göre daha kalın görünüyor. [benim-ki-n-e göre "compared to mine", a comparison]
The book that you are reading looks thicker than mine.

Bu gazeteye göre hiç yeni haberi daha çıkmamış. [gazete-y-e göre]
According to this newspaper no more new news has happened yet.

-e karşı *against.*

duvara karşı [duvar-a karşı] *against the wall*
rüzgara karşı [rüzgar-a karşı] *against the wind*

Garajın kapısına karşı bisikletimi bırakmışım.
I believe I left my bicycle against the garage door.

-e rağmen *in spite of*

This can be replaces by **-e karşın** the speaker has the choice as the meaning is the same.

It translates as *despite* in negative sentences

buna rağmen *in spite of this*
bunlara karşın *in spite of these*
şuna rağmen *in spite of that*
şunlara rağmen *in spite of those*
ona karşın *in spite of that*
onlara rağmen *in spite of those*

In English there are many types of **-e rağmen** *although, though, in spite of, despite, notwithstanding, albeit etc.*. In Turkish however there are only two words: **-e rağmen** or **-e karşın**. When using **-e rağmen** or **-e karşın** the sentence should contain *contrast, insistence, regret, tenacity or hope.*

Examples of contrast.

Her şeye rağmen başarabilirdik. [şey-e rağmen]
In spite of everything we were able to succeed.

Havanın kararmasına rağmen, yollarına hâlâ yürüyerek devam ediyorlardı. [kararma-sı-n-a rağmen]
Despite the weather getting worse, they still carried on walking along the road.

Bütün bu olumsuz koşullara rağmen yine de başarabiliriz. [koşul-lar-a rağmen]
Despite all these negative circumstances, we were able to succeed again

Akşam saat 7'den sonra yemek yemenin sağlığa zararlı olduğunu bilmesine rağmen, her gece yatmadan önce atıştırmaktan kendini alamıyordu. [bilme-si-n-e rağmen] ("kendini alamamak" "can't help")
In spite of knowing that eating after 7 o'clock in the evening is dangerous to health, he could not help taking a snack before going to bed.

-e rağmen *despite* in negative sentences.

Ben hiçbir suçum olmamasına rağmen pişmanım, ya sen? [olma-ma-sı-n-a rağmen]
Despite not being at fault, I am sorry, how about you?

Kalan benzinimizin şehre varmaya yeteceği belli olmamasına rağmen, ısrarla yola devam ettiler. [olma-ma-sı-n-a rağmen]

Despite us not having petrol left to get to town, they insisted on continuing on the road.

[olma-ma-sı-n-a] This is Negative Infinitive of "olmama(k)" "to not be", with the addition of -(s)ı making it a specific definite noun described by "Kalan benzinimiz" "which-remains petrol-our", which is further suffixed with -(n)-a to make it part of "rağmen" clause.

An actual newspaper article Peugeot Crisis.

İSTANBUL, 5 Mart (Reuters) Fransız otomotiv üreticisi Peugeot'nun CEO'su Jean Philleppe Colin, krize rağmen Türkiye'ye ilişkin yatırım projelerinin devam ettiğini, kompakt sedan sınıfı araçların Türkiye'de üretimi için fizibilite çalışmaları yaptıklarını söyledi.

ISTANBUL, 5 March (Reuters) *The CEO of French car producer Peugeot Jean Philleppe Colin has said that in spite of the crisis, that the investment project concerning the compact sedan class vehicles' production in Turkey feasibility studies are on-going.*

Peugeot krize rağmen (kriz-e rağmen) Türkiye'ye yatırım projesini sürdürüyor.
In spite of the Peugeot crisis the investment project is still carrying on for Turkey.

Dependent Adverbs with "-den/-dan".

These adverbs require that the preceding noun have the motion away **-den/-dan, -ten/-tan** *from* suffix:

-dan dolayı *because of.*
-dan başka *except for, apart from, other than.*
-dan beri *since.*
-dan önce *before (in time).* [Modern Turkish]
-dan evvel *before (in time).* [Older Turkish, still in use]
-dan sonra *after(wards)*

Bundan dolayı *because of this.*

Mehmet'in yaptıklarından dolayı asla başaramayız! [Mehmet'-

in yaptık-lar-ı-n-dan]
Because of what Mehmet did we will never be able succeed!

Ondan başka *except for that.*

Piyanomdan başka her şeyi geri bırakacağım. [Piyano-m-dan başka] *Except for my piano I will leave everything behind.*

Ondan beri *since then.*

saat üçten beri *since 3 o'clock.* [üç-ten beri]

Saat üçten beri sizi arıyordum.
I have been looking for you since three o'clock

Geçen haftadan beri hastayım. [hafta-dan beri]
I have been ill since last week./I have been ill for a week.
(This means that I am still ill.)

Şundan önce, Şundan evvel *before that* (in time).

Mayıs ayından önce mühendis olarak çalışıyordum.
(or **çalışmaktaydım.**) [ay-ı-n-dan önce]
Before May I was working as an engineer.

Ondan evvel lokantaya gidelim. [On-dan evvel]
Before that, let's go to the cafe.

Ondan sonra after that.

Haziran ayından sonra emekli olacağım. [ay-ı-n-dan sonra]
After (the month of) July I shall retire (from work).

61

6 THE ARTICLES

Definite and Indefinite Articles.

The Subject Definite Article "THE".

There is no Turkish word for the subject definite article only the context tells us when to insert *"THE"* in English:

Çay pahalı. *Tea is expensive.* (Here "tea" is in general. The Definite Article is not required.)
Çay soğuk. *The tea is cold.* (Here the "tea" is particular. The Definite Article is required.)
Araba caddede. *The car is in the road.*

The Subject Definite Article *"the"* does not exist in Turkish as a word or a suffix, but it does exist as a Direct Objective Suffix. When the noun is an object of a verb as in "Mehmet mended *the* radio" then Turkish does use an Objective Suffix *"the"*.

The Direct Object Suffix "the".

Turkish Grammar calls it the Noun Object Condition (accusative). The direct object suffix which makes the object substantive is one of the most difficult hurdles for English Speakers to surmount when speaking, reading and understanding the Turkish Language.

It has the form of a suffix:
-i -ı -u -ü used with bare nouns which end in a consonant.
-yi -yı -yu -yü used with bare nouns which end in a vowel.
-ni -nı -nu -nü used with extended (already suffixed) nouns ending in a vowel.

In English both the Subject and Object of a sentence are made substantive by the use of the same Definite Article *"the"*. This "doubling" causes many learning problems for English Speakers.

Adam kapıyı (kapı-*yı*) **kapattı.**
The (subject substantive) *man closed the* (object substantive) *door.*

The subject is already understood as substantive in Turkish. Unlike English, the Definite Article *"the"* does not exist in Turkish. There is no *"the man"* as the subject definite article *"the"* is already understood.

However, there is an Object Definite Article *"the"* in Turkish which appears as the suffix **-i** (governed by Vowel Harmony).

To form an object **-i** is added to a bare noun stem: **ev** house (subj.) becomes **evi** *the house* (obj.) and when added extended (already suffixed) nouns which terminate in a consonant .

evim [ev-im] *my house* (subj.) becomes **evimi** [ev-im-i] *my house* (obj.)

-yi buffer letter **-y** is used when added to a bare noun stem ending in a vowel: **oda** *room* becomes **odayı** [oda-yı] *the room.*

-ni buffer letter **-n** is used when added to an already extended (suffixed) nouns which end in a vowel: **odası** [oda-sı-nı] *his room* becomes **odasını** [oda-sı-nı] *his room* (obj.)

The Direct Object is suffixed according to Vowel Harmony Rules.

Simple noun ending in a consonant:

Adam kilidi (kilid-i) **kapattı.** *The man locked the lock.*
The **-i** suffix makes the bare noun *"the lock"* substantive as a Direct Object.

Extended noun ending in a consonant:

Adam kilidimi (kilid-im-i) **kapattı.** *The man locked my lock.*
The **-i** suffix makes the extended noun *"my lock"* substantive as a Direct Object.

Simple noun ending in a vowel:

Adam kapıyı (kapı-yı) **kapattı.** *The man closed the door.*
The **-yı** suffix makes the bare noun *"the door"* substantive as a

Direct Object.

Extended noun ending in a vowel:

Adam kapısını (kapı-sı-nı) **kapattı.** *The man closed his door.*
The **-nı** suffix makes the extended [already suffixed] noun *"his door"* substantive as a Direct Object.

To sum up:

As objects of a verb nouns needs an object pointers (Objective Condition) in Turkish. This is the suffix **–(y)i -(y)ı -(y)ü -(y)u** using buffer letter **-y-** after vowels. However if the object pointer follows another suffix then the buffer letter becomes **-n-** and thus the object pointer suffix is **–ni -nı -nü -nu** when attached to possessed objects.

Some examples of Objective Condition.

onun *of him* and **onların** *of them* has been used here to make the meaning clear. Examples using the verb **boyamak** *to paint* and **boyamamak** *not to paint*.

Direct Object pointer **-i** for Simple Noun.
Evi boyuyorum. [ev-i] *I am painting the house.*

Direct Object pointer **-n-i** for Extended Noun.
(onun) Evini boyuyorum. [ev-i-n-i] *I am painting his house.* [the house of him]

Direct Object pointer **-y-i** for Simple Noun.
Arabayı boyuyorum. [araba-y-ı] *I am painting the car.*

Possessive Pronoun **-s-ı** plus Direct object pointer **-n-ı** for Extended Noun.
(onun) Arabasını boyuyorum. [araba-s-ı-n-ı] *I am painting his car.* [the car of him]

Possessive pronoun **-ları** plus Object Pointer **-nı** for Extended Noun.
(onların) Arabalarını boyuyoruz. [araba-ları-n-ı] *We are painting their car.* [the car of them]

Possessive Pronoun **-sı** plus Direct object pointer **-nı** for Extended Noun.

(onun) Arabasını boyuyor musunuz? [araba-s-ı-n-ı] *Are you painting his car?*

Possessive Pronoun **-ınız** plus Direct object pointer **-ı** for Extended Noun.
Mehmet, arabanızı boyamıyor mu? [araba-nız-ı] *Isn't Mehmet painting your car?*

Possessive Pronoun **-si** plus Direct object pointer **-ni** for Extended Noun.
(onun) Kedisini aramıyor muyum? [kedi-s-i-n-i] *Aren't I looking for his cat?*

Direct Object Pointer **-i** for Personal Pronoun.
Beni istiyor musun? [ben-i] *Do you want me?*
Seni istemiyor muyum? [sen-i] *Don't I want you?*

The Indefinite Article.

The Singular Indefinite Article is: **bir** *a, an, one.*

bir kapı *a gate.*
bir elma *an apple.*
bir bardak *one glass.*
Caddede bir araba var. *There is a car in the road.*

The Positive Plural Indefinite Article is: birkaç *some.*

In English the Article *some* is only used in Positive Statements whereas *any* is used in Negative Statements and also both in Positive and Negative Questions.

Positive Statements use *some* in English:

Bahçede birkaç kapı var.
There are some gates in the garden.
Bahçede birkaç kedi var.
There are some cats in the garden.
Caddede birkaç araba var
There are some cars in the road.

The Negative Singular Indefinite Article is "hiçbir" *not one.*

Negative Statements use *any* (usually with the plural) in English.

Bahçede hiçbir kapı yok.
There is not a gate in the garden at all./There aren't any gates in the garden.

Bahçede hiçbir kedi yok.
There is not a (single) cat in the garden./There aren't any cats in the garden.

Caddede hiçbir araba yok.
There is not a car in the road./There aren't any cars in the road.

Both Positive and Negative Questions use "hiçbir" *a (single)?, at all?* in English:

Bahçede hiçbir kapı yok mu?
Isn't there a (single) gate in the garden?

Bahçede bir kedi var mı?
Is there a cat in the garden?

Caddede hiçbir araba yok mu?
Isn't there a car in the road at all?

Caddede bir araba var mı?
Is there a car in the road?

The Negative Plural Indefinite Article is "hiç"- *any, none at all.*

Negative Statements use *any* in English:

Bahçede hiç kapı yok.
There are not any gates in the garden.

Bahçede hiç kedi yok.
There are not any cats in the garden.

Caddede hiç araba yok.
There are not any cars in the road.

Both Positive and Negative Questions use "hiç" *not any?* in English:

66

Bahçede hiç kapı yok mu?
Aren't there any gates in the garden?

Bahçede birkaç kedi var mı?
Are there any cats in the garden?

Caddede hiç araba yok mu?
Aren't there any cars in the road?

Caddede birkaç araba var mı?
Are there any cars in the road?

birkaç *some* and **hiç** *not any* always take a singular noun in Turkish but the meaning is plural in both Turkish and English:

birkaç kadın *some ladies*
hiç ev *not any houses*

From the previous section we can see that **hiçbir** *not a single one* is used for the singular both in Turkish and English:

Caddede hiçbir araba yok.
There is not a car in the road?

Hiç meaning *ever* or *never.*

In normal verbal *positive questions* **hiç** translates as *ever.*
Hiç Alanya'ya gittiniz mi?
Have you ever been to Alanya?

In normal verbal *negative questions* **hiç** translates as *never.*
Hiç Alanya'ya gitmediniz mi?
Have you never been to Alanya?

Other Indefinites are:

bazı *some*
Caddedeki bazı arabalar artık yok.
There were some cars in the road. (now there are none).

bazı *some* always takes the plural.
bazı kadınlar. *some ladies.*
bazı evler. *some houses.*

67

birçok *a lot of or many.*

Caddede birçok araba var.
There are a lot of cars on the road.
Caddede birçok araba var.
There are many cars on the road.

biraz. *a little, a small amount.*

Biraz şeker, lütfen.
A little sugar, please.

About Gender.

Generally Turkish has no gender. There is only one form of the noun, no masculine as *author, hero* and feminine as *authoress, heroine.* English has two forms of these nouns. When gender distinction is necessary Turkish uses locutions:

kız *girl* or **kadın** *lady* can be placed in front of the noun to show human femininity:
terzi *tailor* **kadın terzi** *tailoress.*
arkadaş *friend* **kız arkadaş** *girl friend.*

dişi *female* can be used before nouns to show a female animal :
köpek *dog* **dişi köpek** *bitch.*

erkek *male/man* can be used to show maleness :
kardeş *sister/brother* **erkek kardeş** *brother.*

kız *girl/maiden* can be used to show femininity :
kardeş *sister/brother* **kız kardeş** *sister.*
This method is used whenever it is necessary to differentiate between the sexes of brothers and sisters.

The Exceptions of Family Relationships.

Although there is generally no gender distinction in Turkish This does not apply to close family relationships. Relationships on the mother's side will have a different word than those of the father's side.

amca. *uncle.* [father's brother] and
dayı. *uncle.* [mother's brother]

teyze. *aunt.* [mother's sister] and
hala. *aunt.* [father's sister]

A word list of Turkish Family Relations

anne	*mother*
bebek	*baby*
erkek kardeş	*brother*
kız kardeş	*sister*
abı (ağabey)	*elder brother*
abla	*elder sister*
oğul, erkek çocuk	*son*
kız, kız çocuk	*daughter*
teyze	*aunt (mother's side)*
hala	*aunt (father's side)*
dede, büyükbaba	*grandfather*
nine, büyükanne	*grandmother*
anneanne	*grandmother (mother's side)*
baba anne	*grandmother (father's side)*
yeğen	*nephew; niece*
amca	*uncle (father's side)*
dayı	*uncle (mother's side)*
kuzen	*cousin*
kayınbaba, kayınpeder	*Father-in -law*
kaynana, kayınvalide	*Mother-in-law*
baldız	*Sister-in-law*
bacanak	*Sister-in-law's husband*
damat	*Son-in-law*
gelin	*Daughter-in-law;bride*
enişte	*sister's husband*
torun	*grandson; grand-daughter*
ikiz	*twin*

ikiz kardeş	*twin brother; twin sister*
eş, hanım, karı	*wife*
koca	*husband*
üvey anne	*stepmother*
üvey baba	*stepfather*

Turkish Conjunctions.

The Particle de or da *and, also, too.*

This is not a Static Position Suffix but written separately and it is translated *too, also, and, both.* It is a word in its own right but it does follow Vowel Harmony rules, hence the choice of **de** or **da**. It is always written separately as **de** or **da** and pronounced as **de** or **da**. It does not show any Consonant Mutation to "te" or "ta".

The following examples show this clearly:
Dolapta bir çanta var. *There is a bag in the cupboard.*
Bu dolap da küçükmüş. *This cupboard is small too.*

Conversational Stress.

The Static Position suffix **-de** is stressed, but the separate particle **de** the stress occurs on the preceding syllable.

Dolapta bir çanta var. *There is a bag in the cupboard.*
Bu dolap da küçükmüş. *This cupboard also seems (to be) small.*

The translations of the Static Position suffix **-de/-da** and of the particle **de** have two very different meanings.

Ali bey de odada. *Ali bey is also in the room.*
Benim de param yok. *I also have no money.*
Benim param var. *I have money.*
Benim de param var *I have got money too.*
Bahçedeki çocuklar da top ile oynuyorlar. *The children in the garden are playing with a ball too.*

Ali bey de ben de sigara içeriz. *Both Ali bey and I smoke (cigarettes).*

70

Here that the particle **de** *also* is repeated after each individual subject.

Hem... Hem... *both, both of.*

Hem bunu hem şunu al. *Take both this one and that one.*
Hem bu hem şu tamam. *Both this and that are OK.*

Ya... ya... — *either... or...*

Ya benimle gel ya onlu git. *Either you come with me or you go with him.*
Ya girin ya çıkın. *Either go in or come out.*

Ne... ne... — *neither... nor...*

Ne bunu ne şunu istiyorum. *I want neither this or that.*
Mehmet, ne beni ne seni seviyor. *Mehmet loves neither me nor you.*

Some Other Conjunctions.

ve *and*
veya *or*
fakat, ama *but*
ayrıca *moreover, furthermore*
bari, hiç olmazsa *at least*
çünkü *because*
ancak *scarcely, hardly, except*
yalnız *only*
yoksa *if not, otherwise*
öyleyse *if so*
mesela, örnek *for example*
mademki *seeing that, since*
halbuki *whereas*
sanki *as if..*
bu sebeple *in consequence*
bununla beraber *nevertheless*

neyse *whatever*
ise *as for*
zaten *besides*

Translation of "ile" *and, also.*

When **ile** stands between two nouns it can be used to translate
and when the basic meaning is *with, also.* Even when it is suffixed
as **-le/-la** or **-yle -yla**, when added to vowel, it is still translated
as *and* meaning "also".

Masada fincanla tabaklar var.
There are cups and plates on the table.

Ali ile arkadaşı, odaya girdi.
Ali and his friend entered the room.

Mustafa ile Selim partiye gitti.
Mustapha and Selim went to the party.

However if the suffix **-le/-la** does not come between the nouns then
it is translated as *with, together with.*

Mehmet benimle geldi. M*ehmet came with me.*
[Lit: Mehmet me-with came.]

Ali arkadaşıyla, odaya girdi.
Ali entered the room with his friend.

Mustafa, Selim 'le partiye gitti.
Mustapha went to the party with Selim.

Explanation:

If **ile** is in between two people or things as in **Ali ile arkadaşı** or
Mustafa ile Selim then these sentences are translated into English
by the conjunction "and", *Ali and his friends; Mustafa and Selim.*
If **ile** does not in between two nouns it is translated by "with" *Ali
went to party with his friend.*

Toplantıya sekreterimle katıldım.
I attended the meeting with my secretary.

Patron ile adamları aniden silahlarını çektiler.
The boss and his men suddenly pulled their guns.

In this type of sentence **ve** *and, also* could be used in place of **ile.**

Ali ve arkadaşı odaya girdi. [meaning: *and*]
Mustafa ve Selim partiye gitti. [*and*]
Masada fincan ve tabak var. [*and*]

For the other sentences we can not use "ve" in place of "ile".

Mehmet benimle geldi. [meaning: *with*] ("ve" cannot be used)
Ali, arkadaşıyla odaya girdi. [*with*] ("ve" cannot be used.)

7 TURKISH NOUNS

Formation of Nouns.

Formation of Nouns from Adjectives the suffix "-lik."
This suffix is vowel harmonized forms are **-lik -lık -luk -lük.**
The suffix **-lik** is very heavily used in Turkish. It has four main uses in Turkish as follows.

Formation of Abstract Nouns from Adjectives.

güzel *beautiful*
güzellik *beauty*

mutlu *happy*
mutluluk *happiness*

iyi *good*
iyilik *goodness*

çocuk *child*
çocukluk *childhood*

zor *difficult*
zorluk *difficulty, complication*

Some English abstract nouns end in *-ness, -tion, -ity.* These abstract nouns can be further suffixed in Turkish according to their function in meaning:

Hepimiz, çocukluğumuzu mutluluk içinde geçirdik. ["çocuk-luğ-umuz-u" "our childhood" (obj.), "mutlu-luk" "happiness"] *All of us passed our childhood in happiness.*

O zamanlarda mutluluğum sonsuzdu. [O zaman-lar-da mutlu-luğ-um (my happiness) son-suz-du.] *At that time my happiness was endless.*

Formation of Collective Nouns.

74

genç *young*
gençlik *youth*

yaşlı *old*
yaşlılık *age*

insan *person*
insanlık *human-kind*

Bakan *Minister*
Bakanlık *Ministry*

balık *fish*
balıkçı *fisherman* becomes **balıkçılık** *Fishing Club, Group, Association.*

This last example shows that noun suffixes can be chained to produce further extended meanings.

Forming Nouns of Usage.

Adding **-lik** to concrete nouns or verb stems forms nouns and adjectives meaning *"suitable for, intended for, place of"*.

tuz *salt*
tuzluk *salt cellar*

biber *pepper*
biberlik *pepper shaker*

göz *eye*
gözlük *spectacles*

kira *hire*
kiralık *for hire*

yağmur *rain*
yağmurluk *raincoat, mackintosh*

Forming Nouns of Location.

Bakan *Minister*
Bakanlık *Ministry*

çamaşır *linen, laundry items*
çamaşırlık *a laundry*

orman *forest*
ormanlık *forest place*

In this example of *forest* Turkish uses **-lik** to make a Substantive Noun of Location: **O tepenin arkasında büyük bir ormanlık bulunur.** *There is a large forest (to be found) behind that hill.* Here the word **ormanlık** is used as a general Substantive Noun of Location.

We may go on to talk about this particular **orman** itself:
O ormanda çok yabani hayvan varmış. *There are (probably) many wild animals in that forest. [yabani wild, savage, feral]*

Many place names (see a Turkish map) often end in the suffix **-lik**.
Ayvalık *Place of the Quince* ["ayva" "quince"] **Değirmenlik** *Place of the Mill* ["değirmen" "mill"] It is difficult to translate this suffix directly into English, we can only say "Quince" or "Quinceville" and "Milltown" or "Millhill" or similar. Arising from the above it also form nouns of "Place of" as follows:

elmalık *apple orchard* from **elma** *apple.*
sebzelik *vegetable garden, stall* from **sebze** *vegetable.*
çiçeklik *flower garden, stall* from **çiçek** *flower.*
kitaplık *book case, book store* from **kitap** *book.*

The Suffix "-lik" with Numbers.

A number is normally used as an adjective thus the number 10 (as an adjective) **On yumurta** *-Ten eggs.* Turkish changes numbers and numeric expressions into nouns by the addition of the **-lik** suffix thus the number 10 **on** becomes **onluk** *the amount of 10.* This similar to *"Lend me a 'tenner'"* in English where the number 10 has become a noun "of the amount ten". In English when saying *"I want a ten egg box."* we understand that our requirement is *"A box that will contain the amount of ten eggs"*

Turkish is more precise:

On yumurta bir kutu Lit: *"Ten eggs, one box".* This example has no meaning in Turkish it is just two items "ten eggs" and "one box". The suffix **-lik** is added to numbers to produce a complex counted noun. For the example of **on yumurta** *ten eggs*. Turkish will use a counted noun **on yumurtalık** *ten eggs-amount* thus *I want a ten egg box* becomes **On yumurtalık bir kutu istiyorum.** [Lit: "I want a ten egg-amount box"] To say *I want a box of ten eggs* the Turkish uses the **-li** *furnished with, containing* suffix:

On yumurtalı bir kutu istiyorum. *I want a box containing ten eggs.*

İki kişilik çadır var mı? [Lit: "Is there a tent of two person-amount?"] *Is there a double tent?*

Evet var. Kaç günlük ? [Lit: "Yes, there is. How many day-amount?"] *Yes there is. For how many days?*

Formation of Negative Abstract Nouns.

The suffix **-sizlik** *without*. The **-lik** suffix is often added to the **-siz** *without, lacking in* suffix to form Negative abstract nouns in **-sizlik.**

sabır *patience* becomes **sabırsız** *impatient* and the abstract noun **sabırsızlık** *impatience.*
Bazı kişilerin sabırsızlığını anlayabiliriz. *We can understand some people's impatience.*

istek *wish, desire* becomes **isteksiz** *reluctant, unwilling* and the abstract noun **isteksizlik** *reluctance, unwillingness.*
Onu yapmama isteksizliğimi itiraf etmek zorundaydım. [istek-siz-liğ-im-i] *I had to confess my reluctance to do it.*

Further suffixes can be added to show the noun condition.

mutsuz *unhappy* becomes **mutsuzluk** *unhappiness.*
Mutsuzluğum sonsuza kadar sürer. [Mutsuz-luğ-um] *My unhappiness has no end.*

dikkat *care* becomes **dikkatsiz** *careless* and the abstract noun **dikkatsizlik** *carelessness.*
Demin dikkatsizliğini fark ettim. [dikkat-siz-liğ-i-ni] *I just noticed your carelessness.*

Dikk-at is from an Arabic Feminine Plural and as such it does not follow Turkish Vowel harmony Rules as the final letter -a- is pronounced very long dikkAAt. Consequently any added suffixes take the Dotted form.

Compound Nouns

A noun may take another one or more nouns as describing nouns in order to make its basic meaning clear. These noun groups are called Compound Nouns. The describing nouns are called Completing Nouns and the Noun itself is called a Completed Noun.

Definite Noun Completion.

The first noun possesses the noun it modifies. The second noun is then suffixed as definitive. Both components retain their grammatical function as nouns in their own right.

Bisikletimin garajı. [Bisiklet-im-in garaj-ı.] *My bicycle's garage.* (Lit: "the garage of my bicycle.")

kapının zili. [kapı-nın zil-i.] *the door-bell.* (Lit: the bell of the door.)

Mehmet'in arabası. [Mehmet'-in araba-sı.] *Mehmet's car.* (Lit: the car of Mehmet.)

pencerenin perdesı. [pencere-nin perde-si.] *the window-curtain.* (Lit: the curtain of the window.)

All the above are Definite Compound nouns as they are both particular and both definite.

The last example **pencerenin perdesi** *the window's curtain* [the-curtain of-the-window] is a Definite Noun Compound. It is a particular definite curtain belonging to a particular definite window. However it can also be an Indefinite Noun Compound "any window curtain, window curtaining" **pencere perdesi** *window curtain(ing)*. This is the difference between Definite and Indefinite Compound Nouns.

Definite Noun Compound:

Pencerenin perdelerini yıkamalıyım. [Pencere-nin perde-ler-i-ni yıkamalıyım.] *I must wash the window curtains.* (Here "perdeleri-ni" is in the Object Condition "the curtains".)

Indefinite Noun Compound:

Pencere perdesi ambarda kaldı mı? *Is there any window curtain left in the store-room?*

Further Examples:

Here the Describing (Completing) Noun shows who or what is owned by the Described (Completed) Noun. The Describing Noun is suffixed with **-in -ın -ün -un.** The Described Noun is suffixed with the third person singular **-i -ı -ü -u.**

Konağın bahçesi . *The garden of the mansion, The mansion's garden.* Shows that "the garden belongs to the mansion". Describing Noun Suffix **-ın.** Described noun Suffix **-si** uses buffer Letter **-s** to keep vowels apart.

Çantanın fermuarı. *The zip of the bag, The bag's zip.* Shows that "the zip belongs to (is part of) the bag". Describing Noun Suffix **-nın** uses buffer Letter **-n-** to keep vowels apart. Described Noun Suffix **-ı.**

Bankanın kapısı. *The door of the bank, The bank's door.* Shows that "the door is part of and belongs to the bank". Describing Noun Suffix, **-nın** uses buffer Letter **-n-** to keep vowels apart. Described Noun Suffix, **-sı** uses buffer letter **-s** to keep vowels apart.

Kavanozun kapağı. *The lid of the jar, The jar's lid.* Shows that "the lid belongs to the jar". Describing Noun Suffix **-un.** Described Noun Suffix **-ı.** Its terminal **-k** mutates to **ğ** softened consonant from on addition of a vowel suffix.

More about Compound Nouns.

Bisikletimizi bıraktığımız yeri hatırlayamayacağız. [Bisiklet-imiz-in bırak-tığ-ımız yer-i-ni hatırla-ya-ma-y-acağız] *We will not be able to remember the place where we leave/have left our bicycle(s).* In these sentences **yer** is the "place that we can not remember where we left the bicycle", and **bisiklet** is the "bicycle". They are both in the Object Condition. Whereas *I can't remember my bicycle's place* translates as **Bisikletimin yerini hatırlayamıyorum** In this sentence **Bisikletimin yeri** is a Definite Noun Combination (both nouns are substantive). The "bicycle" is in the Ownership Condition and "place" is made substantive with the Object condition.

Summary of Definite Noun Completion Suffixes.

Describing Noun suffixes are always **-(n)in -(n)ın -(n)ün -(n)un.** Describing Nouns which end in a vowel always use buffer letter **-n-** where required.

The Described Noun suffixes are always **-(s)i -(s)ı -(s)ü -(s)u.** Described Nouns which end in a vowel always use buffer letter **-s-** where required.

A Special case su *water.*

The single exception **su** *water* which takes buffer letter **-y-** as both a Describing or Described Noun. The only noun in Turkish which does not conform to Buffer Letter rules is **su** *-water*. Whether as a Describing (Completing) Noun or as a Described (Completed) Noun it takes the Buffer letter **-y-** instead of the normal **-s-**. This avoids the ugly "susu". **Suyun sesi.** *The sound of the water, The water's sound* The Describing Noun Suffix is **Su-y-un** to make this noun the "owner", with **-y-** buffer letter to keep vowels apart. The Described Noun Suffix is **ses-i** to make this noun substantive.

Indefinite Compound Noun Completion

The first noun acts as an adjective to describe the second noun which is suffixed as a definitive noun.

Only the Completed Noun takes the suffix of the third person singular **-(s)i -(s)ı -(s)ü -(s)u**

Yaz mevsimi . *summer season.*[-i Completed Noun Suffix]
Kış tatili . *winter holiday.* [-i Completed Noun Suffix]
Yolcu gemisi. *ferryboat* .[Lit: traveller boat] [-i Completed Noun
Suffix] (**s** buffer letter for the third person singular.)
Armut ağacı. *the (particular) pear tree.* [-ı Completed Noun
Suffix]

When two nouns are joined as in *lamp-post*, the second noun takes
the third person possessive suffix, e.g. **ışık direği** [ışık direğ-i] *lamp-
post* (Lit: Lamp its-post). Similarly **gece kulübü** [gece kulüb-ü]
nightclub (Lit: night its-club). This is the way that Turkish shows a
connection between the two words to make a complex noun the first
noun "lamp" becomes an adjective to describe the second "post"
which is made into a definitive noun by the addition of the third
person suffix. Further suffixes can be added to this complex noun as
required:

ışık direği. [direğ-i] *lamp post.* [lamp its-post.]
onun ışık direği. [direğ-i] *his lamp post.*
Mehmet'in ışık direği. [direğ-i] *Mehmet's lamp post.*
onun ışık direğinden. [direğ-i-nden] *from his lamp post.*
Mehmet'in ışık direğinden. [direğ-i-nden] *from Mehmet's lamp
post.*

If you say *lamp post* , that is **ışık direği**, and *his lamp post* would be
also **ışık direği**. Why? Because the **-i** at the very end has the
meaning of *"Indefinite Noun Completion"* as in the first phrase, and
"Possession for the 3rd. Person Singular" as in the second. To avoid
doubling only one of them is used. This shows the conflict between
Indefinite Noun Completion Suffix **-i** and 3rd. Person Possessed
Suffix **-i**. But how to distinguish between them? In order to do that,
you should bring **onun** *his, her* at the beginning, thus **onun ışık
direği** is clearly about possession.

bisiklet yeri. [bisiklet yer-i] *the bicycle place.*
kapı kolundan. [kapı kol-u-ndan] *from the door handle.*
yaz okulu. [yaz okul-u] *the summer school.*
yolcu gemisinde. [yolcu gemi-si-nde] *on the ferry boat.*
Ali'nin elma ağacı. [elma ağac-ı] *Ali's apple tree.*
ayakkabı boyası. [ayakkabı boya-sı] *the shoe polish.*
bilgisayar ekranı. [bilgisayar ekran-ı] *the computer screen.*
su borusu. [su boru-su] *water pipe.*

Descriptive (Uncompleted) Compound Nouns.

Neither noun is made definitive thus producing a Descriptive Combined Noun. The first noun acts as an adjective describing the main noun which follows. In this compound neither Completing or Completed Noun take a suffix. It describes the material from which the second noun is made.

el çanta. *handbag.* (hand + bag)
elma ağaç. *apple tree* (apple + tree)
tahta kapı. *wooden door.*
alüminyum pencere. *aluminium window.*
demir köprü. *iron bridge.*
plastik sandalye. *plastic chair.*
pamuk mendil. *cotton handkerchief.*
tahta masa. *wooden table.*
pamuk gömlek. *cotton shirt.*
su bardak. *water glass. (tumbler)*
benzin depo. *petrol dump.*

Some of these compound nouns have formed words through historical usage:

ortaokul. *middle school.* (middle + school)
başbakan . *prime minister* . (head + minister)
ayakkabı. *shoe.* (foot + cover)
Vowel Harmony does not operate as each word is individual.

Compound Noun Chains.

Nouns can be chained together using the Ownership (genitive) suffix as in English:

Arkadaşımın annesinin köpek kulübesi. [Arkadaş-ım-ın anne-si-nin köpek kulübe-si.] *My friend's mother's dog kennel. The dog kennel of friend's mother.*

Kavak ağacının dalları. [Kavak ağac-ı-nın dal-lar-ı] *The poplar tree's branches.*

Ali beyin çaydanlığın kapağı. [Ali bey-in çaydanlığ-ın kapağ-ı] *Ali*

Bey's teapot's lid.

Kitabının sayfaların resimleri. [Kitab-ın sayfa-lar-ın-ın resim-ler-i]
The pictures of the book's pages.

Belediye parkının kapısı. [Belediye park-ı-nın kapı-sı] *The gate of
the corporation park.*

Manisa Trafik Polis karakolu. [Manisa Trafik Polis karakol-u]
Manisa Traffic Police headquarters.

Plural Compound Nouns:

Armut bahçeleri. [bahçe-ler-i] *Plum orchards.*
Müdürler Toplantısı. [Müdür-ler] *Managers Meeting.*
Öğrencinin defterleri. [defter-ler-i] *Student's notebooks.*
Evlerin kapılarının zilleri. [Ev-ler-in kapı-lar-ın-ın zil-ler-i] *house
door bells..*
The last example shows in Turkish "The bells of the doors of the
houses"

Compound Nouns with Suffixes of Condition:

Kiraz bahçeleri güzelce çiçekleniyor. [bahçeler-i] *The cherry
orchards are flowering nicely.* (Subject Condition.)

Çiftçi elma bahçelerini suladı. [bahçeler-i-ni] *The farmer watered
the apple orchards.* (Object Condition.)

Çiftçi portakal bahçesine gitti. [bahçe-si-ne] *The farmer went to
his orange orchard.* (Movement Towards Condition.)

Çocuk sebze bostanında oynuyorlar. [bostan-ı-nda] *The children
are playing in the vegetable garden.* (Static Cond.)

Mehmet belediye parkından çıktı. [park-ı-ndan] *Mehmet came out
from the municipal park.* (Movement Away Condition.)

Compound Nouns with Proper Names.

Şair Eşref Bulvarı *Şair Eşref Avenue* Indefinite Compound Noun
Şair Eşref Describing Noun ("The Poet Eşref") **Bulvarı** Described

Noun.

Apocopating Nouns.

Definition:
Apocopate (verb.) to cut off or drop, to apocopate a word, syllable, letter.
Apocopate (adj.) shortened by apocope, an apocopate form.
A comprehensive list of Turkish apocopating nouns can be found in The Glossary Chap. 43 Page 430.

Nouns which lose an internal vowel in Turkish.

Some Turkish nouns which lose their final vowel (apocopate) when a suffix which itself begins with a vowel is added to the noun.

As an example: **izin** *leave, time off* becomes **izn-im** [NOT izin-im] *my leave.* The final vowel of the noun root is dropped when adding a suffix which begins in a vowel.

Adding a suffix beginning with a vowel *does* affect the Noun.

iznim *my leave* becomes **iznimden** [izn-im-den] *since my time off.* The final vowel in the noun root is lost when adding **-im** *my* suffix (which begins with a vowel).

Adding a suffix beginning with a consonant *does not* affect the Noun.

izindeyim [izin-de-yim] *I am on leave.*
Here the vowel of **izin** is not lost as the first suffix **-de** begins with a consonant.

Some Examples of Possessive Adjectives being added:

fikir *idea* becomes:
fikrimiz *our idea.*
keyif *joy* becomes:
keyfi *his/her joy.*
oğul *son* becomes:
oğlun *your son.*

boyun *neck* becomes:
boynum *my neck.*
nakit *transport* becomes:
onun nakdi *his transport.*
Here, final consonant **-t** has Mutated to its soft form **-d.**
ağız *mouth* becomes:
ağzınız *your mouth.*
kayıp *loss* becomes:
kaybı *his loss.*
This noun also undergoes a softening of the consonant **-p** to **-b.**

The rules of Consonant Mutation are still observed in the reduced form of the noun. There are some nouns which do not soften their root vowel as they may be considered:
(a) Single Syllable Words or
(b) Foreign Word Imports.
As an example: **vakit** (arb.) *time, occasion* which becomes **vaktim** *my time* without any consonant mutation.

Some Examples of Case Suffixes being added:

Mehmet filmi seyretmiş. [film-i] *It seems Mehmet watched the film.* Here the Direct Object suffix **-i** affects the noun **film.**

Ali'nin alnı terliyor. [Ali'nin aln-ı] *Ali's forehead is sweating.* Here the word **alın** *forehead* is in the Possessive Relationship which affects the noun **alın** shortening it to **aln-ı.**

Adding a suffix which begins with a consonant, then the noun root retains its basic form:

ağızda. *in the mouth.*
beyinden. *from the brain.*
kayıptan. *from the loss.*

The noon root is shortened (apocopated) as stated above, if the first added suffix begins with a vowel:

ağzında. [ağz-ı-nda] *in his mouth.*
beynimden. [beyn-im-den] *from my brain.*
kaybımızdan. [kayb-ımız-dan] *from our loss.*

8 TURKISH ADJECTIVES

Adjectives Basic Rules.

Words which describe the condition, colour size, number, position and place of nouns are called adjectives.

Adjectives are invariable. They do not have to agree with the noun they describe in either number or gender as in French or Spanish.
(a) They have no singular or plural form. (Never add a **-lar/-ler** plural suffix to an adjective.)
(b) Adjectives have no gender. There is no masculine, feminine or neuter form.
Adjectives and adjectival phrases precede the noun as they do in English.
Adjectives can be formed from both nouns or verbs as in English.

Position of Adjectives.

Adjectives are words that describe or modify nouns A *blue* house, a *rich* man. The adjective always comes in front of its noun as in English.

Mavi ev. *The blue house.*
Mavi evler. *(The) blue houses.*
Zengin adam. *The rich man.*
Yorgun çocuklar. *(The) tired children.*

When adjectives follow a noun the meaning is entirely different. It becomes a "Statement of Fact". Generally a comma is added after the subject noun:

Ev, mavi. *The house is blue.*
Evler, mavi. *The houses are blue.*
Adam, zengin. *The man is rich.*

Uzun geniş yol. *The long wide road.* is different to **Uzun yol, geniş.**
The long road is wide.
Geniş yol, uzun. *The wide road is long.* is different to:
Yol, uzun geniş. *The road is long and wide.*

Adjectives Emphasized and Public Forms.

Uzun yol, geniştir. *The long road is wide.*
Uzun yol, geniş midir? *Is the long road wide?*
The emphasis is stressed by the use of the verb *to be* suffix **-dir**
(Vowel Harmony and Consonant Mutation are observed), which
makes it a "Statement of Fact" **Yol geniş*tir*.** *The road is wide.*

This shows that the verb *to be* **-dir** is sometimes lacking in the third
person in Turkish, unless it is needed to emphasize the meaning or it
is a public statement such as a notice, as follows:

Bu ev, mavidir. [mavi ev] *This house is blue.*
Giriş Yaşaktır. [yaşak giriş] *Entry is Forbidden.*
These examples are emphasized using the verb "to be" **-dir** *is*.
Normally **-dir** is not required or used in normal conversation.

Adjectives Position of the Article.

bir *a, an, one* can interpose between the adjective and its noun. This
has the effect of putting the emphasis on the adjective and/or causes
the noun it describes to become definite.

Bir güzel kız güldü. *A beautiful girl laughed.*
In this example some girl or other laughed an indefinite girl,
therefore the adjective follows **bir**.

Güzel bir kız gördüm. *I saw a beautiful girl.*
In this example a definite girl was seen and moreover she was
definitely beautiful **güzel** followed by **bir** emphasizes all these
points.

Generally speaking if the indefinite article is used with its noun, then
Turkish will not separate them as we do in English :

Büyük beyaz bir ev(dir). *It is a big white house.*
Yaşlı bir adam. *An old man.*
Boş bir kutu. *An empty box.*

Adjectives used as Nouns.

Turkish adjectives can also be used as nouns:

hasta *ill, sick,* **bir hasta** *a patient.*
Hastalar hastanede. *The patients are in hospital.*

zengin *rich,* **bir zengin** *a rich person.*
Otelde kalan bir zengin var. *There is a rich [person] who is staying at the hotel.*

Intensified and Reducing Adjectives.

Adjective forms which deepen, strengthen and intensify their basic meaning.

Repetition of the adjective intensifies the meaning.

Beyaz beyaz arabalar. *Cars so white.*
Sıcak sıcak çörekler. *Such fresh buns.*
Uzun uzun yollar. *Really long roads.*
Taze taze yumurtalar. *Really fresh eggs.*

Placing the question particle between repeated adjectives intensifies the meaning.

This is similar to saying in English "Is he rich or is he rich?"
Beyaz mı beyaz arabalar *Are the cars white of what?*
Sıcak mı sıcak çörekler *So fresh buns.*
Uzun mu uzun yollar. *The roads are so long.*
Taze mi taze yumurtalar. *Really fresh eggs.*

To intensify an adjective, follow these steps:
(1) Find the first vowel of the plain adjective.
(2) Add one of the letters **(p, r, s, m)** to form a syllable.
(3) Prefix the new syllable to the plain adjective for its Intensified Form.

Beyaz etek. becomes **Bembeyaz etek.** [Be + m + beyaz etek] *Bright white skirt.*

Kırmızı elma. becomes **Kıpkırmızı elma.** [Kı + p + kırmızı elma] *Bright red apple.*

Temiz ev. becomes **Tertemiz ev.** [Te + r + temiz ev] *A squeaky clean house.*

Doğru yol becomes **Dosdoğru yol.** [Do + s + doğru yol] *Dead straight road.*

There are some exceptions **paramparça, çırılçıplak** etc. In these cases more than one letter is used **(p, r, s, m)** as **(-ram-** or **-ril-)** in the examples above. There is no rule for which letter to choose from among **(p, r, s, m)**. It a feeling for the one which sounds correct.

A comprehensive list of Intensified Turkish Adjectives and Adverbs is to be found in the Glossary at Chapter 43 Page 448

Doubled Adjectives and Words.

Turkish has many picturesque doublets similar to English. Some English examples are "pell-mell topsy-turvy, jingle-jangle" etc. These types of words are used extensively in Turkish conversation and reading. We list them here as they are often difficult to "look up" in a dictionary.

A comprehensive list of Turkish Doublets is to be found in the Glossary at Chapter 43 Page 451

Turkish Intensifying Doublets.

There are different intensification of meanings methods in Turkish. Some of them are "doublets":

(1) Repetition of the Same Word.

In the first version the same word is repeated twice:

akşam akşam. *late in the evening(s).*
sabah sabah. *early in the morning(s).*

korka korka. *getting scared.*
yavaş yavaş. *slowing down.*
sıcak sıcak. *really hot and fresh.*
usul usul. *gently, quietly.*

Ahmet'i gördüm sabah sabah nereye gidiyordu merak ettim.? *I saw Ahmet early in the morning and wondered where he was going?*

Akşam akşam konuşmayalım şimdi çok yorgunum. *Let's not chat so late in the evening, I am very tired now.*

İç şu çayı sicak sicak, soğutmadan hadi! *Drink that tea it's hot and fresh, come on don't let it cool down!*

Geldiğinde kapıyı usul usul çal, çocuk uyanmasın. *When you come knock the door gently and quietly so the child does not wake up.*

Burayı sevmediğini biliyorum, ama yavaş yavaş (zamanla) alışacaksın. *I know that you don't like it here, but you'll slowly get used to it (in time).* "Yavaş yavaş" is a little bit different. It indicates that something will happen in time. So we can say: **Yavaş yavaş her şey düzelir, merak etme.** *Don't worry, everything will be alright in (good) time.*

When a "doublet" is used with a verb then it becomes a normal adverb: Double adjectives form mostly adverbs:
ince. (adjective) *thin.*
ince ince. (adverb) *thinly.*
Soğanları ince ince doğramalısın. *You must chop the onions up thinly.* When an adjective is used as an adverb, another word is required to "intensify" its meaning:

(2) Two Different Words are Used Together.

In this version, for strengthening two very similar, sometimes the same, or opposite words are used:

sessiz sedasız. (seda voice) *quietly.*
hesap kitap. *calculate, sort out (finances).*
yok yoksul. *very poor.*

sorgusuz sualsız. (sorgu a question, sual an inquiry) *beyond question, take for granted.*

- e bata çıka. (batmak to sink, çıkmak to get out of takes a Motion Toward Object) *with great difficulty, to wade through*
gire çıka (girmek to enter, çıkmak to get out of) *to frequent a place, come and go.*
utana sıkıla. *timidly, ashamedly.*

Sonunda sessiz sedasız ortadan kayboldu. *In the end he* quietly and silently *slipped away (vanished).*

Geçen yıl aldıkları şoför eve gire çika, evin küçük kızını ayarttı ve bu yıl da evlendiler. *Last year the chauffeur that they had employed* kept coming and going *to their home; he seduced the daughter of the house and this year they got married.*

Utana sikila patronun karşısına çıktı zam istemek için. *He went to the boss* timidly *because he wanted a rise. (zam increase/rise)*

Adamı sorgusuz sualsız içeri attılar, neredeyse 2 haftadır hapiste! *It was 2 weeks in prison, they threw the man inside* without any questioning!

Küçük kız sahilden topladığı irili ufaklı deniz kabukları ile oynuyordu. *The little girl was playing with the shells,* both big and small, *that she had picked up at the shore.*

Yarından önce bu yedek parçaların üretim maliyetini hesap kitap yapmamız lâzım. *We need* to calculate *the production cost of these spare parts before tomorrow.*

Çamurlara bata çıka sonunda ana yola vardılar. *After* wading through *the mud at last they reached the main road.*

(3) Two Different Words are Used Together the Second is Meaningless.

In third version 2 different words are used but the second one is mostly meaningless. It does not exist alone in the dictionary.

karman çorman. *hodge-podge.*
karışık kuruşuk. *all mixed up.*

kayıt kuyut. *restrictions, paper-work.*
zar zor. *hardly, scarcely.*

Eve geldiğimde ortalık öyle karman çormandı ki 2 saattir toparlamaya çalışıyorum. It was such a hodgepodge *around the house that I took two hours to clear it up.*

Bıktım senin bu karışık kuruşuk işlerinden! *I'm fed up with these* mixed up *doings of yours!*

Kayit kuyut tamam, haftaya okula başlıyorsun. All the paper-work *is OK and you'll start school within a week.*

Son zamanlarda çok kilo aldığı için oturduğu koltuktan zar zor kalkabiliyordu. *In the end because he had put so much weight on he could* hardly *get up from his armchair.*

(4) Repeating Words but the Second Word begins with M.

In fourth version 2 different words are used. The second one always begins with "m" and the rest of the word is the same with the first one.

m-doublets.

If a word is doubled and the second of the pair is changed to begin with a letter **-m** then the meaning is "and the suchlike.."

While I was in Turkey I heard a mother say to her small child: **Sokağa çık, oyna moyna!** *Go on the street and* play about! (çıkmak to exit, go out, oynamak = to play)

Cebimde para mara yok. *I have no* cash or suchlike *in my pocket.*

Bugün sokakta araba maraba görülmez. *Today there are no cars or anything to be seen on the street.*

Bira mira'yi ister misin? *Do you want a* beer or anything?

If the original word already begins with an "m" then "filan and/or falan" is used to arrive at the "suchlike" meaning:

Müdürler falan de geliyor. *The managers* and all that lot *are coming as well.*

tahta mahta. *wood, board and things.*
kapı mapı . *doors and things (windows, exits).*
güzel müzel. *good and nice.*

Yasak masak anlamam kardeşim, ben kızımı göreceğim! *I don't understand* all the "forbids" *pal, I am going to see my girl!*

Ben evrak mevrak görmedim masada! *I didn't see the* papers and things *on the table.*

Valla bak sen yaşlı maşlı dinlemem, döverim ha! *Look! I'm not listening about (your) being* old and decrepit, *I'm going to beat you up!*

(5) Only One Word is Used with Meaningless Prefixes.

In fifth version only one word is used with meaningless prefixes.

güpegündüz. *(in) broad daylight.* from: *gündüz*
kıpkırmızı. *bright red.* from: *kırmırzı*
dapdar. *so very narrow.* from: *dar*
sımsıcak. *nice an warm and comfy.* from:*sıcak*
kaskatı. *totally rigid.* from: *katı*
darmadağınık. *in a mess/disheveled.* from: *dağınık*

3 çocuk güpegündüz kaçırıldı. *Three children have been kidnapped in* broad-daylight.

Mehmet'in suratı utançtan kıpkırmızı döndü. *Mehmet's face turned* bright red *with embarrassment.*

Pantolon dapdar, sanıyorum ben kilo almışım. *The trousers are* so narrow, *I think I have put some weight on.*

Sapsarı saçları ile çok alımlıydı. *She was very attractive with* bright yellow hair.

Dudakları kupkuruydu, suya uzandı ve bir şişe suyu bitirdi. *His lips* were so parched *that he reached for a drink of water and* *finished off a whole bottle.*

Hakkındaki onca eleştiriye rağmen o, dimdik ayaktaydı. *Despite all this criticism about his rights,* he stood up dead straight.

Gerçek apaçık ortada, sen suçlusun! *In truth it is* glaringly clear, *you are guilty!*

(6) Two words are Used Both Meaningless Alone.

In sixth version 2 words are meaningless but there are also very little examples for such a strengthening.

hort zort. *like a bull a gate, rudely and noisily.*
paldır küldür. *like a bull at a gate, rudely and noisily, discourteously.*
harala gürele. *hustle and bustle.*
zart zurt. *bluster, loud empty talk, bellow, intimidate.*
zırt pırt. *so often, so frequently.*
palas pandıras. *helter-skelter.*

O edepsiz kabadayı, bizimle tartışınca daima zart zurt eder. *When that nasty bully argues with us he always* blusters and intimidates us.

İşleri hort zortla (paldır küldür/kaba saba bir şekilde) yürütemezsin, biraz daha insancıl ol! *Don't carry on* like a bull at the gate, *be a little more gentlemanly!*

İşte ne yapalım, harala gürele gidiyor hayat. *What ever we do, life goes on* with a hustle and bustle.

Zirt pirt telefon etmesene, patron kızıyor! *Don't keep using the telephone* so often, *the boss is getting angry!*

Tatile bir anda, palas pandiras gittik ama buna rağmen çok iyi geçti. *We left* helter-skelter *for a holiday at the drop of a hat (bir anda), but in spite of this it went well.*

(7) "mi" Interrogative Particle" is Used.

In seventh version "mi interrogative particle" is used.

çırkın mı çırkın. *really ugly.*
kötü mü kötü . *really bad.*
tipsiz mi tipsiz. *not an oil painting, so unattractive.*

Kız çırkın mı çırkındı! *Is that girl ugly or is she ugly!, That girl is* really *ugly.*

Ali tipsiz mi tipsiz! *Ali is* no oil painting*!, Ali is quit unattractive.*

Mehmet zengin mi zengin! *Mehmet is* really loaded*!*

Film korkunç mu korkunçtu! *The film was* so *scary!*

No other intensification should be used with this form: "Mehmet o kadar zengin mi zengin." is incorrect.

(8) Normal Intensifying Words are Used "very, quite, etc.".

In eighth version: Normal strengthened sentences are used.

çok. *much, many.*
epey. *a good deal of, goodish amount.*
hayli. *fair amount, pretty much.*
hatırı sayılır miktarda/oranda. *considerable amount.*
bayağı. *common, quite, a sort of.*

Aşağıda bayağı bir çuval var, artık yarın taşırız. *Downstairs there is a* sort of *sack, and we'll take it with us tomorrow.*

Üzerinden epey (hayli, çok) zaman geçti tam hatırlayamıyorum şimdi. *Since than* quite a lot of time *has passed I cannot remember completely now.*

Üyelerimiz hatırı sayılır bir oranda yurtdışı gezisine katılacaklarını belirttiler. *They have indicated that a* considerable number *of our members will join the overseas tour.*

Elde edilen verilerin hatırı sayılır bir miktarı yanlıştı. *A considerable amount of what has been acquired is incorrect.*

Reducing Adjectives:

Adjective forms which weaken their basic meaning.

Reducing adjectives are formed by adding the suffixes **-ce, -cik** to qualifying adjectives or **-(i)msi, -(i)mtırak** to colours.

Güzel araba **güzelce araba** *a niceish car.*
Yeşil elma **yeşilimsi elma** *a greenish apple.*
Mavi çanta **mavimsi çanta** *a bluish bag.*
Kısa pantolon **kısacık pantolon** *little short pants.*
Küçük masa **küçücük masa** *a smallish table.*
Köpeğim **köpeciğim** [köpek+cık+im] *my little dog.*
Sarı elma **sarımtırak elma** *a yellowish apple.*

Recognising Adjectives.

In Turkish, words can often be recognized as adjectives by their endings. This is similar to English where words can also be recognized as adjectives by their endings. For instance the ending -*ful* in the word *beautiful "They built a beautiful house in the hill."* Thus the -*ful* adjective adds the concept of *beauty* to the house.

There are other adjectival endings in English where English speakers recognize instantly the attribute being added by its ending. One of these adjectival endings is used above, in the heading *"Attributable"*. The following example also uses the "Ability Attribute" -*able "They have built a beautiful, desirable house on the hill"*.

Some other adjectival endings in English may be:
-*ly* as in *the lovely view.*
-*ing* as in *the shaking branch.*
-*ive* as in *the positive result.*
-*en* as in *the broken arrow.*
and some other forms; each ending giving us a differing degree or meaning in concept.

This is the way that Turkish follows and if one learns the Adjectival Endings it is easier to recognize the concept of meaning as we automatically do in our own tongue.

They are also words in their own right and they should not be considered as adjectives with an added suffix. As with English the (adjectival) ending on the word often points to the type of attribute that the adjective supplies to its noun. For instance in English there is a different type of attribute supplied by the adjectives *lovely, loving, loveable, lovelorn, loved* although the root word carries the same meaning.

The Adjectival Suffix -ik -ık -ük uk

This suffix usually forms adjectives where the described noun is in a state **from which it cannot return** that is it has assumed a permanent state. From **yanmak** *to burn* the adjective **yanık** is formed meaning *burnt* (as a permanent state).

bir düşük yaprak. *a fallen leaf* [from **düşmek** *to fall*]
bazı kırık tabaklar. *some broken plates.* [**kırmak** *to break*]
kesik parçalar . *cut (up) parts.* [**kesmek** *to cut*]
By recognizing the **-ilk** suffix we can see a permanent adjectival state has been attained. We must take care however not to mistake nouns which end in **-ilk** such as **balık** *fish* or **sözlük** *dictionary* as being adjectives.

The different Forms of Adjectives.

Using the Present Participle **düşen** *which falls/which is falling* as an adjective then the meaning changes.

Bir düşen yaprak. *A falling leaf.* [Lit: A which-is-falling leaf.]
Düşen yapraklar. *Falling leaves.*

Similarly using the past participle:
düşmüş olan *which has fallen.*
düşmüş olan yaprak nemlidir. *The leaves which have fallen are damp/the fallen leaves are damp.*

Common Adjectives and their Opposites.

beautiful	**güzel**	*ugly*	**firkin**
better	**daha iyi**	*worse*	**daha koru**

big	**büyük**	*small*	**küçük**
cheap	**ucuz**	*expensive*	**pahalı**
early	**erken**	*late*	**geç**
easy	**kolay**	*difficult*	**zor**
free	**serbest**	*occupied*	**meşgul**
full	**dolu**	*empty*	**boş**
good	**iyi**	*bad*	**kötü**
heavy	**ağır**	*light*	**hafif**
here	**burada**	*there*	**orada**
hot	**sıcak**	*cold*	**soğuk**
near	**yakın**	*far*	**uzak**
next	**gelecek**	*last*	**son**
old	**ihtiyar/yaşlı**	*young*	**genç**
old	**eski**	*new*	**yeni**
open	**açık**	*shut*	**kapalı**
quick	**çabuk**	*slow*	**yavaş**
right	**doğru**	*wrong*	**yanlış**
left	**sol**	*right*	**sağ**

The Comparison of Adjectives.

The Degree of Equality.

This Degree of Comparison uses **kadar** [Lit: "its amount"] *as.*

Londra İstanbul kadar güzeldir. *London is as beautiful as Istanbul.*

Mehmet Ali kadar zengindir. *Mehmet is as rich as Ali.*

Kar kadar beyaz. *As white as snow.*

Also used ...**ile aynı** *the same as.*

Ali, Mehmet'ile anyı yaştadır. *Ali is the same age as Mehmet.*

Araban, bemimkiyle aynı renktedir. *Your car is the same colour as mine.*

The use of *"-dir" - "is"* in some these sentences makes a Statement of Fact. It is not always necessary if the Fact is "understood" as in **Kar kadar beyaz.** *As white as snow.*

The Negative Equality.

The negative comparison is marked by the use of **değil** *is not* placed after the comparison.

Londra İstanbul kadar güzel değil. *London is not as beautiful as Istanbul.*

Ayşe Deren kadar boylu değil. *Ayşe is not as tall as Deren.*

The Degree of Comparison:

This comparison is made by using **daha** *more* and suffixing the object being compared with **-dan** or **-den** *from* thus giving the sense *"than"* in the comparison.

Mehmet Ali'den daha zengin. *Mehmet is richer than Ali.*

İstanbul Londra'dan daha güzel. *Istanbul is more beautiful than London.*

Demir sudan daha ağır. *Iron is heavier than water.*

The Negative of Comparison.

The Negative First Degree Comparison uses **az** *less.*

Londra İstanbul'dan az meşgul. *London is less busy than İstanbul.*

Bulmacalar Türkçe derslerden az ilginç. *Crosswords are less interesting than Turkish lessons.*

The Superlative.

The Third Degree of Comparison is obtained by using **en** *the most.*

Mehmet en zengin adam. *Mehmet is the richest man.*

Dünyanın en güzel şehri, İstanbul. *Istanbul is the world's most beautiful city.*

The Negative Superlative.

The Negative uses **en az** *the least.* [Lit: the most less].

Dünyanın en az zengin memleketleri Afrika'da. *The least richest countries of the world are in Africa*

However, the fact is that although possible, usage of **en az** for negative superlatives is not common. The preferred way is to use the superlative form of opposite adjective. So, the preferred way of the example is:

Dünyanİn en fakir memleketleri Afrika'da. *The world's poorest countries are in Africa.*

The more common usage of **en az** is *at least.*

Ahmet en az Mehmet kadar zekidir. *Ahmet is at least as intelligent as Mehmet.*

Sen de en az benim kadar yeteneklisin. *You are at least as talented as me.*

kadar iyi. *as good as.*
Bu, o kadar iyi. *This, is as good as that.*
Bu onun kadar iyi *This is as good as that*

-dan daha iyi *better than*
Bu, ondan daha iyi *This, is better than that.*

en iyisi *the best*
Bu, en iyisi(dir) [Lit: iyisi the best] *This, is the best of all*

Further Shades of Degree Positive.

çok. *too, very, many.*

Çok para istiyor. *He wants a lot of money.*
Çok mutluyum. *I'm very happy.*
çok odalı bir otel. *a hotel containing many rooms.*

en çok . *the most.*
en çok para. *the most money.*
Ali'nin en çok parası var. *Ali has got the most money.*
Tepede en çok ev var. *Most of the houses are on the hill.*

daha. *more.*
İki çay daha, lütfen. *Two more teas, please.*
Daha beş bira, lütfen. *Five beers more, please.*

fazla. *too much, excessive.*
Fazla yemek geldi. *Too much food has arrived.*
Fazla para istediler. *They wanted too much money.*

daha fazla *much more.*
daha fazla yemek geldi. *much more food has arrived.*
daha fazla para istediler. *they wanted much more money.*

Further Shades of Degree Negative.

az, biraz. *a little.*
Az sonra çarşıya gidiyorum. *I'm going to the shops a little later on.*
Biraz tuz istiyorum. *I want a little salt.*

daha az. *lesser.* [Lit: more less(er)]
Yemeğe daha az tuz koyunuz. *Put less salt on the food.*
Buralarda, daha az polis var. *There are less policemen around here.*

pek az. *very little.* [Lit: a bit less(er)]
Pek az sigara kullanıyorum. *I smoke (cigarettes) just a little,*
Pek az şeker istiyorum. *I only want a little sugar.*

çok az. *extremely little* [lit: a lot little(er)]
Çok az benzin kalıyor. *Just a small amount of petrol is left.*
Çok az para istedi *He only wanted a very small amount of money.*

The Demonstrative Adjectives *"this, these, that, those" are discussed in Chapter 36 Demonstratives.*

9 PERSONAL PRONOUNS

Personal Pronouns *I, you, he.*

In Turkish basic pronouns are divided into two categories:
(1) Stand-alone Pronouns **Ben gidiyorum** *I am going.*
(2) Pronouns in suffix form (extended words). **Gidiyorum** [gidiyor-um] *I am going.*

The stand-alone personal pronouns are not used widely as the person is evident from the personal verb ending. They are used for emphasis only in their simple form as the verb form itself already points to the person. This is similar to Spanish where a person will say *comprendo I understand* instead of *Yo comprendo I understand.* However they are used in their extended forms when suffixes are added for all those important little words *to, from, with, etc.*

Simple Personal Pronouns.

ben *I*
sen *you* [familiar/informal]
o *He, she, it*
biz *we*
siz *you* [plural/formal singular]
onlar *they*

Examples of Emphasis.

Gidiyorum *I'm going.* Emphasized **ben** **gidiyorum** *I am going.*
Kaldık *We stayed.* Emphasized **Biz** **kaldık** *We stayed.*

Suffixed (Extended) Pronouns First Person.

ben *I*
bana *to me* (irregular NOT "bene".)
benim *of me, my* (irregular NOT "benin".)

103

beni *me (obj.)*
bende *on me*
benden *from me*
benimle or benle *with me*

biz *we*
bize *to us*
bizim *our* (irregular NOT "bizimiz".)
bizi *us (obj.)*
bizde *on us*
bizden *from us*
bizimle or bizle *with us*

Second Person Singular (familiar/informal).

sen *you*
sana *to you* (irregular NOT "sene".)
senin *of you, your*
seni *you (obj.)*
sende *on you*
senden *from you*
seninle or senle *with you*

Second Person Plural (polite/formal/public).

siz *you*
size *to you*
sizin *your*
sizi *you (obj.)*
sizde *on you*
sizden *from you*
sizinle or sizle *with you*

Third Person Singular.

o *he, she, it*
ona *to him, her, it*
onun *of him, his, her, its*
onu *him, her, it (obj.)*
onda *on him, her, it*
ondan *from him, her, it*
onunla or onla *with him, her, it*

onlar *they*
onlara *to them*
onların *their*
onları *them (obj.)*
onlarda *on them*
onlardan *from them*
onlarla *with them*

The Third Person spelling changes. All extended forms of **O** use buffer letter **-n-**. The third person singular pronoun **O** *he, she, it* adds letter **-n-** when adding further suffixes. The third person plural is also irregular, **Onlar** *they.*

Irregular Personal Pronouns.

The personal pronouns show some changes in spelling. These changes have naturally occurred over a period of historical daily usage:
ben *I*:
to me becomes **bana** (NOT bene).
of me, my becomes **benim** (NOT benin).

biz *we*:
of us, our becomes **bizim** (NOT bizimiz).

sen *you (sing.)*:
to you (singular) becomes **sana** (NOT sene).

Extended Forms of the Personal Pronouns.

The main use for the Suffixed Personal Pronouns is to extend them with all the important little words (prepositions in English) *to, from, with etc.*, which are suffixes in Turkish.

Motion Toward Suffix -e/-a to, towards.

bana *to me*
sana *to you*
ona *to him/to her/to it*
bize *to us*
size *to you*

onlara *to them*

The first and second person singular forms are **bana** and **sana** are irregular where "bene" and "sene" would have been expected. This is a shift that has happened historically but some of the Turkic Languages have not made this Vowel Shift. "bene" and "sene" are still used in the Kazakh and Uzbek tongues.

Examples With the -a -e suffix:

Bana onu verin. *Give it to me.* This can also mean *"Give that to me."* as **O** translates as *he/she/it* and as a demonstrative pronoun. *that.*
Onlara onu verin. *Give it to them.*

Bize inanıyorlar *They believe us.* [lit: believe to us.]
The word **inanmak** *to believe* takes the Dative Case as its Object, hence Turkish says **bize inanın** *believe to us.* English uses the direct object for the verb *to believe believe us.* In a similar fashion there are certain verbs in English that do not take the direct object case as in "I am frightened **of** the dark." where the literal translation of Turkish is "I am frightened **from** the dark" [**Karanlıktan korkuyorum.** *Darkness-from I am frightened.*]

Static Suffix -de/-da.

With the **-de -da** Static Condition suffix *in, on, at.*

bende *in, on, at me*
sende *on you*
onda *on him/on her/on it*
bizde *on us*
sizde *on you*
onlarda *on them*

Examples with the -de/-da suffix:

Bende para yok. *I've got no money.* [lit: on me]
Sende para var mı? *Have you got any money?* [lit: on you]
Bizde para var mı? *Have we got any money?* [lit: on us]

Motion Away Suffix -den/-dan.

With the **-den -dan** Movement Away suffix *from, via, movement away.*

benden *from me*
senden *from you*
ondan *from him/from her/from it*
bizden *from us*
sizden *from you*
onlardan *from them*

Examples with the -den suffix:

Benden bir şemsiye alabilirsiniz. *You can have an umbrella off me.* [lit: from me]
Senden bir sigara alır mıyım? *Can I have a cigarette off you?* [lit: take from you]
Ondan korkuyorum. *I am frightened of him.* [lit: frightened from him] As mentioned previously this last example shows where Turkish uses a different suffix to the English preposition for this verb.

Ownership Suffix *-in -ın -un -ün.*

With the **-in -ın -un -ün** Ownership suffix *of, belonging to.*

benim *my, of me*
senin *your, of you*
onun [o-n-un] *his/hers/its of him, her, it*
bizim *our, of us*
sizin *your, of you*
onların *their, of them*

Examples with the -in suffix:

Benim şemsiyemi alabilirsiniz. *You can take my umbrella.*
[şemsiye-m-i] "my umbrella" as a Direct Object.
Senin araban yeni mi? *Is your car new?*
Onların arabası eskidir. *Their car is old.*

Object Suffix *-i -ı -u -ü.*

With the **-i -ı -u -ü** Objective suffix which signifies the Direct Object.

beni *me*
seni *you*
onu *him/her/it* (obj.)
bizi *us*
sizi *you*
onları *them*

Examples with the -i Direct Object Suffix:

Mehmet, beni vurdu. *Mehmet shot me.* [ben-i *me* as a Direct Object]
Ali, arabanı onardı mı? *Did Ali repair your car?* [araba-n-ı *your car* as a Direct Object]
Mustafa, onu yaptı. *Mustapha did it.* [on-u *it* as a Direct Object]

To reiterate:

In English both the Subject and Object of a sentence are made substantive by the use of the same Definite Article *the* as in "*The* man closed *the* door."

The Subject is already understood as substantive in Turkish so it does not need a Definite Article. The Subject Definite Article *"the"* does not exist in Turkish. There is no *"the man"* as a subject. It is already substantive simply **"Adam"**.

However there is an Object Definite Article *"the"* in Turkish. The Objective Condition suffix **-(y)i** is added, according to Vowel Harmony Rules.

Adam kapıyı kapattı. [kapı-yı] *The* man closed *the* door.
Öğrenci mektubu yazdı. [mektub-u] *The* student wrote *the* letter.

The Direct Object Suffix which makes the Object substantive is a major difficulty when leaning Turkish as it is does not exist in English.

The Suffix -le/-la *"with, by"*.

With the **-le -la (ile)** suffix *with, and, together with.*

benimle/benle. *with me.*
seninle/senle. *with you.*

onunla/onla. *with him/with her/with it.*
bizimle/bizle. *with us.*
sizinle/sizle. *with you.*
onlarla. *with them.*

Adding the **-le -la** suffix can be considered as an exception: When adding the **-le/-la** suffix **ben(im)le, sen(in)le, on(un)la, biz(im)le, siz(in)le** are alternatives. The third person plural **onlarla** is the only alternative, however. It is not correct to say "onlarınla". The preferred version is *benimle, seninle* etc.

Examples with the -le/-la suffix:

Mehmet, benimle geldi. *Mehmet came with me. Mehmet and I came.* ["ben-im-le" "with me".]
Mustafa, bizimle kalacak . *Mustapha will stay with us.* ["biz-im-le" "with us."]
Ali, onlarla geldi mi? *Did Ali come with them?* ["onlar-la" "with them".]
For the preferred version the **-le** or **-la** *with* suffix is added to the Ownership condition, except for the third person plural which retains the basic form **onlarla** *with them.*

The Reflexive Pronoun "kendi" *self/own.*

As an adjective **kendi** means *own.*
The person agrees with the thing which is owned:

kendi bahçem. [kendi bahçe-m] *my own garden.*
kendi evin. [kendi ev-in] *your own house.*
kendi evi. [kendi ev-i] *his own house.*
kendi arabaları. [kendi araba-ları] *their own car.*

Personalised Forms **kendi** *self.*

kendim. *myself.*
kendin. *yourself.* (familiar)
kendi(si)/kendi. *himself/herself/itself.*
kendimiz. *ourselves.*
kendiniz. *yourselves* or *yourself.* (polite form)
kendileri. *themselves.*

The third person singular is almost always in the short form **kendi** as the **-si** suffix is dropped in use.

Kendi is also used in its extended (suffixed) forms:

kendime. *to myself.*
kendinden. *from yourself.*
kendinde or **kendisinde.** *on himself.*
For the Third Person Singular the **-si** suffix can be used when further suffixes are added to *kendi(si).*
kendimizle. *with ourselves.*
kendinizin. *of yourselves.*
kendilerinden. *from themselves.*

Kendi is used in many different contexts, especially for emphasizing purposes.

(a) Meaning *myself, yourself, himself.*
Kendime bir bilgisayar aldım. *I bought a computer for myself.*
Bence kendini biraz küçümsüyorsun. *I think you underestimate yourself a bit.*

(b) Meaning *own* (as an adjective).
kendi evim or **benim kendi evim.** *my own house.*
kendi düşüncesi. onun kendi düşüncesi. *her own opinion.*

(c) Meaning *on my own* or in order to emphasize the subject.
Bu resmi ben kendim yaptım. *I made this picture on my own (by myself).*
Bunu biz kendimiz düşündük. *We thought that on our own (by ourselves).*

(d) To give a formal impression, used for 3rd person singular and plural, always as **kendisi** or **kendileri.**
Size Mr. Jones'u takdim etmek istiyorum. Kendisi daha önce bir şirkette CEO olarak çalışıyordu. *I would like to present you Mr. Jones. He used to work [lit: was working before] as a CEO in a company.* To use **O** *he* instead of **kendisi** sounds too informal.
Kendisi *he himself* suits the formal situation in a better way.

(e) Duplication of **kendi.** Has an adverbial meaning:
Bilgisayar bozuktu. Ama daha sonra kendi kendine çalıştı. *The*

computer had broken down. But a little later, it worked by itself.
Kendi kendime konuşuyorum. *I am talking to myself.*

Türkçe'yi kendi kendime öğrendim. *I learned Turkish by myself.*
(meaning, "I did not have a teacher"). This usage is similar to Irish,
where they may say "Is it yourself that is going to town now?" for
"Are you going to town now?"

Reflexive Verbs and the usage of **kendi** should not be confused.
I had a wash translates as **Yıkandım.** *I washed myself. I had a wash.*

Reflexive Verbs are dealt with in Chapter 24

Reflexive verb "yıkanmak" "to wash oneself".
Whereas **Yıkadım** *I washed (something else).*
Çamaşırı yıkadım. [Çamaşır-ı (obj.)] *I did the washing* . [Lit: I
washed the washing.]

Transitive verb "yıkamak" "to wash something".
The addition of the **-n** serves as a suffix with a reflexive meaning.
"Kendimi yıkadım." is incorrect, **Yıkandım.** is correct. Similarly
"kendimi ısladım." is incorrect, **Islandım** is correct for *I got wet.*

Interrogative Pronoun *who?*, *whom?* kim?, kimler?

The pronoun **kim?** *who?* has a plural in Turkish: **kimler?** *who?*
English makes do with one form who for both singular and plural.

Singular Meaning Plural.
kim *who?* **kimler.**
kime *to whom?* **kimlere.**
kimin *whose?* **kimlerin.**
kimi *whom?* (obj.) **kimleri.**
kimde *on whom?* **kimlerde.**
kimden *from whom?* **kimlerden.**
kiminle or **kimle** *with whom?* **kimlerle.**

Interrogative Pronoun Examples:

Kimi gördünüz? *Whom did you see?* [Objective Singular]

Kimleri gördünüz? *Whom (what people) did you see?* [Objective

Plural]

Arabayı kimlerden aldınız? *From whom (plural) did you buy the car?*

Parayı kime verdiniz? *To whom did you give the money?*

Bu gözlük kimin? *Whose are these glasses?*

Kiminle geldi? *Whom did he come with?*

kimse *somebody, anybody/anybody?, nobody.*

The translation of the *somebody, anybody, nobody* is:
biri (positive singular general) *somebody.*
birisi (positive singular particular) *somebody.*
birileri (positive plural) *somebody.*
kimse *nobody* (negative).
kimse *anybody* (negative).
kimse? *anybody?* (positive or negative question).

The word **kimse** (which is used for both singular and plural) is very much that same as "personne" in French. It can mean *nobody* [negative] or *anybody?* [positive and negative questions] according to the sentence context. These examples show that the word *somebody* in Turkish can be a singular *somebody* **biri, birisi** or some plural *somebodies* **birileri.**

Examples of Usage

Biri var, Birisi var, Birileri var all mean *There is somebody there.* [In English a Positive statement uses "somebody"]. In Turkish it can be singular "somebody" or plural "somebodies"

Kimse var mı?, Kimseler var mı? *Is there anybody there?* [Positive question uses *anybody?* in English.]

Kimse yok. *There is nobody there.* [Negative statement uses *nobody* in English.]

Kimse yok mu? *Isn't there anybody there?* [Negative question uses *anybody?* in English.

Şimdiden evde biri (birileri) olmalı. *There must be somebody at home by now.* [Positive Statement.]

Saat sekizde parkta kimse görünmedi. *At eight o'clock there was nobody to be seen in the park.* [Negative Statement.]

Saat sekizde parkta kimse var mıydı? *Was there anybody in the park at eight o'clock?* [Positive Question.]

Şu anda ofisinizde kimse yok mu? *Isn't there anybody in your office at the moment?* [Negative Question.]

The Diminutive Form kimsecik, kimsecikler.

If the diminutive form **kimsecik, kimsecikler** is used with the negative as in: **kimsecik yok** the meaning becomes *nobody at all.*

Odanın içerisinde (or içinde) kimse var mı? *Is there anybody inside the room?* ["oda-nın içeri-si-nde" "room-of inside-its-at" is a Possessive Relationship *See Chapter 11*]

Odada kimsecik/kimsecikler yok. *There is nobody at all in the room.* ["oda-da" "the room-in"]

Rules to remember **kimsecik, kimsecikler** is only used with negative verbs. The word and **kimsecik, kimsecikler** is invariable, it does not take any further suffixes.

10 POSSESSIVE ADJECTIVES

Possessive Adjectives my, your, her.

The Possessive Adjective *my, your, his, her ,our, their* is a suffix which obeys vowel harmony rules. It is called a Possessive Adjective because it shows possession and describes a noun. *Which cat?* The answer *my cat.* The word *my* is a Possessive Adjective describing the noun *cat.*

Examples of the Possessive Adjective *my* as a suffix:

The suffix **-ım -im -um -üm** *my* is added to words ending in a consonant or just **-m** when added to words ending in a vowel.

The E-Dotted Vowels Singular.

el *hand* becomes **elim** *my hand.*
iş *job* becomes **işim** *my job.*
göz *eye* becomes **gözüm** *my eye.*
gül *rose* becomes **gülüm** *my rose.*

The E-Dotted Vowels Plural.

eller *hands* becomes **ellerim** *my hands.*
işler *jobs* becomes **işlerim** *my jobs.*
gözler *eyes* becomes **gözlerim** *my eyes.*
güller *roses* becomes **güllerim** *my roses.*

The A-UnDotted Vowels Singular.

ay *month, moon* becomes **ayım** *my month.*
kız *girl, daughter* becomes **kızım** *my daughter.*
tost *toast* becomes **tostum** *my toast.*
sabun *soap* becomes **sabunum** *my soap.*

The A-UnDotted Vowels Plural.

aylar *months, moons* becomes **aylarım** *my months.*
kızlar *girls, daughters* becomes **kızlarım** *my daughters.*
tostlar *toasts* (slices of) becomes **tostlarım** *my toast(s).*

sabunlar (bars of) *soap(s)* becomes **sabunlarım** *my soap(s)*.

The Plural is always the First Suffix Added. The Possessive Suffix follows the Plural Suffix. Examples of the plural and additional suffixes:
ellerim [el-ler-im] *my hands.*
odalarımız [oda-lar-ımız] *our rooms.*

Adding the Possessive Adjective to words that end in a vowel.

When the word ends in a vowel then the Possessive Suffix drops its own initial vowel.
kedi *cat.*
kedim [kedi-m] *my cat.*

But the Possessive Suffix does not lose a vowel when attached to the plural of a noun as it follows the final consonant of **-ler.**
kediler *cats.*
kedilerim [kedi-ler-im] *my cats.*

Possessive Adjective Reference Summary.

The suffixes for all the persons viz: *my, your, his, our, your, their* are as follows. They all obey Vowel Harmony Rules.

Suffixed to Consonants: **-ım -im -um -üm** *my.*
Suffixed to Vowels: **-m.**

Suffixed to Consonants: **-ın -in -un -ün** *your.*
Suffixed to Vowels: **-n.**

Suffixed to Consonants: **-ı -i -u -ü** *his, her, its.*
Suffixed to Vowels: **-sı -si -su- -sü.**

Suffixed to Consonants: **-ımız -imiz -umuz -ümüz** *our.*
Suffixed to Vowels: **-mız -miz -muz -müz.**

Suffixed to Consonants: **-ınız -iniz -unuz -ünüz** *your.*
Suffixed to Vowels: **-nız -niz -nuz -nüz.**

Suffixed to Consonants: **-ları -leri** *their.*
Suffixed to Vowels: **-ları -leri** (no change).

Possessive Adjective single exception su *water*.

The word **su** *water* is the single irregular noun in Turkish. It takes a buffer letter **-y-** with all its suffixes which begin with a vowel.

su *water.*
suyum *my water.*
suyun *your water.*
suyu *his water.*
suyumuz *our water.*
suyunuz *your water.*
suları *their water.*

Possessive Adjectives Suffixed.

Consonant Mutation and Vowel Harmony when adding Suffixes.

The Third Person Singular Possessive Suffix **-i** becomes **-si** (Buffer Letter **-s-**) when added to a noun ending in a vowel.

oda *room.*
odası [oda-s-ı] *his room.*
This example shows the addition of the buffer letter **-s-** in order to keep two vowels apart.

palto *overcoat.*
paltom *my overcoat.*
paltolarım *my overcoats.*

sokak *street.*
sokağım *my street.*
sokaklarım *my streets.*

göz *eye.*
gözün *your eye.*
gözleriniz *your eyes.*

armut *pear.*
armudu *his pear.*
armutları *his pears/their pear(s).*

The last example (**armutları** *his pears/their pear(s)*) above can be construed three ways:
armutlar -ı *his pears.*
armut -ları *their pear.*
armut -ları *their pears.*
"armutlarları" is wrong, the **-lar** suffix cannot be duplicated. The context of conversation is usually enough for the correct interpretation to be understood. It seems that "their pears" should be "armutlarları", but **-lar** suffixes are never doubled. To make clear the singularity or plurality of the noun and to be explicit then the Ownership Condition Pronoun **onun** *his* or **onların** *their* can be used accordingly:

onun armudu. *his pear.* [he has singular pear]
onun armutları. *his pears.* [he has plural pears]
onların armudu. *their pear.* [they have a singular pear]
onların armutları . *their pears.* [they have plural pears]

Examples showing difference of singular and plural nouns:

araba *car.*
arabamız *our car.*
arabalarımız *our cars.*

kapı *door.*
kapım *my door.*
kapılarım *my doors.*

domuz *pig.*
domuzu *his pig.*
onun domuzları *his pigs.*
onların domuzları *their pigs.*

oda *room.*
odası *his room.*
onun odaları *his rooms.*
onların odası *their rooms.*

kulak *ear.*
kulağınız *your ear.*
kulaklarınız *your ears.*

aile *family.*
ailesi *his family.*
onların aileleri *their families.*
onların ailesi *their family.*

şemsiye *umbrella.*
şemsiyeniz *your umbrella.*
şemsiyeleriniz *your umbrellas.*

göz *eye.*
onun gözleri *his eyes.*
onların gözleri *their eyes.*

otobüs *bus.*
otobüsümüz *our bus.*
otobüslerimiz *our buses.*

The addition of further suffixes to the possessed noun:

A noun with the possessive suffix being a noun in its own right can be subject to further suffixes. Buffer letter **-n-** is used when adding second suffixes to possessed items for third person singular *his, her, its* and third person plural *their.*

arabasına. [araba-sı-n-a] *to his/her car.*
onların elmalarından. [elma-ları-n-dan] *from their apples.*

Here are some examples of extended possessed nouns where further suffixes have been added to make a new word.

kedi *cat* Singular * **kedi** ends in a vowel so only suffix **-m** is added.
kedim [kedi-m] *my cat.*
kedimden [kedi-m-den] *from my cat.*
kedime [kedi-m-e] *to my cat.*

kediler *cats* Plural * **kediler** ends in a consonant so suffix **-im** is added.
kedilerim [kedi-ler-im] *my cats.*
kedilerimden [kedi-ler-im-den] *from my cats.*
kedilerime [kedi-ler-im-e] *to my cats.*

araba *car* * **araba** ends in a vowel so only suffix **-n** is added.
araban [araba-n] *your car.*

arabana [araba-n-a] *to your car.*
arabanda [araba-n-da] *in your car.*

arabalar *cars* * **arabalar** ends in a consonant so total suffix **-ım** is added.
arabaların [araba-lar-ın] *your cars.*
arabalarına [araba-lar-ın-a] *to your cars.*
arabalarında [araba-lar-ın-da] *in your cars.*

elma *apple* * **elma** ends in a vowel, so third person suffix using buffer letter **-sı** is added.
onun elması [elma-s-ı] *his apple.*
onun elmasında [elma-s-ı-n-da] *in his apple.*
onun elmasından [elma-s-ı-n-dan] *from his apple.*

A noun with the possessive suffix can be subject to further suffixes. Buffer letter **-n-** is used when adding second suffixes third person singular *his, her, its* or third person plural *their.*

elmalar . *apples.*
onun elmaları. [elma-lar-ı] *his apples.*
onun elmalarında. [elma-lar-ı-n-da] *in his apples.*
onların elmasında. [elma-s-ı-n-da] *in their apple.*
onların elmasından. [elma-s-ı-n-da] *from their apple.*
onların elmaları. [elma-ları] *their apples.*
onların elmalarında. [elma-ları-n-da] *in their apples.*
onların elmalarından. [elma-ları-n-dan] *from their apples.*
onların *their* is used to show that this/these apple(s) belongs to more than one person.

köy *village.*
köyümüz. [köy-ümüz] *our village.*
köyümüzde. [köy-ümüz-de] *in our village.*
köyümüzden. [köy-ümüz-den] *from our village.*

köyler. *villages.*
köylerimiz. [köy-ler-imiz] *our villages.*
köylerimizde. [köy-ler-imiz-de] *in our villages.*
köylerimizden. [köy-ler-imiz-den] *from our villages*

köpek *dog.*
köpeğiniz. [köpeğ-iniz] *your dog.*

köpekleriniz. [köpek-ler-iniz] *your dogs.*
köpeğinizde. [köpeğ-iniz-de] *on your dog.*
köpeğinize. [köpeğ-iniz-e] *to your dog.*
The Rule of Consonant Mutation where **-k** changes to **-ğ** is operating here when a vowel suffix is being added to a hard consonant.

köpekler. *dogs.*
köpekleri. [köpek-leri] *his dogs/their dog(s).*
onun köpeklerine. [köpek-ler-i-n-e] *to his dogs.*
onların köpeklerine. [köpek-leri-n-e] *to their dogs.*
onların köpeklerinden. [köpek-leri-n-den] *from their dogs.*

ev. *house.*
onların evi. [ev-i] *their house.*
onların evine. [ev-i-n-e] *to their house.*
onların evinde. [ev-i-n-de] *in their house.*
onların evinden. [ev-i-n-den] *from their house .*

evler. *houses.*
onun evleri. [ev-ler-i] *his houses.*
onların evleri. [ev-leri] *their houses.*
onun evlerinde. [ev-ler-i-n-de] *in his houses.*
onların evlerinde. [ev-leri-n-de] *in their houses.*
onun evlerinden. [ev-ler-i-n-den] *from his houses.*
onların evlerinden. [ev-leri-n-den] *from their houses.*

11 THE POSSESSIVE RELATIONSHIP

All about Possession.

There is a special construction in Turkish which means *"belonging to"*. In English generally only the Possessor is marked as in *Janet's house* where the **'s** tells us that the house belongs to Janet. However, possession can also be marked by both the Possessor and the Possessed in English as in *"The hair of the dog"*. In this case both words *"hair"* and *"dog"* are marked **"THE hair** and **OF THE dog"**.

This then is the way that Turkish uses, both the Possessor and the Possessed are always marked:
Köpeğin tüyü. [Köpeğ-in tüy-ü] *The hair of the dog.* [Lit: dog-the-of hair-its]

The Possessor.

In Turkish the Possessor is suffixed with the Ownership Noun Condition Suffix **-in, -ın, -un, -ün,** or **-nin -etc.** when suffixed to a word which ends in a vowel. The **-in** suffix means *of, belonging to* in English, and is subject to vowel harmony. In grammar this is called the Genitive Case

Formation of the Possessor:

For words ending in a consonant we add The Ownership Suffix **-in -ın -un -ün** according to Vowel Harmony Rules.

adam *man.*
adamın [adam-ın] *of the man, the man's.*

göz *eye.*
gözün [göz-ün] *of the eye, the eye's.*

All plural forms end in a consonant **-ler/-lar.**

adamlar *the men.*
adamların. [adam-lar-ın] *of the men, the men's.*

fareler. *the mice.*
farelerin. [fare-ler-in] *of the mice, the mice's.*

lastikler. *the tyres.*
lastiklerin. [lastik-ler-in] *of the tyres, the tyres'.*

Nouns ending in vowels use buffer letter **-n** to form **-nin.**

banyo. *bath.*
banyonun. [banyo-n-un] *of the bath, the bath's.*

köprü. *bridge.*
köprünün. [köprü-n-ün] *of the bridge, the bridge's.*

The Possessed.

The Possessed Item in Turkish is suffixed with the 3rd person Suffix to show it as a substantive item owned by its Possessor.

Formation of the Possessed.

The Possessed item in Turkish is suffixed with **-i -ı -u -ü** *his, hers, its.* If the word being suffixed already ends in a vowel then the buffer letter **-s-** is used after this final vowel, thus the forms **-si -sı -su -sü** are used. This suffix is also is subject to vowel harmony as shown above. The only exception is **su** *water.* This word historically uses the buffer letter **-y-** producing **suyu.** ["susu" is wrong]

Formation of the Possessive Relationship.

The man's hand becomes in Turkish: **Adamın eli** ["Adam-ın el-i" "the-man-of hand-his"]. The Possessor is marked with the Ownership Suffix and the Possessed is marked with 3rd person suffix to make it substantive.

Both the Possessor and Possessed are suffixed in Turkish as follows:

The Possessor **adam** *man* with the Possessed **el** *hand* becomes:

adamın eli. [adam-ın el-i] *the man's hand, the hand of the man.* [Lit: "man-of hand-his"].

The Possessor **Mehmet** with the Possessed **palto** *overcoat* becomes: **Mehmet 'in paltosu.** [Mehmet-'in palto-su] *Mehmet's overcoat.* [Lit: "Mehmet-of overcoat-his"].

The irregular noun **su** *water* becomes **adamın suyu** [adam-ın su-y-u] *the man's water.*

When adding suffixes to Proper names that the suffix is separated by an apostrophe. The easy way to remember is that any noun beginning with a capital letter should be separated from its suffix. *Londra* [London] becomes **Londra'nın** *London's, of London.*

The Plurals of the Possessive Relationship.

The plurals are formed by the addition of **-ler** or **-lar** to either the possessor or the possessed or to both according to context. The following examples should make this clear:

Both Possessor and Possessed Singular.

adamın arabası. [adam-ın araba-sı] *the man's car.*
evin damı. [ev-in dam-ı] *the roof of the house.*

The Possessor Plural and Possessed Singular.

yıldızların ışığı. [yıldız-lar-ın ışığ-ı] *the light of the stars.*
adamların arabası. [adam-lar-ın araba-sı] *the men's car*

The Possessor Singular and Possessed Plural.

adamın arabaları. [adam-ın araba-lar-ı] *the man's cars.*
odanın duvarları. [oda-nı duvar-lar-ı] *the walls of the room.*

Both Possessor Plural and Possessed Plural.

adamların arabaları. [adam-lar-ın araba-lar-ı] *the men's cars.*
çocukların oyunları. [çocouk-lar-ın oyun-lar-ı] *the children's games.*

The Possessive Relationship in Use.

The Possessive Relationship is Compound Noun in its own right and as such can have further suffixes such as:

-dan/-den *from.*
-da/-de *in, on, at.*
-a/-e *to, towards.*

added to the Possessed item(s) to modify the meaning according to context:

Adamın arkadaşına kitabı verdim. [Adam-ın arkadaş-ı-na kitabı verdim] *I gave the book to the man's friend.* [Lit: "Man-of friend-his-to book-the gave-I"]

Adamın arkadaşından kitabı aldım. [Adam-ın arkadaş-ı-ndan kitabı aldım] *I took the book from the man's friend.* [Lit: "Man-of friend-his-from book-the took-I"]

Suffixed Possessive Relationship Models.

Both the Possessor and the Possessed Singular.

adamın arabası. *the man's car*
adamın arabasının. *of the man's car, the man's car's.*
adamın arabasına. *to the man's car.*
adamın arabasını. *the man's car.* (object)
adamın arabasında. *in the man's car.*
adamın arabasından. *from the man's car.*
adamın arabasıyla. *with the man's car.*

The Possessor Singular and the Possessed Plural.

adamın arabaları. *the man's cars.*
adamın arabalarının. *of the man's cars, the man's car's.*
adamın arabalarına. *to the man's cars.*
adamın arabalarını. *the man's cars (object).*
adamın arabalarında. *in the man's cars.*
adamın arabalarından. *from the man's cars.*
adamın arabalarıyla. *with the man's cars.*

The Possessor Plural and the Possessed Singular.

adamların arabası. *the men's car.*

adamların arabasının. *of the men's car, the men's car's.*
adamların arabasına. *to the men's car.*
adamların arabasını. *the men's car.* (object)
adamların arabasında. *in the men's car.*
adamların arabasından. *from the men's car.*
adamların arabasıyla. *with the men's car.*

Both Possessor and Possessed Plural.

damların arabaları. *the men's cars.*
adamların arabalarının. *of the men's cars, the men's cars'.*
adamların arabalarına. *to the men's cars.*
adamların arabalarını. *the men's cars* (object)
adamların arabalarında. *in the men's cars.*
adamların arabalarından. *from the men's cars.*
adamların arabalarıyla. *with the men's cars.*

The Separation of Possessor and Possessed.

The Possessive Relationship may be separated by other words such as an adjective or an adjectival phrase:

Adamın eski arkadaşından. *From the man's old friend.*

Adamın büyük ve pahalı arabasında. *In the man's large and expensive car.*

Chaining Possessors.

The chaining of Possessors is quite easy in Turkish, as follows:
evin kapısının penceresi. [ev-in kapı-sı-n-ın pencere-si] *the house's door's window.*

And with various plural forms:
evin kapısının pencereleri. *the house's door's windows.*
evlerin kapısının penceresi. *the houses' door's window.*
Each "chained" Possessor takes both the Possessed Suffix **-i** and the Possessor Suffix **-in** hence **kapı-sı-nın** *door-the-of.*

The item Possessed takes the Possessed Suffix in **-i** hence **pencere-si** *window-the* (Sing.) or **pencere-ler-i** *windows-the* (Plural).

Further examples of chaining:

Ali'nin defterinin sayfaları yırtılmıştır *Ali's notebook's pages have been torn.*

Bahçenin duvarlarının tuğlaları kırılmıştır. *The garden's walls' bricks have been broken.*

Mehmet'in bisikletinin lastikleri aşınılmıştır. *Mehmet's bicycle's tyres have been worn down.*

Arabamızın motorunun benzin deposunun doldurma kapağı eksiktir. (-tir makes this a defining statement.) *Our car's engine's petrol tank's filler cap is missing.* [Lit: "is absent"]

In English we would say something like:
Ali's notebook pages are torn.
The garden walls' bricks are broken.
Mehmet's bicycle tyres are worn down.
Our car engine petrol tank's filler cap is missing.

In Turkish the "possessed nouns" have to be made definite by the **-(s)i** suffix.

12 POSSESSIVE CONSTUCTIONS

Formation of Possessive Constructions.

A simple basic Possessive Construction is two nouns where the first noun "owns" the second noun. **Ev** *house* and **duvar** *wall* produces a Possessive Construction **evin duvarı** [ev-in duvar-ı] *the wall of the house* literally in Turkish "the house-of wall-its".

In this Possessive Construction **evin duvarı** [ev-in duvar-ı] *the wall of the house*, the first noun is the Possessor with a Suffix of Ownership (Genitive Suffix) **ev-in** *of the house, the house's*. Whilst the second noun is the Possessed Object and is given the 3rd Person Suffix **duvar-ı** *the (its) wall*.

Extended Forms of Possessive Constructions.

Addition of the Motion Toward, Static or Motion Away Suffix produces:

evin duvarına. *to the wall of the house.* [to the house's wall.]
evin duvarında. *at/on/in the wall of the house* . [in/on/at the house's wall.]
evin duvarından. *from the wall of the house.*

Odanın içinde yer bulup oturdu. *He found a place in the room and sat down.* [In the inside of the room.]

Mehmet'in kutuda ne var? *What is in Mehmet's box?*

Bilmem, onun içine bakmadım. *I don't know, I have not looked (to the) inside (of) it.*

Bankanın içinden bir ses geliyordu. *A sound was coming from (the) inside (of) the bank.*

Bu odanın içindekiler birbiriyle sohbet ediyor. *The people in this room are chatting to each other.* [The people that are in the inside of the room are chatting to each other]

Omission of the Possessive Suffix.

In some cases the suffix of Possession may be omitted from the first noun with very little difference in meaning:

Fabrikanın içinde çok insan çalışıyor.
Fabrika içinde çok insan çalışıyor.

Both the above mean *Many people are working in the factory.* But in other cases there is a distinction in definiteness and specific meaning when the Possession Suffix is omitted from the first noun.

Definite Possession.

Frequently the distinction is one of definiteness (or specificity). If the first noun carries the Possessive Suffix, it is definite (specific) and refers to a particular specific object known to the speaker.

Bu hayvanlar mağaranın içinde yaşar.
These animals live in the cave. [a definite cave.]

Eşyalarımı kutunun içine koydum.
I put my things into the box. [a definite box.]

Indefinite Possession.

If however the Possessive Suffix is absent then the noun becomes indefinite and is often used in a general sense:

Bu hayvanlar mağara içinde yaşar.
These animals live in caves. [caves generally.]

Eşyalarımı kutu içine koydum.
I put my things into a box/boxes. [indefinite box/boxes.]

Idiomatic Forms of Possession.

Sometimes the Possessive Compound corresponds to an idiomatic expression:

Ali'nin dairesi, şehrin içinde. *Ali's office is (right) in the town.*

Ali'nin dairesi, şehir içinde. *Ali's office is in town. ("downtown" USA usage.)*

Metaphorical Sense.

Also the Possessive (genitive) is normally omitted when it is used in a metaphorical instead of actual physical sense:

Bir hafta içinde kitabını bitirecek. *He will finish his book within a week.*

İki gün içinde geri döneceğim. *I'll return in(side) two days.*

Demonstratives are Definite.

However, when the first noun is already definite as in the case of the Demonstrative Pronouns *this* and *that*, then it must have a Possessor Suffix:

Bu şehrin içinde çok insan var. *There are many people (living) in this (particular) city.*

Bu bahçenin içinde çok çeşit çiçek bulunur. *Many type of flowers are to be found in this (particular) garden.*

Yangın, o adamın ofisinin içinde başlamış. *Apparently the fire started in that (particular) man's office.* (chained possession "in the inside of the wall of the office of the man".)

O hayvanlar şu mağaranın içinde yaşar.
Those animals live in that (particular) cave..

13 POSSESSION VAR AND YOK

Possession Var - *There is. Yok - There isn't.*

Present Tense Form.

Both **var** and **yok** are used for either the Singular *there is, there isn't* or the Plural *there are, there aren't.* Basically **var** means *Is existent, It exists, There is, There are*.

Tepede bir lokanta var. *There is a cafe on the hill.*

Bu ağaçta çok meyve var. *There is a lot of fruit on this tree.*

yok means *Is non existent, It does not exist, There isn't, There aren't.*

Bahçede kızlar yok. *There are no girls in the garden.*

Garajda hiç araba yok. *There is/are not any car(s) in the garage at all.*

Yeşil kutuda kibrit yok. *There is/are no match(es) in the green box.*

"People are..." and "Things is..." in Turkish. This is why the last two examples can be singular or plural in meaning.

Present Question Form.

This is formed by adding the Question Particle **mi?** according to Vowel Harmony Rules. The Question Particle is written separately:

var mı? means *Does it exist? Is there? Are there?*

Tepede bir lokanta var mı? *Is there a cafe on the hill?*

Ağaçta meyve var mı? *Is there any fruit on the tree?*

yok mu? means *Doesn't it exist?, Isn't there?, Aren't there?*

Garajda hiç araba yok mu? *Isn't there a/any car(s) in the garage?*

Yeşil kutuda kibrit yok mu? *Are there not any matches in the green box?*

In all cases the Question Particle **mi? mu?** is written separately.

Definite Past Form.

This form is also used for the Past by using the past tense suffix **-di** according to Vowel Harmony and Consonant Mutation Rules:

Thus **var** *There is, There are* becomes **vardı** *There was, There were.*

Tepede bir lokanta vardı. *There was a cafe on the hill.*

Bu ağaçta çok meyve vardı. *There was a lot of fruit on this tree.*

Similarly **yok** *There is not, There are not* becomes **yoktu** *There was not, There were not.*

Garajda hiç araba yoktu. *There wasn't a (single) car in the garage.*

Yeşil kutuda kibrit yoktu. *There were no matches in the green box.*

Past Tense Question.

This is formed by adding the Past Tense Question Particle **miydi?** according to Vowel Harmony Rules. The Past Tense Question Particle is written separately:

Var mıydı? *Did it exist? Was there? Were there?*

Tepede bir lokanta var mıydı? *Was there is a cafe on the hill?*

Ağaçta meyve var mıydı? *Was there is any fruit on the tree?*

Yok muydu? *Didn't it exist? Wasn't there? Weren't there?*

Garajda hiç araba yok muydu? *Wasn't there a car(s) in the garage?*

Yeşil kutuda kibrit yok muydu? *Weren't there (any) matches in the green box?*

Beware of the Dog!

This sign clearly shows that **var** (and **yok**) always come at the end of the sentence in Turkish. You can see that the writer of the sign has literally translated into English *Care! Dog there is!* thus conserving the natural Turkish word order.

```
CARE DOG
THERE IS!


DİKKAT!
KÖPEK VAR.
```

Extended Forms of "Var" and "Yok".

Besides the basic forms of *there is, there are* many other extended forms are in constant use in daily Turkish conversation explained below.

"Var" and "Yok" The Formal Form.

vardır. *definitely, surely.*

The formal form acts a "Statement of Fact" and is suffixed with the verb *to be* **-dir.** **Vardır** means *Is (definitely) existent, It (definitely) exists, There (definitely) is, There (definitely) are.* This form is used in Public Notices and Advices.

A Traffic Propaganda Advertisement.

Here is an actual example from a roadside notice.

Unutma! Her trafik kuralının bir nedeni vardır. *Don't forget,* *every traffic law has a reason!* Thus showing **vardır** as *definitely, surely.*

UNUTMA!
HER TRAFİK
KURALININ BİR
NEDENİ VARDIR.

Tepede bir lokanta vardır. *There must be a cafe on the hill.* [definitely.]

Bir kiloda bin gram vardır. *There are 1000 grams in a Kilogram.* [Statement of Fact.]

yoktur. *definitely not, surely not.*

yoktur means *Is (definitely) non existent, It (definitely) does not exist, There (definitely) isn't, There (definitely) aren't.*

Garajda hiç araba yoktur. *There is (surely) not a (single) car in the garage.* [Statement of Fact.]

Yeşil kutuda kibrit yoktur. *There is not a (single) match in the green box.* [Definite Statement.]

Var Present Tense Conditional.

The Present Conditional *If there is, If there are* is formed by adding the Conditional Suffix **-sa/-se** *if* as the following examples show:

varsa. *If there is, If there are.*

Tepede bir lokanta varsa, orada yiyelim. *If there is a cafe on the hill, let us eat there.*

Ağaçta meyve varsa, onu koparırım. *If there is any fruit on the*

133

tree, I will pick it.

yoksa. *If there is not, If there are not.*

Garajda hiç araba yoksa, o zaman bir taksi tutun. [taxi tutmak to take/catch a taxi.] *If there isn't a car in the garage, then catch/take a taxi.*

Yeşil kutuda kibrit yoksa, çakmağını kullan. [familiar imperative] *If there are no matches in the green box, use your lighter.*

Yeşil kutuda kibrit yoksa, çakmağınızı kullanın [polite imperative.] *If there are no matches in the green box, use your lighter.*

Var Past Conditional Form.

The Conditional Past *If there was, If there were* the forms with **var** becoming **varsaydı** and **yok** becoming **yoksaydı** are not widely used. The forms with the verb **olmak** *to be/to become* and **olmamak** *not to be/not to become* may be used instead.

olsaydı. *If there was, If there were.*

Tepede bir lokanta olsaydı, orada yerdik. *If there had been a cafe on the hill, we would have eaten there.*

Tepede bir lokanta olmuş olsaydı, orada yerdik *If there had been a cafe on the hill, we would have eaten there.* [the addition of **olmuş** *been* makes this statement a little more formal.]

Ağaçta meyve olsaydı, onu koparırdım. *If there had been any fruit on the tree, I would have picked it.*

olmasaydı. *If there was not, If there were not.*

Garajda hiç araba olmasaydı, taksi tutacaktım. *If there had not been a car in the garage, I would have taken a taxi.*

Garajda hiç araba olmamış olsaydı, taksi tutacaktım. *If there had not been a car in the garage, I would have taken a taxi.* [the addition of **olmamış** *not been* makes this statement a little more formal.]

Yeşil kutuda hiç kibrit olmasaydı, çakmağımı kullanırdım. *If there weren't any matches in the green box, I would have used my lighter.*

Yeşil kutuda hiç kibrit olmamış/olunmamış olsaydı, çakmağımı kullanırdım. *If there weren't/had not been any matches in the green box, I would have used my lighter.*

Kırmızıda geçmemiş olsaydım, kadın yaşayacaktı.
Kırmızıda geçmiş olmasaydım, kadın yaşayacaktı.
Kırmızıda geçmeseydim, kadın yaşayacaktı. are all different ways of saying:
If I had not passed on the red light, the lady would have still lived.

Var The Inferential Form.

The Inferential *It seems that there is/was* is used when the subject has no eyewitness knowledge. It is used for reporting and inference. The Inferential is simply formed by adding the Inferential Suffix -**miş** as the following examples show. The Inferential Suffix -**miş** is used for both the Present Tense and the Past tense:

varmış. *It seems that there is/was, It seems that there are/were.*

Deniyor ki tepede bir lokanta varmış, [eğer] öyleyse orada yiyelim. *It is said there is a cafe on the hill, if so let us eat there.*

Ağaçta çok meyve varmış. *It seems there is a lot fruit on the tree.*

yokmuş. *It seems that there is/was not, It seems that there are/were not.*

Garajda araba yokmuş. *(I think that) there is not a car in the garage.*

Yeşil kutuda kibrit yokmuş. Mavi olanına [olan-ı-n-a] bakın. *(I think that) there are no matches in the green box. Have a look in the blue one.*

At the beginning of fairy tales Turkish usually says **Bir varmış, bir**

yokmuş where English says *Once upon a time.*

Explanation about olan *the which.*

olan *the which one.*

olanı. *One [the one that]* [lit: that which is] as an item.
olanları. *Ones [the ones that]* [lit: those which are] as items.

Hangi tişörtü istiyorsunuz? *Which tee-shirt do you want?*
Mavi olanı(nı) lütfen. *The blue one, please.*

Hangi ayakkabıları istiyorsunuz? *Which shoes do you want?*
Siyah olanları(nı) lütfen. *The black ones, please.*

The verb **istemek** *to want* does not take an Object Condition in questions but in answers the direct object ending is grammatically correct and the verb **istemek** *to want* is understood. As with all languages sometimes the easy way is used and the direct object suffix is discarded though constant daily conversational usage.

Forms with "iken" *"while"*.

varken. *While there is, As there is*
yokken. *While there isn't , As there isn't.*

This formation is **var + iken** *(while)* producing **varken** and similarly **yok + iken** producing **yokken.**

varken. *While/As there is, While/As there are.*

Tepede bir lokanta varken, başkasını açmıyorlar. *While there is a cafe on the hill, they will not open another one.*

Ağaçta çok meyve varken, onu koparalım. *While there is a lot fruit on the tree, let us pick it.*

yokken. *While/As there is not, While/As there are not.*

Hazır garajda araba yokken, haydi oraya bisikletimizi bırakalım. *As there is not a car in the garage, let us put our bicycles in it.*

Yeşil kutuda kibrit yokken ateşi yakamam. *While there are no matches in the green box I cannot light the fire.*

Enumeration using Var and Yok.

When enumerating lists of things **var** or **yok** are placed after each item. In English the greengrocer may tell us that he has *apples, tomatoes, onions, cherries, etc.* In Turkish he will say **elma var, domates var, soğan var, kiraz var, vs.**

If a question is asked that contains a **var mı?** or a **yok mu?** the answer must always be **var** or **yok**, whereas in English we tend to use *Yes* or *No* as an answer, but the Turk does not usually use the words **hayır** or **evet** in answer to a question that contains a **var** or a **yok.**

Dolapta bir bardak yok mu? *Isn't there a tumbler in the cupboard?* Answer: **var/evet var** or **yok/hayır yok** accordingly.

Kilitte anahtar var mı? *Is the key in the lock?.* Answer: **var** or **yok** accordingly.

The English answers can be *Yes [it is]* or *No [it isn't].* However the Turkish answers must simply be **Var** *there is* or **Yok** *there isn't.*

Ownership *"I have/haven't got".*

Explanation of Usage: There is no verb *to have* or *to have got* in Turkish for "to have something" as in *I have a new car.* or *Have you got a new car?* or *Do you have any anything cheaper?*

All these kinds of sentences use **var** or **vardır** for *to have (got)* and in the negative sense **yok** or **yoktur** for *not to have (got).* The addition of **-dır** or its vowel harmonic equivalents does not alter the meaning, its use is optional, but it does show that the Statement is a Fact. It is seen as **vardır** *there (definitely) is* or **yoktur** *there (definitely) is not* in Public Notices and Advices.

In general conversation the simple form is the commonly used. To say *I have a cat* or *I have got a cat* the possessive adjective Suffix *my, your, his, our* is attached to the item which is possessed with **var** *to have* or **yok-** *not to have.*

Positive Examples **var** *there is, there are, have got.*

Kedim var. [kedi-m var] *I have a cat, I have got a cat.*
Köpeğin var. [köpeğ-in var] *You have a dog, You've got a dog.*
Arabası var. [araba-s-ı var] *He/she has a car, He's got a cat.*
Evimiz var. [ev-imiz var] *We have a house, We have got a house.*
Bahçeniz var. [bahçe-niz var] *You have a garden, You have got a garden.*
Şişeleri var. [şişe-leri var] *They have a bottle, They have got a bottle.*

Negative Examples **yok** *there is not have not got.*

Kedim yok. [kedi-m yok] *I do not have a cat, I have not got a cat*
Köpeğin yok. [köpeğ-in yok] *You do not have a dog, You have not got a dog.*
Arabası yok. [araba-s-ı yok] *He/she doesn't have a car, He has not got a cat.*
Evimiz yok. [ev-imiz yok] *We do not have a house, We have not got a house.*
Bahçeniz yok. [bahçe-niz yok] *You do not have a garden, You have not got a garden.*
Şişeleri yok. [şişe-leri yok] *They do not have a bottle, They have not got a bottle.*

Explanation of Difference in Turkish English for *to have, to have got.*

kedim var. *I have a cat, I have got a cat.* [Lit: There is a my cat.]

In the sentence above the first person singular Possessive Adjective suffix **-im** states "whose cat it is", and in this case it tells us that - *I have a cat* by using **var.**

kedin yok. *You haven't got a cat.* [Lit: There isn't a your cat.]

Similarly in the second sentence the Second Person Possessive Adjective suffix **-in** states that *You haven't got a cat* by using **yok.** It is the Possessive Suffix which tells us WHO OWNS the object.

Positive Questions.

Using the Positive Question **var mı?** *Is there? Are there?*

Evin var mı? *Have you got a house?* [Lit: Is there a your house?]

In the first example above the literal translation is *Is there a your house?* but in English we must say *"Have you got a house?"*

Kedisi var mı? *Has he/she got a cat?* [Lit: Is there a his cat? Is there a her cat?].

Here the Third Person Singular Possessive Adjective Suffix **-(s)i** tells us whose cat it is, and in this case it asks us if *Has **he/she** got a cat?*

Evleri var mı? [Ev-leri their house] *Have they got a house?* [Lit: Is there a their house?]

Negative Questions.

Using the Negative Question **yok mu?** *Isn't there?, Aren't there?*

Evimiz yok mu? *Haven't we got a house?* [Lit: Isn't there an our house?]

In the sentence above the First Person Plural Possessive Adjective suffix **-imiz** asks us whose house it is, and in this case it asks *"Haven't we got a house?"*

Eviniz yok mu? *Haven't you got a house?* [Lit: Isn't there a your house?]. Similarly in the last sentence the Second Person Possessive Adjective suffix **-iniz** asks us *"Haven't **you** got a house?"*

Evleri yok mu? [Ev-leri their house] *Haven't they got a house?* [Lit: Isn't there a their house?]

All the above sentences have been turned into question form by adding the question tag **-mi?** according to Vowel Harmony Rules.

Positive Examples: **var mı?** *is there?, are there?*

Kedim var mı? [kedi-m var mı?] *Do I have a cat?, Have I got a*

139

cat?

Köpeğin var mı? [köpeğ-in var mı?] *Have you a dog?, Have you got a dog?, Do you have a dog?*

Arabası var mı? [araba-s-ı var mı?] *Has he/she a car? Has he/she got a car?*

Evimiz var mı? [ev-imiz var mı?] *Have we a house? Have we got a house?*

Bahçeniz var mı? [bahçe-niz var mı?] *Have you a garden? Have you got a garden?*

Şişeleri var mı? [şişe-leri var mı?] *Have they a bottle? Have they got a bottle?*

Negative Examples: **yok mu?** *isn't there?*

Kedim yok mu? [kedi-m yok mu?] *Have I not got a cat? Do I not have a cat?*

Köpeğin yok mu? [köpeğ-in yok mu?] *Do you not have a dog? Have you not got a dog?*

Arabası yok mu? [araba-s-ı yok mu?] *Doesn't he/she have a car? Has he/she not got a car?*

Evimiz yok mu? [ev-imiz yok mu?] *Have we not a house? Have we not got a house?*

Bahçeniz yok mu? [bahçe-niz yok mu?] *Do you not have a garden? Have you not got a garden?*

Şişeleri yok mu? [şişe-leri yok mu?] *Do they not have a bottle? Have they not got a bottle?*

Some Examples of Possession.

The Conditional **var: varsa, varmış etc.** and of **yok: yoksa, yokmuş, etc.** can be used with the Possessive Forms.

Yeni bir arabanız var mı? *Have you got a new car?*

140

Yeni bir arabamız olsaydı, beraber/birlikte kasabaya gidebilecektik. *If we had a new car, we could have gone to town together.*

Orhan'ın yeni arabası varmış. *(It seems that) Orhan has/had a new car.*

Şekeriniz var mı, lütfen? *Do you have any sugar, please?*

Şekeriniz yoksa, sade içeyim. *If you do not have sugar, I'll drink it without (sade plain).*

Boş vaktimiz var mı? *Have we got time to spare?*

Boş vakitleri/zamanları olsaydı, bize gelirdiler/gelirlerdi. *If they had had time, they would have come to us.*

vakit *"a point in time"* is one of the nouns which loses final vowel (apocopates) when suffixed with another vowel. *See Apocopating Nouns Chapter 7 Page 84*

Cevabı yok. *He/she hasn't got the answer.*
Cevabı yoksa. *If he/she hasn't got the answer.*

Elmaları yok. *They haven't got any apples.*
Elmaları yokmuş. *(It seems that) they haven't got any apples.*
Elmaları yok mu? *Haven't they got any apples?*

Mehmet'in kedisi var. *Mehmet has got a cat.*
Mehmet'in kedisi varken, köpeğimi onunla bırakamam. *While Mehmet has got a cat, I cannot leave my dog with him.*

Sadece az param var. *I've only a little money.*
Ali'nin parası var mı? *Has Ali got any money?*

Yeterli param varsa, yeni araba alırım. *If I have enough money, I'll buy a new car.*

Ama o kadar yokmuş gibi geliyor. *But it seems that (like) I have not got that much (money).*

"Var and Yok" Personalised.

141

Var and **yok** can also take the personal endings of the verb **to be** *"I am, you are, etc."*

The Personalised "Var" and "Yok" with *"to be"* suffixes added.

varım. *I am there/I'll be there.*
yokum. *I am not there/I'll not be there.*

varsın. *You are there/You will be there.*
yoksun. *You are not there/You will not be there.*

var. *He/She/It is there He/She/It will be there.*
yok. *He/She/It is not there He/She/It will not be there.*

varız. *We are there/We will be there.*
yokuz. *We are not there/We will not be there.*

varsınız. *You are there/You will be there.*
yoksunuz. *You are not there/You will not be there.*

varlar. *They are there/They will not be there.*
yoklar. *They are not there/They will not be there.*

When stating the future **olmak** *to become* can also be used **var olacağım** *I will be there.* But in practice the shorter way as in the table above is used in conversation.

The words here used like **varım, varsın, var, varız** can also have the meaning *I am in!*, when talking about interference into an issue. For instance, **Bugün "raftinge" var mısın?** *Are you in for "rafting today?* can be answered *Evet, varım.* or *Hayır, ben yokum.*

"Open the Box!".

This was a TV show in Turkey. The contestant has a closed box. There are also 20 other closed boxes. Every box contains an amount of money. Some boxes contain 1 million TL, some 250.000, some 100.000, some 1.000, some 250, some 50, some 10 and some 1 TL. The contestant does not know which boxes, including his own, contain which amount. In first round, 6 boxes are opened, next round 5, then 4,and then 3 and then 2. At the end of each round a proposal of money is made. The contestant can choose to go on for his own box, or accept these proposals. The moderator asked the contestant at the end of each round, **"Bu para için var mısın, yok musun?".** *"Are you in or out for this money?" The answer* **Yokum!** *"Im out!",* **Varım!** *"I'm in!" The TV show was called* **Var mısın? Yok musun?**

"Varsa" and "Yoksa" Present Conditional Personalised.

Varsa and Yoksa *"If I'm there/If I'm not there".*

varsam. *If I am there/I'll be there.*
yoksam. *I am not there/If I'll not be there.*

varsan. *If you are there/If you'll be there.*
yoksan. *If you are not there/If you will not be there.*

varsa. *If he is there am there/If he'll be there.*
yoksa. *If he is not there/If he will not be there.*

varsak. *If we are there/If we'll be there.*
yoksak. *If we are not there/If we will not be there.*

varsanız. *If you are there/If you'll be there.*
yoksanız. *If you are not there/If you will not be there.*

varsalar. *If they are there/If they will be there.*
yoksalar. *If they are not there/If they will not be there.*

Olsaydı and Olmasaydı Past Conditions Personalised.

In Past Conditions **var** and **yok** are replaced by the verb **olmak** *to be/become.*

olsaydım. *If I'd been there.*
olmasaydım. *If I'd not been there.*

olsaydın. *If you had been there.*
olmasaydın. *If you not been there.*

olsaydı. *If he had been there.*
olmasaydı. *If he had not been there.*

olsaydık. *If we had been there.*
olmasaydık. *If we had not been there.*

olsaydınız. *If you had been there.*
olmasaydınız. *If you had not been there.*

olsaydılar. *If they had been there.*
olmasaydılar. *If they had not been there.*

"Varmış" and "Yokmuş" the Indefinite "-miş" form Personalised.

varmışım. *possibly I am/was there/I'll be there.*
yokmuşum. *possibly I am/was not there/I'll not be there.*

varmışsın. *possibly you are/were there/you'll be there.*
yokmuşsun. *possibly you are/were not there/you'll not be there.*

varmış. *possibly he is/was there/he'll be there.*
yokmuş. *possibly he is/was not there/he'll not be there.*

varmışız. *possibly we are/were there/we'll be there.*
yokmuşuz. *possibly we are/were not there/we'll not be there.*

varmışsınız. *possibly you are/were not there/you'll not be there.*
yokmuşsunuz. *possibly you are/were not there/you'll not be there.*

varmışlar. *possibly they are/were there/they'll be there.*
yokmuşlar. *possibly they are/were not there/they'll not be there.*

This form, which is in constant use, actually means something like *I am there, I'll be there, I'll not be there.*

Some examples of these forms.

Yarın ofiste yokum. *I will not be at the office tomorrow.*
Yarın ofiste yokmuşum. *I will probably not be at the office tomorrow.*
Evde var mısın? *Are you at home?*
Kimse var mı? *Is anybody there?*
Kimse yokmuş. *It seems there is nobody (here).*
Kimse yok. *There is nobody (here).*

Yalnız mıyız? *Are we alone?*
Hayır. Onlar da var. *No, there's them as well.*
Gelecek toplantıda ben de varım. *I'll be at the next meeting as well.*

Var Idiomatic Use.

Neyimiz var neyimiz yok depremde kaybettik. *We lost everything what we had/have in the earthquake.*

Could also be stated thus:
Varımızı yoğumuzu depremde kaybettik. *We lost everything what we had/have in the earthquake.*

yok softens its final **-k** to **-ğ** when adding a suffix which begins with a vowel [yoğ-umuz-u = *our nothings* (obj.)]

Vaktin varsa, sonra görüşelim. *Let us meet later on, if you have time.*

Saat onda ofiste yokmuşsun. *It seems you were not at the office at 10 o'clock.*

There is also another usage of **var/yok**: Namely **Varsa yoksa**
Varsa yoksa annesi. meaning that person is very keen on his mother (a little exaggeration and derision also exists). **Varsa yoksa bilgisayar** is suitable when talking about someone who spends a lot of time in front of the computer.

Finally, the "Yok Yok" Shop.

YOK YOK PAZAR

What's in a name? This shop really does belie its name *"the shop with no stock"*, but you would be wrong in that assumption: Here is a typical usage, **"yok" yok**. The notion "yok" is "yok means "yok" doesn't exist.

145

Hence, everything exists! You can say for instance, **Bugün pazara gittim, pazarda yok yoktu.** This expresses that there were plenty of things in the bazaar.

14   VERBS THE INFINITIVE

The Infinitive A description.

The infinitive is the form of a verb that has no inflection to indicate person, number, mood or tense. It is called the infinitive because the verb is usually not made finite, or limited by inflection (change in meaning, tense, person). The Infinitive is the name of a verb, therefore it is a noun.

The Turkish Infinitive has four forms of the infinitive, all of which can be used as nouns and can therefore take case endings and personal pronouns when required. The Standard Infinitive ending in **-mek** or **-mak** which is often abraded to **-me** or **-ma** by dropping the final **-k**.

Forming the Infinitive of Turkish Verbs.

To form the Infinitive of Turkish Verbs **-mek** or **-mak** is added to the verb stem **gelmek** [gel-mek] *to come*, **almak** [al-mak] *to take.* The choice of adding **-mek** or **-mak** is bound by the Rules of Vowel Harmony.

There is a separate Infinitive form for the negative verb.

The negative is characterized with the negative particle **-me-** or **-ma** (according to vowel harmony rules) added to the positive verb stem. Thus the negative verb root becomes **gelme-** *not come* or **alma-** *not take*. By adding the infinitive suffix **-mek** or **-mak** we arrive at the negative verbs **gelmemek** [gelme-mek] *to not come* and **almamak** [alma-mak] *to not take.* This method of forming the negative is true for all verbs in Turkish.

E-Dotted Verbs.

For verbs of the E-Dotted Group with **e i ö ü** in verb stem the suffix **-mek** signifies the positive verb and **-memek** signifies the negative of the verb.

147

Applying Vowel harmony rules then **-mek** is added to verbs whose final root vowel is **-e.**

vermek. [ver-mek] *to give.*
vermemek. [verme-mek] *not to give.*

-mek is added to verbs whose root vowel is **-i.**

bilmek. [bil-mek] *to know.*
bilmemek. [bilme-mek] *not to know.*

-mek is added to verbs whose root vowel is **-ö.**

görmek. [gör-mek] *to see.*
görmemek. [görme-mek] *not to see.*

-mek is added to verbs whose root vowel is **-ü.**

gülmek. [gül-mek] *to laugh.*
gülmemek. [gülme-mek] *not to laugh.*

A-UnDotted Verbs.

For verbs of the A-UnDotted Group with **a ı o u** in verb stem the suffix **-mak** signifies the positive verb and **-mamak** signifies the negative of the verb. Applying Vowel harmony rules then **-mak** is added to verbs whose root vowel is **-a.**

yapmak. [yap-mak] *to do, make, perform.*
yapmamak. [yapma-mak] *not to do.*

-mak is added to verbs whose root vowel is **-ı.**

ağrımak. [ağrı-mak] *to ache.*
ağrımamak. [ağrıma-mak] *not to ache.*

-mak is added to verbs whose root vowel is **-o.**

kopmak. [kop-mak] *to snap.*
kopmamak. [kopma-mak] *not to snap.*

-mak is added to verbs whose root vowel is **-u.**

kurumak. [kuru-mak] *to dry.*

148

kurumamak. [kuruma-mak] *not to dry.*

The Infinitive as an Object of a Verb.

The Infinitive being a noun can take all the suffixes that any other noun takes. Here is the infinitive of some verbs in the Object case (suffix **-(y)ı -(y)i -(y)u -(y)ü** as an object of the main verb **unutmak** *to forget.*

Often the main verb has two objects with the **-i** suffix. For instance in the last example below "The window " together with "its opening" are both in the Objective case of being "forgotten" as the main verb. If you inspect the other examples below you will see many double objects similarly.

Geçen hafta ödevimi yapmayı unuttum. *I forgot to do my homework last week.*

Garajdan arabamı almayı unuttum. *I forgot to pick up (take) my car from the garage.*

Ali, sana söylemeyi unuttu. *Ali forgot to tell you.*

Affedersin, seni aramayı unuttuk. *We're sorry, we forgot to call you.* (a secondary meaning of **aramak** is *to call (on the telephone).*

Filmi izlemeyi unuttum. *I forgot to watch the film.*

Kediyi beslemeyi unuttum. *I forgot to feed the cat.*

Mehmet'i sormayı unuttunuz *You forgot to ask Mehmet.*

Kapıyı kapamayı unuttum. *I forgot to close the door.*

Pencereyi açmayı unuttular. *They forgot to open the window.*

About Verbal Objects.

Some main verbs take Movement Towards suffix **-(y)e/-(y)a** as their objects when the verb itself signifies movement towards. In English saying *she is starting to write* then the infinitive **yazmak** *to write* is the object of the verb *she is starting,* and consequently must be suffixed to show its relationship to the verb.

As the verb **başlamak** *to start, begin* signifies movement of some sort it governs the Movement Towards Condition in Turkish **-a** or **-e**. To effect the addition of the Movement Towards suffix to **yazmak** the final **-k** of **-mek** or **-mak** is dropped and the resulting verbal noun **yazma** is treated as a normal object by the addition of the Movement Towards Condition suffix **-(y)a** so **yazmak** *to write* becomes **yazmaya başladı** *she started to (to) write/she started writing.*

While translating in English we use The Present Continuous Participle in *-ing* (another noun) so the above is often rendered in the following manner: **yazmak** *to write* becomes **yazmaya başladı** *she started (the) writing.*

Special Case istemek *to want.*

The verb **istemek** *to want* is a special case as it causes no modification of the verb it governs:

yazmak istiyorum. *I want to write.*
içmek istiyorlar. *they want to drink.*
kalmak istemedin. *you didn't want to stay.*
çalışmak istemeyecekler. *they will not want to work.*

This also applies in English, we also cannot say *I want writing* or *they want drinking.* The object pointer is not required by **istemek** *to want* as the concept of "wanting." does not affect the verb being governed in any way.

However if **istemek** governs anything other than a verb then the objective case must be used. We can see from the examples below that **istemek** is not governing the verb **kalmak** directly, but it governs **a person**. Hence the direct object pointer is required.

Kalmamanızı istiyoruz. [Kalma-ma-nız-ı] *We want you not to stay.*

Kalmanızı istemiyoruz. [Kalma-nız-ı] *We do not want you to stay.*

Kalmasını istemiyorlar. [Kalma-sı-n-ı] *They don't want him to stay.*

Kalmamalarını istemiyorum. [Kalma-ma-ları-n-ı] *I don't want them not to stay.*

Formation of the Short Infinitive Verbal Noun.

To effect the addition of the suffixes to the infinitive, for instance the verb **içmek**, then the final **-k** of **-mek** or **-mak** is dropped and the resulting verbal noun then ends in **-ma** or **-me** becoming **içme** in this case. It is treated as a normal object the addition of the suffix **-(y)i** thus becoming **içmeyi**. Similarly the Movement Toward Object is formed in the same manner: The infinitive **yazmak** *to write* forms Verbal Noun **yazma** *the writing* thence forms the Movement Toward Condition Object **yazmaya** [yazma-y-a] *to the writing.*

Examples of Verbal Nouns in English.

Unfortunately we do not realize when we are using Verbal Nouns, but if you want to understand Turkish both written and spoken then we must learn to recognize them.

The writing is on the wall.
The drinking of this water is prohibited.
Smoking is allowed.
Leave your suitcase in the waiting room.
He is working in the drying shed.

Explanation of the Short Infinitive.

The Positive Verb **içmek** *to drink* or *to smoke a cigarette* drops it final **-k** and is used to form **içme** *drinking, smoking* as a noun. With the addition of the accusative case it becomes **içmeyi** *the drinking, the smoking* as the object of a verb. With the addition of the dative case it becomes **içmeye** *to the drinking, the smoking* as the dative object of a verb.

The Negative Verb forms its Verbal Noun by dropping its terminal -k in a similar fashion **içmemek** *not to drink* forms **içmeme** *not drinking, not smoking* as a noun. The Negative Accusative then becomes **içmemeyi** *the not drinking, the not smoking* as a direct object and the Movement Toward Object becomes **içmemeye** *to the not drinking, to the not smoking.*

About Conversational Stress.

This could mistaken for the negation suffix **-me** but the difference is hidden in the stress. When it is a Positive Verbal Noun then the stress is on itself as in **içMEyi**. However when it is a Negative Verbal Noun, then the stress is on the preceding syllable **İÇmemeyi**. The negative suffix **-me/-ma** itself is never stressed in conversation but always throws the stress on to the previous syllable.

Examples of Suffixed Infinitives.

Vowel Harmony and Consonant Mutation rules are followed when adding the standard suffixes, also the buffer letter **-y-** is used to keep vowel suffixes apart.

gelmeye çalıştı. *he tried [to] to come.* [Movement Towards Suffix as the verb **çalışmak** takes a Movement Toward Suffix *to try to.*]

Yüzmeyi severim. *I like to swim.* [I like the swimming.]

Onu yapmaktayım. *I am just doing it.* [in/at doing it.]

Sigara içmeyi bıraktım. *I have given up [the] smoking.* [Direct Object suffix.]

Adding Suffixes to the Standard Infinitive in -mek.

The infinitive is a noun. Consequently it can be suffixed with any of the case suffixes. We are taking for our model the Positive Infinitive **gelmek** *to come* and the Negative Infinitive **gelmemek** *not to come.*

The Extended Infinitive Forms.

Positive.
gelmek *to come.*
gelmeye *to come.*
gelmeyi *to come.* (obj.)
gelmekte *in coming.*
gelmekten. *from coming.*
gelmekle. *by/with coming.*

Negative.

152

gelmemek. *not to come.*
gelmemeye. *to not to come.*
gelmemeyi. *not to come.* (obj.)
gelmemekte. *in not coming.*
gelmemekten. *from not coming.*
gelmemekle. *by/with not coming.*

Examples of the various infinitive forms.

Kesmeyi bıraktı. *He stopped [the] cutting.*

Sürmeyi öğreniyorum. *I am learning [the driving] to drive.*

Gülmemeye çalışıyorlar. *They are trying not to [to] laugh.*

The Personalised Infinitive.

When the standard infinitive takes the personal pronoun endings it drops its final **-k** of **-mek** or **-mak** in all persons.

Positive Infinitive Personalized.

gitmek *to go*
gitmem *my going*
gitmen *your going*
gitmemiz *our going*
gitmeniz *your going*
gitmeleri *their going*

Negative Infinitive Personalized.

gitmemek *not to go*
gitmemem *my not going*
gitmemen *your not going*
gitmememiz *our not going*
gitmemeniz *your not going*
gitmemeleri *their not going*

The Abilitative *(can, can't)* Infinitive Form.

gidebilmek *to be able to go.*
gidememek *to not be able to go.*

gidebilmem *my being able to go.*
gidemememiz *our not being able to go.*
gidebilmesi *his being able to go.*
gidememeleri *their not being able to go.*
These personal forms can further be extended by the addition of noun condition suffixes:

Gitmesini bekledim . *I expected him to go.* [gitme-si-ni Objective Condition.]

Kalmanızı istiyorum *I want you to stay.*
Kalabilmenizi istiyorum *I want you to be able to stay.*
Kalmamanızı istiyoruz *We want you not to stay.*
Kalmanızı istemiyoruz *We do not want you to stay.*
Kalmasını istemiyorlar *They don't want him to stay.*
Kalmamalarını istemiyorum *I don't want them not to stay.*

The Little Used Heavy Infinitive.

This is formed by affixing **-lık** or **-lik** to the standard Infinitive for the positive verb. The final **-k** of **-mek** is often dropped when adding the **-lik** suffix. The negative is slightly different in that the **-mek** or **-mak** changes to **-mez** or **-maz**.

gelmek becomes **gelme(k)lik.**
bakmamak becomes **bakmazlık.**

The meaning of the heavy infinitive is the same as the standard infinitive and is only used when there may be ambiguity in the context. The heavy infinitive is little used. The heavy infinitive can also have personal pronouns and or case endings added to it. It does not however drop its final **-k** of **-lik** as does the common infinitive when suffixes are added although this final **-k** will mutate to a final **-ğ** when necessary before an added vowel.

Positive Negative Forms Heavy Infinitive.

gelme(k)lik *to come.*
gelmezlik *not to come.*

gelme(k)liğim *my coming.*

gelmezliğimiz *our not coming.*

gelme(k)likleri *their coming.*
gelmezliği *his not coming.*

How to say "To pretend (not) to".

The heavy infinitive is little used except for the following "special case": The use of the Negative of the Heavy Infinitive in the ablative case followed by the verb **gelmek** means *to pretend not to.* This "pretend not to" form is a reduplicated negative ie: **bakmazlık** becomes **bakMAmazlık** meaning *to not NOT to see* It is mentioned here because in this form it is daily use.

Bana görmemezlikten geldi. *He pretended (not) see me.*

Onu görmemezlikten geliyorsunuz. *You are pretending (not) to see it.*

Ayşe hanımı sevmemezlikten gelir misiniz? *Are you pretending (not) to like Miss Ayşe?*

This construction is a special locution and only used with **gelmek** as an auxiliary verb.

It is used widely to mean *To pretend not to.*

görmemezlikten gelmek *ignore.*
görmemezlikten gelmek *turn a blind eye.*
görmemezlikten gelmek *overlook.*
görmemezlikten gelmek *look through.*
görmemezlikten gelmek *give someone the go by.*
görmemezlikten gelmek *close one's eyes to.*
görmemezlikten gelmek *pretend not to see.*

15 THE VERB "TO BE"

The Verb "to be" Positive.

From the History of Turkish.

The verb "to be" is a now defective verb "imek" whose stem was "i-" which is found in four forms of vowel harmony "i ı u u". It also mutates to "-y" in the past and other forms when being suffixed to a word. This is no longer important in learning Turkish, but it does give the reason for many of the suffixes in modern use for the verb "to be".

The verb *"to be"* is used to describe a State of Being.
The house is blue.
Mehmet was ill.
It will be a quick journey.
If it is a big house.
If it had not been out of sight.

The Verb "to be" takes the form of a suffix in Turkish. It is subject to Vowel Harmony, and Consonant Mutation when added to words ending in a hard consonant. In the Present only 3rd person singular has consonant mutation.

Present Tense "to be".

The Present Tense verb "to be" takes the form of a suffix as follows:

I am: **-im -ım -üm -um.**
After vowels: **-yim -yım -yüm -yum.**

you are: **-sin -sın -sün -sun.**

he/she/it is: **-dir -dır -dür -dur.**
After [ç f h k p s ş t]: **-tir -tır -tür -tur.**

156

We are: **-iz -ız -üz -uz.**
After vowels: **-yiz -yız -yüz -yuz.**

you are: **-siniz -sınız -sünüz -sunuz.**

they are: **-dirler -dırlar -dürler -durlar.**
After [ç f h k p s ş t]: **-tirler -tırlar -türler -turlar.**

The First Persons use Buffer **-Y-** when added to a vowel.

The Third Person **-dir/-dirler** suffix changes to **-tir/-tirler** when added to unvoiced consonants **ç f h k p s ş t** due to Consonant Mutation.

  The Third Person suffix is often omitted in conversation. It is only used for emphasis or official advice and public notices. It is also used when stating an actual fact, **Elma meyve***dir. Apples are fruit.* This omission not does not apply to the past tense as shown below.

Past Tense Definite and Indefinite "to be".

The past tense endings are used in all persons although sometime the **-ler/-lar** of the plural form is omitted in conversation. The Buffer Letter **-y-** is used in the formation of the Past Tense for Verb stems which end in a vowel. This is to keep the final vowel of the verb stem separated by mutating the first vowel of the Past Tense endings **-idim etc.** to **-ydim etc.** As every person suffix in the past tense begins with a **-d** then it follows that every person can be subject to consonant mutation to **-t** when added to a word ending in a hard consonant.

The Definite Past tense endings are used for Statements of Fact and events witnessed by the speaker: ("Mehmet is/was a in his garden.") means: "I saw him there a moment ago."

"To be" Definite Past Suffixes.

I was: **-(y)dim -(y)dım -(y)düm -(y)dum.**
After (ç f h k p s ş t): **-tim -tım -tüm -tum.**

you were: **-(y)din -(y)dın -(y)dün -(y)dun.**

After (ç f h k p s ş t): **-tin -tın -tün -tun.**

he/she/it was: **-(y)di -(y)dı -(y)dü -(y)du.**
After (ç f h k p s ş t): **-ti -tı -tü -tu.**

we were: **-(y)dik -(y)dık -(y)dük -(y)duk.**
After (ç f h k p s ş t): **-tik -tık -tük -tuk.**

you were: **-(y)diniz -(y)dınız -(y)dünüz -(y)dunuz.**
After (ç f h k p s ş t): **-tiniz -tınız -tünüz -tunuz.**

they were: **-(y)diler -(y)dılar -(y)düler -(y)dular.**
After (ç f h k p s ş t): **-tirler -tırlar -türler -turlar.**

The Indefinite Past suffixes are used for hearsay, supposition and unwitnessed events: ("Mehmet is/was probably in his garden.") supposition "Because he is nearly always there".

"To be" Indefinite Past Suffixes.

(It seems) I was: **-(y)mişim -(y)mışım -(y)müşüm -(y)muşum.**

(It seems) you were: **-(y)mişsin -(y)mışsın -(y)müşsün - (y)muşsun.**

(It seems) he/she/it was: **-(y)miş -(y)mış -(y)müş -(y)muş.**

(It seems) we were: **-(y)mişiz -(y)mışız -(y)müşüz -(y)muşuz.**

(It seems) you were: **-(y)mişsiniz -(y)mışsınız -(y)müşsünüz - (y)muşsunuz.**

(It seems) they were: **-(y)mişler -(y)mışlar -(y)müşler - (y)muşlar.**

Past Tense "to be" Independent Standalone Form.

The Past Tense Positive also has an independent form which is not subject to vowel harmony, but takes its form from the defunct verb "imek". It is written separately after the word it affects. Using this form is a matter personal taste, but it is often found in newspapers and books. The Present Tense does not have an independent form, it is always as suffix.

"to be" Past Singular Independent Standalone.

Person Definite Indefinite.

I was: **idim imişim.**
you were: **idin imişsin.**
he/she/it was: **idi imiş.**
We were: **idik imişiz.**
you were: **idiniz imişsiniz.**
they were: **idiler imişler.**

Vowel Harmony of the Verb "to be".

Both the present and past obey the rules of vowel harmony, which are summed up as follows:

The A-UnDotted Group -"to be" examples.

Final vowel **-a** or **-ı** is followed by **-ı** in suffix.

yaşlıyız. [yaşlı-yız] *we are old.*
yaşlıydık. [yaşlı-ydık] *we were old.* independent form **yaşlı idik.**
yaşlıymışız. [yaşlı-ymışız] *probably we were old.* independent form
yaşlı imişiz.

hastayım. [hasta-yım] *I am ill.*
hastaydım. [hasta-ydım] *I was ill* independent form **hasta idim.**
hastaymışım [hasta-ymışım] *probably I was ill* independent form
hasta imişim.

Final vowel **-o** or **-u** is followed by **u** in suffix.

bir vazodur. [vazo-dur] *it is a vase..*
bir vazoydu. [vazo-ydu] *probably it was a vase.* independent form
bir vazo idi.
bir vazoymuş .[vazo-ymuş] *it was a vase.* independent form -**bir
vazo imiş.**

yorgunsun. [yorgun-sun] *you are tired.*
yorgundun(uz). [yorgun-dun(uz)] *you were tired.* independent form
 yorgun idin(iz).
yorgunmışsın(ız). [yorgun-mışsın(ız)] *probably you were tired.*

independent form **yorgun imişsin(iz).**

The E- Dotted Group -"to be" examples.

Final vowel **-e** or **-i** is followed by **i** in suffix.

bir deredir. [dere-dir] *it is a stream.*
bir dereydi. [dere-ydi] *it was stream.* independent form **bir dere idi.**
bir dereymiş. [dere-ymiş] *it was stream.* independent form **bir dere imiş.**

zenginsin. [zengin-sin] *you are rich.*
zengindin(iz). [zengin-din(iz)] *you were rich.* independent form
zengin idin(iz).
zenginmişsin(iz). [zengin-mişsin(iz)] *you were rich.* independent
form **zengin imişsin(iz).**

Final vowel **-ö** or **-ü** is followed by **ü** in suffix.

bir gözdür. [göz-dür] *it is an eye.*
bir gözdü. [göz-dü] *it was an eye.* independent form **bir göz idi.**
bir gözmüş. [göz-müş] *it was an eye.* independent form **bir göz imiş.**

Türk' türler. [Türk'-türler] *they are Turkish.*
Türk' tüler. [Türk'-tüler] *they were Turkish.* independent form
Türk idiler.
Türk' müşler. [Türk'-müşler] *they were Turkish.* independent form
Türk imişler.

Consonant Mutation of the Verb "to be".

The present and past tense suffixes which begin in **-d-** undergo
consonant mutation **-dir** becomes **-tir** and all the past tense suffixes
beginning in **-di** become **-ti** after a final hard consonant the letters **ç f
h k p ş s t.**

Consonant Mutation Present Tense and Past Tense -"to be".

The suffixes in brackets are omitted in familiar conversation.
büyük(tür). *it is large.*

160

büyüktü büyükmüş. *it was large.*

genç(tirler). *they are young.*
gençtik gençmişiz. *we were young.*

yavaşsın(ız). *you were slow.*
çabuktun(uz) çabukmuşsun(uz). *you were quick.*

sabah(tır). *it is morning.*
sabahtı sabahmış. *it was morning.*

bir mektup(tur). *it is a letter.*
bir mektuptu bir mektupmuş. *it was a letter.*

Mehmet('tir). *It is Mehmet.*
Mehmet' ti Mehmet' miş. *It was Mehmet.*

bir sepet(tir). *it is a basket.*
bir sepetti bir sepetmiş. *it was a basket.*

bir virüs(tür). *it is a virus.*
bir virüstü bir virüsmüş. *it was a virus.*

felaket(tir). *it is a disaster.*
felaketti felaketmiş. *it was a disaster.*

polis(tirler). *they are policemen.*
polistiler polismişler. *they were policemen.*

Proper names with the verb "to be".

Suffixes are not fixed directly to Proper Names (words which begin with a capital letter), an apostrophe comma is used instead:

Mehmet' tir. *It is Mehmet.*
İstanbul' dur. *It is Istanbul.*
Hükümet' tir. *It is the Government.*

Some Examples of the verb "to be".

zengin. *rich.*
zenginim. *I am rich.*
zengindim. *I was rich.*

yorgun. *tired.*
yorgunum. *I am tired.*
yorgundun. *you were tired.*

pahalı. *dear, expensive.*
pahalı(dır). *it is dear.*
pahalıydı . *it was dear.*

küçük. *small.*
küçük(tür). *it is small.*
küçüktü. *it was small.*

hasta. *ill.*
hastayız. *we are ill.*
hastaydık. *we were ill.*

yaşlı. *aged/old.*
yaşlısın. *you are old.*
yaşlıydı. *he was old.*

yoksul. *poor.*
yoksul(durlar). *they are poor.*
yoksuldular. *they were poor.*

genç. *young.*
genç(tirler). *they are young.*
gençti. *he was young.*

Interrogative Form of the Verb "to be".

Asking questions, the interrogative particle **-mi?** is used to form questions. It is placed after the word it affects, personal endings added according to Vowel Harmony Rakes:

"to be" Questions Present Positive.

am I? **mıyım? miyim? muyum? müyüm?**

are you? **mısın? misin? musun? müsün?**

is he/she/it? **mı? mi? mu? mü?**

is he/she/it? (formal, public) **mıdır? midir? müdür?**

are we? **mıyız? miyiz? muyuz? müyüz?**

are you? **mısınız? misiniz? musunuz? müsünüz?**

are they? **-lar mı? -ler mi? -lar mu? -ler mü?**

are they? (formal/public) **mıdırlar? midirler? mudurlar? müdürler?**

Except for the 3rd person form **-lar mi?** the positive form of the interrogative is written separately from the word it affects, but obeys the rules of Vowel Harmony. The longer forms which end in **-dir** are more formal and are used in instructions and public notices. They are not usually used in general conversation.

Interrogative Present Tense Positive examples "to be".

zengin miyim? *am I rich?*
yorgun musun? *are you tired?*
pahalı mı? *is it dear?*
büyük mü? *is it big?*
hasta mıyız? *are we ill?*
yaşlı mısınız? *are you old?*
gençler mi? *are they young?*
yoksullar mı? *are they poor?*

The question tag is written separately from the verb, but still obeys vowel harmony rules.

Interrogative Past Tense Positive examples "to be".

The Past tense personal endings are added to the question particle -mi and obeys Vowel harmony but is written separately.

"to be" Questions Past Positive.

was I? **mıydım? miydim? muydum? müydüm?**

were you? **mıydın? miydin? muydun? müydün?**

is he/she/it? **mıydı? miydi? muydu? müydü?**

were we? **mıydık? miydik? muyduk? müydük?**

were you? **mıydınız? miydiniz? muydunuz? müydünüz?**

are they? **mıydılar? miydiler? muydular? müydüler?**

The Buffer Letter -y- is used in the formation of the Past Tense Questions. This is to keep the final vowel of the question tag **-mi** by mutating the first vowel of the Past Tense endings **-idim etc** to become **-ydim etc.**

Interrogative Past Tense Positive examples "to be".

acı mıydı? *was it bitter?*
sıcak mıydı? *was it hot?*
hava soğuk muydu? *was the weather cold?*
mutlu muyduk? *were we happy?*
yorgun muydular? *were they tired?*
hasta mıydınız? *were you ill? or have you been ill?*
güzel miydi? *was she beautiful?*
ev büyük müydü? *was it a large house?*

The question tag is written separately from the verb, but still obeys vowel harmony rules.

The Future of the Verb "to be" will be.

The Future Tense of Verbs is discussed in Chapter 19. Page 192

The Future of the verb "to be" is lacking in Turkish. It place is taken by the Future Tense of the Verb **olmak** *to be, to become.*

Yarın hazır olacağım. *I will be ready tomorrow.*

Er geç zengin olacaksın. *You will become rich sooner or later.*

Bu gece parti çok güzel olacak. *It will be a great party tonight.*

All these are "state of being" sentences but Turkish uses the verb **olmak** *to become* to convey the future of the verb *"to be"*

The Verb "*not to be*" Negative.

The Negative Particle is **değil** *not.*

The Negative *not to be* is formed by using the negative particle **değil** *not.* This word is invariable and not subject to vowel harmony rules. To form the negative the personal present tense endings are affixed to **değil** *not.* The resulting verb *not to be* is written separately from the verb root, whereas the positive forms *to be, am, is, are, etc.* being added to the root word, are subject to both Vowel Harmony and Consonant Mutation.

Present Tense Negative "not to be".

ben değilim. *I am not.*
zengin değilim. *I am not rich.*

sen değilsin. [Familiar, Usual] *you are not.*
yorgun değilsin. *you are not tired.*

değildir. *he/she/it is not.*
pahalı değildir. *it is not dear.*

o değil. *he is not.*
o şişman değil. *she is not fat*

biz değiliz. *we are not.*
hasta değiliz. *we are not ill.*

siz değilsiniz. [Public, Official] *you are not.*
yaşlı değilsiniz. *you are not old.*

değildirler. *they are not.*
genç değildirler. *they are not young.*

değiller. *they are not.*
çirkin değiller. *they are not ugly.*

Generally the third person forms using **-dir** are not used in day to day conversation. However they are used in Public Signs and Warnings as a reinforcement. The shortened form should always be used in general conversation. However the use of the **-dir** form is apparent in Public Signs, Official Instructions and in newspaper reports. For these reasons this longer form is included here.

Using The Personal Pronouns for emphasis:

The Personal Pronouns are only used for emphasis, as the person of the verb is already apparent from the verb ending.

ben zengin değilim. *I AM not rich.*
zengin değilim. *I'm not rich.*

o hasta değil. *HE is not ill .*
hasta değil. *he's not ill.*

Interrogative Present Tense Negative "not to be".

To form Negative Questions the positive interrogative verb is added after **değil** *not*, but written separately.

zengin değil miyim? *am I not rich? aren't I rich?*

yorgun değil misin? *aren't you tired?*

büyük değil mi? *isn't it big?*
pahalı değil mi? *isn't it dear?*

hasta değil miyiz? *aren't we ill?*

yaşlı değil misiniz? *aren't you old?*

genç değiller mi? *aren't they young?*
yoksul değiller mi? *aren't they poor?*

Interrogative Past Tense Negative "not to be".

To form the Past Tense of *"not to be"* the Personal Past Tense endings are added to **değil** *not.*

değildim. *I was not.*
zengin değildim. *I was not rich.*

değildin. *you were not.*
hasta değildin. *you were not ill.*

değildi. *he was not.*
yorgun değildi. *he/she was not tired.*

değildik. *we were not.*
mutlu değildik. *we were not happy.*

değildiniz. *you were not.*
aç değildiniz. *you were not hungry.*

değildiler. *they were not.*
yoksul değildiler. *they were not poor.*

Examples of Negative Questions regarding Past Time formed with **değil** *not* followed by the question tags written separately.

açık değil miydi? *wasn't it open?*
mutlu değil miydik? *weren't we happy?*
hava soğuk değil miydi? *wasn't the weather cold?*
zengin değil miydiler? *weren't they rich?*
emin değil miydim? *wasn't I sure?*
Mehmet meşgul değil miydi? *wasn't Mehmet busy?*
yorgun değil miydiniz? *weren't you tired?*
çocuklar mutlu değil miydiler? *weren't the children happy?*

Question Tags in Turkish.

The question tags that we use in English: *Isn't it?, Aren't you?, Aren't they?, Can't we?, Weren't they?, Didn't they?. etc* are all translated by the single tag **değil mi?** in Turkish for all Persons and all Tenses.

Hava soğuk, değil mi? *The weather is cold, isn't it?*
Hava soğuktu, değil mi? *The weather was cold, wasn't it?*
Mutlusunuz, değil mi? *You are happy, aren't you?*
Mutlu olacaksın, değil mi? *You will be happy, won't you?*
Hastadırlar, değil mi? *They are ill, aren't they?*
Mehmet kazanabilir, değil mi? *Mehmet can win, can't he?*

"to be" Examples.

The word **pek** *very, hard, firm, quite* is often used as an intensifier

167

especially in negative sentences. The word **çok** *very* can also be used as an intensifier in positive sentences although it is a little more direct as **pek** is a more gentle word.

Mutluyum. I am happy.
İyisiniz. You are good.
Bozuk(tur). It is spoiled, broken, no good.
Kolay(dır). It is easy.
Neşeliyiz. We are merry.
İngilizsiniz. You are English.
Zeki(dirler). They are clever.
Pek/Çok şişmansınız. You are very fat.
Çok/Pek naziksiniz. You are very nice.
Mehmet pek hasta(dır). Mehmet is quite ill.
Genç değilim. I am not young.
Hasta değilsiniz. You are not ill.
Pek aç değilim. I am not very hungry.
Yüksek değil(dir). It is not high.
Deli değiliz. We are not crazy.
Pek/Çok çabuk değil(dir). It is not very quick/fast.
Pek nazik değilsiniz. You are not very nice.
Pek zeki değil(dirler). They are not very clever.
Zengin miyim? Am I rich?
Zengin değil miyim? Am I not rich?
Hasta mısınız? Are you ill?
Ali bey genç mi(dir)? Is Ali Bey young?
Kolay mı(dır)? Is it easy?
Zeki miyiz? Are we clever?
Zeki değil miyiz? Aren't we clever?
Deli misin? Are you crazy?
Arkadaşınız yaşlı mı(dır)? Is your friend old?
Arkadaşım yaşlı değil(dir). My friend is not old.
Evet, arkadaşım genç(tir). Yes, my friend is young.
Mehmet mutlu mudur? Is Mehmet happy.
Evet, mutlu(dur). Yes, he is happy.
Hayır, mutlu değil(dir). No, he is not happy.
Hazır mısın? Are you ready?
Hazır değil misin bile? Aren't you ready yet?

16 THE PRESENT CONTINUOUS TENSE

Present Continuous iyor "doing, saying"

This tense takes the form of "be doing, be not doing, be saying, be not saying, be going". *I am going, Are you thinking?, We are not staying, Are they not trying?*

The Tense sign of the Present Continuous Tense is **-iyor- -ıyor- -üyor- -uyor-** which is added to the verb root. The tense endings are completed by adding the personal suffixes.

When the verb root itself ends in a vowel, as in **bekle-mek** *to wait, expect* becoming **bekl-iyor**, then this vowel is also dropped as the head vowel of the **-iyor** tense sign replaces it. The first letter **-i-** of **-iyor-** is subject to vowel harmony with the verb stem's final vowel. The Tense Sign **-iyor-** can be likened to the English Tense sign *"-ing"*.

Spelling Exceptions of Verb Roots.

Only five verbs change their root spelling from **-t** to **-d** when adding a vowel (the "famous" five!).

gitmek *to go* becomes
gidiyorum *I am going*

ditmek *to shred* (verb used in recipes) becomes
didiyor *he/it shreds*

tatmak *to taste (of)* becomes
tadıyor *it tastes (of)*

etmek *to do/perform* becomes
ediyorum *I am doing*

gütmek *to nourish, feed*
güdüyor *he nourishes, feeds*

The verb **etmek** includes all verbs containing **etmek** as a compound:

kaybetmek *to lose* **kaybediyor.**
affetmek *to pardon, to excuse* **affeder.**

All other verbs retain their original spelling, examples:

bitmek *to end.*
bitiyor *it is finishing.* [NOT "bidiyor"]

batmak *to sink.*
batıyor *it is sinking.* [NOT "badıyor"]

Formation of the Present Continuous Tense.

The Personal Endings -Present Continuous.

geliyorum. [gel-iyor-um] *I am coming.*
bakıyorsun. [bak-ıyor-sun] *you are looking.*
giriyor. [gir-iyor] *he, she, it is entering.*

çıkıyoruz. [çık-ıyor-uz] *we are going out.*
buluyorsunuz. [bul-uyor-sunuz] *you are finding.*
gülüyorlar. [gül-üyor-lar] *they are laughing.*

Positive Present Continuous Tense Conjugated.

Positive Infinitive: gelmek. [gel-mek] *to come.*

geliyorum *I am coming.*
geliyorsun *you are coming.*
geliyor *he is coming.*

geliyoruz *we are coming.*
geliyorsunuz *you are coming.*
geliyorlar *they are coming.*

Negative Present Continuous Tense Conjugates.

Negative Infinitive: gelmemek. [gelme-mek] *not to come.*

gelmiyorum. *I am not coming.*
gelmiyorsun. *you are not coming.*
gelmiyor. *he is not coming.*

gelmiyoruz. *we are not coming.*
gelmiyorsunuz. *you are not coming.*
gelmiyorlar. *they are not coming.*

The vowel of **gelmek** (E-Dotted group) is **-e-** therefore the tense sign begins with a Dotted-i **-iyor-** The infinitive verb ending **-mek** is dropped from the verb stem and **-iyor-** is added together with the personal endings to form the tense.

All Negative Verb roots that end in a vowel as in: **gelmemek** [gelme -mek] *not to come* also drop this final vowel from the vowel stem so that when the tense sign **-iyor-** is added two vowels do not occur together. [gelmeiyorum is incorrect]. The Rule is that Negative Verbs drop the final vowel of the root along with **-mek** or **-mak.**

The final vowel of any verb stem is dropped when adding **-iyor** in order to keep two vowels apart. This applies to *all negative* Verbs in both the A-UnDotted Vowel and the E-Dotted Groups as they all end in a vowel of the **-me** or **-ma** negative particle.

Examples of the E-Dotted vowel group of Verbs.

Continuous Tense Positive Verbs.

vermek *to give*
veriyor *giving*

bilmek *to know*
biliyor *knowing*

görmek *to see*
görüyor *seeing*

gülmek *to laugh*
gülüyor *laughing*

Continuous Tense Negative Verbs.

vermemek *not to give*

vermiyor *not giving*

bilmemek *not to know*
bilmiyor *not knowing*

görmemek *not to see*
görmüyor *not seeing*

gülmemek *not to laugh*
gülmüyor *not laughing*

The final vowel of any verb is dropped when adding **-iyor** in order to keep two vowels apart. This applies to all positive Verbs in both A-UnDotted and E-Dotted Groups. As an example see **kuru -mak** becomes **kur-uyor** and **ağrı-mak** becomes **ağr-ıyor** in table above. All negative verb stems lose their final stem vowel as they end in the negative particle **-me** or **-ma**.

Examples of the A-UnDotted vowel group of Verbs.

Continuous Tense Positive Verbs.

yapmak *to do, make, perform*
yapıyor *doing*

ağrımak *to ache*
ağrıyor *aching*

kopmak *to snap*
kopuyor *snapping*

kurumak *to dry*
kuruyor *drying*

Continuous Tense Negative Verbs.

yapmamak *not to do*
yapmıyor *not doing*

ağrımamak *not to ache*
ağrımıyor *not aching*

kopmamak *not to snap*
kopmuyor *not snapping*

172

kurumamak *not to dry*
kurumuyor *not drying*

Examples of Verb Root ending in a Vowel.

Continuous Tense Positive Verb.

Positive Infinitive: beklemek *to wait, expect.*

bekliyorum *I am waiting*
bekliyorsun *you are waiting*
bekliyor *he/she/it is waiting*

bekliyoruz *we are waiting*
bekliyorsunuz *you are waiting*
bekliyorlar *they are waiting*

The root of this verb is **bekle-** but we must also drop this final vowel
-**e** before adding the tense sign-**iyor-** in order that two vowels do not
occur together. ("bekleiyorum" would be incorrect). The Rule is that
the final vowel of verb stem is dropped along with -**mek** or -**mak**.

Continuous Tense Negative Verb.

Negative Infinitive: beklememek *to not wait, expect.*

beklemiyorum *I am not waiting*
beklemiyorsun *you are not waiting*
beklemiyor *he/she/it is not waiting*

beklemiyoruz *we are not waiting*
beklemiyorsunuz *you are not waiting*
beklemiyorlar *they are not waiting*

A-UnDotted Verbs Ending in a Consonant.

Continuous Tense Positive Verb.

Positive Infinitive: bakmak *to look, to look at.*

bakıyorum *I am looking*
bakıyorsun *you are looking*
bakıyor *he is looking*

bakıyoruz *we are looking*
bakıyorsunuz *you are looking*
bakıyorlar *they are looking*

Continuous Tense Negative Verb.

Negative Infinitive: bakmamak *not to look, not to look at.*

bakmıyorum *I am not looking*
bakmıyorsun *you are not looking*
bakmıyor *he is not looking*

bakmıyoruz *we are not looking*
bakmıyorsunuz *you are not looking*
bakmıyorlar *they are not looking*

For verbs of the A-UnDotted Group with **a i o u** in verb stem the suffix -**mak** signifies the positive verb and -**mamak** is used for the negative verb. The positive verb is **bakmak** *to look*. The negative verb is **bakmamak** *not to look.*

Bakmak *to look* is a verb of the A-UnDotted Group therefore the tense sign also begins with an UnDotted-ı -**ıyor**-

E-Dotted Verbs Ending in a Vowel.

Continuous Tense Positive Verb.

Positive Infinitive: yürümek *to walk.*

yürüyorum *I am walking*
yürüyorsun *you are walking*
yürüyor *he is walking*

yürüyoruz *we are walking*
yürüyorsunuz *you are walking*
yürüyorlar *they are walking*

Continuous Tense Negative Verb.

Negative Infinitive: yürümemek *not to walk.*

yürümüyorum *I am not walking*

yürümüyorsun *you are not walking*
yürümüyor *he is not walking*

yürümüyoruz *we are not walking*
yürümüyorsunuz *you are not walking*
yürümüyorlar *they are not walking*

For verbs of the E-Dotted Group with **e ı ö ü** in verb stem the suffix -**mek** signifies the positive verb and -**memek** is used for the negative verb. The positive verb is **yürümek** *to walk*. The negative verb is **yürümemek** *not to walk*.

Yürümek *to walk* is a verb of the E-Dotted Group therefore the tense sign also begins with a Dotted -**üyor**- This verb also has a final vowel in the verb stem which is dropped along with the infinitive sign -**mek**. The tense sign -**üyor**- is then added under vowel harmony rules.

Interrogative Present Continuous.

To form questions the question particle **mi?**, subject to Vowel Harmony, is used after -**iyor**. It is written separately and the personal ending is added making a question tag. The Third Person Plural is slightly different in that the question particle **mi?** is always placed last for reasons of ease of pronunciation.
The question particle **mi?** is subject to Vowel Harmony so can have four forms **mi? mı? mu? mü?**. It retains its vowel harmonization even when not attached as a suffix.

Question Formation Generally.

The Question Particle **mı? mi? mu? mü?** is placed after the item that you are questioning: It is not always the verb that is in question. This is the same for English.

Question Particle Positioning.

Mehmet, şimdi eve gidiyor mu? *Is Mehmet going home now?*
"Mehmet, is he going home now?" Question on the verb "gitmek" "to go".

175

Mehmet, eve mi gidiyor? *Is it home that Mehmet is going to?*
Question on the object "ev" "home."

Mehmet mi, eve gidiyor? *Is it Mehmet who is going home?*
Question on The subject "Mehmet".

Bisiklet, ters mi duruyor? *Is the bicycle upside down?*
"The bicycle, is it upside down?" The position of the bicycle is in
question.

Mehmet, kemen mi çalıyor? *Is Mehmet playing the violin?*
"Is it the violin? That he is playing". The "keman" "violin" is in
question.]

The verb **çalmak** has two meanings:
(1) To play a musical instrument.
(2) To steal something.

O, kemen mi çalıyor? could mean *Is it a violin that he is
stealing?* or *Is it a violin that he is playing?*

Bir hırsız arabamı çaldı. *A thief stole/has stolen my car.*

Bir kız piyanoyu güzelce çaldı. *A girl played the piano well.*

Question Tags in Turkish.

Forming the Interrogative.

Positive Infinitive: gelmek *to come.*

geliyor muyum? *am I coming?*
geliyor musun? *are you coming?*
geliyor mu? *is he coming?*

geliyor muyuz? *are we coming?*
geliyor musunuz? *are you coming?*
geliyorlar mı? *are they coming?*

Negative Infinitive: gelmemek *to not come*

gelmiyor muyum? *aren't I coming?*

gelmiyor musun? *aren't you coming?*
gelmiyor mu? *isn't he coming?*

gelmiyor muyuz? *aren't we coming?*
gelmiyor musunuz? *aren't you coming?*
gelmiyorlar mı? *aren't they coming?*

The question tags **muyum?, musun?** etc are always written separately from the verb itself. The tags do however follow vowel harmony rules even that they are not directly suffixed to the verb stem itself. The negative questions are formed in the same manner using the negative verb stem. The vowel harmonized question tag is still written separated from the verb stem.

Yarın şehre gidiyorum. *Tomorrow I am going to town.*

Yarın şehre gitmiyorum. *Tomorrow I am not going to town.*

Benimle gelmiyor musunuz? *Aren't you coming with me?*

Küçük odada uyumuyorlar mı? *Aren't they sleeping in the small room?*

Evi boyuyor. *He is painting the house.* ["ev-i" Lit: the house direct object.]

Mehmet kendi evini boyamıyor. *Mehmet is not painting his own house.* ["ev-i-n-i" Lit: the house of him possessed direct object.]

In the first example above it can be seen that Turkish uses the Present Continuous Tense as a Future Tense of Intention, just as we do in English: ***We are going to Turkey*** *next month.* ["We will go to Turkey" Future of Intention]

The Present Progressive Tense "- makta".

This tense is coming into use more and more each day. It is especially used in newspapers, but is also now being used in conversation. Its base is formed by adding the locative suffix to the infinitive, to which the personal endings of the verb "to be" are then added.

It means *"I am presently doing something and I am still doing it at the moment"*. It is best translated into English as *"I have been doing (and am still doing)"*

As an example **beklemek** *to wait*

beklemekteyim. [beklemek-te-yim] *I have been waiting* (and am still waiting)

beklemektesin. [beklemek-te-sin] *you have been waiting.* (and are still waiting)

beklemektedir. [beklemek-te-dir] *he has been waiting.* (and is still waiting)

beklemekteyiz. [beklemek-te-yiz] *we have been waiting.* (and are still waiting)

beklemektesiniz. [beklemek-te-siniz] *you have been waiting.* (and are still waiting)

beklemekteler. [beklemek-te-ler] *they have been waiting.* (and are still waiting)

Saat:14:30-15:00 saatleri arasında spor salonunda voleybol oynamaktaydık. *Between 2:30 and 3 o'clock we had been playing volley-ball in the sports salon.*

Saat beşten beri bankada seni beklemekteyim. *I have been waiting for you in the bank since five o'clock* (and I am still waiting)

A newspaper might print:

Şimdilik futbol takımınız İtalya'da oynamaktadır. *Our football team are presently playing in Italy.* (and are still there)

The past tense endings can also be added to change the tense:

Evde Mehmet'i belemekteydim. *I had been waiting for Mehmet at home.*

Mehmet evde beni belemekteydi. *Mehmet had been waiting for me at home.*

Sabırsızlıkla bu filmi beklemektelerdi. *They had been waiting for this film with impatience.*

Here is an example in the Passive Mood and Past Indefinite Tense.

Bu akşam üzeri ülke genelinde sağnak yağış beklenmekteymiş. *In the evening scattered showers may be expected over the countryside.*

17 SIMPLE TENSE POSITIVE

Habitual, Consent, Uncertain Future Tense.

The Simple Present Tense is also known as the Aorist (Boundless) Tense in some grammar books. It does not specify a time of the present, past or future.

This tense is known as the Wide Tense in Turkish grammatical terms as it signifies an unbounded time situation. In Turkish it is called "Geniş Zaman" "The Wide Tense". It is also considered as a gentle tense and is used as a polite imperative or polite request. The three uses of the Simple Present are as follows:

(1) Habitual Action.

This tense is used where verbs are required to signify a timeless situation in meaning:

Her gün denizde yüzerim. *I swim in the sea every day.*
Ayşe hanım dondurmayı çok sever. *Miss Ayshe likes ice cream a lot.*
Her gece eve dönerim. *I come back home every night.*
Her gün düzenli olarak traş olur. *He shaves regularly each day.*
Genelikle et yeriz. *Generally we eat meat.*
Her hafta sonunda futbol oynarlar. *They play football every weekend.*

In the sentences above there is no indication of future, past or present time. The tense then is used to denote action that is habitual or ongoing.

(2) Consent or Willingness.

The tense also shows consent or willingness. It is a "gentle" tense.

Kapıyı açar mısınız? *Would you open the door please?* [a polite request.]

180

Buna bakar mısınız? *Would you look at this please* [a polite command.]
Evet, onu yaparım. *Yes, I will do the job* [a willing consent.]
İki gecelik bir oda tutarız *We will take a room for two nights.*

In Turkish *would you?* *and please* are not translated as it is inherent within the tense itself. This tense is a polite tense.

The Polite Command.

Bakar mısınız? *Would you look, please?*

This is the polite way to get attention of a waiter or any person. It is similar to the Welsh *Look you?* in that it is not rude.

The Polite Request.

Bir çay rica ederim. *A tea, please.* [Lit: I request a tea.]
Pencereyi kapatır mısınız? *Would you close the window, please?*

This is the polite way of asking questions or giving minor orders to strangers.

The Polite Consent.

Ben onu yaparım. *I'll do it.*

This is a nice way of accepting the responsibility of something.

(3) Uncertain Future.

The Simple Present is used for future events which are un-timed.

Saatin altında seni beklerim. *I'll be waiting under the clock for you.*
Parkın yanındaki bankayı tabii ki bulursunuz. *You'll find the bank all right, next to the Park.*
Yarın ofiste buluşuruz. *We'll see each other in the office tomorrow.*

Simple Present Positive Tense Formation.

The tense sign is **-r** which is added directly to the verb stem as follows:

181

Single Syllable Verbs.

For verbs of one syllable which end in a consonant the positive tense sign is **-ar** or **-er**. There are some exceptions to this general rule. This tense is the only one which shows some irregularity in its formation.

Multi Syllable Verbs.

For verbs consisting of more than one syllable the tense sign is **-ir -ır -ür -ur**, according to Vowel harmony.

Verb Stems ending in a Vowel.

For all verbs ending in a vowel the tense sign is **-r-**. The Personal suffixes are added to the tense sign to complete the verb in number.

Single Syllable Verb Root ending in a Consonant.

For A-UnDotted Group verbs **-ar** is added after dropping infinitive sign **-mak.**

Positive Infinitive: yapmak *to do, to make.*

yaparım *I do*
yaparsın *you do*
yapar *he does*

yaparız *we do*
yaparsınız *you do*
yaparlar *they do*

For E-Dotted Group verbs **-er** is added after dropping infinitive sign **-mek.**

Positive Infinitive: kesmek *to cut.*

keserim *I cut*
kesersin *you cut*
keser *he cuts*

keseriz *we cut*
kesersiniz *you cut*
keserler *they cut*

The Five Verbs which Show Root Consonant Mutation.

Remember also that the five verbs that soften their final **-t** to **-d** when a vowel is added in the suffix:

gitmek *to go* **gider** *he goes.*
etmek *to do* **ederim** *I do.*
tatmak *to taste of* **tadarlar** *they taste of.*
ditmek *to shred* **didersin** *you shred.*
gütmek *to nourish* **güderim** *I nourish.*

Exceptions to Single Syllable Verbs.

Some 13 single syllable verbs take the tense sign as **-ir -ır -ür -ur.** These verbs are listed below. All these verb stems end in **-r** or **-l** except one, **sanmak** *to suppose.* These verbs should be learned as exceptions. They are in daily use.

almak	*to take*	**alırım**	*I take*
bilmek	*to know*	**bilir**	*he knows*
bulmak	*to find*	**bulur**	*he finds*
durmak	*to stop, halt*	**dururuz**	*we stop*
gelmek	*to come*	**gelirsiniz**	*you come*
görmek	*to see*	**görürler**	*they see*
kalmak	*to stay*	**kalırım**	*I stay*
olmak	*to become*	**olursun**	*you become*
ölmek	*to die*	**ölür**	*it dies*
sanmak	*to suppose*	**sanırız**	*we suppose*
vermek	*to give*	**verirsiniz**	*you give*
varmak	*to arrive*	**varırlar**	*they arrive*
vurmak	*to hit*	**vururum**	*I hit*

Verb Stems which end in a Vowel.

In these cases the Tense sign **-r** is added after dropping **-mak.**

Positive Infinitive: anlamak *to understand.*

anlarım *I understand*
anlarsın *you understand*
anlar *he understands*

anlarız *we understand*
anlarsınız *you understand*
anlarlar *they understand*

In these cases the Tense sign **-r** is added after dropping **-mek.**

Positive Infinitive: demek *to say, mean.*

derim *I say*
dersin *you say*
der *he says*

deriz *we say*
dersiniz *you say*
derler *they say*

Simple Present Tense Examples. The tense sign is **-r.**

demek der *to say.*
Dünya yuvarlaktır derler. *They say the world is round.*

yemek yer *to eat.*
Her gün ekmek yeriz. *We eat bread every day.*

beklemek bekler *to wait.*

Her gün köşede beklersiniz, değil mi? *Every day you wait at the corner, don't you?*

söylemek söyler *to speak.*
Her zaman "hayır'ı" derler *They say "No" every time.* [the word "hayır'ı" is a Direct Object]

Multi Syllable Vowels ending in a Consonant.

Verbs consisting of more than one syllable in the verb stem take tense sign **-ir -ır -ür -ur** according to vowel harmony.

Positive Infinitive: kazanmak *to win.*

kazanırım *I win*
kazanırsın *you win*
kazanır *he wins*

kazanırız *we win*
kazanırsınız *you win*
kazanırlar *they win*

Positive Infinitive: göndermek *to send.*

gönderirim *I send*
gönderirsin *you send*
gönderir *he sends*

göndeririz *we send*
gönderirsiniz *you send*
gönderirler *they send*

Examples the tense sign is **-ir -ır -ür -ur.**

kazanabilmek kazanabilir *to be able to win*
Her hafta Milli Piyango'yu kazanabilirsin *You can win the lottery every week.*

-a tırmanmak *to climb (to, up to).*
Her yıl Nemrut Dağı'na tırmanırız. *We climb (to)Mount Nemrut every year.*

The verb **tırmanmak** *to climb (to, up to)* takes a Motion Towards Object in **-a** or **-e**.

götürmek götürür *to bring.*
Mehmet, yemeğini her gün evden götürür. *Mehmet, brings his lunch from home every day.*

beğenmek beğenir *to like, approve.*
Türk kahvesini beğenirler. *They like Turkish coffee.*

Translation of "used to".

If the past tense endings are added to the Wide Tense Positive **-r** verb stem then the meaning is habitual in the past. This is translated by *used to* in English. However in Turkish the Simple Present Tense is used with the past tense personal endings habitual in the past.

Sık sık buraya gelirdim. *I used to come here very often.*

Gençken çok gülerdin. *You used to laugh a lot when* [Lit: while..] *you were young.*

Kuşadası'nda kalırken her zaman denizde yüzerdi. *He always used to swim in the sea when staying at Kuşadası.*

1950 yılından önce (1950'den önce) Türkiye'de kola içilirdi. *Coca-cola used to be drunk in Turkey before 1950.*

Dersler bittikten sonra uzun zaman/süre beni beklerdin. *You always used to wait for me a long time after school finished.*

Tatilde kamp yaparken hep/daima iyi uyurlardı. *They always used to sleep very well while on holiday while camping.*

Although **iken** translates as *while* in English, it is very often better to translate it as *"when"*, although this is not literally correct.

Positive Proverbs *"Atasözler"*.

Turkish Proverbs are usually written in the Wide Tense. Here are some examples in the positive form of the timeless tense. These translations are not literal showing the difficulty of such interpretation from Turkish to English.

Acele işe, şeytan karışır. *If you hurry, the devil intervenes.*
Çabuk parlayan çabuk söner. *A flash is quickly extinguished.*
Damlaya damlaya göl olur. *Lakes form drop by drop.*
Fakirlik ayıp değil tembellik ayıp. *Poverty is no shame but idleness is.*
Ne ekersen onu biçersin. *You reap what you sow.*
Önce düşün sonra söyle. *Think first, speak later.*

18 SIMPLE TENSE NEGATIVE

Timeless Tense Negative Form.

The negative of the Simple Present tense translates as:
I don't go to work on Saturdays.
He doesn't like ice cream.
We don't keep a pet.
They never take a holiday.
We'll not see each other for some time.
The simple present tense is used in situations in both the present and the future that are un-timed.

The Negative Wide Tense tense sign is **-maz/-mez.** This tense is not based on the normal negative infinitive "gelmemek" "not to come". In this tense the word **gelmek** *to come* becomes **gelmez** *does not come.* The first person singular and plural have lost the "z" and have become abraded to **-me/-ma.**

Some Examples of The Simple Present Negative.

The Wide Tense Negative Infinitive **gitmez** *not to go.*
The First Persons Singular and Plural are abraded to **-me-**

Negative Infinitive: gitmemmek *to not go.*

gitmem *I don't go* [not "gitmezim"]
gitmezsin *you don't go*
gitmez *he doesn't go*

gitmeyiz *we don't go* [not "gitmeziz"]
gitmezsiniz *you don't go*
gitmezler *they don't go*

The first persons **gitmem** *I do not go* and **gitmeyiz** *We do not go* drop the **-z** when adding the personal endings to the negative verb stem, all other persons preserve the **-z.**

tanımamak. *not to know somebody.*
Beni tanımazsınız. *You don't know me.*
Beni tanımaz mısınız? *Don't you know me?*

içmez . *does not to drink.*
O bira içmez. *He doesn't drink beer.* [generally]
Mehmet, bira içmez mi? *Doesn't Mehmet drink beer?* [usually?]

If you were to use Direct Object Condition **birayı** in the example above, the object becomes a definite object, but here we are talking about generally the drinking of beer.

O bira içmez. *He doesn't drink beer.* [generally]
Mehmet birayı içmez mi? *Doesn't Mehmet drink the (or that) beer?* [particular beer]

konuşmamak. *not to talk.*
Onun hakkında konuşmayız. *We don't talk about it.*

giymemek. *not to wear.*
Genellikle bir şapka giymez misiniz? *Don't you generally wear a hat?*

seyretmemek. *not to watch.*
Televizyonu seyretmezler. *They don't watch the television.* [in particular]
Televizyon seyretmezler. *They don't watch television.* [generally]

Timeless tense The Negative Interrogative Form.

The interrogative is formed by adding the personalized question particles after the verb stem ending in **-z.**
They are written separately, but follow vowel harmony rules.

bakmamak *not to look.*
bakmaz mıyım? or **bakmam mı?** *don't I look?*

kalmamak *not to stay.*
kalmaz mısın? *don't you stay?*

bitirmemek *not to finish.*
bitirmez mi? *doesn't he finish?*

yazmamak *not to write.*
yazmaz mıyız? *don't we write?*

koşmamak *not to run.*
koşmaz mısınız? *don't you run?*

yürümemek *not to walk.*
yürümezler mi? *don't they walk?*

Her gün saat beşte seni görmez miyim? *Don't I see you every day at five o'clock?*

Londra'da oturmaz mısınız? *Don't you live in London?*

Ali bey bir bankada çalışmaz mı? *Doesn't Ali Bey work in a bank?*

Hepimiz bir parti sevmez miyiz? *Don't we all love a party?*

Saying *I didn't used to* **-mezdim.**

When the past tense endings are added to the Wide Tense negative -
mez verb stem then the meaning is habitual in the past, which is
translated by *didn't used to* in English. In Turkish the Negative
Simple Present Tense is suffixed with the Past Tense Personal
endings for Habitual in the Past:

Sık sık buraya gelmezdim. *I didn't used to come here very often.*

Genç iken o kadar gülmezdin. *You didn't used to laugh very much when you were young.*

Kuşadada kalırken denizde yüzmezdi. *He never used to swim in the sea when staying at Kuşadası.*

1950 yıldan önce Türkiye'de kola içilmezdi. *Coca-cola did not used to be drunk in Turkey before 1950.*

Derslerimiz bittikten sonra yeterli zaman için beni beklemezdiniz. *You didn't used to wait long enough for me after our lessons l finished.*

Tatilde kamp yaparken o kadar iyi uyumazdılar. *They didn't used* *to sleep very well while on holiday while camping.*

Question Form: *Didn't you used to?* **-mez miydin(iz).**

Her gün çarşıya gitmez miydim? *Didn't I used to go to the shops everyday?*

Hatice'yi sevmez miydin? *Didn't you used to love Hatice?*

Ummaz mıydı? *Didn't he used to hope?*

Cuma günleri açmaz mıydık? *Didn't we used to open on Fridays?*

Soğan satmaz mıydılar? *Didn't they used to sell onions?*

Here **soğan** is not in the direct object case nor is it plural in Turkish, but it is a non-specific object of the family of "onion". In Turkish "things is" and "people are".

Çıkmaz mıydılar? *Didn't they used to go out?*

Her gün seni görmez miydim? *Didn't I used to see you every day?*

Bıkmaz mıydık? *Didn't we used to get fed up?*

Londra'da oturmaz mıydın? *Didn't you used to live in London?* **oturmak** means *to sit (down)* or *to live (at a place).*

Ali İstanbul'da oturur. *Ali lives in Istanbul.*

Atlara binmez miydiniz? *Didn't you used to ride horses?*

binmek *to get on, to ride, to board* takes the Motion Toward **-e** or **-a** as "movement towards" is implied in the verb **binmek**.

Conversational Turkish: *"used to"* and *"didn't used to"* In daily speech the Past Imperfect Tense will often be used:

Yıllar önce Manisa'da çalışıyordum *Many years ago I was working in Manisa*

Proverbs in the Negative "Atasözler".

190

Turkish Proverbs are usually written in the Wide Tense. Here are some examples in the negative form of the timeless tense. These translations are not literal showing the difficulty of such interpretation from Turkish to English.

Boş çuval ayakta durmaz. *An empty sack does stand up.*

Mum dibine ışık vermez. *The bottom of a candle sheds no light.*

Havlayan köpek ısırmaz. *A barking dog does not bite.*

Küçük suda büyük balık olmaz. *There are no big fish in small pools.*

Yuvarlanan taş yosun tutmaz. *A rolling stone gathers no moss.*

19 VERBS FUTURE TENSE

Future Tense will, shall (y)ecek, -(y)acak.

The future tense sign is **-ecek-** or **-acak-** to which the personal suffixes are attached. When a personal ending which begins in a vowel is suffixed then the final **-k-** of this tense sign is softened to a **-ğ-** thus producing the forms to **-eceğ-** or **-acağ-**

Use of the Future Tense.

Decisions:
İlerde doktor olacağım. *I'm going to be a doctor.*

Offers and Promises:
Sana bisiklet alacağım. *I will buy you a bicycle.*

Predictions:
Hava yarın çok güzel olacak. *The weather will be fine tomorrow.*

Commands:
İlk önce bunu bitireceksin. *First of all you will finish this.*

Obligations:
Yarına ödeviniz bitecek. *By tomorrow our duty must finish.*

Conjugation of the Future Tense.

Positive Infinitive: gelmek *to come.*

geleceğim *I shall come*
geleceksin *you will come*
O gelecek *he will come*

geleceğiz *we shall come*
geleceksiniz *you will come*

gelecekler *they will come*

Negative Infinitive: gelmemek *not to come.*

gelmeyeceğim *I shall not come*
gelmeyeceksin *you will not come*
O gelmeyecek *he will not come*

gelmeyeceğiz *we shall not come*
gelmeyeceksiniz *you will not come*
gelmeyecekler *they will not come*

In pronunciation the Future Negative is often pronounced
gelmiyeceğim. The Negative Particle **-me-** or **-ma-** abrades to **-mi-**
or **mı-**

Verb Stem ends in a Vowel.

The buffer letter **-y-** is used if the verb stem ends in a vowel in order
to keep the vowels apart when the **-acak/-ecek** future suffix is added
the verb.

Positive Infinitive: aramak *to seek, look for.*

arayacağım [ara-y-acağım] *I shall look for*
arayacaksın *you will look for*
O arayacak *he will look for*

arayacağız *we shall look for*
arayacaksınız *you will look for*
arayacaklar *they will look for*

Negative Infinitive: aramamak *to not look for.*

aramayacağım [arama-y-acağım] *I shall not look for*
aramayacaksın *you will not look for*
O aramayacak *he will not look for*

aramayacağız *we shall not look for*
aramayacaksınız *you will not look for*
aramayacaklar *they will not look for*

Pronunciation in Conversation.

If a verb stem ends in **-a** or **-e** as does **ara-mak** above, then the final **-a** or **-e** is sometimes pronounced as **-ı** and **-i** the positive future tense as in **arıyacağım.**

Some Examples of this Vowel Change.

söyleyecek *he will speak* (as written), becomes **söyliyecek** *he will speak* (as spoken).
oksayacaklar *they will caress/stroke* (as written), becomes **oksıyacaklar** *they will caress* (as spoken).

However, the verb stems which end with a final vowel **-ı -i -o -ö -u -ü** do not mutate in conversation and retain their original vowel when the Future Tense Sign is added to the verb stem. For instance **yürümek** *to walk* retains its final **-ü** in the future tense **yürüyecek** and **uyumak** *to sleep* becomes **uyuyacak.**

In fast, local talk (also in television programmes the **-ecak/-acak** Future Suffix often gets abraded in conversation thus:

Gideceğim becomes *gidicem I will go.*
Gideceğiz becomes *gidicez we will go.*
Yazacağım becomes *yazıcam I will write.*
Yazacağız becomes *yazıcaz We will write.*
Güleceğim becomes *gülecem I will laugh.*
Güleceğiz becomes *gülecez We will laugh.*

Uyuyakaldım koşa koşa ofise gidicem şimdi. *I overslept, now I'll go to the office in a hurry (running).*

The Interrogative of the Future Tense.

The interrogative is formed as usual by placing the interrogative personal pronouns after the future tense verb root written separately but observing vowel harmony rules.

The Positive Interrogative Future Tense.

Positive Future Verb Stem.

yürümek *to walk* becomes **yürüyecek.**

yürüyecek miyim? *Shall I walk?/Am I going to walk?*
yürüyecek misin? *Will you walk?/Are you going to walk?*
O yürüyecek mi? *Will he walk?/Is he going to walk?*

yürüyecek miyiz? *Shall we walk?/Are we going to walk?*
yürüyecek misiniz? *Will you walk?/Are you going to walk?*
yürüyecekler mi? *Will they walk?/Are they going to walk?*

The Negative Interrogative Future Tense.

Negative Future Verb Stem.

yazmamak *to not write* becomes **yazmayacak.**

yazmayacak mıyım? *Shall I not write?/Am I not going to write?*
yazmayacak mısın? *Will you not write?*
O yazmayacak mı? *Will he not write?*

yazmayacak mıyız? *Shall we not write?*
yazmayacak mısınız? *Will you not write?*
yazmayacaklar mı? *Will they not write?*

The Future of the verb *"to be".*

In the Present Tense **hazırım** *I am ready*, and the Past Tense
hazırdım *I was ready* the verb "to be" is a suffix, which is added to
the word it modifies. However, here is no future tense of the verb "to
be" in suffix form, it does not exist. The future of the verb **olmak** *to
become* is employed to form the future tense of the verb "to
be" **hazır olacağım** *I shall be ready*. The verb **olmak** *to become* is a
word in its own right. It is not affixed as a suffix to the word it
modified, but is written separately.

Positive Future Tense of the Verb *to be*.

The Verb **olmak** *"to be/to become"*. One of its most important
auxiliary functions is its use as the Future Tense of the verb *"to
be"*. **Olmak** being a verb in its own right is not a suffix, so is written
separately.

Present Tense Positive *"to be"*.

hazırım *I am ready.*
zenginsin *you are rich.*
yoksuldur *he is poor.*
yoksuldurlar *they are poor.*

Şimdilik İstanbul'dayım. *Just now I am in Istanbul.*

Future Tense Positive *"to be"* with "olmak."

hazır olacağım. *I shall be ready.*
zengin olacaksın. *you will be rich.*
yoksul olacak. *he will be poor.*
yoksul olacaklar. *they will be poor.*

Yarın İstanbul' da olacağım. *Tomorrow I shall be in Istanbul.*

Negative Future Tense of the Verb *"to be"*.

The Negative Verb **olmamak** *"not to be/not to become"*. One of its most important auxiliary functions is its use as the Negative Future Tense of the Verb *will not be*. **Olmamak** being a verb is not a suffix, is written separately.

Negative Present Tense *"to be"*.

hazır değilim *I am not ready.*
zengin değilsin *you are not rich.*
yoksul değildi *he was not poor.*
yoksul değiller *they are not poor.*

Şimdi İstanbul'da değilim. *I am not in Istanbul now.*

Negative Future "to be" with "olmak".
hazır olmayacağım *I shall not be ready.*
zengin olmayacaksın *you will not be rich.*
yoksul olmayacak *he will not be poor.*
yoksul olmayacaklar *they will not be poor.*

Yarın İstanbul' da olmayacağım. *I shall not be in Istanbul tomorrow.*

Future Tense Active and Passive Mood

Active: kesmek. *to cut.*
O, yarın onu kesecek. *He will cut it tomorrow.*

Passive; kesilmek . *to be cut.*
O, yarın kesilecek. *It will be cut tomorrow.*

Active Potential Future: kesebilmek. *to be able to cut.*
O, yarın onu kesebilecek. *He, will be able to cut it tomorrow.*

Passive Potential Future: kesilebilmek. *To be able to be to be cut.*
O, yarın kesilebilecek. *It will be able to be cut tomorrow.*

20 VERBS PAST TENSE

The Past Tenses Definite and Indefinite.

The Definite Past Tenses *"It was personally witnessed."*

There are two Past Tenses in Turkish. The Definite Past Tenses "Seen Tenses" are used when you have personal knowledge and witness of the action. These Definite Past tenses are like the English:
Past Perfect Tense *I have made it.*
Past Simple Tense *I made it.*
Past Imperfect Tense (Past Continuous) *I was making it.*
Past Pluperfect Tense *I had made it.*

The Indefinite Past Tenses *"It was heard about."*

The Indefinite Past Tenses "Heard Tenses" are used by inference to transfer information that you have not actually seen and witnessed yourself. There is no inferential tense in English, not many languages have one, consequently the idea of inference is communicated by other ways. English speakers do this automatically:

I think that I went out [doubt]
Presumably you have left. [possibility]
He has left as far as I know. [reportative]
I think that we left at. [uncertainty]
They say that you went out. [hearsay]
Its pretty sure that they have left. [probability]

All the examples above show that this tense is used whenever the speaker has not been an eyewitness to the past events. The Inferential Tense is used for reporting un-witnessed events, or implying possibility, doubt or uncertainty. It is often used in telling jokes as the content of the joke is just a story.

Definite Past Tense Formation.

The Tense Sign is the suffix **-dı- -di- -du- -dü-** or **-tı- -ti- -tu- -tü-**
when added to verb root ending in **p ç k t ş** plus the personal
pronoun are added to the verb stem. Vowel Harmony and Consonant
Mutation rules are applied. There is no buffer "-y-" used with the
verbal past tense suffixes as there is with the past tense of the verb
"to be", the defunct "imek". *See Chapter 15.*

Continuous Past:
Geliyordum. [Geliyor-dum] *I was coming.*
Past Tense suffixes are added to Continuous Tense base.

Simple Past:
Gelirdim. [Gelir-dim] *I used to come.*
Past Tense suffixes are added to Simple Tense base.

Future Past: (Future in the Past)
Gelecektim. [Gelecek-tim] *I was going to come, I would have come.*
Past Tense suffixes are added to Future Tense base.

Pluperfect: (Past in the Past)
Gelmiştim. [Gelmiş-tim] *I had come.*
Past Tense suffixes are added to Past Participle Tense base.
The **-miş** suffix here does not convey any inferential meaning in the
Pluperfect Tense as the final Past Tense Suffix in **-di/-ti** is definitive.

Necessitative Past: (Obligation in the Past)
Gelmeliydim. [Gelmeli-ydim] *I had to come.*
"to be" Past Tense suffixes are added to Necessitative Mood base.

Conditional Past:
Gelseydim. [Gelse-ydim] *If only I had come.*
"to be" Past Tense suffixes are added to Conditional Mood base.

Definite Past Tense A-UnDotted Vowel Group.

Infinitive Verb Stem (a): anlamak *to understand.*

anladım [anla-dı-m] *I understood.*
anladın [anla-dı-n] *you understood.*
(o) anladı [anla-dı] *he understood.*

anladık [anla-dı-k] *we understood.*
anladınız [anla-dı-nız] *you understood.*
anladılar [anla-dı-lar] *they understood.*

Infinitive Verb Stem (ı) çıkmak *to go out/exit.*

çıktım [çık-tı-m] *I went out.*
çıktın *you went out.*
(o) çıktı *he went out.*

çıktık *we went out.*
çıktınız *you went out.*
çıktılar *they went out.*

Infinitive Verb Stem (o) koşmak *to run.*

koştum [koş-tu-m] *I ran.*
koştun *you ran.*
(o) koştu *he ran.*

koştuk *we ran.*
koştunuz *you ran.*
koştular *they ran.*

Infinitive Verb Stem (u) bulmak *to find.*

buldum [bul-du-m] *I found.*
buldun *you found.*
(o) buldu *he found.*

bulduk *we found.*
buldunuz *you found.*
buldula. *they found.*

Definite Past Tense E-Dotted Vowel Group.

Infinitive Verb Stem (e) gelmek *to come.*

geldim [gel-di-m] *I came.*
geldin [gel-di-n] *you came.*
(o) geldi [gel-di] *he/she/it came.*

geldik [gel-di-k] *we came.*

geldiniz [gel-di-niz]*you came.*
geldiler [gel-di-ler] *they came.*

Infinitive Verb Stem (i) içmek *to drink/smoke.*

içtim [iç-ti-m] *I drank/smoked.*
içtin *you drank/smoked.*
(o) içti *he drank/smoked.*

içtik *we drank/smoked.*
içtiniz *you drank/smoked.*
içtiler *they drank/smoked.*

Infinitive Verb Stem (ö) görmek *to see.*

gördüm [gör-dü-m] *I saw.*
gördün *you saw.*
(o) gördü *he/she/it saw.*

gördük *we saw.*
gördünüz *you saw.*
gördüler *they saw.*

Infinitive Verb Stem (ü) gülmek *to laugh.*

güldüm [gül-dü-m] *I laughed.*
güldün *you laughed.,*
(o) güldü *he/she/it laughed.*

güldük *we laughed.*
güldünüz *you laughed.*
güldüler *they laughed.*

Indefinite Past. (Inferential)

*Inferential: [adj.] of reasoning; proceeding from general premises
to a necessary and specific conclusion.*
*Inference: [noun] The reasoning involved in drawing a conclusion
or making a logical judgment on the basis of circumstantial evidence
and prior conclusions rather than on the basis of direct observation.
Based on interpretation; not directly expressed.*

The Sign of the Indefinite (Inferential) Past is the addition of the suffix **-miş- -mış- -müş- -muş-** according to Vowel harmony and Consonant Mutation Rules, to which the Past Tense Personal suffixes are added.

Past Inferential:
Gelmişim [Gel-miş-im] *It seems (they say) I came.*
Inferential Tense suffixes are added to the Root Verb base.

Past Continuous Inferential:
Geliyormuşum [Gel-iyor-muş-um] *It seems (they say) I am coming.*
Inferential Tense suffixes are added to the Continuous Tense base.

Future in the Past Inferential:
Gelecekmişim.[Gel-ecekm-miş-im] *It seems I would have come.*
Inferential Tense suffixes are added to the Future Tense base.

Simple Present Inferential:
Gelirmişim [Gel-ir-miş-im] *It seems I come.*
Inferential Tense suffixes are added to the Simple Tense base.

Necessitative Inferential:
Gelmeliymişim [Gel-meli-ymiş-im] *They say I must come.*
"to be" Inferential Tense is added to the Necessitative Mood base.

Conditional Inferential:
Gelseymişim [Gel-se-ymiş-im] *If only I had come.*
"to be" Inferential Tense suffixes is to the Conditional Mood base.

There are many ways of modifying our speech in English to show these various nuances of doubt, uncertainty or hearsay. All these modifications and nuances are inherent in the Turkish Inferential -miş- Tense itself so extra words of explanation are not required for inference as in English.

Indefinite Past Tense Examples.
The Tense Sign suffix **-miş- -mış- -müş- -muş-** and the personal ending are added to the verb stem. Vowel Harmony and Consonant Mutation rules are applied.

Indefinite Past Tense A-UnDotted Vowel Group.

anlamak *to understand.*

anlamışım [anla-mış-ım] *I have understood it seems.*
anlamışsın [anla-mış-sın] *you have understood is seems.*
(o) anlamış [anla-mış] *he has understood it seems.*

anlamışız [anla-mış-ız] *we have understood it seems.*
anlamışsınız [anla-mış-sınız] *you have understood it seems.*
anlamışlar [anla-mış-lar] *they have understood it seems*

çıkmak *to go out/exit.*

çıkmışım [çık-mış-ım] *I have gone out it seems.*
çıkmışsın *you have gone out it seems.*
(o) çıkmış *he has gone out it seems.*

çıkmışız *we have gone out it seems.*
çıkmışsınız *you have gone out it seems.*
çıkmışlar *they have gone out it seems.*

koşmak *to run.*

koşmuşum [koş-muş-um] *I have run it seems.*
koşmuşsun *you have run it seems.*
(o) koşmuş *he has run it seems.*

koşmuşuz *we have run it seems.*
koşmuşsunuz *you have run it seems.*
koşmuşlar *they have run it seems.*

bulmak *to find.*

bulmuşum [bul-muş-um] *I have found it seems.*
bulmuşsun *you have found it seems.*
(o) bulmuş *he has found it seems.*

bulmuşuz *we have found it seems.*
bulmuşsunuz *you have found it seems.*
bulmuşlar *they have found it seems.*

Indefinite Past Tense E-Dotted Vowel Group.

gelmek *to come.*

gelmişim [gel-miş-im] *I have come it seems.*

gelmişsin [gel-miş-sin] *you have come it seems.*
(o) gelmiş [gel-miş] *he/she/it has come it seems.*

gelmişiz [gel-miş-iz] *we have come it seems.*
gelmişsiniz [gel-miş-siniz] *you have come it seems.*
gelmişler [gel-miş-ler] *they have come it seems.*

içmek *to drink/smoke.*

içmişim [iç-miş-im] *I have drunk/smoked it seems.*
içmişsin *you have drunk/smoked it seems.*
(o) içmiş *he has drunk/smoked it seems.*

içmişiz *we have drunk/smoked it seems.*
içmişsiniz *you have drunk/smoked it seems.*
içmişler *they have drunk/smoked it seems.*

görmek *to see.*

görmüşüm [gör-müş-üm] *I have seen it seems.*
görmüşsün *you have seen it seems.*
(o) görmüş *he/she/it has seen it seems.*

görmüşüz *we have seen it seems.*
görmüşsünüz *you have seen it seems*
görmüşler *they have seen it seems.*

gülmek *to laugh.*

gülmüşüm [gül-müş-üm] *I have laughed it seems.*
gülmüşsün *you have laughed it seems.*
(o) gülmüş *he/she/it has laughed it seems.*

gülmüşüz *we have laughed it seems.*
gülmüşsünüz.*you have laughed it seems.*
gülmüşler *they have laughed it seems.*

Negative Forms of Past Tenses.

For the **Perfect Past Tense Definite Witnessed** the suffix **-dı- -di- -du- -dü-** is added to the negative verb form.

For the **Perfect Past Tense Indefinite (Un-witnessed)** the suffix -mış- -miş- -muş- müş- is added to the negative verb form. Personal pronouns are then added to complete the personalized verb.

Past Definite Signifies Reality.

anlamadım *I didn't understand / I have not understood.*
anlamadın *you didn't understand / you have not understood.*
(o) anlamadı *he, she, it didn't understand /he has not understood.*

anlamadık *we didn't understand / we have not understood.*
anlamadınız *you didn't understand / you have not understood.*
anlamadılar *they don't understand / they have not understood.*

Past Inferential Signifies Conjecture.

anlamamışım *I have not understood it seems.*
anlamamışın *you have not understood it seems.*
(o) anlamamış *he has not understood it seems.*

anlamamışız *we have not understood it seems.*
anlamamışsınız *you have not understood it seems.*
anlamamışlar *they have not understood it seems.*

Past Definite Reality.

gitmedim *I didn't go / I have not gone.*
gitmedin *you didn't go / you have not gone.*
(o) gitmedi *he, she, it didn't go / he has not gone.*

gitmedik *we didn't go / we have not gone.*
gitmediniz *you didn't go / you have not gone.*
gitmediler *they don't go / they have not gone.*

Past Inferential Possibility.

gitmemişim *I probably did not go.*
gitmemişsin *you probably did not go.*
(o) gitmemiş *he probably did not go.*

gitmemişiz *we probably did not go.*
gitmemişsiniz *you probably did not go.*
gitmemişler *they probably did not go.*

The inferential suffix in **-miş** is understood in context in Turkish. I can mean *"it seems, it is not known, may be, might be, could be"* and any meaning that cannot be stated as definite.

Definite Past Continuous Tense.

This is formed in a similar way to English. The Turkish Forms are suffixed. Positive Verb stem + Present Tense suffix **"-iyor-"** + Past Tense suffix **"-di-"** + Personal ending.

Positive Verb: gelmek *to come.*

geliyordum [gel-iyor-du-m] *I was coming.*
geliyordun *you were coming.*
(o) geliyordu. *he/she/it was coming.*

geliyorduk *we were coming.*
geliyordunuz *you were coming.*
geliyorlardı/geliyordular *they were coming.*

Negative Verb: gitmemek *to not go.*

gitmiyordum [gitm-iyor-du-m] *I wasn't going.*
gitmiyordun *you weren't going.*
(o) gitmiyordu. *he/she/it wasn't going.*

gitmiyorduk *we weren't going.*
gitmiyordunuz *you weren't going.*
gitmiyorlardı/gitmiyordular *they weren't going.*

All the meanings above must be construed as witnessed (definite). It is true.

Questions in the Definite Past Tenses.

The **mi?** question particle follows the full verb in the Past Tense.

Okula gittin mi? *Did you go to school?*
Okula gitmeli miydin? [*the Necessitative See Chap. 27*] *Did you have to go to school?*

Henüz Ayşe hanım ders çalıştı mı? *Has Miss Ayshe done her lesson yet?*
Henüz Ayşe hanım ders çalışmadı mı? *Hasn't Miss Ayshe done her lesson yet?*

Mehmet televizyon seyrediyor muydu? *Was Mehmet watching television?* [television generally without object pointer]
Mehmet televizyonu seyrediyor muydu? *Was Mehmet watching THE television?* [a particular television with object pointer]

Kemal gazete okudu mu? *Did Kemal read a newspaper?* ["gazete" unspecified object.]
Kemal gazeteyi okudu mu? *Did Kemal read **THE** newspaper?* ["gazete-yi" specified object.]
Kemal bu gazeteyi okudu mu? *Did Kemal read **THIS** newspaper?* ["bu gazeteyi" demonstrated specific object.]

Serhan içki içti mi? *Did Serhan drink alcohol?* ["içki" "alcoholic drink"]
Serhan içki içiyor muydu? *Was Serhan drinking alcohol?*

Faruk Ankara'ya gitti mi? *Has Faruk gone Ankara?*
Faruk Ankara'ya gidebildi mi? *Was Faruk able to go Ankara?*

Definite Past Perfect. *"had done.."*

This tense signifies the Past in The Past. English says:
"I had done it." Past Perfect Definite.
"I thought I had done it." Past Perfect Indefinite.

The Past Perfect Definite is formed by adding the definite past tense suffix to the Indefinite Past Tense -miş form of the verb. There is no hearsay or doubt in the meaning of this tense as it is made definite and specific by the addition of the Past definite suffix in **-di**

gelmiştim [gelmiş-tim] *I had come.*
unutmuştun [unutmuş-tun] *you had forgotten.*
yürümüştü [yürümüş-tü] *he had walked.*
bilmiştik [bilmiş-tik] *we had known.*
çıkmıştınız [çıkmış-tınız] *you had gone out.*
anlamıştılar [anlamış-tılar] *they had understood.*

Indefinite Past Perfect. *"maybe he had done".*

The Past Perfect Indefinite is formed by adding the indefinite past tense suffix "-miş" to the Indefinite Past Tense "-miş" form of the verb. There is hearsay or doubt in the meaning of this tense as it is made indefinite and unspecific by the addition of the Past Indefinite suffix in **-miş.**

In English this tense can be translated as:
I believe that he had gone.
We think that he had arrived.
Presumably the train had been on time.
All showing some uncertainty or lack of prior knowledge.

This tense is widely used on a daily basis in spoken and written Turkish. It is used all the time in daily conversation. Some of the English shades of meaning are shown here by example: These examples show that this tense is used whenever the speaker has not been an eyewitness to the past events.

çıkmışmışım *I think that I had gone out.* [doubt]
çıkmışmışsın *Presumably you had left.* [possibility]
çıkmışmış *He had left as far as I know.* [reportative]
çıkmışmışız *I think that we had left.* [uncertainty]
çıkmışmışsınız *They say that you had gone out.* [hearsay]
çıkmışmışlar *It was pretty sure that they had left.* [probability]

If we are asked the question:
Mehmet çıktı mı? *Has Mehmet gone out?*

We could answer in the Past Definite Tense:
O çıktı. *He has gone out.* meaning "Yes he has gone out for sure, I saw him go."

Or we may answer in the Past Inferential Tense:
O çıkmış. *He has gone out.* meaning "As far as I know he has left, but I did not actually see him go myself."

All this meaning is within the **-miş** Inferential Past Tense itself.

Negative Indefinite Past Perfect.

Examples of the Negative Verb yapmamak *to not do*
Here the words "I think that" are not required in Turkish. The
Inferential "-miş" is used instead.

Ben yapmamışım ki. *(I think that) I did not do it.*
Sen yapmamışsın ki. *(They say that) You did not do it.*
O yapmamış ki. *(It seems that) He did not do it.*
Biz yapmamışız ki. *(They say that) We did not do it.*
Siz yapmamışsınız ki. *(It is reported that) You did not do it.*
Onlar yapmamışlar ki. *(Apparently) They did not do it.* (but they
might have).

Here "ki" is an object "it, that" which completes the sentence by
providing an object for a transitive verb. *See Chapter 35 about "ki"*

Indefinite Past Questions.

Positive Interrogative Inferential.

The English inference shown does not need to be said in Turkish. It
is already understood in the "-miş" suffix. The Personalized
Interrogative Particle **-mi -mı -mü -mu** is written separately and
follows the verb.

Onu yapmış mıyım? *Have I done it?* [I wonder]
Did I do it? [I'm not sure]

Onu yapmış mısın? *Have you done it?* [at all]
Did you do it? [any rate]

Onu yapmış mı? *Has he done it?* [then]
Did he do it? [yet]

Onu yapmış mıyız? *Have we done it?* [I wonder]
Did we do it? [I'm not sure]

Onu yapmış mısınız? *Have you done it?* [at all]
Did you do it? [any rate]

Onu yapmışlar mı? *Have they done it?* [surely]
Did they do it? [yet]

Negative Interrogative Inferential.

There are many ways of showing inference in English, even the tone of the voice can be enough, and we have only shown a few ways in these examples above and below to show doubt, uncertainly and lack of prior knowledge which the Turkish Inferential Tense already inherently contains within itself.

Onu yapmamış mıyım? *Haven't I done it?* [I wonder] *Didn't I do it?* [I'm not sure…]

Onu yapmamış mısın? *Haven't you done it?* [at all] *Didn't you do it?* [any rate]

Onu yapmamış mı? *Hasn't he done it?* [then] *Didn't he do it?* [yet]

Onu yapmamış mıyız? *Haven't we done it?* [I wonder] *Didn't we do it?* [perhaps not]

Onu yapmamış mısınız? *Haven't you done it?* [at all] *Didn't you do it?* [any rate]

Onu yapmamışlar mı? *Haven't they done it?* [surely] *Didn't they do it?* [yet]

Çıkmış mi? *Has he (seemingly) left?* [would you know? possibility.]

Gülmüşler mi ? *Did they laugh? (at all?)* [a question asking for a report.]

Onu yapmamış mısınız? *Haven't you done it?* [at all? uncertainty.]

Onu yapmamış mısınız? *You haven't (gone and) done it have you?* [doubt and incredulity]

Indefinite Past Continuous.

This Tense is used regularly in Turkish whereas in English its use is occasional. Formed with the Negative Verb Stem + Present Tense suffix **"-iyor-"** + Inferential Tense suffix **"-miş-"** + Personal ending.

Positive Inferential bilmek *to come.*

biliyormuşum. [bil-iyor-muş-um] *(it seems that) I was knowing.*
biliyormuşsun *you were knowing.*
(o) **biliyormuş** *he/she/it was knowing.*

biliyormuşuz *we were knowing.*
biliyormuşsunuz. *you were knowing.*
biliyorlarmış/biliyormuşlar. *they were knowing.*

Negative Inferential okumamak *to not read.*

okumuyormuşum [okum-uyor-muşum] *(it seems that) I wasn't reading.*
okumuyormuşsun. *you weren't reading.*
(o) **okumuyormuş** *he/she/it wasn't reading.*

okumuyormuşuz *we weren't reading.*
okumuyormuşsunuz *you weren't reading.*
okumuyorlarmış/okumuyormuşlar *they weren't reading.*
The meaning is indefinite and un-witnessed "It may or may not be true".

anlamamak. *to not understand.*

anlamıyormuşum *it seem that I was not understanding.*
anlamıyormuşsun *it seem that you were not understanding.*
anlamıyormuş *it seem that he was not understanding.*

anlamıyormuşuz *it seem that we were not understanding.*
anlamıyormuşsunuz *it seem that you were not understanding.*
anlamıyorlarmış *it seem that they were not understanding.*

gitmemek. *not to go.*

gitmiyormuşum *I do not think that I was going.*
gitmiyormuşsun *I do not think that you were going.*
gitmiyormuş *I am pretty sure that he is not going.*

gitmiyormuşuz *I think that we are not going.*
gitmiyormuşsunuz *I believe that you are not going.*
gitmiyorlarmış *apparently they are not going.*

Definite and Indefinite Past Tense Examples.

almak *to take.*
Definite Positive: **aldı** *he took.*
Indefinite Positive: **almış** *probably he took.*

almamak *to not take.*
Definite Negative: **almadı** *he did not take.*
Indefinite Negative: **almamış** *he probably did not take.*

aramak *to look for.*
Definite: **aradı aramadı.**
Indefinite: **aramış aramamış.**

bitmek *to end.*
bitti bitmedi.
bitmiş bitmemiş.

içmek *to drink/smoke.*
içti içmedi.
içmiş içmemiş.

başlamak *to start.*
başladı başlamadı.
başlamış başlamamış.

çalışmak *to work.*
çalıştı- çalışmadı.
çalışmış çalışmamış.

gelmek *to come.*
geldi- gelmedi.
gelmiş gelmemiş.

görmek *to see.*
gördü görmedi.
görmüş görmemiş.

gülmek *to laugh.*
güldü- gülmedi.
gülmüş gülmemiş.

kızmak *to get angry.*
kızdı kızmadı.
kızmış kızmamış.

okumak *to read.*
okudu okumadı.
okumuş okumamış.

vermek *to give.*
verdi vermedi.
vermiş vermemiş.

yapmak *to do/make.*
yaptı yapmadı.
yapmış yapmamış.

A Joke in the Inferential Tense.

This is not a true event and the use of the inferential shows this.

Temel İngiltere'ye gitmişti.
It seems Temel had gone to England.

Arkadaşları Temel'e İngilizce bilmezdin İngiltere'de çok sıkıntı çektin mi? demişler.
Temel's friends said "You didn't know English. In England did you have a lot of trouble?"

Temel Hayır, sıkıntıyı asıl İngilizler çekti. demiş.
Temel said "No. It was the English who had the trouble."

21 VERBS CONDITIONAL TENSE

Saying "if" using -se and -sa.

In English the Conditional Tenses are formed with that very important little word - "if".

Conditional *if* sentences are often introduced with the word **eğer** *if,* and less commonly **şayet** *lest, unless*. In Turkish these words are pointers alerting the listener that a Condition and Result are following. They do not have any direct meaning, they are "alerters" or "markers".

Condition and Result Real and Unreal.

We recognize and use Conditional Sentences with ease in our Mother Tongue, English. However, Conditional Sentences are not so easy to recognize in Turkish as they appear as a Mood of the verb itself.

If we leave at noon, we will arrive on time.
If you pass the exam, I shall give you a present.
If you had passed the exam, I would have given you a present.
Unless you pass the exam, you can not apply for a university place.
Unless you work hard, you will not be successful.
Take whichever one that you want.
If you want that one then take it.

There are many ways of introducing the Conditional in English *"if, if ever, whenever, whatever, whichever, however"* and the simple forms *"when, what, which, how"*. In the negative *"if not"* can be replaced with *"unless"* and the older *"lest"*. All the mood forms of the verb can be used *"can, must, would, might, may, should"*. The same is true for Turkish.

The Real Conditional.

This is used to express condition and result based on fact in both the Present and the Future.

Erken kalkarsan, kahvaltıyı yapabilirsin. *If you get up early, you can make the breakfast.*

Erken kalkarsan, bizi beklersin. *If you get up early, wait for us.*

Sana yardım edebilirsem, memnun olacağım. *If I can help you, I will be happy.*

The Unreal Conditional.

Is used to express unreal results or wishes and desires in the Present and Future.

Çok antrenör edemezsen, asla koşu kazanmayacaksın. *If you do not train a lot, you will never win the race.*

Sigaradan vazgeçersen, daha sıhhatli kendi kendine hissedersin. *If you give cigarettes up you will feel healthier.*

The Past Conditional.

Is used to state Conditions in the Past that did not happen. Often use to express criticism or regret.

Erken kalksaydın, bizi bekleyecektin. *If you had got up early, you would have waited for us.*

Kötü hava olmasaydı, çarşıya gidecektik. *If the weather had not been bad, we would have gone to the shops.*

Bu lokantaya gelmeseydim, senle görüşemedim. *If I had not come to this cafe, I would not have been able to meet you.*

O lokantaya gitseydim, senle görüşürdüm. *If I had gone to that cafe, I would have met you.*

The changes of tense and mood of the verbs show the meaning in

English. The same is true for Turkish, the correct tenses and moods of condition and result must be used to adequately communicate the correct meaning of the statement. English uses its normal tenses and the condition is produced by insertion of that little word *if.* Turkish however, together with many other languages, has a special Conditional Tense Form. The Conditional mood sign is **-se-/-sa-**

Forming the Conditional.

The Turkish Conditional is characterized by the suffix **-se-** or **-sa-** according to Vowel Harmony rule. A simple example is **var** *there is, there are* which becomes **varsa** *if there is, if there are* with the addition of the **-sa** Conditional Suffix. The negative is based on **yok** *there isn't, there aren't* which becomes **yoksa** *if there isn't, if there aren't.*

Paranız varsa bana verin. *If you have (any) money (then) give it to me.*

Bir taksi yoksa burada kalalım. *If there isn't a taxi (then) let's stay here.*

For verbs the Conditional Tenses are formed by adding the Conditional Personal endings to the **-se-** or **-sa-** suffix to the verb in any suitable tense or mood. The mark of the Conditional Suffix follows Vowel Harmony Rules, therefore there are two forms **-se** or **-sa** to choose from.

The Conditional Suffix

If I: **-sem** or **-sam**
If you: **-sen** or **-san**
If he: **-se** or **-sa**
If we: **-sek** or **-sak**
If you: **-seniz** or **-sanız**
If they: **-seler** or **-salar**

The Conditional suffix can be added to most tenses and moods. Some examples:

yaparsam. [yap-ar-sam] *if I do.*

giriyorsan. [gir-iyor-san] *if you are entering.*
kesilecekse. [kes-il-ecek-se] *if it will be cut, if it is to be cut.*
anlaşmasaydık. [anlaşma-sa-ydık] *if we have not agreed.*
mutlu olmayacaksanız. [olma-y-acak-sa-nız] *if you will not be happy.*
gelebilecekseler [gel-ebil-ecek-se-ler] *if they will be able to come.*

The Simple Present Conditional.

gelsem *if I come*
yazsan *if you write*
gülse *if he laughs*

içsek *if we drink*
görebilirseniz *if you can see*
yaparsalar *if they do*

The Present Continuous Conditional.

geliyorsam *if I am coming*
yazmıyorsan *if you are not writing*
gülüyorsa *if he is laughing*

içiyorsak *if we are drinking*
görmüyorsanız *if you are not seeing*
yapıyorsalar *if they are doing*

The Conditional Positive.

Simple Actual Conditional of **gelmek** *to come.*

gelsem *if I were to come*
gelsen *if you were to come*
gelse *if he were to comes*

gelsek *if we were to come*
gelseniz *if you were to come*
gelseler *if they were to come*

Present Continuous Conditional of **gelmemek** *not to come.*

gelmiyorsam *if I am not coming*
gelmiyorsan *if you are not coming*

gelmiyorsa *if he is not coming*
gelmiyorsak *if we are not coming*
gelmiyorsanız *if you are not coming*
gelmiyorsalar *if they are not coming*

Simple Habitual Conditional of **gelmek** *to come.*

gelirsem *if I (usually) come*
gelirsen *if you (usually) come*
gelirse *if he (usually) comes*

gelirsek *if we (usually) come*
gelirseniz *if you (usually) come*
gelirseler *if they (usually) come*

Future Intention Conditional of **gelmek** *to come.*

geleceksem *if I (will) come*
geleceksen *if you (will) come*
gelecekse *if he (will) come*

geleceksek *if we (will) come*
gelecekseniz *if you (will) come*
gelecekseler *if they (will) come*

Real Past Conditional of **gelmek** *to come.*

geldiysem *if I came*
geldiysen *if you came*
geldiyse *if he came*

geldiysek *if we came*
geldiyseniz *if you came*
geldiyseler *if they came*

Unreal Past Conditional of **gelmek** *to come.*

gelseydim *If only I had come*
gelseydin *If only had come*
gelseydi *If only had come*

gelseydik *If only we had come*
gelseydiniz *If only you had come*

gelseydiler *If only they had come*

Conditional Negative Tenses.

Negative Simple Actual Conditional.

gelmesem *if I were not to come*
gelmesen *if you were not to come*
gelmese *if he were to not comes*

gelmesek *if we were not come*
gelmeseniz *if you were not to come*
gelmeseler *if they were not to come*

Negative Present Continuous Conditional.

gelmiyorsam *if I am not coming*
gelmiyorsan *if you are not coming*
gelmiyorsa *if he is not coming*

gelmiyorsak *if we are not coming*
gelmiyorsanız *if you are not coming*
gelmiyorsalar *if they are not coming*

Negative Simple Habitual Conditional.

gelmezsem *if I (usually) do not come*
gelmezsen *if you (usually) do not come*
gelmezse *if he (usually) do not comes*

gelmezsek *if we (usually) do not come*
gelmezseniz *if you (usually) do not come*
gelmezseler *if they (usually) do not come*

Negative Future Conditional.

gelmeyeceksem *if I (will) not come*
gelmeyeceksen *if you (will) not come*
gelmeyecekse *if he (will) not come*

gelmeyeceksek *if we (will) not come*
gelmeyecekseniz *if you (will) not come*

gelmeyecekseler *if they (will) not come*

Negative Past Real Conditional.

gelmediysem *if I had not come*
gelmediysen *if you had not come*
gelmediyse *if he had not come*

gelmediysek *if we had not come*
gelmediyseniz *if you had not come*
gelmediyseler *if they had not come*

Negative Past Unreal Conditional.

gelmeseydim *If only I had not come*
gelmeseydin *If only you had not come*
gelmeseydi *If only he had not come*

gelmeseydik *If only we had not come*
gelmeseydiniz *If only you not had come*
gelmeseydiler *If only they had not come*

Conditional Examples in other Tenses.

There are other tense form (such as the Inferential Tense) which are used in conditional sentences and one should learn to recognize the -se- or -sa- form of the verbal suffix to realize that the conditional *"if"* should be used.

Erken varırsanız, beklemelisiniz. *If you arrive early, you will have to wait.*

Erken varırsanız, beklersiniz. *If you arrive early, you would have to wait.*

Erken varsaydınız, bekleyecektiniz. *If you had arrived early, you would have had to wait.*

Sana yardım edebilirlerse, yardım edecekler. *They will help you if they can.*

Sana yardım etseler, yardım ederler. *They would help you if they* *could.*

Sana yardım edebilseydiler, (yardım) ederlerdi. [or "edeceklerdi"] *They would have helped you if they could have.*

Fazla içersen sarhoş olursun. *If you drink too much you get drunk.*

Çok çalışmazsan, sınavı geçemeyeceksin. *Unless you work hard you will not be able to pass your test.*

Sigara içmeyi bırakırsan, daha uzun yaşarsın. *If you stop smoking you will live longer.*

Yağmur yağmasaydı dışarı çıkamayacaktık. *We would have not been able to go out if it had not stopped raining.*

Eğer buradan gitseydim sana yazardım. *If I had gone away, I would have written to you.*

Verbs of Condition.

There are some verbs in the Turkish vocabulary that already have a "conditional feeling" within themselves. The can be recognized as they contain "-sa-/-se-" conditional sign within the verb stem itself. The meaning of these verbs is best translated as "to regard as + verb".

An example of this effect is the verb **gülümsemek** *to smile* which becomes **gülümsiyorum** *I am smiling*. The "conditional sign" -se- is part of the verb stem, so the verb itself can have the meaning "to regard as laughing". If this method is applied to other "conditional verb stems", then very often we can translate the Turkish easily.

küçümsemek. *to belittle.* [to consider as small]
kötümsemek. *to disparage.* [to consider as bad]
benimsemek. *to appropriate.* [to consider as personal]
çekimsemek. *to refrain from.* [to consider as absent]
gereksemek. *to consider as necessary.*
hafifsemek. *to take s.o lightly.* [to consider as light]
yakınsamak. *to converge.* [to consider as nearing]
umursamak. *to care.* [to have consideration]

çıkarsamak. *to infer, to deduce.* [to consider as resulting in...]

Although this is not really part of the conditional tense itself, it is mentioned here as an aid for understanding when reading Turkish.

22 VERBS AUXILIARY VERBS

Auxiliary (Helping) Verbs.

There are two main auxiliary verbs in Turkish:
(1) etmek *to do, to make, to perform.* This auxiliary is used to make Active Tenses.
Babamı mutlu ettim. *I made my father happy.*

(2) olmak *to be, to become, to happen, to occur.* This auxiliary is used to make Passive Tenses.
Seni görünce mutlu oldum. *I became happy on seeing you.*

etmek *to do/to perform.*

etmek makes verbs from nouns.
telefon etmek *to telephone.*
dans etmek *to dance.*
şikâyet etmek *to complain.*
tereddüt etmek *to hesitate.*
zannetmek [zan etmek] *to suppose.*
sabretmek [sabir etmek] *to be patient.*
affetmek [af etmek] *to pardon.*
seyretmek [seyir etmek] *to watch.*
kaybetmek.[kayıp etmek] *to lose.*
hissetmek [his etmek] *to feel.*

The auxiliary **etmek** is directly joined to single syllable word stems otherwise **etmek** is written separately. The verb **dans etmek** is an irregularity (being added to a foreign imported word), as is **park etmek**, these are written separately.

etmek is also used with many Arabic and Persian words to form verbs where none exist in modern Turkish:

teşekkür. *(arabic) a thanking.*

223

teşekkür etmek *to thank somebody.*
teşekkür ederim *(I) thank you.*

Many Arabic words do not follow the rules of vowel harmony within themselves but any Turkish suffixes added will always be governed by the final vowel in the word, although there are a few exceptions to this. One we have already met **saat** *hour* becomes **saatler** *hours*.

Sometimes in Turkish there are two words in general use for the same meaning, one Arabic using **etmek** to form its verb, whilst the Turkish rooted word will follow normal rules of conjugation.
tamir etmek [Arab] *to repair* or **onarmak** [Turk] *to repair*

The policy has been to attempt to gradually purify the language by replacing foreign words with a native Turkish vocabulary, but it should be realized that there are many words in daily use where both Arabic or Turkish vocabulary may be used:

kara [Turk] *black* or **siyah** [Arab] *black*.
yıl [Turk] *year* or **sene** [Arab] *year*.

etmek is an important verb, it has may shades of meaning:

"to do, make, perform" **servis etmek** *to serve.*

"to do well or badly" **iyi etmek** *To do well.*
- **iyi ettin!** *you did well!*
- **iyi etmedin!** *you did not do well!*

"to equal. (in numbers)" **Beş üç daha sekiz eder.** *5 plus three makes 8.*
"to be worth." **Bu masa yüz elli bin eder.** *This table is worth 150,000.*
"to amount to." **Toplam yüz elli lira ediyor.** *The total amounts to 150 lira.*

Single Syllable Verb Roots with "etmek".

If verbs are formed with a single syllable root then **etmek** is affixed directly to that root, which if it ends in a consonant will generally double that consonant.

af *pardon* [Arabic]

224

affetmek *to beg pardon* **affedersiniz!** *Pardon!*

ret *a refusal.* [Arabic]
An arabic root takes a doubled "-dd" when adding a verb form
reddetmek *to refuse* **reddederim!** *I refuse!*

etmek as a verb of completion.

Etmek being an auxiliary verb in Turkish, helps the completing of other verbs. Its basic meaning when it is used alone, is *to do, perform, commit an action* as in **intihar etmek** *to commit suicide.*

Ben ettim, sen etme, ne olur! *I did, (but) please you, don't, whatever happens!*
kastetmek *to intend, to mean.*
bahsetmek *to mention.*
terketmek (terk etmek) *to leave, to quit.*
yardım etmek *to help, to aid.*
kabul etmek *to accept.*
farketmek (fark etmek) *to notice, to realize.*

Etmek is also used to make Turkish verbs from imported foreign words:

izole etmek *to isolate, to insulate.*
Şu fişi izole ettim. *I have isolated that plug.*

download etmek *to download.*
Bunu da download edelim. *Let's download this as well.*

farketmek (fark etmek) *to notice, to realize.*
O köşeyi farketmedim. (fark etmedim). *I did not notice that corner.*

Park etmek *to park.*
Arabayı tam buraya park etmiştim. *I had just parked my car right here.*
park yapmak is also found. Turkish has not yet settled on which auxiliary verb to use in this case.

Although **etmek** is an auxiliary verb, it is not used like the auxiliary verbs in English. English: *Are you coming to the party tonight? Yes I am.* Turkish: **Bu akşamki partiye geliyor musun? Evet geliyorum.**

Here, the English short answer includes only *I am* without the verb "coming". Turkish has to include the **geliyorum** verb since it does not include an auxiliary like the "to be" verb of English.

English: *Did you accept this after all? Yes I did.* Turkish: **Herşeye rağmen kabul ettin mi onu? Evet ettim.** The short answer in English is *I did* without the verb "accept". The short answer in Turkish is **ettim** without the noun "kabul". In this case **etmek** can be used alone as a short answer.

Etmek and Vowel Harmony.

etmek being a verb in its own right does not change its own vowels when suffixed to Turkish or foreign roots. When it is used as an auxiliary to nouns of more than one syllable then it is written separately and conjugated in the normal manner:

Etmek forms transitive Verbs.

Transitive verbs have an object.

ayıp *a shaming* **ayıp etmek** *to cause/make a shame.*
Onun için Mehmet bana ayıp etti. *Because of it/that Mehmet shamed me.* ["ayıp etmek" takes a Motion Toward (Dative Object). In this case "bana to me"]

teslim *a delivering* [Arabic] **teslim etmek** *to deliver.*
Mektubu teslim ettim. *I delivered the letter.*
Koliyi teslim ettirdiniz. *You had the parcel delivered.* ("et-tir-mek" Causative Verb form)

tamir *a repairing* [Arabic] **tamir etmek** *to repair.*
Onu tamir etsek. *If we repair it/that.*
Onu tamir edemem. *I can't repair it/that.*

kontrol *a checking* [Eng. Fr.] **kontrol etmek** *to check.*
Onu kontrol ettiler. *They checked it/that*
Onu kontrol edebilir misiniz? *Would you check it/that?*

ret *a refusing* [Arabic] **reddetmek** *to refuse.*
Onu reddedeceğiz. *We shall refuse it/that.*
Onu reddedelim. *Let's refuse it/that.*

takdir *an appreciation* [Arabic] **takdir etmek** *to appreciate.*
Ahmet, onu takdir etti. *Ahmet appreciated it/that.*
Ali, onu takdir edememiş. *(Probably) Ali couldn't have appreciated it/that.*

Active and Passive Auxiliaries.

etmek *to do, to perform, to make* forms verbs which are transitive (ie verbs which have a direct object). Also the use of **olmak** *to be, to become* causes the same verb to be intransitive *(a verb which does not have an object)*. Using the passive form causes the sense to become intransitive.

Examples with the passive auxiliary verb **edilmek**:

teslim *a delivering* **teslim etmek** *to delivered* . [Transitive form takes an object.]
Ali, mektubu teslim etti [Active Sense] *Ali delivered the letter.* [Transitive with **mektubu** in the objective case.]

teslim edilmek *to be delivered.* [Intransitive form takes no object.]
dün teslim edildi. *It was delivered yesterday.* [Intransitive takes no object.]
mektup teslim edildi. *The letter has been delivered.* [Passive with **edilmek** and **mektup** as the subject.]

tamir *a repairing* **tamir edilmek** *to repair.* [passive]
O tamir edilecek. *It (as subject.) will be repaired.*
O tamir edilemedi [ed-il-e-me-di] *It (as subject) could not have been repaired.*

kontrol *a checking* **kontrol edilmek** *to be checked.*
O kontrol edildi. *It has been checked.*
Onu kontrol edilebilecek mi? [ed-il-ebil-ecek mi?] *Can it be repaired?*

ret *a refusing* **reddedilmek** *to be refused.*
Ben, reddedildim. *I was refused.*
O, reddedilince. *On it being refused.*

takdir *an appreciation* **takdir edilmek** *to be appreciated.*

227

Ahmet, takdir edildi. *Ahmet was appreciated.*
Ali, takdir edilecek. *Ali will be appreciated.*

The Passive can be formed with the Passive of **etmek edilmek** but is often replaced by the verb **olmak** *to become* or its Passive Form **olunmak** *to become* without any change in meaning.

olmak *to be/become.*

This verb meaning *to be/to become* is also used as an auxiliary with foreign loan words. It is also attached directly to single syllable roots or written separately when used with roots of more that one syllable. It does not change its own vowels as it is a verb in its own right. One of its most important auxiliary functions is its use as the Future Tense and Potential Mood of the verb *to be.*

hazır *ready.*
hazırım *I am ready.*
hazır olacağım *I shall be ready.* [Future]

zengin *rich.*
zenginsiniz *you are rich.*
zengin olsaydınız *If you had been rich.* [Conditional]

yoksul. *poor.*
O yoksul *he is poor.*
O yoksul olabilir *He may be poor* [Potential]

The Passive use of olmak.

When used with loan word to form verbs it gives the sense of *being in a state of.*

pişman *a regretting* **pişman oldum** *I regret/I was sorry.* [Lit: I was sorry]

fena *bad/ill* **fena oluyorum** *I feel ill.*

memnun *pleased* **memnun oldum** *I'm pleased.* [Lit: I was pleased]

Other Auxiliaries.

yapmak *to do as an action.*
gelmek *to come.*
kalmak *to remain/stay.*
bulunmak *to be found/to be* .[Passive of **bulmak**]
eylemek *to carry out* [equates with **etmek** but not common.]
eylemek can be used as a substitute for **etmek** and serves the same purpose. It is usually restricted to the written word and is seldom used in conversation.
demek *to say.*
dilemek *to wish.*
söylemek *to speak.*
durmak *to stop.*
vermek *to give.* [used as an Accelerative Auxiliary thus speeding the action of the verb]
yazmak *to write.* [but means "almost to" when used as an auxiliary verb] **düşeyazdım** *I almost fell.*

Continuative Verbs - *"to keep on doing"*

-akalmak "continue, keep on doing".
-adurmak "continue, keep on doing".
-ayazmak "almost to do".
-ivermek "to act hurriedly, urgently".

kalmak and **durmak** are used to form a continuing action of the main verb giving the sense *to keep on doing* or to *remain in a condition of.*

Only the first vowel follows the vowel harmony rules. Hence "-ekalmak, -edurmak, -eyazmak, -ıvermek, -uvermek, -üvermek etc". As these are verbs in their own right they retain their spelling. This is similar to the Potential Verb Suffix "-abilmek/-ebilmek"

Formation of the Continuative Verbs.

The Infinitive of **kalmak** or **durmak** is added directly to the Wish/Desire Root of the main verb *(See Chapter 29)*. The root is formed by suffixing **-e** or **-a** to the basic Verb Stem **yüzmek** to swim **yüze-** Wish/Desire stem. Then with the direct addition of **kalmak** *to remain*:

yüzekalmak *to keep on swimming.*
yüzekaldı *He kept on swimming.*

alakalmak *to keep on taking.*
alakalacağım *I will keep on taking.*

durakalmak *to keep on stopping.*
durakalıyorsun *You keep on stopping.*

bekleyedurmak.*to keep on waiting.*
bekleyedurabilecek misiniz? *Will you be able to keep on waiting?*

uyuyakalmak *to oversleep.*
uyuyakalmak *I overleapt.*

kalakalmak *to stand aghast, to be astounded.*
kalakaldım *I was astounded.*

donakalmak *to petrify.*
donakaldım *I was petrified, I was scared stiff.*

The Accelerative Verb *"to hurry along"*.

The Wish/Desire Mood. See Chapter 29

The Mood Sign is **-a** or **-e** which is added to the basic verb stem according to Vowel Harmony Rules. If the bare verb stem ends in a vowel then theWish/Desire Mood Sign becomes **-ya** or **-ye** (Uses buffer letter **-y-**).

When adding the auxiliary **vermek** the **-a/-e** ending often abrades according to vowel harmony rules. As an example: **koşa** [the Wish/Desire root of **koşmak** *to run*] follows vowel harmony and abrades to **koşuvermek** [koş-u-vermek].

The verb **vermek** *to give* is added to the **-a/-e** verb stem and in this case it gives a sense of urgency and speed of action to the main verb. In this case **vermek** loses its meaning *to give*. Then with the direct addition of **vermek** it implies "to 'get a move on'".

koşmak *to run* becomes **koşuvermek** *to hurry up and run.*
yazmak *to write* becomes **yazıvermek** *to scribble/scrawl.*

Koşuverin! [Imperative] *Hurry up and run!*
İçkisini içiverdi. *He gulped his drink down.*
Gelivereceğim. *I'll dash along and come.*

When adding the Accelerative **vermek** to a verb then the vowel of the ending **-e** narrows to **-i** or **-ü** thus:

güle becomes **gülüverin** *Laugh!*
kese becomes **kesiverin** *Cut (it)!*

The ending **-a** narrows to **-ı** or **-u** thus:

baka becomes **bakıverin** *Look!*
tuta becomes **tutuverin** *Get hold!*

23 MOODS THE IMPERATIVE

The Imperative Mood

The Imperative Mood is used in issuing commands. It is formed by using the verb in its simplest root form: "Listen!, Sit!, Eat!" The Imperative Mood in English occurs only in the second person but "you" is usually not stated. Whenever the speaker gives a command regarding someone else, it is still directed at the second person as though it were a request for permission, although it may be a rhetorical statement.

The Imperative is used for giving direct orders, requests, suggestions and in some cases warnings, or even a mixture of all these to a second person.

(You) Look at that.) [order]
Don't (you) leave your valuables in the car. [suggestion]
(You) Bring me another fork please. [request]
(You) Take us to Taksim Square. [order]
(You) Be careful in the traffic. [warning]
(You) Get Mehmet to clean the room. [3rd person order]

The Imperative does not seem so abrupt in Turkish as it is in English, and it would be difficult to upset anyone when using the Imperative.

First Person "pseudo" Imperative *let me.., let us..*

The First person "pseudo" forms are not true imperatives as this is mood of "wish and desire". They are included here as they are heavily used in daily speech. Vowel Harmony operates on these suffixes. The Wish/Desire is discussed in Chapter 29.

The First Person *let me, let us.*

The "pseudo" Imperative in the first person singular adds the suffix **(y)ayım/-(y)eyim.**

almak becomes **alayım** [al-ayım] *let me buy/take.*
beklemek becomes **bekleyeyim** [bekle-y-eyim] *let me wait.*
bakmak becomes **bakayım** [bak-ayım] *let me look.*

The first person plural adds **(y)alım/-(y)elim.**

alalım [al-alım] *let us buy/take.*
bekleyelim [bekle-y-elim] *let us wait.*
görelim [gör-elim] *let's see.*

This form is in daily constant use. It is often used when shopping **onu alayım!** *I'll take it!*

Second Person Imperative *let you.., you do..*

The Second Person *let you.*

The Direct (true) Imperative, the second person singular familiar and immediate for addressing friends or showing urgency. It is formed using the basic verb stem after dropping the Infinitive Sign **-mek** or **-mak.**

Positive Imperative Familiar.

Bak *Look!*
Gel *Come!*

Negative Imperative Familiar.

Bakma *Don't look!*
Gelme *Don't come!*

This is the familiar form. It is also used in some daily "Formula Speak" expressions.

Polite and Public Imperative.

There are two forms of the second person:

The Formal Imperative is used for addressing strangers or being polite. It is formed by adding **-(y)in** to the root verb stem.

The Public Imperative is used for notices and being very polite. It is formed by adding **-(y)iniz** to the root verb stem.

The buffer letter **-y-** is used for verb roots which end in a vowel. The Imperative suffix is subject to Vowel Harmony rules.

Positive Imperative Polite Negative Verb Polite.

Bakın *Look!* becomes **Bakmayın** *Don't look!*
Gelin *Come!* becomes **Gelmeyin** *Don't come!*

This Polite Form is used for addressing one person or a number of people in a group. In all the above forms the Negative Particle **-me** or **-ma** always remains in it absolute form, it does not close to -*mi* or -*mı* etc. The Verb Stem is always accented in speech.

Public Imperative.

This form is characterized by the addition of the suffix **-yiniz** in its various forms. It is used mainly in Public Notices and signs and also in newspapers and on the television. The examples then become:

Positive Verb Public Negative Verb Public.

Bakınız *Look!* becomes **Bakmayınız** *Don't look!*
Geliniz *Come!* becomes **Gelmeyiniz** *Don't come*!

The Public Form is the most polite of all, and can also be used in direct conversation if you wish to be extra polite. In all the above forms the Negative Particle **-me** or **-ma** always remains in it absolute form, it does not close to -*mi* or -*mı* etc. The Verb Stem is always accented in speech.

When speaking the Imperative there is always heavy vocal stress on the last syllable of the verb stem as shown below in capital letters.

Written: **Yapmayın onu** *Don't do that!*
Spoken: **YAPmayın onu!** *Don't DO that!*

Written **Çiçeklere dokunmayınız** *Don't touch the flowers.*

Spoken: **Çiçeklere doKUNmayınız** *Don't touch the flowers.*

The verb **dokunmak** takes a Dative Object "Çiçekler-e".

Third Person Imperative *let him.., let them..*

The Third Person *let him, let her.*

Some examples in English:
(You) Let him do the talking.
(You) Let them build the bridge.
(You) Give him an allowance.
(You) Let sleeping dogs lie.

Turkish uses the second person endings **-sin -sın -sün -sun** and its plural forms **-sinler -sınlar -sünler -sunlar** as a request for the third person imperative by attaching this suffix directly to the Verb stem. [Tense signs like **-iyor-** or **-ar** etc. are not used.]

baksın *(You) let him look* **bakmasın** *(You) let him not look*
girsin *(You) let him enter* **girmesinler** *(You) let them not enter.*

The third person form of verbs widely used especially in "formula speak". To re-iterate, **-sin** (singular) or **-sinler** (plural) are added directly to the basic verb stem; there is no tense sign intervening. Although this form of the verb appears to be of the second person in **-sin** it actually is not. It cannot be construed as so because the **-sin/-sinler** suffix is added directly to the verb stem and not to a verb tense base.

olmak *to become, to happen.*
olsun *let it be*
olmasın *let it not be*

Singular Forms **koşmak** *to run.*
koşsun *let him run*
koşmasın *let him not run*

Plural Forms **koşmak** *to run.*
koşsunlar *let them run*
koşmasınlar *let them not run*

While in the "Hamam" "Turkish Bath" one might say **Keseci gelsin.** *I am ready for the masseur.* [Lit: Let the masseur come] It can also be in question form: **Keseci gelsin mi?.** *Should the masseur come (now)?*

The Third Person Imperative ending is added directly to the verb stem **Yazsın** *Let him write* but if it is added to a tense sign as in **yazıyorsun** then it is the Second Person tense sign *You are writing.* It is easy to get these forms mixed.

Positive Imperative Summary.

1st. Singular: **geleyim.** *Let me come!*
Kasabaya seninle geleyim. *Let me come with you to the shops.*
1st. Plural: **gelelim.** *Let us come!*
Bu akşam televizyonu seyredelim. *Let's watch TV this evening*

2nd. Familiar: **gel.** *Come (you)!*
Buraya gel! *(You) Come (to) here!*

2nd. Polite and Plural: **gelin.** *(Please) come (you)!*
Girin! *(You, Please) come in!*

2nd. Public and Formal: **Durunuz.** *(You) Stop, Halt !* (on a "Stop" sign.)
Onu yapınız *(You) Do that!*

3rd. Singular: **Partiye gelsin.** *(You) Let him come to the party!*
Mehmet, pikniğe arabayı sürsün. *(You) Let Mehmet drive the car to the picnic.*

3rd. Plural: **gelsinler.** *let them come!*
Kızlar dans etsinler. *Let the girls dance.*

Negative Imperative Summary.

1st. Singular: **gitmeyeyim.** *Let me not go!*
Saçımı kestireyim mi kestirmeyeyim mi? *Should I get my hair cut or not?* [Lit: Let me?, Let me not?]

1st. Plural: **gitmeyelim!** *Let us not go!*
Bugün yüzmeyelim. *Let's not go swimming today.*

2nd. Familiar: **gitme!** *Don't go (you)!*
Sakın ha, onu yapma! *(You) Careful, don't do that!*

2nd. Polite: **Girmeyin!** *(Please) Don't come in (you)!*
Sakın ha, onu yapmayın! *(You, please be) Careful, don't do that!*

2nd. Public, Formal: **gitmeyiniz!** *(You) Don't Go!*
Sigara İçmeyiniz *(You) No Smoking.* [on a public sign.]

3rd. Singular: **gitmesin!** *let him not go!*
Mehmet, Ayşe'yi öpmesin. *Don't let Mehmet kiss Ayshe.*

3rd. Plural: **gitmesinler!** *let them not go!*
Çocuklar mesajımı görmesinler. *Don't let the children see my message.*

Vowel Harmony operates on the Imperative Suffixes.

görsün *let him see!*
alın *Take (you)!*
bulsunlar *let them find!*
bulmasınlar *let them not find!*
onu yapmayın *Don't do it (you)!*
gülünüz. *Laugh (you)!*

"Formula Speak" Imperatives.

(1) Sağ ol (Sağol), Sağ olun, Sağ olunuz! *Thanks very much!*

This form is used to thank anyone for extra service over accepted levels. It is stronger than **Teşekkür ederim** *Thank you.*

If you ask a stranger for the time of day you could answer **Sağol** [Lit: Be healthy.] *Stay healthy!* as a thank you for his trouble.

(2) Eksik olmayın(ız)! *Don't go missing!*

This is used for telling someone you like their company and they should "stick around".

(3) Sakın!, Sakınınız! *Be careful! Watch out!*

The Imperative of the reflexive verb **sakınmak** *to avoid, to beware* is used as an interjection to warn or advise.

Sakın ha! *Just mind out!, Just watch it!*
Onu yapmaktan sakınınız! *Be careful of doing that!*

Sakın bunu bir daha yapma! *Don't you ever do that (this) again!* [This is said to warn somebody of a disaster waiting to happen!]

Do not mix **Sakın!** *Mind! Beware!* (UnDotted I) with **sakin** (Dotted İ) *calm, quiet,* as in **Sakin olun!** *Calm down!, Quieten down!*

(4) Geçmiş olsun! *May it pass (from you)!*

A formula used to people who are ill. *Get better soon!* or to people who have had an accident or encountered a problem in life, *Bad luck!*

(5) Kolay gelsin! *May it come easy!, Take it easy!*

This is usually said to people who are carrying out a duty or their work.

(6) Neden olmasın? *Why let it not be? Why not?*

This is the same as *Why not?* in English. New learners often say "Neden yok" for "Why not?" but this actually means "There is not a reason!"

There are many other Formula Speak with this aspect of the verb in daily use in Turkey and a good dictionary or phrase book will always contain them. As the barber might say to you when he has finished cutting your hair **Sıhhatler olsun!** *Good health to you!* said to one after having a bath, a haircut or a shave. This expression is used wrongly by many people. It should be **Sıhhatler olsun. Sıhhat** is the Arabic for **Sağlık**. When people say this expression quickly, it sounds like "Saatler olsun" which is incorrect.

The Accelerative Imperative with vermek.

Another form of the imperative involves the use of an auxiliary verb **vermek** *to give (See Chapter 22).*

Postaneye koşuverin! *Run (along) to the Post Office!*

koşuvermek [from "koşmak to run" + "vermek to give."] *to run hurriedly.*

Onu yapıver! *Do it quickly!, Just get it done right now!* [from "yapmak + vermek."]

Imperative Showing Impatience -sene, -sana.

There is another form of the imperative which can be a little petulant or sound impatient. It may be used if you have been waiting too long or in cases where notice has not been taken. This form should be used with care by the learner. It is at first best translated as: *Why do you?* or *Why don't you?*

Formation of the Extended Imperative (Showing Impatience).

The suffix **-sana** or **-sene** is added to the Positive Verb stems, this becomes **-sanıza** or **-senize** when addressing a group of people.

Positive Verb. (Impatient Form.)

Baksana! *Now look here!*
Gelsene! *Come on then!* or *Come along!*
Otursanıza! *Oh do sit down!* or *Why don't (you all) sit down!!*

Here we can see that although there is only a Positive Form in Turkish we can sometimes translate it as negative in English to arrive at the meaning.

24 MOODS THE CO-OPERATIVE

Co-operative and Reflexive Verbs.

The Co-operative form of the verb is where the sense given is that the action is performed with another person or persons. The co-operation may be contrary in meaning. "They fought *each other*". In this case Turkish the co-operative form of the verb **vurmak** *to hit* becomes **vuruşmak** meaning *to fight "each other"*. Many verbs in daily are of the co-operative form.

In English it is not always apparent when a verb is co-operative, for instance the verb *to collide*. You can collide "with a wall" (an active occurrence) or "with another car" (an "in concert" co-operative occurrence).Turkish does make this distinction:

Active Verb: **çarpmak.** *to bump, collide.*
Bir duvara çarptım. *I bumped a wall.*

Co-operative Verb: **çarpışmak.** *to bump, collide with.*
Bir arabayla çarpıştım. *I collided with a car.*

Co-operative Verb Formation with the suffix -iş.

The Co-operative verb sign is **-iş** which is added to the verb stem and it is subject to Vowel harmony so the suffix can take the following forms: **-ış** or **-iş** or **-uş** or **-üş** and **-ş** is added to verb stems which end in a vowel.

Active Verb.
vurmak *to hit.*
ona vurdum. *I shot him.*

Co-operative Verb.
vuruşmak *to hit.*
Birbirleriyle vuruştular. *They fought each other.* [Lit: hit each

240

other.]

görmek *to see.*
Memet'i gördüm. *I saw Mehmet.*

görüşmek *to see each other/to meet.*
Mehmet ile görüşeceğim. *I'm going to meet Mehmet.* [Lit: I will meet (see each other) with Mehmet.]

anlamak *to understand.*
Ali'yi anlıyoruz. *We understand Ali.*

anlaşmak *to understand each other/to agree.*
Anlaşıyoruz, değil mi? *We agree, don't we?*
Ali ile anlaşıyoruz. *We agree with Ali.* ["understand each other."]

Birbirleriyle *with each other.*
ile *with* is often used with co-operative verbs, since the action is performed mutually.

About the verb **vurmak.**

When used with The Motion Toward (Dative Suffix **-a/-e**) it means *to strike, to hit.*
Mehmet bana vurdu. *Mehmet hit me.* [to me]

When used with Direct Object (Accusative Suffix **-ı/-i/-u/-ü**) it means *to shoot dead, to kill.*
Mehmet kuşu vurdu. *Mehmet shot the bird. [dead]*

Many Co-operative verb forms are in regular use, **konuşmak** *to speak* is a co-operative verb that is in daily use. In Turkish verbs the **-iş** suffix signifies an action, either with or against, that is done in concert. The **-iş** suffix also makes certain nouns to show "a doing together". The "in concert" suffix show in these nouns **giriş** *entrance* which can be construed to mean "an entering in concert" together. Similarly **çıkış** *exit* .["a leaving in concert."]

Some verbs with regular use are in their Co-operative form:

anlaşmak *to agree.* [to understand together.]
sevişmek *to make love* .[with each other.]
öpüşmek *to kiss.* [with each other.]

Although **konuşmak** *to speak* [with each other] and **çalışmak** *to work* [with or at something or other] are not really co-operative verbs we can see that **-iş-** shows that these verbs show "a doing together".

The Reflexive Form of the Verb.

The reflexive form of the verb is used when the action of the verb refers back to the subject as opposed to the object. In English this is usually shown by the use of the reflexive pronouns *myself, yourself, ourselves etc.* However in Turkish the feeling of "self" is understood by using the reflexive form of the verb. **Mehmet yıkandı** *Mehmet washed himself.*

Other Examples of Reflexive Forms in English.

I shaved myself.
He washed himself.
You have cut yourself.
We helped ourselves.

This reflexive form of the verb stem is used to convey the reflexive meaning and takes the form of the suffix **-in** (subject to vowel harmony) or **-n** after verb stems ending in a vowel. The reflexive sign **-n** is the same as the passive form for those verbs whose stems end in a vowel but the context of the sentence is usually enough to make the meaning passive or reflexive quite evident.

Rarely, the **-il** suffix is used for the reflexive meaning. The verb **üzmek** is *to make someone sad* and its reflexive/passive **üzülmek** is *to get sad (oneself).* **Katmak** is *to add/join* and its reflexive/passive **katılmak** is *to get added, hence to join, to attend.* This is really a "grey area" between passive and/or reflexive.

Examples of Use for the Reflexive Verb.

If we take the verb **yıkamak** *to wash* we would say:
Çamaşırı yıkadım. *I washed the shirt.*
However if we say *I washed myself, I had a wash* then the reflexive form must be used **yıkandım**:

Henüz yıkandım! *I've just had a wash!*

Similarly the verb **soymak** *to undress.*

soymak. *to undress somebody.* [Active]
soyunmak. *to undress oneself.* [Reflexive]

25 MOODS THE PASSIVE

The Passive Mood.

The Passive Mood: signifies that the verb acts upon the **subject** of the sentence: *"The man (subj.) was bitten by the dog."*

The Active Mood: signifies that the verb acts on the **object** of the sentence: *"The dog bit the man (obj.)"*

In Turkish the passive verb stem is formed by adding the passive suffix **-il** or **-in** to the basic verb stem. The verb stem of course can be an indicative, co-operative or a causative verb stem.

Order of Verbal Mood Suffixes.

The order that the suffixes are added to the verb as follows:
1. Reflexive.
2. Co-operative.
3. Causative. (*See Chap.26.*)
4. Passive.

acımak *to feel pain.* (active)
acınmak *to feel pain in oneself, to grieve.* (reflexive)
acındırmak *to cause to grieve.* (reflexive causative)
acındırılmak *to be made to grieve* (reflexive causative passive)

tanımak *to know .*(active)
tanışmak *to know one another.* (co-cooperative)
tanıştırmak *to introduce.* (co-cooperative causative)
tanıştırılmak *to be introduced.* (co-cooperative causative passive)

Negation **-me-** plus ability **-ebil-** and inability **-eme-** are added after these. After which the tense suffixes: **-iyor- -ir- -ecek- -di- -miş-** are further added to complete the verb.

Active Present Continuous.

yapmak *to do.*
yapıyorum *I am doing.*

Passive Present Continuous.
yapılmak *to be done.*
yapılıyor *It is being done.*

Active Potential Simple Present.
yapabilmek *to be able do.*
yapabilirim *I can do.*

Passive Potential Simple Present.
yapılabilmek *to be able to be done.*
yapılabilir *it can be done.*

Negative Active Present Continuous.
yapmamak *to not do.*
yapmıyorum *I am not doing.*

Negative Passive Present Continuous.
yapılmamak *to not be done.*
yapılmıyor *it is not being done.*

Negative Passive Potential Future.
yapılamamak *to not be able to be done.*
yapılamayacak *it will not be able to be done.*

Active Future Potential.
yapabilme. *to be able to do.*
Onu yapabileceğiz *we will be able to do it.*

Causative Future Potential Active.
yaptırabilmek *to be able to get it done.*
Onu yaptırabileceğiz *we will be able to get it done.*

Causative Future Potential Passive.
yaptırabilmek *to be able to have it done.*
Onu yaptırabileceğiz. [yap-tır-abil-eceğ-iz] *we will be able to have/get it done.*

There are many other tenses and persons that can be built up using the causative and cooperative verbs in all tenses and persons. This is one of the difficulties for Turkish learners, to use and recognize the verb forms and their meanings easily. It takes practice new learners, but it is second nature to a Turkish national.

Verb Forms of the Passive Mood Explained.

The Passive Mood signifies that the verb acts upon the subject of the sentence whereas in the Active Mood the verb acts on the object of the sentence.

The Active Sentence.

The Active Verb with the subject *Kemal* and the object *the street*.
Kemal swept the street yesterday.

The Passive Sentence.

The Passive Verb. Here *The street* is the subject and *Kemal* (the person doing the sweeping) is called "the agent".
The street is being swept by Kemal.

The Impersonal Passive.

The Passive Verb *The street* is the subject without any agent operating on it.
The street will be swept every day.
Or in the Past Tense:
The street was swept yesterday.

Formation of the Passive.

In Turkish the passive verb stem is formed by adding the passive suffix **-il** or **-in** to the basic verb stem. The verb stem of course can be an indicative, co-operative or a causative verb stem.

Passive: Verb stems terminating in a Consonant add "-il".

For verbs ending in a consonant **(Except -l)** the suffix **-il** ,subject to Vowel Harmony, is added to the verb stem. For those verb stems which themselves end in **-l** then the suffix **-in**, subject to vowel harmony, is added.

Active Mood Positive Passive Mood Positive.

yapmak *to do* **yapılmak** *to be done.*
kesmek *to cut* **kesilmek** *to be cut.*
kırmak *to break* **kırılmak** *to be broken.*

Active Mood Negative Passive Mood Negative.

yapmamak *to not do* **yapılmamak** *to be not done.*
kesmemek *to not cut* **kesilmemek** *to be not cut.*
kırmamak *to not break* **kırılmamak** *not to be not broken.*

Causative and Potential Passive Verbs Positive.

The Causative and Co-operative verbs form their Passive with **-il** in the usual way:

Active Verb Passive Verb..
yapmak Active *to do* **yapılmak** Passive *to be done.*
yaptırmak Active Causative *to get something done.*
yaptırılmak Passive Causative *to cause be done.*
yapabilmek Active Potential *to be able to do s.o.*
yapılabilmek Passive Potential *to be able get s.o. done.*

Causative and Potential Passive Verbs Negative.

Active Verb Passive Verb.
yapmamak *not to do* **yapılmamak** *not to be done.*
yaptırmamak *not to get something done.*
yaptırılmamak *to not to cause to get s.o. done.*
yapamamak *not to be able to do s.o.*
yapılamamak *not to be able get s.o. done.*

Causative Passive Verb Examples.

anlamak *to understand* Active Verb.
anlatmak *to explain* Active Mood Causative.
anlatılmak *to be understood* Passive Verb Causative.

kırmak *to break* Active Verb.
kırdırmak *to break something* Active Mood Causative.
kırılmak *to be broken* (itself in a broken state) Passive Verb.
kırdırılmak *to be broken by somebody* Passive Mood Causative.

Co-operative Passive Verb Examples.

bulmak *to find* Active Verb.
buluşmak *to meet/to find each other* Co-operative Active.
buluşulmak *to be met/to be found together* Co-operative Passive.

anlamak *to understand* Active Verb.
anlaşmak *to agree/understand each other* Co-operative Active.
anlaşılmak *to be agreed.*

çarpmak *to hit, collide* Active Verb.
çarpışmak *to collide with something* Co-operative Active.
çarpışılmak *to be in collision with something* Co-operative Passive.

Passive: Verbs whose stem ends in -L add "-in".

None of these Causative or Co-operative Verbs have a stem which ends in **-l**, therefore the **-il** passive suffix is used. From the examples above it can be seen that by the use of short suffixes Turkish can say in one word which would take many more in English. The use of the differing verb forms is rather difficult at first, but by practice and reading the logic of them quickly becomes clear to the student.

When the verb stem ends in **-L** then the passive mood is formed by the addition **-in**, subject to vowel harmony.

Active Mood Passive Mood.
delmek *to pierce* **delinmek** *to be pierced.*
bilmek *to know* **bilinmek** *to be known.*
almak *to take* **alınmak** *to be taken.*
bulmak *to find* **bulunmak** *to be found.*

Passive: Verbs whose stem ends in a vowel add "-n".

When the verb stem ends in a vowel then the passive sign is **-n**.

Active Mood Passive Mood.
beklemek *to wait/to expect* **beklenmek** *to be waited for/to be expected.*
kapamak *to close* **kapanmak** *to be closed.*
yemek *to eat* **yenmek** *to be eaten.*

The Passive Agent tarafından *who.*

Active Verb Ali, pencereyi kapadı. *Ali closed the window.*
Impersonal Passive Verb Pencere kapandı. *The window was closed.* (ie. not open)
Passive Verb Ali tarafından pencere kapandı. *The window was closed by Ali.*

In the last example above we can see that it was Ali who closed that window. Ali is the agent by which the window was closed. Turkish has a particular construction in the Passive to denote the agent acting on the subject.

For the pronouns *my, your, his, our their*, the agent (the pronoun itself) is placed in the Ownership Condition (Genitive) and followed by **tarafından** meaning *by.* All other common and proper nouns, as in, **"Ali tarafından"** *by Ali* are not suffixed by the genitive **-in.**

An Example in the Causative Active.

O Pencereyi kapattı. *He closed the window.*
The object is *"window"* and the verb is Causative Active.

This Example in the Causative Passive.

Pencere onun tarafından kapatıldı. *The window was closed by him.* The pronoun "onun of him" is suffixed with the Ownership condition **onun.**

Pencere Mehmet tarafından kapatıldı. *The window was closed by Mehmet.*

Here the subject is *"window"* and the verb is Causative Passive. The proper noun "Mehmet" is not suffixed with the genitive **-in** as he is just the agent who is "closing the window".

To reiterate: In the last two examples the agent "who closes" the window is mentioned. Turkish has a particular construction in the Passive to denote the agent acting on the subject. For pronouns such as *my, your, his, our their* the agent (the pronoun itself) is placed in the Ownership Condition (Genitive) and followed by **tarafından** *by.*

However all other nouns are not suffixed with the genitive **-in.**

Pronouns Examples including the agent as a Pronoun.

Hesap, benim tarafımdan ödenecek. *The bill will be paid by me.*

Kitap, onların tarafından yazılacak. *The book will be written by them.*

Proper Nouns Examples including the Agent in the Subject Condition.

Top, Mustafa tarafından bulundu. (not: "Mustafa 'nın".) *The ball was found by Mustapha.*

Araba, Ali tarafından temizleniyor. *The car is being cleaned by Ali.*

If the agent is a Proper Noun it is in the Subject Condition, but if it is a Pronoun the Ownership Condition is used.

In Turkish the Subject of a sentence is usually followed by a comma. This is a good policy to follow when writing Turkish. If a break is not put after the subject there is the possibility of being misunderstood as "nick-names". "Top Mustafa Fatty Mustapha", "Araba Ali Taxi Ali" may be nick-names so used.

26 MOODS THE CAUSATIVE

The Causative Verb.

The active form of the verb gives the sense of: "doing something" and the passive form "something is being done". The Causative sense is "to have something done by somebody, to get something done by something." In the case where English uses "get done by" or "to have done by" Turkish uses the Causative form of the verb.

In English one might say:
The Active Verb *I'm going to clean the car* . [to clean it myself.]
The Causative Form *I'll get John to clean the car.* [to get, to cause John to clean it.]

Use of the Causative.

One of the duties that the Causative Verb form carries out is to make intransitive verbs, which do not take an object into a transitive verbs, which do take an object.
The verb **durmak** *to stop/to halt* is such a word:
Araba caddede durdu. *The car stopped in the street.* There is no object in this sentence, it is intransitive.
Mehmet, arabayı caddede durdurdu. *Mehmet stopped the car in the street.* The object in this sentence is **arabyı** *the car.* It is a transitive sentence.

Causative Verb Formation.

The Causative verb stem is usually formed by adding **-dir** to the basic verb stem or **-tir** if the verb stem ends in an unvoiced consonant. The suffix follows Vowel Harmony Rules and is subject to Consonant Mutation. Therefore the Causative Suffix possibilities due to the above rules are:
-dir-/-tir- -dır-/-tır- -dur-/-tur- -dür-/-tür-
The resulting causative verb stem can have all mood and tense

251

endings added as required. There are some exceptions to this rule.

Regular Causative Verb Formation.

Most verbs are regular in their causative formation even if they are single syllable and end in an unvoiced consonant.

Active Verb Causative Verb.

bakmak *to look.*
baktırmak *to cause to look.*

itmek *to push.*
ittirmek *to cause to push.*

koşmak *to run.*
koşturmak *to cause to run.*

satmak *to sell.*
sattırmak *to cause to sell.*

sevmek *to love.*
sevdirmek *to cause to love.*

Verbs ending in -k take -it as their Causative Sign.

Active Verb Causative Verb.

akmak *to flow.*
akıtmak *to cause to flow.*

sarkmak *to hang down.*
sarkıtmak *to hang s.o. up.*

ürkmek *to have a scare.*
ürkütmek (Vowel Harmony operates on the suffix **-üt**.) *to startle.*

Verbs which take -ar or -er as their Causative sign.

Active Verb Causative Verb.

çıkmak *to go out/to exit.*
çıkarmak *to send out, to extract.*

gitmek *to go.*
gidermek *to send away/to remove/to expel.*

kopmak *to snap itself.*
koparmak *to break s.o.off.*

onmak *to mend.*
onarmak *to have repaired.*

One verb is completely irregular.

Active Verb. Causative Verb.

görmek *to see.*
göstermek *to show.*

All these are common verbs and should be learnt as irregularities.

Regularly Formed Causative Verbs.

Basic Verb.
gülmek *to laugh.*
Ona güldüm. *I laughed at him.* ["gülmek" takes a Motion Toward (dative) object.]
Bana güldü. *He laughed at me.*

Causative Form.
güldürmek *to make laugh/cause to laugh.*
Onu güldürdüm. *I made him laugh.*
Beni güldürdü. *He made me laugh.*

Basic Verb.
bilmek *to know.*
Onu biliyorum. *I know that.*

Causative Form.
bildirmek *to make known.*
Mehmed' e haberi bildirdik. *We made the news known to Mehmet.*

Basic Verb
çalışmak.*to work.*
Bugün çalışıyorum. *I am working today.*

Causative Form.
çalıştırmak *to cause to work.*
Bugün, Mehmed'e çalıştırıyorum. *I am getting Mehmet to work today.*

Basic Verb.
unutmak *to forget.*
Çantamı unuttum. *I forgot my bag.*

Causative Form.
unutturmak *to cause to forget.*
Mehmet'e çantasını unutturduk. *We've let Mehmet forget his bag.*

Examples in the Potential Mood.

Onu güldürebilirsiniz. *You can make her laugh.*
Beni güldüremeyecek. *he will not be able to make me laugh.*
Bizi güldüremediler. *they couldn't make us laugh.*

Examples in the Necessitative Mood.

Mehmet seni güldürmeliydi. *Mehmet should have made you laugh.*
Onu yaptırmalıyım. *I should have it done.*

Irregular Causative Forms.

Basic verb Stems ending in a **vowel** or **-r** form their causative by the addition of the suffix **-t** to produce the causative verb stem.

Active Verb Causative Verb.

oturmak *to sit* **oturtmak** *to seat somebody.*
Sıra sıra öğrencileri oturttum. *I seated the students ın rows.*

anlamak *to understand* **anlatmak** *to make understand/to explain.*
Onu Mehmet'e anlattım. *I explained it to Mehmet.*

boyamak *to paint* **boyatmak** *to get something painted.*
Ön kapımızı boyatmalıyız. *We must get our front door painted.*

Single Syllable Causative Verb Forms.

Some verbs mainly of a single syllable root form their causative by the addition of -ır, that is the initial -d- or -t- of the causative verb sign is dropped. This generally happens when the basic verb stem terminates in -ç or -ş but there are other verbs included in this group. Some verbs which end in -ç or -ş take the full -tir suffix. However the problem of these irregularities is not too great as the number of verbs involved is quite small although some of them are fairly common. These are best learned separately.

Basic Verb Irregular Causative Verb.

artmak *to increase.*
artırmak *to cause to increase.*

batmak *to sink.*
batırmak *to cause to sink.*

bitmek *to finish.*
bitirmek *to finish off.*

doğmak *to be born.*
doğurmak *to give birth.*

doymak *to be filled.*
doyurmak *to fill up s.o.*

düşmek *to fall.*
düşürmek *to cause to fall/to drop s.o.*

geçmek *to pass.*
geçirmek *to cause to pass.*

göçmek *to move/migrate.*
göçürmek *to evict.*

içmek *to drink/smoke.*
içirmek.*to cause to drink.*

kaçmak *to escape.*
kaçırmak *to miss/let escape.*

pişmek *to cook.* (by itself.)
pişirmek *to cook something.*

şaşmak *to be surprised.*
şaşırmak *to surprise s.o.*

şişmek *to swell.*
şişirmek *to cause to swell.*

taşmak *to overflow.*
taşırmak *to cause to overflow.*

uçmak *to fly.*
uçurmak *to cause to fly.*

Using the Causative to form Transitive Verbs.

The Causative makes transitive verb which takes an object out of an intransitive verb which has no object.

Pişmek *to cook (by itself) The eggs are cooking in the pan.* (intransitive The eggs are cooking by themselves.)

Pişirmek *to cook something Ali is cooking the eggs in the pan.* (transitive Ali (the subject) is cooking the eggs. (object)

Inspecting the examples it can be seen that some of the active forms are intransitive whilst their causative Form is the transitive Verb.

This is the reason that the Turkish verb *to eat* is **yemek yemek**. The first **yemek** is a noun meaning *food* and the second **yemek** is the infinitive verb *to eat*. **Yemek** is a transitive verb in Turkish so therefore must always take an object. In English the verb *to eat* can be transitive, "I ate lunch" or intransitive, "I ate well on while on holiday".

Ali, lokantada yemek yiyor. *Ali is eating food in the cafe.* (transitive), whereas in English we say *Ali is eating in the cafe.* (intransitive).

Turkish and English Verb Differences.

The causative verb is used when an instrument or a person causes a verb action. A different verb may be used in English to show the causative sense. It is therefore sometimes difficult to select the correct English verb in translation from Turkish.

Mutfakta yemek pişiyor. *The food (subject) is cooking in the kitchen.* [Intransitive Verb the food is cooking by itself]

Mehmet, mufakta yemeği pişiriyor. *Mehmet (subject) is cooking the food.* [Transitive Causative Verb Mehmet is cooking the food.] The same verb "to cook" is used in English for both intransitive and transitive (causative) meanings.

However a different verb may be used in English:

Active Verb **anlamak** *to understand.*
Cevabı anladım. *I understood the answer.*

Causative Verb **anlatmak** *to explain.* [Lit: to cause to understand.]
Cevabı anlattım. *I explained the answer.*

In English the causative verb often differs from the active verb whereas Turkish uses its causative form of the active Form.

Examples of Different Verb Use in English.

Active Causative Literal

to die to kill/to murder. [Lit: to cause to die.]
to see to show. [Lit: to cause to see.]
to halt to stop. [Lit: to cause to halt.]

Causing a Third Party to Act.

This is a doubled causative verb formed by adding **-t** or sometimes -**tir** to the regular causative verb.

I made him paint the car
I got him to paint the car.
I had him paint the car.

All the above are translated: **arabayı ona boyattırdım.** [boya-t-tır-dım]. In this case we are causing a third party to act as an agent. In these type of sentences the agent has the **-a** or **-e** (indirect object) case endings: ie. "I caused for him to paint the car". The verb is basically a doubled causative form "boya-t-tir-mak". Other doubled causatives are formed similarly:

The doubled causative is used when you get someone else to do the job. You cause them to have the job done.

I got my car repaired at the garage. **Arabamı garajda tamir ettirdim.** uses a single causative.

I got the garage to repair my car. **Arabamı garaja tamir ettirttim.** uses a double dausative.

anlattırmak. [anla-t-tır-mak.] *to have something explained.*
tamir ettirtmek. [et-tir-t-mek.] *to have something repaired.*
yaptırtılmak. [yap-tır-t-ıl-mak.] *to have something done.* (a passive mood example.)

If two letters **-tt-** occur together, then they are both pronounced individually. These forms do crop up quite regularly, especially in newspaper reports about agencies, ministers, governments etc. having something carried out by a third party.

27 MOODS OBLIGATION

Expressing Obligation.

I must go.
I ought to go.
I should go.
I have to go.
I have got to go.

Expressing obligation using **lazım, gerek, şart** and **mecbur.**

Nouns: **şart.** *a condition.*
gerek. *a necessity, a must, a need.*

Adjectives: **mecbur** *forced, compelled.*
gerekli. *necessary, needed.*
lâzım. *necessary, needed.*

These words are used with the short infinitive in **-ma/-me** which is personalised with Possessive Pronouns.

Sabahları saat sekizde okulda olmam lâzım (olmam gerek). *I have to be at school at eight o'clock every morning.*

Yarın sabah erkenden atölyede olman gerek. *You need to be at the workshop very early tomorrow morning.*

Mehmet'in bir saat içinde bürosunda olması gerekiyor (gereklidir). *Mehmet needs to be at his office in an hour's time.*

Saat tam sekizde avukatın ofisinde olmamız şart. *We've simply got to be at the solicitor's office right on eight o'clock.*

şart and **mecbur** are the strongest expressions:

Gelmeniz lazım. *You must come.*
Şart mı? *Is it absolutely necessary?*
Mecbur. *Yes it is necessary.*

The verb **gerekmek**, is often used for the past and future requirements.

Onların her gün işte olması gerekır. (Habitual Simple Tense.) *They need to be at work every day.*

Onların işte olması gerekiyor. (Continuous Present Tense.) *They should be at work now.*

Yarın Ali'nin işte olması gerekecek. (Future Tense.) *Ali will have to be at work tomorrow.*

Dün benim işte gitmem gerekti. (Past Tense.) *I had to go to at work yesterday.*

There are a number of other ways to express obligation in Turkish:

zorunda *"compulsion"*

Using the noun **zor** *trouble, difficulty, worry, problem, difficult, hard* produces **zorunda** *"compulsion"* which is used with a suitable verb:

zorunda kalmak. *to be left no choice but (to do something).*
zorunda olmak. *to have to, be obliged to (do something).*

It is also used with the verb "to be" suffixes:

oynamak zorundayım. *I have to play.*
oynamak zorunda kaldım. *I had to play.*
oynamak zorunda oldum. *I was obliged to play.*
oynamak zorundasın. *you have to play.*
o oynamak zorunda(dır). *he has to play.*
oynamak zorundayız. *we have to play.*
oynamak zorundasınız. *you have to play.*
oynamak zorundalar. *they have to play.*

mecbur -*"necessary to, need to"*

One can also use an arabic word **mecbur** *necessary to, need to.*

mecbur olmak /-a/ (demands a Motion Towards Object.) *to be forced to, be obliged to, have to (do something).*

Bakmaya mecbur oldum. *I had to look.*

mecbur kalmak -/a/ (demands a Motion Towards Object.) *to feel obliged to, feel that one has to (do something).*
Bakmaya mecbur kaldım. *I felt (that) I had to look.*

Mecbur kalmadıkça sıcak havada dışarı çıkmayın. *Unless it is necessary do not go out in hot weather.*

Example with **düşünmek** *to think.*
düşünmeye mecburum. *I should, must, ought to think.*
düşünmeye mecbursun. *you should think.*
o düşünmeye mecbur. *he should think.*
düşünmeye mecburuz. *we should think.*
düşünmeye mecbursunuz. *you should think.*
düşünmeye mecburlar. *they should think.*

Use of -meli/-mali as a tense mood.

kitap okumalıyım. *I must, have to, should read a book.*
kitap okumalısın. *you must, have to, should read a book.*
Ali kitap okumalı . *Ali must, have to, should read a book.*

kitap okumalıyız. *we must, have to, should read a book.*
kitap okumalısınız. *you must, have to, should read a book.*
onlar kitap okumalı(lar). *they must, have to, should read a book.*

In this example "kitap" "book" is not specific, it is any book, a book generally. If we add the direct object suffix it becomes a specific book **kitabı okumalıyım** *I must read the book*, **o kitapı okumalıyım** *I must read that book.*

Use of **lâzım** *need* or **gerek** *necessity* as an auxiliary.

Benim kitap okumam lâzım. [lit: "My reading book is needed".] means *I should read a book.* The Possessive pronoun *my, your, his, etc.* is added to personalize the verb infinitive.

Benim kitap okumam lâzım. *I should read a book.*

Senin kitap okuman lâzım. *you should read a book.*
Ali'nin kitap okuması lâzım. *he should read a book.*

Bizim kitap okumamız lâzım. *we should read a book.*
Sizin kitap okumanız lâzım. *you should read a book.*
Onların kitap okuması (or okumaları) lâzım. *they should read a book.*

Benim kitap okumam gerek. *I should read a book.*
Senin kitap okuman gerek. *you should read a book.*
Ali'nin kitap okuması gerek. *he should read a book.*

Bizim kitap okumamız gerek. *we should read a book.*
Sizin kitap okumanız gerek. *you should read a book.*
Onların kitap okuması (or okumaları) gerek . *they should read a book.*

The Possessive Personalized **-in** is used with both **gerek** and **lâzım** but not with **-meli,-malı** tense suffix.

Turkish **gerek** is now used in preference to the Arabic **lâzım**, although the latter is often used in daily conversation. These methods are widely used especially in notices and newspapers, but the verb itself has a Mood of Obligation which is explained below. There may be some fine differences in meaning and intent within these various methods of expressing obligation, but they can only be learned by experience and observation.

Use of İhtiyaç *need.*

"İhtiyaç"- noun "İhtiyacı Olmak"- verb are old Turkish but still widely used.

Using İhtiyaç (the last syllable is stressed) *need.* The item in need take the **-e/-a** Movement Toward Suffix as in the following sentence. **Arabaya** [araba-ya] **ihtiyacım var.** *I need a car.*

It is used with the personal suffixes for possessions and the words **var** and **yok.**

ihtiyaç var. *There is need.* Positive Statement.

ihtiyaç var mi? *Is there need?* Positive Question.

It uses the Possessive Pronoun for the person "in need of"

For asking Positive questions use the appropriate variant **of var mı?, varmış mı?** and in the past tense **var mıydı?, var mıymış?**

Samimi bir arkadaşına [arkadaş-ı-n-a] **ihtiyacın var.** *You need a close friend.*

Mehmet'in yeni bir işe [iş-e] **ihtiyacı varmış.** *It seems Mehmet needs a new job.*

Dinlenmeye [Dinlenme-y-e] **ihtiyacımız var.** *We need to rest.*

Annemizin artık bir bakıcıya [bakıcı-y-a] **ihtiyacı var.** *Apparently our mother needs a caretaker.*

İhtiyacınız olduğu sürece yanınızda olacağım. *I will be with you when you need me.*

Eşini kaybettiğinden beri çok üzgün, sanırım sana şimdi daha çok ihtiyacı var. *She is so sad since her husband has died, I think she needs you more and more.*

Dün fabrikaya arabayla götürülmeye [götürülme-y-e] **ihtiyacınız var mıydı?** *Did you need to be bought to the factory yesterday? ie did you need "a lift to".*

Onların yardıma [yardım-a] **ihtiyacı var mı?** *Do they need help?*

Bugün bankaya gitmeye [gitme-y-e] **ihtiyacım yok.** *I do not need to go to the bank today.*

Üstünü değiştirmeye [değiştirme-y-e] **ihtiyacın yoktu.** *You did not need to change your clothes.*

Mehmet'in hastaneye gitmeye [gitme-y-e] **ihtiyacı yokmuş.** *It seems Mehmet does not need to go to hospital.*

Acele etmeye [etme-y-e] **ihtiyacımız yok.** *We do not need to hurry.*

Yarınki piknikten önce şu ihtiyaç alışveriş listesini bugünden almamız (halletmemiz) gerek. *Today, we had better buy what we* *need from this shopping-list before tomorrow's picnic.*

Instead of "ihtiyaç" as a name and a verb "gerek, gereksinim, gereksinim duymak" are also used. While the meaning is exactly the same, usage is slightly different.

Bana gerek duyduğunuz sürece yanınızda olacağım.
I'll be with you as long as you need me.

Eşini kaybettiğinden beri çok üzgün, sanırım sana şimdi daha çok gereksinim duyuyor.
Since he lost his wife he's been very sad, I think he needs you now more and more. [This sentence can also be used for the opposite sex "Since she lost her husband etc."]

Annemizin artık bir bakıcıya gereksinimi var.
Our mother needs a care-giver from now on.

The Simple Mood of Obligation -meli/-malı explained.

This mood conveys a necessity. English has many ways of conveying necessity "I must, I ought to, I should, I have (got) to do it." All these methods are translated by the **-meli-/-malı-** mood suffix in Turkish. Each method in English may have a slightly different meaning. These fine meaning are understood "in context" when speaking Turkish.

Obligation Mood A-Dotted Verb.

The Short infinitive is formed by dropping the final **-k** from the Full Infinitive thus giving **bakma** for the Positive Verb stem while the Negative Verb Stem produces **bakmama** from **bakamamak** *not to see.* Then adding of the UnDotted **-lı** Suffix of Obligation we arrive at the necessitative mood verb roots **bakmalı-** for the Positive and **bakmamalı-** for the Negative. The obligation mood is completed by adding the personal endings of the verb *to be.*

Positive Obligation.

bakmalıyım. *I ought to see/I must see.*
bakmalısın. *You ought to see/You must see.*

O bakmalı(dır). *He ought to see/He must see.*

bakmalıyız. *We ought to see/we must see.*
bakmalısınız. *You ought to see/you must see.*
bakmalı(dır)lar. *They ought to see/They must see.*

Negative Obligation.

bakmamalıyım. *I ought not to see.*
bakmamalısın. *You ought not to see.*
O bakmamalı(dır). *He ought not to see.*
bakmamalıyız. *We ought not to see.*
bakmamalısınız. *You ought not to see.*
bakmamalı(dır)lar. *They ought not to see.*

Obligation Mood E-Dotted Verb.

Adding of the Dotted **-li** Suffix of Obligation we arrive at the necessitative mood verb roots **gitmek** *to go* becomes **gitmeli-** for the Positive and **gitmemeli-** for the Negative.

Mood of Obligation Conjugation Examples.

Positive Statement Present Tense.

Ben gitmeliyim. *I must go.*
Sen gitmelisin. *You ought to go.*
O gitmeli(dir). *He, She, It should go.*

Biz gitmeliyiz. *We have to go.*
Siz gitmelisiniz. *You have got to go.*
Onlar gitmeli(dir)ler. *They have to go.*

Positive Interrogative Present Tense.

Ben gitmeli miyim? *Must I go?*
Sen gitmeli misin? *Ought you to go?*
O gitmeli mi? *Should he go?*

Biz gitmeli miyiz? *Have we to go?*
Siz gitmeli misiniz? *Have you got to go?*
Onlar gitmeliler mi? *Have they got to go?*

Negative Statement Present Tense.

Ben gitmemeliyim. *I must not go.*
Sen gitmemelisin. *You ought not to go.*
O gitmemeli. *He should not go.*

Biz gitmemeliyiz. *We have not to go.*
Siz gitmemelisiniz. *You have not got to go.*
Onlar gitmemeliler. *They have not got to go.*

Negative Interrogative Present Tense.

Ben gitmemeli miyim? *Must I not go?/Mustn't I go?*
Sen gitmemeli misin? *Ought you not to go?/Oughtn't you to go?*
O gitmemeli mi? *Should he not go?/Shouldn't he go?*

Biz gitmemeli miyiz? *Have we not got to go?/Haven't we got to go?/*
Siz gitmemeli misiniz? *Have you not to go?/Haven't you got to go?*
Onlar gitmemeliler mi? *Have they not got to go?/Haven't they got to go?*

Past Definite of Obligation -/melı/-mali .

The necessitative past definite relates to an actual situation *I should have gone, He must have gone.*

Positive Statement Past Tense Definite.

Ben gitmeliydim. *I must have gone.*
Sen gitmeliydin. *You ought to have gone.*
O gitmeliydi. *He should have gone.*

Biz gitmeliydik. *We had to go.*
Siz gitmeliydiniz. *You had got to go.*
Onlar gitmeliydiler. *They had to go.*

Positive Interrogative Past Tense Definite.

Ben gitmeli miydim? *Must I have gone?*
Sen gitmeli miydin? *Ought you to have gone?*
O gitmeli miydi? *Should he have gone?*

Biz gitmeli miydik? *Had we to go?*
Siz gitmeli miydiniz? *Had you got to go?*
Onlar gitmeliler miydi? *Had they got to go?*

Negative Statement Past Tense Definite.

Ben gitmemeliydim. *I must not have gone.*
Sen gitmemeliydin. *You ought not to have gone.*
O gitmemeliydi. *He should not have gone.*

Biz gitmemeliydik. *We had not to go.*
Siz gitmemeliydiniz. *You had not got to go.*
Onlar gitmemeliydiler. *They had not got to go.*

Negative Interrogative Past Tense Definite.

Ben gitmemeli miydim? *Must I not have gone?/Mustn't I have gone?*
Sen gitmemeli miydin? *Ought you not to have gone?/Oughtn't you to have gone?*
O gitmemeli miydi? *Should he not have gone?/Shouldn't he have gone?*

Biz gitmemeli miydik? *Had we not got to go?/Hadn't we got to go?*
Siz gitmemeli miydiniz? *Had you not got to go?/Hadn't you got to go?*
Onlar gitmemeliler miydi? *Had they not got to go?/Hadn't they got to go?*

Obligation in the Future.

The **-meli/-malı** necessitative has no future form. If you want to say in English "I will have to do it", then you cannot use **-meli/-malı** in Turkish. Instead **gerek, zorunda** is used for Future Obligation.

Bunu yapmak zorunda olacağım. *I will have to do this.*
Onu yapman gerekecek. *You will have to do that.*

Obligation Past Indefinite with -miş.

267

The necessitative past indefinite relates to an assumption *I suppose that I should have gone, I suppose that he should have gone, etc.*

Positive Indefinite (presumption).

Ben gitmeliymişim. *(I suppose that) I must have gone.*
Sen gitmeliymişsin. *(I believe that) you ought to have gone.*
O gitmeliymiş. *(Presumably) he should have gone.*

Biz gitmeliymişiz. *(In reality) we had got to go.*
Siz gitmeliymişsiniz. *(It seems that) you had to go.*
Onlar gitmeliymişler. *(Probably) they had got to go.*

Positive Interrogative of Presumption.

Ben gitmeli miymişim? *Ought I to have gone? (at all?)*
Sen gitmeli miymişsin? *Should you have gone? (possibly?)*
O gitmeli miymiş? *(I wonder?) Did he have to go?*

Biz gitmeli miymişiz? *(I wonder?) Did we have to go?*
Siz gitmeli miymişsiniz? *(It seems that?) Did you have to go?*
Onlar gitmeli miymişler? *(Surely by now?) Must they have gone?*

Negative Statement of Presumption.

Ben gitmemeliymişim. *(I suppose that) I must not have gone.*
Sen gitmemeliymişsin. *(I believe that) you ought not to have gone.*
O gitmemeliymiş. *(Presumably) he should not have gone.*

Biz gitmemeliymişiz. *(In reality) we had not got to go.*
Siz gitmemeliymişsiniz. *(It seems that) you had not to go.*
Onlar gitmemeliymişler. *(Probably) they did not have to go.*

Negative Interrogative of Presumption.

Ben gitmemeli miymişim? *Ought I not to have gone? (at all?)*
Sen gitmemeli miymişsin? *(I think that?) Should you not have gone?*
O gitmemeli miymiş? *(I wonder?) Did he not have to go?*

Biz gitmemeli miymişiz? *(I wonder?) Had we not got to go?*
Siz gitmemeli miymişsiniz? *(It seems that?) Did you not have to go?*

Onlar gitmemeli miymişler? *(Surely?) must they not have gone?*

The Verb "Gerekmek" *to be required/to need.*

Gerekmek *to need, to want to* is a verb in Turkish. It is used in all tenses and moods:

Present Continuous.

Saatimin ayarlanması gerekiyor. *My watch needs adjusting.*

Otobüse binmem gerekiyor mu? *Do I have to get on a bus?*

Mehmet'e yardım gerekiyor. *Mehmet needs help.*

Bir vize gerekiyor mu? *Is a visa necessary?*

Kışın kar yağması gerekmiyor mu? *It's supposed to snow in winter, right?*

Hakkımda hiçbir şey öğrenmen gerekmiyor. *You do not need to learn anything about me.*

Ondan korkmamız gerekmiyor. *We have no need to be frightened of that/it.*

Simple Present.

İstanbul'a gitmek gerekmez. *It is not necessary to go to Istanbul.*

Bunun üzerinden gümrük ödemeniz gerekir. *Because of this it will be necessary to pay Customs Duty.*

Gülmek gerekir bazen. *One should laugh sometimes.*

On dakika beklemeniz gerekebilir. *It may be necessary for you to wait ten minutes.*

Indefinite Past Tense.

Mutlu olmak için mutlu etmek gerekmiş. *In order to be happy it may be (-miş) necessary to make happiness.*

Bir bilene sormak gerekmiş. *It seem it is necessary to ask someone who knows.*

Çok şey gerekmezmiş mutlu olmaya. *Many things are not needed to become happy.*

Sevmek için sebep gerekmezmiş. *No reason is necessary to love.*

Hatta kimseye bir şey anlatması gerekmezmiş. *It seems it is not even necessary to let anybody know.*

Definite Past Tense.

Kalemler pahalı olunca, ek iş bulma gerekti. *As the items were expensive, a spare time job was necessary.* ("Kalem" also means "pencil".)

Öyle olması gerekti. *It had to be like that.*

Başarmamız gerekti aslında. *Really, we had to succeed.*

Oraya buraya gitmem gerekti. *I had to go here and there.*

Senin iyi olduğunu görmem gerekti. *I had to see that you were alright.*

Üçüncü kez denemem gerekmedi. *I did not have to try a third time.*

Vitesten yukarı çıkmam gerekmedi. *It wasn't necessary to change up (a gear).*

Bir defa bile kutusunu açmam gerekmedi. *I did not even have to open the box.*

Future Tense.

Bu adamların adını hatırlamam gerekecek. *I will have to remember these gentlemen's names.*

Eşme'ye yeni bir yatak almam gerekecek. *I will have to get a new bed for Esme.*

İlk önce siteden şifre almanız gerekecektir. *Firstly you must obtain a password from the site.*

Boyut değiştirmemiz gerekecektir. *We will have to change the dimensions.*

Hap kutusuyu bitirdikten sonra yeniden doktorunuza görünmeniz gerekecektir. *After finishing the pill- box it will be necessary to see the doctor again.*

Present Participle in "-en".

İzlenilmesi gerekilen bir filim. *A film which must be seen.*

Ankara'ya gidince uğranılması gerekilen bır yer olduğunu düşünüyorum. *I think that it is a place that must be visited when going to Ankara.*

Gerçekten öğrenmesi gerekilen çok şeyler var. *Truly there are many things which are necessary to be learned.*

Gümrük vergisi ödenmesi gerekmeyen ki arabamla geldim. *I came in my car for which customs duty was not necessary.*

Sebzelerin tüketiminde dikkat edilmesi gerekilen konusu. *The steps that are necessary for the conservation of vegetables.*

Conditional mood *if, whether.*

O an ne yapılması gerekiyorsa onu yaparım. *I'll do whatever is necessary to do at that moment.*

Eğer gitmem gerekiyorsa giderim. *I will go if it is necessary.*

Her ne gerekiyorsa yaparım. *I will do whatever is necessary.*

Öyle olması gerekiyorsa öyle olur. *If it has to be like that then let it be so.*

Her Türk asker doğar, gerekirse vatan için şehit olur. *All Turks are born soldiers and if necessary will die as a martyr for the country.*

Kısaca anlatmak gerekirse böyle onu yazayım. *Let me write it down like this if it needs to be explained in short.*

Gerekmezse konuşmam. *If it is not necessary, I will not speak.*

A Special use of "Gerek" *as well as.*

gerek, gerek ise *as well as.*

Gerek göklerdeki kuşlar, gerek denizdeki balıklar, gerek yerdeki hayvanlar.
This means "all of them" *The birds in the sky, the fishes in the sea and also the animals on land, all of them*, it is similar to "not only but also" in English.

28 MOODS -THE POTENTIAL

The Potential Mood Positive *"to be able"*

The Potential Mood (tense) indicates: **ability** *to be able, can* or **disposition** *may, might.*

yetenek *ability, accomplishment, acumen, adequacy, aptitude, aptness, artistry, bent, calibre, capability, capacity, competence, competency, dexterity, disposition, efficiency, endowment, facility, faculty, fitness, flair, genius, gift, instinct, knack, merit, predisposition, prerogative, qualification, quality, resource, skill, talent, turn, vocation.*

The Potential Mood uses the addition of **bilmek** *to know* to form its sense of meaning. It always takes the form with a **dotted i** and is not subject to vowel harmony, as **bilmek** is a word in its own right. This is similar to the Scottish use of *ken can, be able to* as in *Do you ken the swimming?* "Do you know how to swim?"

Formation of the Positive Potential Mood.

Verb Stems Ending in a Consonant.

The suffix **-ebil-** or **-abil-** is affixed to the positive verb stems which end in a consonant.

gelmek *to come* forms a new verb and becomes **gelebilmek** *to be able to come.*

yazmak *to write* forms a new verb and becomes **yazabilmek** *to be able to write.*

yazılmak *to be written* [Passive Mood] forms a new verb and becomes **yazılabilmek** *to be able to be written.*

gülmek *to laugh* forms a new verb and becomes **gülebilmek** *to be*

273

able to laugh.

güldürmek *to make s.o. laugh* [Causative Verb] forms a new verb and becomes **güldürebilmek** *to be able to make s.o. laugh.*

Verb Stems ending in a Vowel.

Verb Stems ending in a vowel add **-yebil-** or **-yabil-** using buffer letter **-y.**

yürümek *to walk* forms a new verb and becomes **yürüyebilmek** *to be able to walk.*

taşımak *to carry* forms a new verb and becomes **taşıyabilmek** *to be able to carry.*

The various tenses can be formed as normal after dropping **-mek** or **-mak** which are replaced by **-e-** or **-a-** to which the verb **bilmek** *to know* is suffixed thus forming **-ebil-** or **-abil-** as the Potential Mood Suffix. In essence what is really being formed is a new verb altogether. This is different from English which uses the auxiliary verb "to be able".

Potential Mood Examples.

Present Continuous Tense:
gelebiliyorum *I can come, I am able to come, I may come, I might come.*

Present Simple Tense:
gelebilirim *I can come, I am able to come, I may come, I might come.*

Future Tense:
gidebileceksiniz *you will be able to go, etc.*

Past Tense:
başlayabildik *we were able to start, etc..*

Potential Present Continuous.

Basic Verb: **görmek** *to see.*
Potential Verb: **görebilmek** *to be able to see.*

görebiliyorum. *I can see, I am able to see, I may see, I might see.*
görebiliyorsun. *you can see, you are able to see.*
görebiliyor. *he can see, he is able to see.*

görebiliyoruz. *we can see, we are able to see.*
görebiliyorsunuz. *you can see, you are am able to see.*
görebiliyorlar. *they can see, they are able to see.*

Potential Present Interrogative.

The Interrogative is formed in a similar manner as the basic verb with the addition of the personalised question tag written separately:

gelebiliyor muyum? *Can I come?*
gelebiliyor musunuz? *Can you come?*

Potential Future Tense.

Basic Verb **kalmak.** *to stay, to remain.*
Potential Verb **kalabilmek.** *to be able to stay, remain.*

kalabileceğim. *I will be able to stay.*
kalabileceksin. *you will be able to stay.*
kalabilecek. *he will be able to stay.*

kalabileceğiz. *we will be able to stay.*
kalabileceksiniz. *you will be able to stay.*
kalabilecekler. *they will be able to stay.*

Potential Future Interrogative.

gidebilecek misiniz? *will you be able to go?*

Potential Past Definite Tense.

beklemek *to wait, to expect* becomes in the Past Definite Potential Form -**bekleyebilmek** *to be able to wait, expect.*

bekleyebildim. *I was able to wait.*
bekleyebildin. *you were able to wait.*
bekleyebildi. *he was able to wait.*

bekleyebildik. *we were able to wait.*
bekleyebildiniz. *you were able to wait.*

bekleyebildiler. *they ere able to wait.*

If we insert the **-ir** of the Habitual present, then the meaning becomes "unreal".

beklemek *to wait, to expect* becomes in the Past Definite Potential Unreal **-bekleyebilirmek** *to be able to wait, expect.*

bekleyebilirdim. *I could have waited.*
bekleyebilirdin. *you could have waited.*
bekleyebilirdi. *he could have waited.*

bekleyebilirdik. *we could have waited.*
bekleyebilirdiniz. *you could have waited.*
bekleyebilirdiler. *they could have waited.*

Potential Past Indefinite Tense.

Basic Verb **düşünmek** *to think.*
Potential Verb **düşünebilmek.** *to be able to think.*

düşünebilmişim. *it seems I was able to think.*
düşünebilmişsin. *it seems you were able to think.*
düşünebilmiş. *it seems he was able to think.*

düşünebilmişiz. *it seems we were able to think.*
düşünebilmişsiniz. *it seems you were able to think.*
düşünebilmişler. *it seems they were able to think.*

Potential Past Interrogative.

bekleyebildi mi? *could he have waited?*

Potential Past Continuous.

Basic Verb **yapmak.** *to do, to make.*
Potential Verb **yapabilmek.** *to be able to do.*

yapabiliyordum. *I was able to do.*
yapabiliyordun. *you were able to do.*
yapabiliyordu. *he was able to do.*

yapabiliyorduk. *we were able to do.*
yapabiliyordunuz. *you were able to do.*

yapabiliyorlardı. *they were able to do.*

Potential Past Continuous Interrogative.

durabiliyorlardı mı? *were they able to stop, halt ?*

This example clearly shows that **bilmek** *to know* keeps its **dotted i** as it is not subject to vowel harmony rules, being a separate word in its own right.

Negative Potential Formation - *"to not be able".*

This mood is formed in all tenses by inserting an **-e-** or **-a-** before the negative suffix of any negative verb whether it be active, passive, reflexive, reciprocal or causative. It is a completely new verb with its own infinitive.

Negative Potential A-UnDotted Verbs.

Active Verb **bakmamak.** *to not look.*
Negative Potential Verb **bakamamak.** *not to be able to look.*

Some Examples of Various Tense Formation:

bakamıyorum. *I can't look.*
bakamadın or **bakamıyordun.** *you could not look.*
bakamıyordu. *he was not able to look.*

bakamazsak . *if we cannot look .* (Conditional Form)
bakamayacaksınız. *you will not be able to look.*
bakamadılar or **bakamıyorlardı .** *they could not look.*

The tense and personal endings are added to make the full verb form which includes the "if" forms of the Conditional Mood.

Negative Potential E-Dotted Verbs.

Active Verb **çekmemek.** *to not pull.*
Negative Potential Verb **çekememek.** *not to be able to pull.*

çekemem. *I can't come.* (Simple Present Negative Potential.)

çekemiyorsun. *you cannot pull.* (Present Continuous Negative

Potential.)

çekilemedi. *it could not be pulled.* (Passive form Past Definite Negative Potential.)

çekemeyeceğiz. *we will not be able to pull.* (Future Tense Negative Potential.)

çekememiştiniz. *you had not been able to pull.* (Pluperfect Negative Potential.)

Negative Potential A-UnDotted Verbs Ending in a Vowel.

The buffer letter **-y-** is used to keep the last vowel of the verb stem separate from the **-e-** negative potential particle that has been added to the normal negative infinitive.

Basic Verb **anlamamak.** *to understand.*
Negative Potential Verb **anlayamamak.** [anla-y-a-ma-mak.] *not to be able to understand.*

anlayamadım. [anla-y-a-ma-dım.] *I could not understand.*

anlamasaydın. [anla-ma-sa-y-dın.] *if you did not understand.*

anlayamasaydın. [anla-y-a-ma-sa-y-dın.] *if you could not understand.* (adding the Negative Potential.)

anlayamamış. [anla-y-a-ma-mış.] *it seems he could not understand.* (Inferential Tense.)

anlaşılamayacaksak. [anla-şı-la-ma-y-acak-sak.] *if we will not be able to understood.* (Reciprocal Passive form.)

anlayamazsınız. [anla-y-a-maz-sınız.] *you cannot understand.*

anlaşamadılar. [anlaş-a-ma-dılar.] *they could not agre.e* -[lit: understand each other.] (Reciprocal form.)

Negative Potential E-Dotted Verbs Ending in a Vowel.

Basic Verb **beklemek** . *to wait, expect.*
Negative Potential Verb **bekleyememek.** [bekle-y-e-memek.] *not to be able to wait.*

bekleyemesem. *if I cannot wait.* (Conditional Tense.)

bekletemeyeceksin. *you will not be able to let (it/him) wait.* (Causative Form.)

beklenemedi. *it could not have been expected* . [lit: awaited] (Passive Form.)

bekleyemeyeceğiz. *we will not be able to wait.*

bekleyemezdiniz. *you couldn't have waited.*

bekleyememişler. *it seems that they could not wait.* (Inferential Tense.)

In speech this negative potential particle **-a- (-ya-)** or **-e- (-ye-)** is heavily accented in order to draw the attention of the listener.

29 MOODS WISH AND DESIRE

The Mood of Wish and Desire.

In Turkish Grammar this is called the *İstek Kipi* the Mood of Wish or Desire.

This mood is used quite widely in daily conversation, especially the first person singular and plural forms. The *İstek Kipi* gives a sense of doubt, uncertainty or wish *Let me..., Let us...* or in the negative *Let me not..., Let us not...*

The third person forms are also used regularly. Should a secretary say to the boss that *Ahmet bey* has arrived then the answer might be *Let him wait...* or *Let him come in...* then in these cases the *İstek Kipi* would be used.

For instance if a person is ill we will say *I hope you get better soon.* Turkish however will say **Geçmiş olsun** *Let it pass from you...*

The Personal Endings İstek Kipi

-eyim *let me or* **-ayım** *let me*
Ofiste bekleyeyim. [bekle-y-eyim] *Let me wait in the office.*
Nerede bekleyeyim sizi? *Where should I wait for you?*
Ne yapayım, dilimi mi keseyim? *What should I do, should I shut up?* [lit: cut my tongue.]
Batinin tekniğini alalım kültürünü almayalım. [alma -y -alım] *Let us take western technics, let us not take the culture.*

-sin -sın sun -sün *let him*
Olsun! Let it be! (so)
Olmasın!- Let it not be! (so).
Neden olmasın? *Why not?*

Çocuk kendini suçlu hissetmesin. *Let the child not feel guilty.*

-elim -alım *let us...*
Gidelim *Let us go; We better go!*
Birlikte bir kahve içelim mi? *Should we drink a coffee together?*
Neden egzersiz yapmayalım ki? *Why shouldn't we do that exercise?*
Ukrayna bizi etkileyecek ama panik yapmayalım. *Ukraine will affect us but let us not panic.*

-sinler -sınlar sünler -sunlar *let them...*
Gelsinler! *Let them come; They ought to come!*
Ondan korksunlar! *Let them fear that!*
Kaldırımlara arabaları park etmesinler, trafik kurallarına uysunlar. *They should not park on the pavement, let them conform to the traffic regulations.*

Negative Forms

Oraya gitmeyelim *Lets not go there.*
Ahmet mektuba bakmasın. *Let Ahmet not look at the letter*
Onu bulmasınlar *Hopefully they won't find it.*
Beklemeyeyim! *I'd better not wait.*

İstek Kipi Interrogative

The Interrogative Particle **mi?** or **mı?** is written separately but obeys Vowel Harmony Rules:
Geleyim mi? *Should I come (too)?*
Araba kullanalım mi? *Should we use the car?*
Kasabaya yürümeyelim mi? *Shouldn't we walk to town?*
Partiye gelsinler mi? *Should they come to the party?*

How to say Since...

This structure has the suffix **-eli -alı** *containing* added to the Verb Stem. The subject person is also stated and the tense is taken from the final main verb

Other ways of saying *since* are as follows:
-eli, -eli beri, -eliden beri *since*
All these mean *Since we came to Istanbul it has not rained.*
Biz İstanbul'a geleli hiç yağmur yağmadı.
Biz İstanbul'a geleli beri hiç yağmur yağmadı.
Biz İstanbul'a geleliden beri hiç yağmur yağmadı.

Since I, you, he etc. can also be translated as **-di(X) -eli** where the (X)-person is taken from the tense sign:
Mehmet İstanbul'a geldi geleli hiç yağmur yağmadı.
(Ben) İstanbul'a geldim geleli hiç yağmur yağmadı.
(Siz) İstanbul'a geldiniz geleli hiç yağmur yağmadı.
(Biz) İstanbul'a geldik geleli hiç yağmur yağmadı.
(Onlar) İstanbul'a geldiler geleli hiç yağmur yağmadı

These examples do not really need the subject **ben, sen, o, biz, siz, onlar** stated, as it is already evident from the verb endings **geldi, geldim, geldiniz, geldik, geldikler.**

30 PARTICIPLES

Participles, Verbal Adjectives and Nouns.

Participles are adjectives and nouns formed from verbs. *Learning can be fun.* "Learning" is a Verbal Noun. *The boiling kettle. The kettle which is boiling.* "Boiling" is a Verbal Adjective.

About Verbal Adjectives Nouns.
The most important function of participles is to form modifying phrases or adjectives equivalent to the relative clauses, "who, that, which, when" found in English languages. The use of participles in Turkish is rather different than in English and at first sight is difficult to understand. This is mainly due to the fact that the Relative Pronouns *who, what, which, where* are not used in Turkish as in English. Instead Turkish uses participles of its verbs as adjectives and nouns to show interrelation in sentences.

Subject Relative Participles -an/-en, -yan/-yen.

This Participle means "who does/that goes/which comes".
Example **gelen adam** *the man who comes/who is coming.*

Strip the **-mek** or **-mak** ending from the infinitive of any verb. Add **-(y)en** or **-(y)an** to the remaining verb stem. The buffer **-y-** is inserted if the verb stem ends in a vowel to avoid the occurrence of two consecutive vowels.

Subject Participle Positive Forms.

gelmek gelen [gel-en] *coming* [who/whom/that/which comes.]

sarılmak sarılan [sarıl-an] *hugging* [who/whom/that/which hugs.]

anlamak anlayan [anla-y-an] *understanding* [who/whom/that/which understands.]

beklemek bekleyen [bekle-yen] *waiting* [who/whom/that/which waits.]

Subject Participle Negative Forms.

gelmemek gelmeyen [gelme-y-en] *not coming* [who/whom/that/which is not coming.]

sarılmamak sarılmayan [sarılma-y-an] *not hugging* [who/whom/that/which is not hugging.]

anlamamak anlamayan [anlama-y-an] *not understanding* [who/whom/that/which is not understanding.]

beklememek beklemeyen [bekleme-y-en] *not waiting* [who/whom/that/which is not waiting.]

The buffer **-y-** is inserted in negative verbs all verb stems end in a vowel.

Examples of Relative Verbal Adjectives.

Öğle yemeğe gelen adamı tanırım. [#1 used as an adjective "gelen adam".] *I know the man who is coming to lunch.*

Akşam yemeğe geleni tanır mısınız? [#2 used as an noun "geleni" direct object.] *Do you know who is coming to dinner?*

Gelenlerden biri tanıyorum. *I know one of those who are coming.*

Bekleyenlere her şey gelir. *Everything comes to those who wait.*

Zengin olanlar çok şanslıdır. *Those who are rich are very lucky.*

The Relative Participle can be used as an adjective as in #1 above : **gelen adam** [the *coming* man] or as a noun as in #2 above: **Geleni tanır mısınız?** [gelen-i "the comer, who comes".]

Relative Participle Examples.

The suffix **-an** or **-en** is added to the verb stem or **-yan** or **-yen** after vowels.

yürümek. *to walk.*

284

yürüyen. [yürü-yen.] *who walks, who is walking.*
yürümemek. *not to walk.*
yürümeyen. [yürüme-yen.] *who doesn't walk, who is not walking.*

beklemek. *to wait.*
bekleyen. [bekle-yen.] *who waits, who is waiting.*
beklememek. *not to wait.*
beklemeyen. [beklemе-yen.] *who doesn't wait, who is not waiting.*

bakmak. *to look.*
bakan. [bak-an.] *which looks, who is looking.*
bakmamak. *not to look.*
bakmayan. [bakma-yan.] *which doesn't look, who is not looking.*

görmek. *to see.*
gören. [gören.] *who sees, who is seeing.*
görmemek. *not to see.*
görmeyen. [görme-yen.] *who doesn't see, who is not seeing.*

Relative Participle an actual example of a shop window

BİLGİSAYAR BİLEN BAYAN ELEMAN ARANIYOR.

advertisement: *"Computers who knows about [bilen] lady worker is being sought."*

The Relative Participle an Explanation.

Consider the sentences:
I know the man who is sitting in the chair.
I know the man sitting in the chair.

Here "who" is a relative pronoun referring to "the man" which may be omitted in English, as in the second version above. The word "sitting" is a present participle or verbal adjective describing the state of the man. The sentence above can be broken down to:

(1) The man is sitting in the chair.
(2) I know him.

One could also say:
I can see the bird that is flying in the sky,
I pulled the rope which was hanging down.

In these cases "which" and "that" are relative pronouns whilst "flying" and "hanging down" are present participles used as adjectives. In Turkish the present participle does the job of both the relative pronoun and the adjective. If we transpose the examples above to the form that Turkish exhibits, then they would convert as follows:

Sandalyede oturan adamı tanıyorum. *Chair-in sitting-who-is man-the know-I.*

Gökte uçan kuşu görebilirim. *Sky-in flying-which-is bird-the see-can-I.*

Sarkan ipi çektim. *Hanging down-which-was rope pulled-I.*

This last example is in the Past Tense. This is taken from the final verb of the sentence. The present participle "sitting" translates the relative pronoun by implication, "who is sitting, which is flying". It is important to understand that Turkish uses the verbal adjective as a relative pronoun "who, what, that, which", so it is always best to add "who is, which is, that is," in the English translation.

Other Examples.

Beni arayan kimse var mı? *Is there anybody (who is) looking for me?*

Ayakları kırılmış olan sandalye onarılmalıdır. *The chair whose legs are broken should be mended.*

Dışarıdaki oturan kız seni bekliyormuş. *The girl who is sitting outside is (apparently) waiting for you.*

Taksi isteyen adam bize demin eli salladı. *The man who wanted a* *taxi waved his hand at us just now.*

Arka bahçeye bakan pencere kırıldı. *The window facing the back garden is broken.* [Lit: Back garden-to looking-at-which-is (facing) broken-is.]

Mektup yazan adam çok yaşlıdır. *The man writing the letter is very old.* [Lit: Letter-the writing-who-is man-the old-is.]

Here is a sign in shop window.

"Experienced lady worker *who knows* **[bilen]** English is being sought."

İNGİLİZCE BİLEN TECRÜBELİ BAYAN ELEMAN ARANIYOR.

Examples in the Potential Mood:

The suffix **-an** or **-en** is added to the verb stem, (or either **-yan** or **-yen** after vowels.)

yürüyebilmek. *to be able to walk.*
yürüyebilen. [yürü-y-e-bil-en.] *who can walk.*

yürüyememek. *not to be able to walk*
yürüyemeyen. [yürü-y-e-me-y-en.] *who can't walk.*

The Relative Participle as a Noun.

As the Participle formed is a Verbal Noun, then we can add suffixes to it to change the meaning as we do with all Nouns in Turkish

Noun as Direct Object.

oturmak. *to sit. (or to live at.)*
oturan. *who is sitting / sitting .*(adj.)
oturanı. [otur-an-ı.] *who sits / sitter.*

Noun in Movement Toward Condition Singular.

uçmak. *to fly.*
uçan. *which is flying / flying.* (adj.)
uçana. [uç-an-a.] *to that flying / to the flier.*

Noun in Movement Toward Condition Plural.

yemek yemek. *to eat (food).*
yemek yiyen *who is eating / eater* (adj.)
yemek yiyenlere [yi-y-en-ler-e] *to those eating / to those who eat*

Noun in Movement Away Condition.

sarkmak. *to hang down.* (**sarkıtmak** causative *to dangle.)*
sarkan. *which is hanging down / hanging down.* (adj.)
sarkandan. [sark-an-dan.] *from that which is hanging down.*

Example of a Causative Verb.

Noun in Ownership Condition.

güldürmek. *to cause to laugh.*
güldüren. *which makes one laugh/comic, funny* (adj.)
güldürenin. [güldür-en-in.] *of that which makes one laugh/comic, funny.*

Example of a Passive Verb.

Noun in Movement Away Condition Plural.

kesilmek. *to be cut.*
kesilen. *which is being cut.* (adj.)
kesilenlerden. [kesil-en-ler-den.] *from those that are being cut.*

Adjectival Participle.

Then we can translate adjectivally, for the singular:

Masaya oturan adamı tanırım. *I know the man who is sitting at the table.* [Lit: Table-to (at) sitting man-the know-I.]
In this case **oturan** is an adjective describing *the man.*

And in the plural:

Masaya oturan adamları tanırım. *I know the men who are sitting at the table.* [Lit: Table-to sitting men-the know-I.]
Thus using **oturan** as an adjective describing *the men.*

The Participle as a Noun.

However we could say in Turkish as a noun for the singular:

Masaya oturanı tanıyorum. *I know (he) who is sitting at this table.*
[Lit: Table-to sitting-he-who-is know-I.]
Thus using **oturanı** as a relative pronoun. (singular direct object.)

And in the plural:

Masaya oturanları tanırdım. *I knew those who were sitting at the table.* [Lit: Table-to sitting-they-who-were knew-I.]
Thus using **oturanları** as a relative pronoun (plural direct object.)
The Past tense of this sentence is taken from the final verb.

Suffixed Participles.

The Relative Participle can be declined in both Singular and Plural Positive and Negative and in the Passive and Potential Moods of the verbs. The suffix **-an** or **-en** is added to the verb stem, and **-yan** or **-yen** after vowels.

Active Mood Subject Participles.

Positive Participle Active.

vermek. *to give.*
veren. *who gives.*
verenler. *those who are giving.*

Negative Participle Active.

vermemek. *not to give.*
vermeyen. *who doesn't give.*

vermeyenler. *those who don't give.*

Oğluma, hediye veren adam onun amcasıydı. *The man who gave the present to my son was his uncle.* [Lit: Son-my-to, present gave-who man-the his uncle-was.]

Ankara'ya giden otobüslerin hepsi doludur. *All of the buses which are going to Ankara are full up.* [Lit: Ankara-to of- going-which-are buses all full-are.]

Ankara'ya gidenlerin hepsi erkek. *All of those who are going to Ankara are male.* [Lit: Ankara-to of-going-those-who-are all male-are.]

Passive Mood Subject Participles.

Positive Participle Passive.

beklenmek. *to be expected.*
beklenen. *which is expected.*
beklenenler. *those who are expected.*

Negative Participle Passive.

beklenmemek. *not to be expected.*
beklenmeyen. *which is not expected.*
beklenmeyenler. *those which are not expected.*

The resulting **-an** or **-en** Relative Adjective is used to describe nouns, and can be used as a noun in its own right.

Potential Mood Active Examples.

The Positive Verb.
çalışabilmek. *to be able to work.*
çalışabilen. *who is able to work.*
çalışabilenler. *those who are able to work.*

The Negative Verb.
çalışamamak. *not to able to work.*
çalışamayan. *which is not able to work.*
çalışamayanlar. *those who are not able to work.*

The resulting **-an** or **-en** Relative Adjective is used to describe nouns, and can be used as a noun in its own right.

Participle Examples.

> # GÜNEŞ SİTESİNDE
> # AİT OLMAYAN
> # ARAÇLARIN PARK
> # ETMESİ YASAKTIR.

Here we see a sign at Ladies Beach in Kuşadası for restricted entry into the **Güneş (Sun) Site of Apartments**.

This sign shows how difficult Turkish can be to understand as the grammatical construction is alien to English Speakers. So let us explain what is happening:

Güneş sitesine. [Güneş site-si-ne.] *(In) to the Güneş Site.*
ait olmayan. *who is not concerned.* (with the site anyway.)
araçların park etmesi. *their car's its-parking.*
yasaktır. *is prohibited.*

Yüzebilenlere bir madalya verelim. *Let us give a medal to those who can swim.*
In this example the Relative Adjective is used as a noun with the Dative Suffix **-e** *to* added. [yüz-ebil-en-ler-e.]

Sokağımızda çalışamayan bir engelli oturuyor. *A disabled man who is unable to work is living in our street.*
In this example the Relative Adjective [çalış-a-ma-y an.] *who is unable to work / who can not work* is used to describe the noun **engelli** *invalid/cripple.*

Süremeyenlerden arabaları geri alınız. *Take away the cars from those who can't drive.*
In this example the Relative Adjective [sür-e-me-y-en-ler-den.] *from*

those who can not (are not able to) drive is used as noun with the addition of the suffix **-den** *from.*

Potential Mood Passive Examples.

This is an example of Turkish turning everything into an adjectival description wherever possible.

sürülememek. *not to be able to be driven.*
sürülemeyen. *which can not be driven.*
sürülemeyenler. [sürül-e-me-y-en-ler.] *those which can not be driven.*

Sürülemeyen arabaları çıkarınız. *Take away the cars which can not be driven.*
In the above example the Relative Adjective is used. [sürül-e-me-yen.]

yapılabilmek. *to be able to be done / made.*
yapılabilen. *which can be done.*
yapılabilenler. [yapılabil-en-le.r] *those which can be done.*

Yapılabilenleri bitirelim. *Let's finish those that can be done.*
In the above example the Relative Adjective [yap-ıl-abil-en-ler-i.] *those that can be done* (object) is used as a direct object noun.

Participle of "Olmak" olan *which is.*

The Verb **olmak** *to be, become.*

It can be deduced that the present participle of the verb **olmak** is **olan** meaning *which, is being* or if used as a pronoun means "that, who, which, what is" This is used with the Infinitive in the Locative Case to form a present continuous participle:

Yüzmekte olanları. (obj.) *those who are presently swimming.*
Denizde yüzmekte olanları tanırım. [olan-lar-ı.] *I know those who are presently swimming in the sea.*

Kalmakta olanlardan. *from those who are presently staying.*
Hırsızlar, otelde kalmakta olanlardan para çaldılar. [olan-lar-dan.] *The thieves stole money from those who are staying at the*

hotel.

Beklemekte olana. *to he who is waiting and still is waiting.*
Bu koliyi, beklemekte olana verin. [olan-a.] *Give this parcel to the man (he who is) waiting.*

About **olan** *being.*

Another use of **olan** is with normal adjectives to describe people and events as the following examples show. In these cases **olan** can sometimes be translated as *being, as a.* [Lit: "who is".]

Satılık olan bir ev arıyorum. *I am looking for a house which is for sale.* [Lit: For sale being a house look for-I.]

Çok pahalı olan bir fotoğraf makinesini aldım. *I have bought a camera which was very expensive.* [Lit: Very dear being a camera bought-I.]

Babası kasap olan bir arkadaşım var. *I have got a friend whose father is a butcher.* [Lit: Father-his butcher being a friend-mine there-is.]

Use of **olan** to mean *the one that.*

An explanation of **olan** *the which one.*

olanı. *One, the one that.* [lit: that which is.] as an item.
olanları *Ones, the ones that* [lit: those which are.] as items.

Hangi tişörtü istiyorsunuz? *Which tee-shirt do you want?*
Mavi olanı(nı) lütfen *The blue one, please.*

Hangi ayakkabıları istiyorsunuz? *Which shoes do you want?*
Siyah olanları(nı) lütfen. *The black ones, please.*

The **-ni** as an direct object ending is grammatically correct in the answers as the verb **istemek** *to want* is understood. But as with all languages sometimes the easy way is used and the direct object suffix is discarded though constant daily conversational usage.

The Participle of "bulunan" *which is (to be found)..*

The Verb **bulunmak** *to be found, to be.*

This verb "to be found" is the passive form of **bulmak** *to find.* It is used very much as in English. One might say to a friend you are meeting later on:

Bu akşam otele geldiğinde, ben barda bulunurum. *When you get to the hotel tonight, I'll be found in the bar.* [i.e. I'll be in the bar.]

Otelde bugünkünün gazeteleri bulunur mu? *Are there any of today's newspapers "to be found" in the hotel?* This construction is used is often in Turkish and is translated more easily by the verb *to be.*

The use of *bulunan* with adjectives:

Similarly another use of **bulunan** is used with adjectives to describe people and events as the following examples show. In these cases **bulunan** can sometimes be translated as *having a, containing a.*

İçinde beş kitap bulunan kutuyu getirin. *Bring along the box containing the five books.* [Lit: Inside five books-the found-which-are-to-be (containing) bring along.]

Bahçemizde bulunan güzel çiçekleri sana göstereyim. *Let me show you the beautiful flowers (which are) in our garden.* [Lit: Garden-ours-in found-which-are-to-be beautiful flowers you-to show-let-me.]

Verbal Adjective Future and Past Forms.

These participles are discussed in detail in the next chapters.

Present/Past Relative Participle
with the suffix **-(y)en/-(y)an.**

Future Relative Participle
with the suffix **-(y)ecek/-(y)acak.**

Past Direct Participle
with the suffix **-dik/-tik -dık/-tık -duk/-tuk -dük/-tük.**

Past Indirect (Inferential) Participle
with the suffix **mış -miş -muş -müş.**

Simple Present Positive Participle (Simple Tense)
with the suffix **-r/-er/-ar/-ir/-ır/-ur/-ür.**

Simple Present Negative Participle (Simple Tense)
with the suffix **-mez/-maz.**

These forms can function as either adjectives: **oynamayan çocuklar** *children who do not play* or as nouns: **oynamayanlar** *they/those who do not play.* The most important function of participles is to form modifying phrases or adjectives equivalent to the relative clauses found in English.

The relative pronouns "who, what, which, where" are not used in Turkish. Turkish uses participles of its verbs as adjectives or nouns. English relative construction "he man who sits." becomes "The sitting man." in Turkish by using the verbal adjective to describe the noun.

Past Tense Participles Direct and Indirect.

There are two types of Past Participle in Turkish: The first type is formed by suffixing **-miş** to the verb stem and is used when the participle is subject of the sentence. The second type is formed by the addition of **-dik** to the basic verb stem which is used as an Objective Participle for both the Present and Past Tenses.

The -*miş* Relative Past Participle.

The Relative Participle in **-miş** is used when the action is definitely completed. The **-miş** suffix does not take on a dubative or reportative sense when used as a participle. As with the present continuous participle the relation is completed by using the relative participle **olan** *that, who, which, is.*

vermiş olan. *given, which is given .*
verilmiş olan. *given, which has been given.*

vermemiş olan. *not given, which has not given.*

295

verilmemiş olan. *not been given, which has not been given.*

boyamış olan. *painted, which is painted.*
boyanmış olan. *painted, that has been painted.*

seçmiş olan. *chosen, which is chosen.*
seçilmiş olan. *chosen, that has been chosen.*

Seçilmiş olan şapkayı beğenirim. *I like the hat that has been chosen.*

Seçmiş olanı beğenirim. *I like the one who has chosen.*

Henüz gelmiş olan adamı tanırım. *I know the man who has just come.*

The **-miştir** Past Participle Official and Public Use.

The **-miştir** Past Participle is a happening which is definite in the past **kırılmıştır** *which has been broken* although we usually say in English *which is broken.*

Mavi kapı kırılmıştır. *The blue door is broken.* [Lit. has been broken.]

The **-miş** Past Participle is also used with suffix **-dir** to make an official definite statement.

Türkiye'de yapılmıştır. *Made in Turkey.* [Lit: Turkey-in made-which-has-been-is.]

Paslanmaz çelikten yapılmıştır. *Made from stainless steel.* [Lit: Stainless steel-from made-which-has-been-is.]

İzmir' de üretilmiştir. *Produced in Izmir.* [Lit: Izmir-in produced-which-has-been-is.]

31 OBJECT PARTICIPLES

Object Participles in "-dik/-tik" *that which is.*

This Participle is used for both Present and Past Tenses. A participle is an adjective which is formed from a verb, and as such it precedes the noun which it describes. Being a relative participle then it can also serve as a noun and therefore have the personal suffixes and the suffixes of declension added thus forming a relative clause. It is used for both the present and past tenses, only the context of the situation pertaining will tell which tense to use in English.

Object Participle Formation "-dik/-diği, tik/-tiği ".

The **-mek** or **-mak** is dropped from the Infinitive of the Verb and is replaced by the suffix **-dik/-tik** which is subject to vowel harmony.

Object Participle the E-Dotted Vowels.

gelmek. *to come.*
geldik. *that came/that which is coming.*

girmek. *to enter.*
girdik. *that which entered/that which is entering.*

bölmek. *to divide.*
böldük. *that which divided/that which is dividing.*

gülmek. *to laugh.*
güldük. *that which laughed/that which laughs.*

Object participle the A-UnDotted Vowels.

bakmak. *to look.* (Uses Consonant Mutation -tık.)
baktık. *that which looked at/that which looks at.*

çıkmak. *to exit.*

çıktık. *that which went out/that which is exiting.*

donmak. *to freeze.*
donduk. *that which froze/that which is freezing.*

tutmak. *to hold.*
tuttuk. (tut-tuk.) *that which held/that which is holding.*

Generally this participle is not used in its pure form as above but is always personalized. This participle just happens to be the same as the 1st Person Plural of the Simple Past Definite Tense, the suffix -**dik/-tik** or **-dık/-tık** or **-duk/-tuk** or **-dük/-tük** according to Vowel Harmony and Consonant Mutation Rules, but as it seldom used in its simple form then it is not possible to mistake it. Being a Participle (verbal adjective) it describes a noun so therefore it precedes its noun, and as it is not a verb then it does not stand in final position in the sentence. From this is becomes easier to recognize it as a verbal adjective by its position in any sentence.

Oynadığım park bu köşede. [Oyna-dığ-ım.] *The park where I play is on this corner.*

En çok sevdiğin kitap nedir? [sev-diğ-in.] *Which book do you like best?*

Gönderdiği koliyi aldım. [Gönder-diğ-i koli-yi.] *I have received the parcel that he sent.*

Geldiğimiz araba yepyenidir. [Gel-diğ-imiz.] *The car in which we came is brand new.*

Beğendiğiniz perdeleri bulamadım. [Beğen-diğ-iniz.] *I could not find the curtains that you liked.*

Bu çocukların her gün yaptıkları şey nedir? [Yap-tık-ları.] *What is it that these children do every day.*

The **-dik** Objective Participle is used for both present and past time. When suffixed with personal pronouns it is equivalent to the English relative participle "who, that, which, where, when".

The final **-k** changes to **-ğ** before the possessive suffix, except when adding "-lar" third person plural suffix.

Oturduğumuz ev budur. *This is the house in which we live.*
Oturduğunuz ev budur. *This is the house in which you live.*
Oturdukları ev budur. *This is the house in which they live.*

Adjectives can be turned into nouns in Turkish.

Mehmet, kendiye verdiğim hediyeyi beğendi. *Mehmet liked the present that I gave to him(self).*

Here the participle **verdiğim.** *that which I gave* describes **hediyeyi** [hediye-yi] *the present* which the object of the final verb **beğendi** *he liked.*

In Turkish the participle "verdiğim" can be turned into a noun and placed in the objective case itself: **Mehmet, verdiğimi beğendi.** *Mehmet liked what I gave.*

The Object Participle used as a Noun.

Let us give some examples in both present and past in all persons. These relative pronouns are in the objective case as a direct object of the verb **bilmek** *to know.* The pronoun, object and the verb are personalised to show "who is loving and who is being lived and who knows".

Seni sevdiğimi biliyorum. [sev-diğ-im-i.] *I know that I love you.*
Seni sevdiğimi bildim. *I knew that I loved you.*

Beni sevdiğini biliyorum. [sev-diğ-in-i.] *I know that you love me.*
Beni sevdiğini bildim. *I knew that you loved me.*

Onun beni sevdiğini biliyorum. [sev-diğ-i-n-i.] *I know that he/she love me.*
Onun seni sevdiği bildim. *I knew that he/she loved you.*
Here **Onun** *his/her* is used to show the third person meaning clearly.

Mehmet'i sevdiğimizi biliyorum. [sev-diğ-imiz-i.] *I know that we love Mehmet.*

Mehmet, seni sevdiğimizi bildi. *Mehmet knew that we loved you.*

Mehmet'i sevdiğinizi biliyorum. [sev-diğ-iniz-i.] *I know that you love Mehmet.*

Mehmet, Ayşe'yi sevdiğinizi bildi. *Mehmet knew that you loved Ayshe.*

Seni sevdiklerini biliyorum. [sev-dik-leri-n-i.] *I know that they love you.*

Mehmet, seni sevdiklerini bildi. *Mehmet knew that they loved you.*

Başkan hiç beklemediği bir sürprizle karşılaşır. *The Prime Minster meets with an unexpected surprise.*

Galatasaray taraftarının beklediği haber çiktı. *The news that the Galatasaray fans were waiting for has arrived.*

Gece karanlığından bıktığımızı bilmezler mi? *Don't they know that we are fed up with the dark nights?*

Gece karanlığından bıktığımızı bilmediler mi? *Didn't they know that we were fed up with the dark nights?*

Otomobilinizle hızla giderken dümdüz bir duvara çarptığınızı hayal edin. *Just imagine colliding head-on with a wall while travelling at speed in your car.*

Otomobilimizle hızla giderken dümdüz bir duvara çarptığımızı hayal edin. *Just imagine that we collided head-on with a wall while travelling at speed in our car. (*See the difference?)

The participle can be past or present in meaning.

Ford yeni bir tasarım ekibi kurduklarını söylüyor. *Ford are saying that they are setting up a new design team.*

Libya, petrol üretimini durdurduklarını bildirdi. *It has been reported that Libya have halted their petrol production.*

Mehmet, seçtiğimi beğenmemiş. *Mehmet did not like what I chose. (seemingly.)*

Mehmet, yaptığını beğenmemiş. *Mehmet did not like what you did.(seemingly.)*

Mehmet, söylediğini beğenmemiş.
Mehmet did not like what he said. (seemingly.)

Mehmet, bulduğumuzu beğenmemiş.
Mehmet did not like what we found. (seemingly.)

Mehmet, aldığınızı beğenmemiş.
Mehmet did not like what you bought. (seemingly.)

Mehmet, değiştirdiklerini beğenmemiş.
Mehmet did not like what they changed. (seemingly.)

Object Participle Usage.

This **-dik/-tik -duk/-tuk -dık/-dık -dük/-tük** suffix is often difficult to recognize as it has so many forms due to vowel harmony operating in its internal vowel and consonant mutation operating on both the initial **-d** and the terminal **-k.**
If a further suffix with a vowel is added the final **-k** is also subject to Consonant Mutation: **-diği/-tiği -duğu/-tuğu -dığı/-tığı -düğü/-tüğü.**

bulmak. *to find.*
Bulduğum şapka. *The hat which I found.*

seçmek. *to choose.*
Seçtiğin kitap. *The book that you are choosing/chose.*

görmek. *to see.*
Gördüğü araba. *The car that he sees/saw.*

yazmak. *to write.*
Yazdığımız mektup. *The letter we are writing/that we wrote.*

demek. *to say.*
Dediğiniz gibi. *Like (what) you say/said.*

sevmek. *to like.*
Sevdikleri dondurma. *The ice cream that they liked.*
Bulduğum mendil beyaz renklidir. *The handkerchief that I found is white coloured.*

Yazdığımız mektuplar burada. *The letters that we wrote are here.*

Çalıştığım büro (ofis) kapalı. *The office where I work is closed/ The office where I worked is closed.*

Söyledikleri mantıklıdır. *What they are saying/said is/was sensible.*

The addition of **-dır** onto **mantıklı** [Lit: logical] makes it a Statement of Fact.

Reiteration: The Subject Participle "-en/-an".

Here we re-iterate about the Subject Participle discussed in the previous Cheaper 30 and Object Participle as it is difficult to realise for English Speakers.

To reiterate; a participle is an adjective so it describes a noun and therefore always precedes the noun (or noun phrase) that it describes. The subject participle describes or signifies the person/thing who is doing something, the subject of the sentence.

Çalan zil *The bell which is ringing..*

This description itself can be an Object of another verb:
Çalan zili duyabiliriyorum. [zil-i.] *I can hear the bell (obj.) which is ringing.*

Çalan zili duyabildim. *I could hear the bell which was ringing.*

The passive of **çalmak** is **çalınmak** so the above sentence in the Passive is: **Çalınan zili duyabiliyorum.** *I can hear the bell that is being rung.*

Çalınan zili duyabildim. *I could hear the bell that was being rung.*

The **-an/-en** Subject Participle being an adjective does not show the tense. The tense is taken from the main verb at the end of the sentence.

Reiteration: The Object Participle "-dik, -duk, dık, -dük".

The Object Participle describes the person/thing that is actioned by something as an Object.

çaldığı zil *the bell that is/was rang.*

This description itself can be an Object of another verb:
Mehmet'in çaldığı zili duyabiliyorum. *I can hear the bell that Mehmet is/was ringing.* Mehmet is actioning the "ringing".

In Turkish if a Participle is put between the nouns composing "possessive construction" there is no need to use a "possessive suffix" at the end of the second noun. "Mehmet'in çaldığı zilini : This is wrong objective "-ni" is not used.

Similarly in the Passive:

Mehmet tarafından çalınan zili duyabiliyorum. *I can hear the bell that is/was being rung by Mehmet.* The bell's ringing is being actioned by Mehmet.

Ayşe'nin okuduğu kitabı sen de okumak istiyor musun? *Do you also want to read the book that Ayshe is/was reading?*

Ayşe'nin okuduğu kitabını sen de okumak istiyor musun? : Is wrong ["kitabı" is correct.]

If an adjective is put between the nouns composing "possessive construction" *it is necessary to use a "possessive suffix"* at the end of the second noun.

Ayşe'nin kalın kitabını bulamıyorum. *I cannot find Ayshe's thick book.*

Annesi, evin küçük odasını ailenin en küçük çocuğuna verdi. *The mother gave the house's small room to the smallest child.*

Lack of Relative Pronouns in Turkish.

As already stated, there is no Relative Participle in Turkish "that, who, which, when"; there are no question marks supplied as these are relative pronouns in English. "Turkishified" English will say:

çalan zili. *the ringing bell/the bell which is/was ringing.*
-en/-an Subjective Participle, *the bell* is the subject.

çaldığı zili. *the bell that he is ringing/that he rung.*
-dik/-dığı Objective Participle.

çalındığı zili. *the bell that is/was being rung.*
This example shows the Passive Verb.

A Further Explanation -dik/-dığı Objective Participle.

In the Object Participle **geldiğim zaman** *When I came* "time" is the object of "my coming."
Using the Subject Participle **gelen zaman** means the *time itself is coming* (the future or next time.)

Tense of Sentence taken from main Verb.

Ali'nin geldiği zaman, çarşıya gidiyoruz. *When Ali comes we ARE GOING to the shops.*

Ali'nin geldiği zaman, çarşıya gittik. *When Ali CAME we WENT to the shops.*

Thus it becomes that both ideas, "Ali" and his "coming" both become a compound participle (verbal adjective) to describe **zaman** *time*. This is more suitable to the Turkish point of view than the relative "when" construction which English uses.

The use of "ki" "that".

The Persian **ki** can be used to produce a relative clause in Turkish but it is alien to the language and this method should be avoided or you will be marked as a foreigner.

Biliyorum ki beni seviyorsun. *I know that you love me.*

The Persian method understandable and often used but wrong. This method is based on Persian Grammar and is more suitable to European thinking. However the construction shown below comes over as more natural to the Turk.

Biliyorum ki beni seviyorsun. Is not the natural Turkish method

Beni sevdiğini biliyorum. Is the correct method according to Turkish Grammar, using the object participle:

Beni sevdiğ-in-i biliyorum. -[Lit: Me that-love-you know I.]

Explanation:

Beni [me] **sevdiğini** [that you love] **biliyorum** [I know].
"sevdik" [that loves] + "-in" [you/your] + "-i" [object marker for the verb] becomes "sevdiğini.".

We can see that the correct method uses the **-dik** Relative Object participle. Thus it becomes that both ideas, the "person" and "their loving" become objects of the verb "I know".

Future Objective Participle (y)ecek.

This Participle in its simple form consists of the verb stem with the addition of the Future Tense Sign **-ecek** or **-acak**. The **-mek/-mak** is dropped from the Infinitive of the Verb and is replaced by the suffix **-ecek/-acak** which is subject to vowel harmony.

gelmek *to come* **gelecek** *which will come.*
girmek *to enter* **girecek** *which will enter.*
bölmek *to divide* **bölecek** *which will divide.*
gülmek *to laugh* **gülecek** *which will laugh.*

bakmak *to look* **bakacak** *that will look.*
donmak *to freeze* **donacak** *which will freeze.*
çıkmak *to exit* **çıkacak** *that will go out.*
tutmak *to hold* **tutacak** *which will hold.*

This **-ecek/-acak** future participle can be used in its pure form and also personalized. This participle happens to be the same as the 3rd person singular of the Future Tense but it is not possible to mistake it. Being an adjective it is never last in the sentence. It usually describes a noun.

Yarınki yapacağım iş önemli. *The work that I will do tomorrow will be important.*

Yapılabilecek bir şey yok. [yap-ıl-ebil-ecek.] *There is nothing that can be done.* (from a future aspect.)

Oturacak değilim. *I don't intend to sit.* [Lit: to sit (as a future aspect.), I am not going to sit down.]

Future Participle Real-life Examples.

"Hayır" diyemeyeceğiniz tek lezzet. *The only taste that you will not be able to say "No" (to).* [Lit: "No" that-you-will-not-be-able-to-say only taste.]

"HAYIR" DİYEMEYECEĞİNİZ TEK LEZZET

Here is a slogan from a famous Nut Spread bottle for sandwiches. It can be seen an all the supermarket shelves.
The only taste that you will not be able to say "No" (to).

Explanation:

As **di-ye-me-y-eceğ-iniz** precedes the noun **lezzet** *taste*, it is a Verbal Adjective or Future Participle describing this noun.

If we break this Future Participle into its components:

di-ye-me becomes *not to be able to say.*
di-ye-me-y-eceğ becomes *will not be able to say.*
di-ye-me-y-eceğ-iniz becomes *that you will not be able to say.*

Thus the whole meaning becomes:
In Turkish English: *"No" that-you-will-not-be-able-to-say only taste.*

In English English: "The only taste that you will not be able to say "No" to.

A "real life" example.

While walking around the market with my wife in Izmir one time, we were dragged into a carpet shop and plied with both cups of tea and a sales pitch from the carpet seller. We "escaped" by saying:

Bey efendi teşekkür ederiz fakat hiç bir şey alacak değiliz. *Thank you sir but we are not about to purchase anything at all.*

Another "real life" example.

Here is an actual email from the web where the writer is asking advice about his employment and it changes. there are many instances of Future Object Participles and Past Tense Object Participles.

"Merhaba, Ben 14 seneden beri ayni firmada sistem mühendisi olarak çalışmaktaydım. Firmam başka bir firma ile birleşince iş hayatıma bu yeni firma altında devam ettim. Bu geçiş surecinde istersek işten **çıkabileceğimiz** ve tazminat *(compensation)* **alabileceğiz** söylendi. Biz istemedik. Aradan gecen 16 ayda yönetim tarafında bir çok değişiklik oldu ve biz artık oluşan bu yeni yönetim organizasyonunda **olmayacağımızı** ve çıkmak **istediğimizi** söyledik."

"Hello, I have been working for the same company for (since) 14 years as a systems engineer. When my company combined with another company, I continued my working life under this new company. In was said during this transition period *that we would be able to leave* the job if we wished and *that we would be able to claim* compensation. We did not want to. A lot of changes were made in the intervening 16 months by the management side, and we said *that we would not be* in [part of] the organization which is comprised of the new management any longer and *that we would wish to leave.*"

"Fakat bize **dedikleri** "Biz sizi bırakmak istemiyoruz, siz bize lâzımsınız. Bizler, sizlerden memnunuz." Biz, işe böyle bir yönetim altında devam **edemeyeceğimizden** dolayı, ayrılmakta **kararlı olduğumuzu** söyledik. Onlarda bize bu şartlarda *(conditions)* **tazminat ve diğer haklarımızın yanacağını** söylediler. Ne yapmamız lazım lütfen yardim."

"But *what they said* to us "We do not want you to leave, you are necessary to us. We are happy with you" Because *we could not continue* under such a management we stated *that our decision was to leave.* They have stated with these conditions *that our compensation and other rights will have become invalid.* "What should we do, please help.?"

How to say *Instead of* with the Future Participle.

There is a special construction in Turkish when making a choice between future actions. This consists of The future Participle + Person + Dative (motion toward) Particle **-a/-e.**

oturacağıma. [oturacağ-ım-a.] *instead of me sitting.* (future participle + person + dative particle.)

Bahçede oturacağımıza salonda oturalım. *Instead of sitting in the garden let us sit in the salon.*

This construction is difficult for English speakers to understand, so it can be considered idiomatic to the Turkish language.

Relative Object Participle Examples.

Oturduğun şehri ziyaret ettim. *I visited the city where you live(d).*

Bana verdiğin hediyeyi kaybettim. *I have lost the present that you gave me.*

İlk karşılaştığımız yeri hatırlıyor musun? *Do you remember the place where we first met?*

İlk karşılaştığımız zaman hatırlıyor musun? *Do you remember the time when we first met?*

Çantanı bıraktığım yere geri dönüyorum. *I am going back to the place where I left your bag.*

Çantası bırakmış olduğu yere geri döndüm.
I went back to the place where he had left his bag.

Future Object Participle Examples.

Londra'ya çıkacağımız zaman saat beş'tir. *5 o'clock is the time that we will leave for London.*

Uçağın kalkacağı zamanı bilmiyorum. *I don't know what time the* *plane will take off.*

Evleneceğim kızı tanıştırmak istiyorum. *I want to introduce the girl that I'm going to marry.*

A Joke: Fakirlik *Poverty*:

This joke shows various examples of Turkish participles.

Günlerden bir gün bir baba ve zengin ailesi oğlunu köye götürdü. Bu yolculuğun tek amacı vardı, insanların ne kadar fakir **olabileceklerini** oğluna göstermek.
Çok fakir bir ailenin çiftliğinde bir gece ve gün geçirdiler.
Yolculuktan **döndüklerinde** baba oğluna sordu:
-İnsanların ne kadar fakir **olabildiklerini** gördün mü?
-Evet!
-Ne öğrendin peki?
Oğlu yanıt verdi:
- Şunu gördüm: Bizim evde bir köpeğimiz var, onlarınsa dört.
- Bizim bahçenin ortasına kadar uzanan bir havuzumuz var, onlarınsa sonu **olmayan** bir dereleri.
- Bizim bahçemizde ithal lambalar var, onlar inşa yıldızları.
- Bizim görüş alanımız on avluya kadar, onlarsa bütün bir ufku görüyorlar.
Oğlu sözünü **bitirdiğinde** babası söyleyecek bir şey bulamadı.
Oğlu ekledi:
-Teşekkürler, baba. Ne kadar fakir olduğumuzu **gösterdiğin** için!

This joke shows that often Turkish will use a dash (-) to introduce speech instead of "inverted commas".

Simple Present Participles.

The Simple Present Tense is called "Geniş Zaman Wide Tense" in Turkish. It is also known as the aorist or timeless tense grammar. This verb tense is used for habitual situations. The tense participle also has this same sense for when used as an adjective and it precedes the noun which it describes. The formation of both the positive **-ir -ır -ür -ur** and negative **maz -mez** participles is the same as their respective simple present tense bases.

Positive Timeless Participle in "-r".

The simple present tense positive sign **-r** is used to mark this type of participle.

akmak *to flow* becomes **akar** *that which flows.* (continually, habitually.)

If we place the tense base after the noun then it is a verb:

Nehir, denize kadar akar. *The river flows as far as the sea.*

However if we use it in front of a noun then it is an adjective meaning *that which flows.*

Yatak odasında akar su var. *There is running water in the bedroom.* [Meaning water is available in that room.]

This is at variance with the Present Participle **akan** *which is flowing.* Here the meaning is different.

Yatak odasında akan su var. *There is water (which is) flowing in the bedroom.* [The meaning here is that there is leak or maybe the roof is leaking.]

It is apparent that the wide tense participle in **-r** describes what generally happens as a rule and the Present Participle in **-an - en** describes what is happening now.

Many Wide Tense Participles have entered the language as common nouns in their own right.

Yazmak *to write.* simple present tense base **yazar** *writer/author.*

Bu kitabın yazarı Orhan Kemal'dır. *The writer/author of this book is Orhan Kemal.*

But if we were to use the Present Participle then the meaning changes.

Bu kitabın yazanı Orhan Kemal'dır *It is Orhan Kemal who wrote* *this book.*

Negative Timeless Participle in "-mez".

The negative participle is also used as an adjective to describe the general state of things. English also uses this construction.

I saw an unbelievable film last night. [which is not able to be believed.]

It was an unforgettable film last night. [which is not able to be forgotten.]

Here we in English are using the negative participle as an adjective by placing it in front of its noun.

But it can also take its verbal form as well:
The film I saw last night was unbelievable. [It could not be believed] as a verb.

The film was unforgettable. [It was not able to be forgotten] as verb.

It is all a matter of position of the participle. Placed before its noun it is an adjectival description. Placed after its noun it becomes a verb. Turkish uses these participles in exactly the same manner as English.

Formation of the Negative Timeless Participle.

The simple present tense negative sign **-maz/-mez** is used to mark this participle.

akmak *to flow.* becomes **akmaz.** [That which does not flow continually, habitually.]

İnanılamaz bir şey oldu! *An unbelievable thing has happened!* ["inan-ıl-a-maz" that which is not able to be usually believed.]

Dün akşam unutulamaz bir filim seyrettik. *We watched an unforgettable film last night.*

Garajınızda kullanılamaz olan eski bir bisiklet buldum. ["kullan-ıl-a-maz olan" that which is unable to be used.] *I found an old* *unusable bicycle in your garage.*

This example shows the addition of **olan** *that which is,* the present participle of **olmak** thus helping the listener to discern that the participle is an adjective.

Common Nouns Negative.

Many of these negative participles have also become nouns in their own right. The usual example of this is **çıkmaz** *that which does not exit.*

This has come to mean a *"cul-de-sac",* so one can often see the sign **çikmaz sokak** *a street with no exit, cul-de-sac.* It can also be found on doors which lead nowhere in public buildings **çikmaz** *no exit .* [Lit Does not exit.]

How to say: *As soon as* **"..-ir ..-mez".**

There is one formula to translate *as soon as* which uses both positive and negative Wide Tense participles in apposition: This formula is quite heavily used in every day speech.

Biz gelir gelmez yemek yiyelim *As soon as we come, lets eat (a meal).*

The translation of *as soon as I come/came.* **Ben gelir gelmez** *As soon as* is translated by using the Wide Tense Positive and Negative Participles in apposition: **...ir ...mez**, as in **Sen gelir gelmez** *As soon as you come/came.*

1. The person (subject) has to be stated as it is not apparent from the verb form.

2. The tense is taken from the verb of the final statement.

3. Very often the word *when* can be substituted for *as soon as* in English.

Examples showing changes in person:

Ben gelir gelmez bir kaza oldu. *As soon as I came an accident happened.*

Sen gelir gelmez bir kaza oldu. *As soon as you came an accident happened.*

O gelir gelmez bir kaza olacakmış. *As soon as he comes an accident will probably happen.*

Mehmet gelir gelmez bir kaza olabilir. *As soon as Mehmet comes an accident may happen.*

Biz gelir gelmez bir kaza oldu. *As soon as we came an accident happened.*

Siz gelir gelmez bir kaza oldu. *As soon as you came an accident happened.*

Onlar gelir gelmez bir kaza oldu. *As soon as they came an accident happened.*

Polis gelir gelmez başka bir kaza oldu. *As soon as the police came another accident happened.*

Biz çıkar çıkmaz annem gelecekmiş. *As soon as (when) we go out my mother may arrive.*

Onlar oraya varır varmaz partı başlayacak. As soon as (when) they arrive there the party will begin.

32 SAYING *"WHILE"* İKEN

Saying *while, when* "iken".

There are various ways of describing time relationships in English, consider:

When I saw him, I waved at him.
When I see him, I shall wave at him.
As soon as I see him I shall wave at him.
Whenever I see him I wave at him.
Every time I see him I wave at him.
If I see him, I shall wave at him.

It can be seen from above that the Adverbial Clause of time has a slightly different sense in relation to tense, time and duration. The Adverbial Clause of Time are best studied by example, as it is sometimes rather difficult at first to relate the English Constructions to the corresponding Turkish ones. Turkish uses the Relative Adjectival Participles widely and at first sight they may be difficult to analyze. They are logical constructions however, and as such a little reading and study will be rewarding in hastening understanding.

Using iken -ken -yken meaning *while.*

iken can stand alone or be suffixed as **-ken** when added to consonants or **-yken** (when added to vowels). It is invariable and does not follow the rules of vowel harmony. It does not take further suffixes. **iken** is used when the verb action is continuous at a point in time. It may also follow an adjective.

iken with the Present Tenses.

-ken is always suffixed to the verb tense sign.

As the subject is not always evident, then it is stated as in the examples below.

Mehmet kasabaya yürüyorken onu gördüm. *I saw Mehmet while (he was) walking to town.*

Sen kasabaya yürüyorken, seni gördüm. *I saw you while (you were) walking to town.*

Ben kasabaya yürüyorken, seni gördüm. *I saw you while (I was) walking to town.*

Biz kasabaya yürüyorken, onu gördük. *We saw him while we were walking to town.*

Siz dans ediyorken, dinleneyim. *Let me rest while you are dancing.*

Onlar dans ediyorken, dinlenelim. *Let's rest while they dance.*

Biz kasabaya yürürken, onu her gün görürüz. *Every day we see him when (while) we walk to town.* Simple present habitual *yürü-r-ken*]

As **iken** can not be suffixed to pronouns the Personal Subject Pronouns have to be used to point to the subject. The last example shows a slight difference in meaning due to the differing use in the Wide Tense and Present Continuous Tenses.

iken with Adjectives.

iken can be used with adjectives, in this case it can stand alone or be suffixed:

Ben, hasta iken (hastayken), uyurum. *I sleep while (when) I am ill.*

Biz, o hastayken, merak ettik. *While he was ill, we worried.*

Onlar, siz uykudayken, meşgul olacaklar. *They will be busy while you are asleep.*

Uykudayken, soyuldular. *They were robbed while they were asleep.*

Here the 3rd Person Plural comes from the last verb. It is in the Passive Mood thus states the subject. The Subject Pronouns are used clarify the meaning.

iken with the Past Tenses.

If the action is continuous in the past then **iken** can be translated into English: *As (subject) was/were (verb) + -ing.*
As I was going to town I saw him.
As we were going to town I saw him.

Past Definite Tense with iken:

Ben İngiltere'deyken, yağmur yağdı . *While I was in England, it rained.*

Past Continuous Tense with iken:
Biz İngiltere'ye giderken, yağmur yağıyordu. *When we were going to England it was raining*

tam iken *just as.*

A further construction with **iken** is *"just as"* or *"right at the moment that"*. This construction uses the word **tam** *complete* to introduce the Adverbial Clause at the point in time:

Biz tam evden çıkarken, yağmur yağmağa başladı. *Just as we were leaving the house it started to rain.*

Onlar tam kapıyı açarken, anahtar koptu. *Just as they were opening the door the key broke.*

Future Tense vith iken -ecekken/-acakken.

When attached to the Future Tense the meaning of **iken** becomes *just as I was about to or instead of.*

İngiltere'ye gidecekken, Türkiye'de kaldık. *Instead of going to England we stayed in Turkey.*
This may seem difficult to understand but it can be analyzed that **iken** *as/while* is suffixed to the Future Participle **gidecek** *that about to go/which will go* and the Turkish aspect becomes apparent. *"We,*

while about to go to England, did something different" (ie. We stayed in Turkey.) This sense is best translated into English as : *instead of -ing.*

Türkiye'de kalacakken, İngiltere'ye gidelim. *Instead of staying in Turkey let's go to England.*

The -miş Past Participle with iken.

This takes to form of: **-mişken -mışken -müşken -muşken.**

This construction produces **-mişken** as in **yapmışken** *having done*
yapmışken. *having done.*
yapılmışken. *having been done.*

görmüşken. *having seen.*
görülmüşken. *having been seen.*

Bu iş bitirilmişken, eve gidelim. *This job having been finished, lets go home.*

Aklıma gelmişken, söyleyeyim. *Having come to (my) mind, let me tell you.*

Hazır gelmişken bir kahveni içelim. *Having already come, let us drink one of your coffees.*

The Negative Simple Present -mazken/-mezken.

-mezken, -mazken means *though not or while it isn't.* This construction is normally used in news and commercials.

Galatasaray'ın yıldız futbolcularından Necati Ateş, kendilerine ödeme yapılamazken, bazı yabancı oyuncuların alacaklarının verildiğini duymanın üzüntü verici olduğunu söyledi. *One of the star players of Galatasaray, Necati Ates, has said that it was disappointing to hear that some foreign players' debts had been paid while there can not be a payment for themselves.*

Konu hakkında henüz herhangi bir bilgiye ulaşılamazken,

araştırmaların devam ettiği bildirildi.
Here is the "Turkish" English:
While any information can't be reached yet about the subject, it has been told that the investigations keep on.
Here is the "English" English:
Although as yet no information can be communicated about the subject, it has been stated that investigations are continuing.

We can see some differences of tense and negation in the change from "Turkish" English to "English" English. This is because of:

(1) Basic grammatical structure differences between the two languages.

(2) The difference in local daily usage of each language.

(3) It also underlines the fact that literal translation between the two languages is often difficult, and it is better to arrive a suitable translation in one's own language.

Of course the above examples could be translated into English in a different way whilst still retaining the intended meaning in Turkish. A positive statement usually follows this negative form.

The Conversational Method.

In order to get the meaning for *Though not, or while it isn't,* The following method is a little formal (although it is correct):

Çalışmazken susuzum. *Although I have not worked I am thirsty.*

Sürmezken yolu bilirim. *Although I do not drive I know the road.*

From the last two examples above it can be seen that **iken** takes its person from the main verb at the end of each sentence.

Substituting *"despite"* for **-mazken** (more informal). To arrive at the meaning *though not or while it isn't* a construction with **-a rağmen** *in spite of, despite* is used:

Çalışmamama rağmen susuzum. *Despite not working I am thirsty.*

Ben sürmememe rağmen yolu bilirim. *Although I do not drive I*

318

know the road.

Explanation:

Sür-me-me-m-e
1st **-me** is short infinitive from "sürmek" "to drive" [sür-me].
2nd **-me** is negative short infinitive from "sürmemek" "to not drive" [sür-me-me].
3rd **-m** is suffix producing a verbal noun for 1st sing. Person "sürmemem" "my not driving" [sür-me-me-m].
And Finally **-e** is suffix for Movement Towards Condition (dative case) "to my not driving" [sür-me-me-m-e] with the addition of "rağmen" to give the meaning of "in spite of/despite".
Conversational stress is on the first syllable, preceding the negation suffix.[**sür**-me-me-m-e.]

Another example: **bilmememe rağmen** means *Although I don't/didn't know.* An analysis of this construction:

Bilmek *to know something.*
Bilme *to know*, short infinitive positive from *bilmek.*
Bilmeme *to not know*, short infinitive negative from *bilmemek.*
Bilmemem *My not knowing.*
-e rağmen *In spite of*

Bilmememe rağmen. *Despite my not knowing/Although I don't/didn't know.*

Mehmet sürememesine rağmen yolu bilirmiş. *Although Mehmet can not drive it seems that he knows the road.* [Inferential Tense]

The basic sentence is "Mehmet yolu bilirmiş." "It seems Mehmet knows the road." to which we add "although he can not drive".

Explanation of Sür-e-me-me-si-n-e.

1st **-e-me** is negation suffix of inability. [sür-e-me-mek.]
2nd **-me** is noun producing suffix. [sür-eme-me.] This is the short Infinitive Verbal Noun from "sürememek" "to not be able to drive".
3rd **-si** is suffix for 3rd. sing. Person [sür-eme-me-si "his (Mehmet's) inability to drive"].

The **-(n)e** is a suffix for Movement Towards Condition (using the buffer letter "-n-") thus producing **sürememesine** [sür-eme-me-si-n-e]. Finally the addition of "rağmen" to give the meaning of "in spite of/despite".

33 VERBAL NOUNS

Verbal Nouns.

Further explanations and examples are in the following Chapter 34.

The suffix -(y)e, -(y)a.

The Wish/Desire Verb sign **-(y)e, -(y)a** [indicates repeated or continuing activity simultaneous with the main verb.]

Gide gide çarşıya mi gittin? *Did you go along to the shops then?* (going and going.)

Göz göre göre onu yaptı. *He did it, eyes wide open.* (open and open.)

Güle güle! *(Leave) Happily!* [said to someone who is departing from "gülmek" "to laugh.".]

Güle güle kullan! *Use it with smile!*
[said to one who has obtained a new item that they will enjoy.]

-(y)erek, -(y)arak by doing.

The addition of the suffix **-rek** or **-rak** Wish/Desire verb base of the verb means "by doing". **bilerek** [bil-e-rek] *knowingly.*

Kapıyı açarak evden gitti. *Opening the door, he left the house.*

Used with Negative Verbs.

bilmeyerek. [bilme-ye-rek.] *unknowingly.*
istemeyerek. *reluctantly.*

Bu yılki üzüm festivali de yapılamayarak, Belediye panayıra dönüştü. [yap-ıl-a-ma-ya-rak.] *Not being able to hold this year's grape festival, the Corporation changed (it) to a street market* *(instead).*

Koşarak gitti. [kös-a-rak.] *He went a-running.*

Gülerek baktı. [gül-e-rek.] *She looked laughingly.*

Teşekkür ederek evden çıktı. [ed-e-rek.] *Thanking (his host), he left the house.*

Telefon ederek sordunuz mu? [ed-e-rek.] *Have you inquired by telephoning?*

Gülümseyerek karşılık vermiş. [gülümse-ye-rek.] *She answered smilingly.*

Yürüyerek gideceğim. [yürü-ye-rek] *I shall go by foot (by walking).*

Otomobile atlayarak kaçmış. [atla-ya-rak] *By jumping into a car he escaped.*

Bavulunu alarak taksiyi bindi. [al-a-rak.] *Taking his luggage, he got on a taxi.*

Kapıyı açarak odama girdim. [aç-a-rak.] *Opening the door I entered the room.*

Special case olarak *as a.., being a.*

olarak "ol-a-rak" from "olmak to become" is widely used. It is best translated by *as a..* or *being a..* The negative form is **olmayarak.** *not being..*

Dost olarak. *As a friend/Being a friend.*
Kesin olarak. *Definitely/Being sure.*
Memur olarak. *As a civil servant/Being a civil servant.*
İlk kez olarak. *For first time/Being the first time.*

Kadın, mutlu olmayarak, boşanma istedi. [ol-ma-y-a-rak.] *The woman, not being happy, wanted a divorce.*

Mehmet, kendisine hakim olamayarak bir yumruk attı. [ol-a-ma-y-a-rak.] *Mehmet, not being able to control himself, threw a punch.*

-(y)erek/-(y)arak shows an action accompanying or preceding that of the main verb in the sentence. The gerund formed by affixing **-rek** or **-rak** to the Wish/Desire Base **(-y)e or -(y)a** is the same for all verbs. The tense and person is taken from the main verb at the end of the sentence.

-(y)ip *and, also.*

The vowel harmony variations are **-(y)ip, -(y)ıp, -(y)up, -(y)üp.**

Used when there are two verbs with identical suffixes joined by "and/also" to simplify the first one.

Kalkıp gittik. [not: kalktık gittik.] *We got up and left.*

Oturup konuşuyorlar. [not: oturuyorlar konuşuyorlar.] *They are sitting and talking.*

Gidip bakmalıyız. *We must go and see.*

If one verb is negative then **de** *also* and is inserted between the them:

Pazara gidip de hiç bir şey almadım. *I went to the market and (also) I bought nothing.*

-(y)ince *on doing/when doing.*

Vowel Harmony variations are **-(y)ince -(y)ınca -(y)ünce -(y)unca.**

Signifies action just prior to the main verb. This often best easily translated by *On doing* or *When* in English:

Otobüs gelince, onu binerım. *When the bus arrives, I will get on it.* [On the bus arriving, I will get on it.]

-(y)inceye kadar, -(y)inceye dek -(y)inceye değin *until..*

The vowel harmonised variations are **-(y)inceye -(y)ıncaya -(y)ünceye -(y)uncaya.**

323

This signifies "until" [lit: to-the-on-doing the-amount]. The tense is taken from the final verb.

Otobüs gelinceye kadar, gidemedik. *We couldn't go until the bus came.* [The amount to the bus on coming, we couldn't go]

Otobüs varıncaya kadar, gidemiyorum. *I cannot go until the bus arrives.* [The amount to the bus on arriving, I cannot go]

Otobüs duruncaya dek, inmeyin. *Don't get off until the bus stops.* [The amount to the bus stopping, do not get off.]

The Turkish here is cumbersome so it is best learned and translated as "until".

-ene kadar, -ene dek, -ene değin *"until"*.

The vowel harmonised variations are **-ene kadar / -ana kadar, -ene dek / -ana dek, -ene değin / -ana değin**.

The meaning is "until" but less formal.

Otobüs gelene kadar, gitmiyoruz. *We are not going until the bus comes.*

Otobüs gelene dek, gidemedik. *We could not go until the bus came.*

-(y)esiye, -(y)asıya *"to the point of.."*

Here the meaning is *to the point of, being..*

Sarhoş olasıya kadar içki içmek. *To drink to the point of becoming drunk.*

O öpücük bitesiye dek sanki cennette kendimi hissettim. *Until that kiss was ending, I felt as though I was in heaven.*

Ben seni seviyorum ölesiye, sen beni sevdin gülesiye! *I love you to the point of dying, you loved me to the point of laughing!*

-(y)eli, -(y)eli beri, -(y)eliden beri, -diX -eli *"since"*.

The vowel harmonised variations are **-(y)alı, -(y)alı beri, -(y)alıdan beri, -diX -eli / -dıX -alı / -düX -eli / -duX -alı.**

All these mean "since" with the **-di** past ending conjugated as needed.

Biz İstanbul'a geleli hiç yağmur yağmadı. *Since we came to Istanbul it has not rained.*

Siz İstanbul'a geleli beri hiç yağmur yağmadı. *Since you came to Istanbul it has not rained.*

Ben İstanbul'a geleliden beri hiç yağmur yağmadı. *Since I came to Istanbul it has not rained.*

Onlar İstanbul'a *geldiler geleli* hiç yağmur yağmadı. [gel-diler geleli.] *Since they came to Istanbul it has not rained.*

Mehmet İstanbul'a *geldi geleli* hiç yağmur yağmadı. [gel-di geleli.] *Since Mehmet came to Istanbul it has not rained.*

-meden/-madan, -mezden/-mazdan *"before, without"*.

Meaning: *before, without* followed by **evvel** or **önce** *before/ago* to mean *before*.

Siz gitmeden evvel beni uyandırınız. *Wake me up before you go.*

Otobüs kalkmadan önce bir çay içelim. *Let's drink a tea before the bus leaves.*

-dikten sonra/-tikten sonra *"after doing"*.

The vowel harmonised and consonant mutated variations are **-dikten sonra/-tikten sonra, -dıktan sonra/-tıktan sonra, -dükten sonra/-tükten sonra, -duktan sonra/-tuktan sonra.**
After the unvoiced consonants **"ç f h k p s ş t"** this suffix is mutated to **"-tikten sonra"** etc.

Beni uyandırdıktan sonra hemen kahvaltı yapabilir misin?

Could you make breakfast straight away after waking me.

-r.. -mez.., -r.. -maz.. *"as soon as"*.

The positive tense base can have the forms **-r -ar -er -ir ir -ur -ur** according to the verb being used in the sentence. Turkish is cumbersome but used regularly. Literally meaning "between doing and not doing": This is the simple present positive an negative tense bases repeated.

Ben oturur oturmaz telefon çaldı. *As soon as (When) I sat down, the telephone rang.*

Mehmet, kapıdan girer girmez cereyan kesildi. *A soon as (Just as) Mehmet entered through the door, the electricity supply was cut.*

-dikçe/-tikçe, -dıkça/-tıkça *so long as, the more that, all the while that.*

Vowel Harmonized forms: **-dukça/-tukça, -dükçe/-tükçe.**
After the unvoiced consonants "ç f h k p s ş t" this suffix is mutated to "-tikçe" etc.

Alışveriş yaptıkça para kazan. *Win money while shopping.* (An advertisement.)

Terör devam ettikçe operasyonlar sürecek. *As terror continues the operations (against it) will go on.* (A short headline form.)

Ali'nin durumu gittikçe kötüleşiyor. *Ali's condition is getting worse as it goes (on).* We can see that **gittikçe** *as it goes* can be translated as "gradually" *Ali's condition is gradually getting worse.*

Fırsatım oldukça fotoğraflarına bakıyorum. *Whenever I have the chance I look at your photographs.* Similarly from **olmak** *to become/to be* we can form **oldukça** *as it becomes/as it is* which can be translated as *quite.*

O kız oldukça güzel görünüyor. *That girl over there is quite good looking.*

Otel postaneden oldukça uzak. *The hotel is quite a way from the* *post office.*

Adam yaşadıkça yaşlanıyor *Man ages as he lives.*

-medikçe, -madıkça *"so long as it is not, unless"*.

To understand how Turkish arrives at this suffix: The "-ça/-çe" suffix means "appertaining to". This is added to the relative participle of the negative verb thus meaning "appertaining to that which is not done" producing the meaning "unless" in English.

Gerçekten gerekli olmadıkça. *Unless it's really necessary.*

Yabancı dil devamlı kullanılmadıkça körelmekte ve unutulmaktadır *Unless a foreign language is not used regularly it dries up and is forgotten.* [kullan-ıl-ma-dık-ça "appertaining to that which is not used" a Passive model.]

-diği müddetçe *"as long as, all the time"*.

The vowel harmonised and consonant mutated variations are **-diği/-tiği, -dığı/-tığı, -düğü/-tüğü, -duğu/-tuğu.**
After the unvoiced consonants "ç f h k p s ş t" this suffix is mutated to "-tiği" etc.

O çalıştığı müddetçe şarki söyler. *He sings all the time he works.*

Fenerbahçe kovmadığı müddetçe buradayım. *As long as Fenerbahçe don't kick me out, I'm (still) here* .(Said by a footballer on the transfer list.)

Yaşadığım müddetçe o doktora minnettar olacağım. *As long as I live I will be indebted to that doctor.* Here we can see it is personalised to the subject "as long as I live".

-diği halde *"although/in a state of"*.

Vowel Harmonized forms: **-diği/-tiği, -dığı/-tığı, -düğü/-tüğü, -duğu/-tuğu.**

After the unvoiced consonants "ç f h k p s ş t" this suffix is mutated to "-tiği" etc.

Bağırdığım halde kimse yardıma gelmedi. *Although I shouted, no one came.*

Bacağı alçıda olduğu halde eve döndü. *He returned home although his leg was plastered.*

Bacağı alçıda olduğu halde eve dönecekmiş. *It seems he will return home although his leg is plastered.*

-diği için, -diğinden *because of the...*

Vowel Harmony and Consonant Mutation Variations also exist.

Bu hali aldığı için, vergi ödemeliyim. *I have to pay taxes because I bought this carpet,*

-diği kadar, -dığı kadar, -duğu kadar, -düğü kadar *as much as.*

Vowel Harmony and Consonant Mutation Variations also exist.

İstediğiniz kadar kalınız. *Stay as long as you want.*

Senin uyuduğun kadar ben uyuyamam. *I cannot sleep as much as you do.*

-eceğine, -acağına, -ecek yerde, -acak yerde *instead of.*

İzmir'e yürüyeceğine, otobüse bineceğim. *Instead of walking to Izmir, I will get on the bus.* (lit: board the bus)

-mekle, -makla *"with/by doing".*

Günümü hep yazı yazmakla geçirdim. *I spent all of my day writing.*

-mektense, -maktansa, -mekten ise/, -maktan ise *rather than.*

doing

Ankara'ya gitmektense, İstanbul'a gittim. *Rather than going to Ankara, I went to Istanbul.*

-meksizin, -maksızın, -meden, -madan *without.*

"-meden" is more frequently used.

Taksiye falan binmeksizin yürüyerek Aksaray'a varabilirdik. *Without getting a taxi or anything we were able to get to Aksaray by walking.*

Para ödemeden, ücretsiz olarak onu kullanabilirsiniz. *Without paying, you can use it free.* [ücretsiz olarak being un-priced.]

Şu resme 10 saniye boyunca gülmeden bakar mısın? *Can you look at this picture for 10 seconds without laughing?.*

-casına/-cesine *"like, as if".*

This suffix is added to a tense base.

-ırcasına. **Yağmur, bardaktan boşanırcasına yağıyordu.** *It rained as if being emptied from tumblers.* [rainng "cats and dogs".]

-mışçasına. **Zavallı, böylesini görmemişçesine bakıyordu.** *The poor chap looked as if he was not seeing.*

-(ı)yormuşçasına. **Anlatılanları alıyormuşçasına kafasını salladı.** *He nodded his head as if he understood what was being said.*

-acakmışçasına. **Burada temelli kalacakmışçasına eşyalarını yerleştirmeye başladı.** *He began to place his belongings as if he would be staying here for good.*

34 ADVERBIAL CLAUSES

Adverbial Clauses Explained.

Order of Main and Subordinate Clauses.

Subordinate clauses are treated differently in Turkish. In English we always put the main part of the meaning at the beginning of a sentence as below:

I shall go home **when** *the party is over.*
I went out to the library **after** *(eating) dinner.*
He put on his pyjamas **before** *he went to bed.*
We can have supper **as soon as** *we arrive at the hotel.*

All the above are ways of describing what will or did happen. Turkish as always says it backwards. The Turkish construction puts the most important part at the end of the sentence with the main verb as the final word.

English Construction: *I shall go home* when the party is over.
Turkish Construction: When the party is over, *I shall go home.*
Parti bitince, *eve gidiyorum.*

English Construction: *I went out to the library* after (eating) dinner.
Turkish Construction: After (eating) dinner, *I went out to the library.*
Yemek yedikten sonra, *kütüphaneye çıktım.*

English Construction: *Ali put on his pyjamas* before he went to bed.
Turkish Construction: Before he went to bed, *Ali put on his pyjamas.*
Ali, yatmadan önce, *pijamasını giydi.*

English Construction: *We can have supper* as soon as we arrive at the hotel.

Turkish Construction: As soon as we arrive at the hotel, *we can have supper.*
Otele varır varmaz (varınca), *akşam yemeğini yiyebiliriz.*
This construction puts the main verb last in the sentence, which of course is one of the main rules of Turkish Grammar.

Differing Aspects of Adverbial Clauses.

"Who did or will do what? and When?"
Time modifying words and clauses, *(before, after, as soon as, etc.)* are also managed differently in Turkish. One of the problems is the relationship of the temporal adverb with the subjects and objects.
English Construction: I went out to the library *after eating dinner.*
Turkish Construction: *After eating dinner* I went out to the library
Yemek yedikten sonra, kütüphaneye çıktım.
The subject or objects an be changed easily in English. The same applies to Turkish, but treats this problem in a different way.

Aspects of Time Clauses.

The locution **-dikten sonra** means *after doing.* As an example **yazdıktan sonra** means *after writing.* The tense and person is taken from the final verb:
Mektubu yazdıktan sonra çıktık. *After writing the letter we went out.*

Mektubu yazdıktan sonra çıkacağım. *After writing the letter I will go out.*

Sen mektubunu yazdıktan sonra çıkabilirsin. *After writing your letter you can go out.*

Odasını temizledikten sonra yatağa girdi. *After cleaning his room he went to bed.*

English Model: *I went out to the library after (eating) dinner.*
Turkish Model: Yemek yedikten sonra, kütüphaneye çıktım.

Mehmet went out to the library after he had (eaten) dinner.
Mehmet, yemek yedikten sonra kütüphaneye çıktı.

You went out to the library after Mehmet had (eaten) dinner.
Siz, Mehmet yemek yedikten sonra kütüphaneye çıktınız.

He went out to the library after (eating/having eaten) dinner.
O, yemek yedikten sonra kütüphaneye çıktı.

I went out to the library after you had (eaten) dinner.
Ben, siz yemek yedikten sonra kütüphaneye çıktım.

They will go out to the library after (having eaten) dinner.
Onlar, yemek yedikten sonra kütüphaneye çıkacaklar.

I used to out to the library after we had (eaten) dinner.
Ben, biz yemek yedikten sonra kütüphaneye çıkardım.

You went out to the library after we had (had) dinner.
Siz, biz yemek yedikten sonra kütüphaneye çıktınız.

In these examples the changes in the final verb tense in Turkish changes the English tense of the actual aspect of "eating dinner". It is not usual for us to state this "eating aspect" in English as it is normally understood and has become redundant. You can see there are many differing aspects of subject, object and tenses in this simple sentence and changes have to be made in Turkish, just as in English. The problem does not end here as it can be applied to any adverbial clause, but the same rules apply.

Clauses of Place *Where, Wherever.*

English Model: *I can not remember where I left my bicycle.*
Turkish Model: Bisikletimin bıraktığım yerini hatırlayamıyorum. [hatırla-ya-m-ıyorum. Negative Potential Present Continuous "I can not remember(ing)."]

I can not remember where you left my bicycle. **Bisikletimin bıraktığınız yerini hatırlayamıyorum.**

I can not remember where he left my bicycle. **Bisikletimin bıraktığı yerini hatırlayamıyorum.**

I can not remember where I left his bicycle. **Bisikletinin bıraktığım yerini hatırlayamıyorum.**

We will not remember wherever our bicycles are. **Bisikletimizin bıraktığımız yerini hatırlayamayacağız.**

He can never remember where to leave your bicycle. **Her zamanki gibi (Asla) bisikletinin bırakacağın yerini hatırlayamaz.**

You could not remember where you left my bicycle. **Bisikletimin bıraktığın yerini hatırlayamadın.**

They can not remember where they left their bicycles.
Bisikletlerinin bıraktıkları yerini hatırlayamıyorlar.
We just need to be aware of what we are trying to say at the time, and use the Turkish Constructions accordingly.

About Noun Clauses and Adverbial Clauses.

Example of a Noun Clause:
I can not remember *where you left my bicycle.*
This is a **Noun Clause** as it can be replaced by pronoun *it*
I can't remember *it.*

Example of an Adverbial Clause:
I can shop *where credit cards are accepted.*
This is an **Adverbial Clause** which is replaced by an adverb.
I can shop *there.*

Adverbial Clauses of Time "when".

There are many ways of saying "when" in English and of course the same applies in Turkish.

When I've painted the house, I am going on holiday.
As soon as I have painted the house, I am going on holiday.
After I have painted the house I am going on holiday.
On the house being painted, I am going on holiday.

These choices in English help us to fine tune our meaning. The Turkish language has similar nuances of intention. In some cases the choice is easy, in others it may alter the meaning slightly. The choice of the expression always relies on the circumstance appertaining at the time. The Turkish word order is contrary to English as the main verb must be last in the sentence:

I shall go to the cafe, when the job is finished. **English Construction**
When the job is finished, I shall to the cafe. **Turkish Construction**
İş bitince, lokantaya gideceğim.

When I got up, it was raining hard. **Yataktan kalktığım zaman çok
yağmur yağıyordu.**

They were dancing while I was playing the piano. **Ben piyano
çalarken onlar dans ediyorlardı.**

I was very tired when I returned from the party. **Partiden
döndüğümde çok yorgundum. (yorgun idim).**

My sister found the money when she was sweeping the carpet. **Kız
kardeşim halıyı süpürürken parayı buldu.**

When the rain stopped we returned home. **Yağmur durunca
evlerimize döndük.**

***before* önce or -meden önce.**

I went out to play before I had dinner. **English Construction.**
Before I had dinner, I went out to play. **Turkish Construction.**
Akşam yemeğini yemeden önce dışarıya oynamaya çıktım.

We must go home before it gets dark. **Hava kararmadan önce eve
gitmeliyiz.**

I will finish everything by the time my father comes home. **Babam
eve gelmeden önce her şeyi bitireceğim.**

If there is no verb in the sentence : **-dan önce/-tan önce** or **-den
önce/-ten önce** is used:
Before May. **Mayıstan önce.**
Before April. **Nisandan önce.**
Before 5 o'clock. **Saat beşten önce.**
Before 2 o'clock. **Saat ikiden önce.**

***because of* -dan dolayı or yüzünden.**

Because of what Mehmet has done we can never succeed.
Mehmet'in yaptığından dolayı asla başaramayız.

Because of what Mehmet has done we can never succeed.
Mehmet'in yaptığı şey yüzünden asla başaramayız.

Because of what Mehmet has done we will never be able to succeed.
Mehmet'in yaptığı şey yüzünden asla başaramayacağız. [wall not
be able to.]

after, afterwards **sonra or -diktan sonra.**

I turned the lights off after my sister went to bed. **English
Construction.**
After my sister went to bed, I turned off the lights. **Turkish
Construction.**
Kız kardeşim yattıktan sonra ışıkları söndürdüm.

After class I'll ask the teacher a question. **Ders bittikten sonra
öğretmene bir soru soracağım.**

After leaving Ankara I'll write a letter to you. **Ankara'dan
ayrıldıktan sonra sana mektup yazacağım.**

as, while **-dığında, or -ınca or iken.**

Ali went to bed as the clock struck ten. **English Construction.**
As the clock struck ten, Ali went to bed. **Turkish Construction.**
Saat onu vurunca Ali yattı.

We saw a man running down the stairs as we were going out. **Evden
dışarı çıkınca merdivenlerden aşağı koşan bir adam gördük.**

The poor man was going home as the snow was falling. **Kar
yağdığında zavallı adam evine gidiyordu.**

The boy met a fisherman as he was walking along the seashore.
Çocuk deniz kıyısına doğru yürürken bir balıkçıya rastladı.

just as **tam or iken.**

The phone rang just as I was leaving the house./Just as I was leaving the house, the phone rang. **Ben, tam evden ayrılırken telefon çaldı.**

It started to rain just as I was leaving home. **Ben, tam evden ayrılırken yağmur yağmaya başladı.**

during **esnasında.**

Necessary actions to take during a heart attack. **Kalp krizi esnasında yapılması gerekenler.**

while **iken.**

We stayed at a hotel while we were in Istanbul **İstanbul'dayken bir otelde kaldık.**

While the children were playing in the garden it started to rain. **Çocuklar bahçede oynarken yağmur yağmaya başladı.**

I will visit my friends while you are in Ankara. **Sen Ankara'dayken arkadaşlarımı ziyaret edeceğim.**

no sooner than, as **-masıyla bir oldu.**

The dance had no sooner started than the lights went out.
No sooner had the dance started then the lights went out.
Dansın başlamasıyla ışıkların sönmesi bir oldu.

I recognised him as soon as I saw him. **Onu görmemle tanımam bir oldu.**

whenever **her ne zaman.**

Whenever I started to speak English, my friend used to laugh.
My friend used to laugh whenever I started to speak English.
Her ne zaman İngilizce konuşmaya başlasam arkadaşım gülerdi.

Whenever I drink too much coffee I cannot sleep well. **Her ne zaman çok kahve içsem iyice uyuyamam.**

every time that, as usual **her bir zaman, her zamanki gibi.**

Every time I meet her we go the cinema. **Onunla her karşıladığım zaman sinemaya gideriz.**

It is not a bad thing to be late every time. **Geç kalmak her zaman kötü değildir.**

Our love is in danger as usual! **Aşkımız her zamanki gibi tehlikede!**

as soon as ...ir ...mez.

Other meanings: "the moment that, directly that, immediately that (once), once, when."

As soon as Ali arrives I'll ring you. **Ali gelir gelmez sana telefon edeceğim.**

The moment I finish this job I'll take a break. **Bu iş bitirir bitirmez bir mola vereceğim.**

I will give him the message directly I get there. **Oraya varır varmaz ona mesajı vereceğim.**

They are going to inform us immediately (once) they hear the news. **Haberi duyar duymaz bize bildirecekler.**

We'll go when my father is ready. **Babam hazır olur olmaz gideceğiz.**

***Now that, When that* -diği zaman.**

Now (that) you mention it, of course I do remember. **Ondan bahsettiğiniz zaman, elbet hatırlıyorum.**

35 ABOUT "Kİ" -*THAT, WHICH, WHO*

The Three Types of Ki and Kiler.

In Turkish there are 3 types of **ki** and its plural **-kiler.**
Conjunction: *that, so that, as, but what, but.*
Pronoun: *that/those which, which, who.*
Idiom: *thus, like that, so it is.*

There are many meanings of **-ki** as a suffix or as a stand alone word:
who, which, that,
so, that, such, that,
seeing, considering that,
as, though, in, of,
when,
I wonder?

Ki as a Conjunction.

This word **ki** replaces the English words *who, that, which* when joining two ideas in relation to each other. A comma is usually placed after the subject before **ki.**

Oran, ki sen bugün gördün, benim en iyi arkadaşım. *Oran, who you saw today, is my best friend.*

Matematik, ki bir çok insan nefret eder, benim en sevdiğim derstir. *Maths, which many people hate, is my favourite class.*

Ki is also used for joining two sentences together.
Biliyorum ki beni seviyorsun.
I know that you love me.
This method is based on Persian Grammar although understandable but is not the natural Turkish method. It is more suitable to European thinking.

The correct Turkish method uses the **-dik** Relative Object participle:
Beni sevdiğini biliyorum.
I know that you love me.
[Lit: Me that-love-you knowing-am-I].
sevdiğ- "that loves" + **-in** "your" + **-i** "object marker".
Both ideas "Beni the person" and "sevdiğini their loving" become
objects of the verb "I know".
Ali'nin arabasını temiz ettiğinizi görüyorum. [et-tiğ-iniz-i.]
I see that you have washed Ali's car.

Ki as a Suffix.

The suffix **ki** *who, that, which* is often used with the Static Position
suffix "-daki/-deki" to show "where an object is".
In Turkish the addition of **ki** to a located object completes the
meaning as it becomes a descriptive adjective of location. In English
the relative pronoun "who" in this relationship is often not included.
Bahçedeki çocuk top oynuyor.
The child (who is) in the garden is playing ball.

The use of the relative **ki** *who, which, that* is necessary in Turkish
although in English it can be omitted. Without "ki" then "Bahçede
çocuk" is meaningless, whereas "Bah**çedeki** çocuk" means "The
child **who is in** the garden" showing that "the child" is specific and
"is in the garden, "-deki" becomes an adjective standing in front of
its noun describing the position of "the child".

Elimdeki kitap eskidir.
The book (that is) in my hand is old.
[Lit: Hand-of-mine-in-which-is book old-is.]
["The "book" is described by an adjective of location.
Yanımdaki para yok.
I don't have money with me.
[lit: Side-of me-at-which-is money there is not.]
Masadaki bardağı bana verin.
Give me the glass (which is) on the table.
[lit: Table-on-which-is the-glass to-me give.]

The cat is sick. **Kedi hasta.**
The sick cat **Hasta kedi.**

Here **hasta** is originally an adjective, so it can be used as an adjective without any change.

The cat is at home. **Kedi evde.**

The cat, (which is) at home **Evdeki kedi**.

Here **evdeki** *which is at home* is an adjectival expression of place describing "where the cat is". To use such an expression as an adjective, the **-ki** *that which* completes the description.

Sokaktaki adam. *The man (who is) in the street.*

Here **sokakta** is not an adjective, but a noun plus a suffix, therefore -*ki* is added to make an adjective.

Adam sokakta. *The man is on the street.*

Here, **sokakta** is not an adjective but a noun indicating the location, therefore -*ki* is not required.

Ki as an Idiom.

This **ki** is often used in comparison as in:

oysa ki. *if it is thus, if that's the way it is, thus, so then.*

hal bu ki. *the condition is this, that is the way it is, so then.*

These locutions are often written as a single word **oysaki** *so, then,* **halbuki** *It's this way, like this.*

Ki as a Relative Pronoun.

In the completion of descriptive nouns, the suffix **-ki** can be added to the completed noun and then used in place of the noun + noun completion.

Ali'nin arabası, Ayşe'nin arabasından daha güzeldir. *Ali's car is better than Ayşe's car.*

Ali'nin arabası, Ayşe'ninkinden daha güzeldir. [Ayşe'nin-ki-nden.] *Ali's car is better than Ayşe's (one).*

Koltuklarımız, Fatma'nınkilerden daha yenidir. [Fatma'nın-ki-ler-den.] *Our chairs are newer than Fatma's ones.*

Bizimkiler, Fatma'nın koltuklarından daha yenidir. [Bizim-ki-ler.] *Our ones are newer that Fatma's chairs.*

Bizimkilerden mi bir tane alırsanız. [Bizim-ki-ler-den.] *Why don't you take one of ours.*

Bahçenin domatesi, seranın domatesinden daha lezzetlidir. *The garden tomatoes are tastier than the greenhouse tomatoes.*

Bahçeninkiler, seranınkinden daha lezzetlidir. *The garden ones are tastier than the greenhouse ones.*

Bahçe domatesi, sera domatesinden daha lezzetlidir. *Garden tomatoes are tastier than greenhouse tomatoes.* (tomatoes generally)

Bahçekiler, serakinden daha lezzetlidir. *Garden ones are tastier than greenhouse ones.*

Ahmet'inkinin yerine Ali'nin kitabını alsana. *Why don't you take Ali's book instead of Ahmet's one.*

Kiler in the plural.

Just as an example:
içindekiler. *contents. [Lit: those which are inside.]*

Odanın içindekileri hepsi kiralamış. *Apparently all the room's contents are on hire.*

In dictionaries the word "contents" is shown as "içindekiler". But it is a string of suffixes added to the basic word "iç". This is the reason that it is difficult to "look up" words in Turkish dictionaries. This in itself is another language hurdle that the Turkish language student has to surmount.

Vowel changes to "ki".

-ki is not usually subject to the vowel harmony changes but with one exception: **-kü** is added to words whose last vowel is **ö** or **ü**.

Bugünkü planımız ki sinemaya gidelim. *Our plan for today is to go to the cinema.*

Bugünkünün filimi güzeldi. [Bugün-kü-nün "today-which-of the-film".] *Today's film was good.*

Dünkü hava çok güzeldi. *Yesterday's weather was nice.*
In both cases, the words **bugün/dün** are used in adjective-like
functions. Without **-kü** then **Dün hava çok güzeldi** would
mean *Yesterday the weather was nice.*

"Ki" as a separate word.

Using "Ki": **Film o kadar üzücüydü ki, ağlamalıydım.**
The film was so sad, that I had to cry.
The Turkish construction: **Film o kadar üzücü olduğundan
ağlamalıydım.**

Using "Ki": **Hava o kadar sisliydi ki, hiç bir şey göremiyordum.**
The weather was so foggy, that I hardly saw anything.
The Turkish way: **Hava o kadar sisli olduğundan, hiç bir şey
göremiyordum.**

Using "Ki": : **Herkes bilir ki, dünya yuvarlaktır.**
Everybody knows that the world is round.
The Turkish way: **Herkes dünyanın yuvarlak olduğunu bilir.**

Using "Ki": **Oturdum ki, biraz dinleneyim.**
I sat down (in order) to have a rest.
The Turkish way: **Dinlenmek için oturdum.**

Using "Ki":. **Odadan içeri girmişti ki telefon çaldı.**
The phone rung just as he entered the room.
The Turkish way: **Odadan içeri tam girdiği zaman telefon çaldı.**

Madem ki geldin o zaman konuşalım.
Seeing that you have come, let's have a chat then.

İyi ki erken gelmişiz, yoksa yer bulamazdık.
*Its a good job that we came early, otherwise we would not have
found a place.*

Neden bu kadar sinirleniyorsun ki?
Why are you getting so upset?
"-ki" at the end of a sentence shows a shock, emphasis, exaggeration
or curiosity.

İçerdeki masanın üzerinde duran gömlekler yeni mi?
Are the shirts lying on top the table (which is) inside new?

Evet bugün aldım. Seninkileri de gördün mü?
Yes I bought Then today. Did you see yours? ("seninkiler senin gömleklerin".)

Yoo, nerede ki?
No, where are they then?
If **ki** does not make an adjective, it should be always written separately.

Ki *"who, which, that"*.

Bir çocuk ki çok yaramaz. *A child who is very naughty.*

Anlaşıldı ki bu işi o yapmış. *Its understood that he's the one who did this.*

Sanmam ki gelecek. *I don't think he'll come.*

Bir şey yapmadım ki pişmanlık duyayım. *I haven't done anything that I should feel sorry about.*

Ki *"so that, such that"*.

Öyle ucuz ki herkes alabilir. *Its so cheap that everyone can afford it.*

Ki *"but, Would you believe it?"*.

Eve geldim ki kapı duvar. *I came home, but (ki? would you believe it?) nobody answered the door.*
Elimi cebime attım ki para yok. *I felt in my pocket for it, but (ki? would you believe it?) the cash wasn't there.*

Ki *"seeing that, considering that"*.

Adam üşümüş ki paltosunu giymiş. *The man must have been cold, seeing that he put on his coat.*

343

Ki *"such as, though"*.

Ne yazık ki! *What a shame!*

Ki *"When"*.

Henüz uykuya dalmıştım ki, bir patlama oldu. *I'd just dropped off to sleep when there was an explosion.*

Ki *"I wonder?"*.

Bilmem ki ne yapsam? What should I do, I wonder?

Ki *"Indicates frustration, disapproval, doubt, or anxiety"*.

O bana inanmaz ki! *She won't believe me at all?*

Ama ona yapamam ki? *But I can not do that anyhow?*

Ki *"Is used for emphasis"*.

Öyle güzel ki! *That is so beautiful!*

Öyle bir para döktü ki! *He spent and spent!*

Araba ki ne araba! *That's some car and a half!*

36 DEMONSTRATIVES

Demonstrative Pronouns and Adjectives.

The Demonstrative Adjectives "this and that, these and those" and Demonstrative Pronouns "this one, that one, these ones, those ones" demonstrate and describe which item is being mentioned.

Simple Forms *this and that, these and those.*

bu *this (here)* or *this (which was just mentioned).*
bunlar *these.*

şu *that (nearby)* or *that (which follows on).*
şunlar *those (nearby).*

o *that (over there, yonder.)*
onlar *those (over there).*

When adding any suffixes including the plural suffix **-lar** buffer letter **-n-** is always used with the demonstratives, thus forming the plurals **bunlar, şunlar, onlar.**

bu kedi *this cat,* **bu kediler, bunlar** *these cats, these (ones)*
şu fincan *that cup* (near to, between us) **şu fincanlar, şunlar** *those cups, those (ones).*
o adam *that man over there, yonder,* **o adamlar, onlar** *those men, those (ones).*

This and These **bu, bunlar, şu, şunlar, o, onlar.**

bu *this* (here) or *this* (which was just mentioned) and the plural **bunlar** *these.*

Turkish has two words for "that, those".

Şu *that* (nearby) **or** *that* (which follows on) and the plural **şunlar** *those* (nearby).

Şu signifies something near by or something between the speakers. **Şu** also means "that which follows" as in **şu tavsiye** *the following recommendation.*

O *that yonder* and the plural **Onlar** *those yonder* signifies items far away or which does not lie between the speakers.

O and **onlar** are often used for descriptions of happenings in foreign countries and cities.

About the usage of "şu" *that nearby.*

Question: **Şu ne?** *What is that (just there)?*
Answer: **O bir gazete** *That is a newspaper.*

As an answer "Şu bir gazete" is incorrect. It is only used as an adjective describing "the newspaper".

The correct answer is **O bir gazete**. As a phrase in its own right **Şu bir gazete** *That (just there) is a newspaper* is used, but not as an answer to a question like **Şu ne?** *What's that?*

If you are asked **Şu masanın üstündeki nedir?** *What is it on that table?* then the answer would be either:
O bir gazete or just **gazete**, not "Şu bir gazete".
If you are describing it **Şu bir gazete** is correct but to ask for it you must say **Nerede o gazete?** not "Nerede şu gazete?"

Summary:

Question: **Şu ne?** *What is that?*
Answer: **O bir gazete.** *That is a newspaper.*
Question of Place: **Nerede o gazete?** not "Nerede şu gazete?"

The disparaging meaning of "Şu".

Although **şunca** and **şunlarca** are not normally in use, they are sometimes used disparagingly. In Turkish they can be used to despise something in quantity or magnitude, muscular power. If someone has a small wound and is complaining too much about it

346

then one could say **Şunca/şuncacik yaradan ölmezsin.** *You won't die from such a small wound (surely not!).*

Care must be taken using **şu** and its extensions as they are used in a derogatory sense according to context:

Şu adama bakın! *Look at that bloke!*
Şunu istemedim! *I didn't want that!* (damn thing.)
Şu kahrolasıca herif kim? *Who is that damn fellow?* [quite strong language.]

This is a "frozen form" **kahrolasıca** [from "kahrolmak" "to be distressed"]. The suffixes are made up **ol-a-sı-ca** where **-ası** is a now defunct ending with an added **-ca** suffix indicating *having the attribute of.* However this word is best learned as a single unit In reality it should not be used as it is considered rather rude. You can also say **kahrolsun!** *Let him be dammed!* It is really like a bad swear word in English and not to be taken lightly. Be careful in its use!

The Suffixed Forms of the Demonstratives.

The Demonstrative Pronouns and Adjectives **bu** *this*, **şu** *that*, **o** *that yonder* use buffer letter **-n-** to become **bun-, sun-, on-** when adding any further suffixes. This includes the plural suffix **-lar** buffer letter **-n-** is always used with the demonstratives, thus forming the plurals **bunlar, şunlar, onlar.**

bu *this, this here*	bunlar *these, these here*
bu *this*	**bunlar** *these*
buna *to this*	**bunlara** *to these*
bunun *of this*	**bunların** *of these*
bunu *this* (obj.)	**bunları** *these* (obj.)
bunda *in/on/at this*	**bunlarda** *in/etc these*
bundan *from this*	**bunlardan** *from these*
bununla *with this*	**bunlarla** *with these*

şu *that, that there*	şunlar *those, those there*
şu *that*	**şunlar** *those*

şuna *to that*	**şunlara** *to those*
şunun *of that*	**şunların** *of those*
şunu *that* (obj.)	**şunları** *those* (obj.)
şunda *in/on/at that*	**şunlarda** *on those*
şundan *from that*	**şunlardan** *from those*
şununla *with that*	**şunlarla** *with those*

o *that yonder,* that over there	onlar *those yonder,* those over there
o *that yonder*	**onlar** *those yonder*
ona *to that*	**onlara** *to those*
onun *of that*	**onların** *of those*
onu *that* (obj.)	**onları** *those* (obj.)
onda *in/on/at that*	**onlarda** *on those*
ondan *from that*	**onlardan** *from those*
onunla *with that*	**onlarla** *with those*

The Suffix -ca bunca, şunca, onca *concerning.*

The addition of **-ca** produces an adjective which means *"all this/that amount of"*. **-ca** is used with the Demonstrative Pronoun to produce **bunca** *all this,* **bunlarca** *all these,* **onca** *all that,* **onlarca** *all those.*

Although "şunca" and "şunlarca" are not normally in use but they are sometimes used disparagingly. However, in Turkish it could be used to despise something in quantity or magnitude, power.

Bunca emeğim boşa gitti. *All this work of mine was in vain.* ["all this amount of my work".]

Bunca kitabı, kitaplıkta dursunlar diye mi aldın? *Did you buy all these books (just) to fill the bookcase?* ["all this amount of books".]

Bunca arkadaşımın arasından onu mu beğendin? *Between all these friends of mine, was it (only) him you liked?* ["all this amount of my friends".]

Bunca yıldır bu okuldayım, böyle olay görmedim. *I was at this* *school all these years and I have not seen such a thing (before).*["all these years".]

Bunca kediyi nasıl besleyeceksin ki? *How do you feed all these cats?* ["all this amount of cats."]

The addition of **bunca** replaces **bu kadar** *this amount of* and **onca** replaces **o kadar** *that amount of.*

The Singular Form.

bunca *all this.*
"şunca" Not usually used.
onca *all that.*

The Plural Form.

bunlarca *all these.*
" şunlarca" Not usually used.
onlarca *all those.*

Bu ne? What's this?
Bu bir büyük kedi *This is a big cat.*
Avluda bunca uzun kuyruklu kedi cirit atıyorlar. *All these long tailed cat are running wild in the yard.* "cirit atmak" Literally "to throw a javelin" but used here idiomatically meaning "run amok, swarm wildly".

Şunca yaradan (Şuncacıktan) ölmezsin . *You won't die from such a small wound (surely not!)* [the "-cik" suffix shows "downsizing."]

bunca and **onca** are plural and they take a singular object. The substantive that it describes is always in the singular.

bunca kedi, onca kedi *all these/those cats* is similar to **Bu kediler, O kediler.** *these cats, those cats.*

O ne? *What is that over there?*
O bir dergi. *That is a magazine.*
Bunca dergiyi nereye koyacaksın? *Where are you going to put all these magazines?* [Plural is assumed from "bunca".]
Bunlar ne? *What are these?*
Bunlar yeşil elma. *These (ones) are green apples.*

Şunlar ne? *What are those?*
Onlar beyaz ev. *Those are white houses.*

Onlar kim? *Who are those (people) over there?*
Onlar genç kızlar. *Those (people) are young girls.*

Yarın onca genç kız Ayşe'nin partiye gidiyormuş. *All those girls are going to Ayşe's party tomorrow.* ["all that amount of girls".]

Should we use **Onlarca kız** or **Onca kız**? **Onlarca kız**, [on means 10] meaning there are some girls but they are in groups containing 10 girls.

Buna bakar mısınız? *Would you look after this?*
[Motion Towards Object: "-a bamak" means "to look after."]
Bunlara bakar mısınız? *Would you look after these?*

Onu bakar mısınız? *Would you look at that?*
[Direct Object "-u bamak" means "to look at".]
Onları bakar mısınız? *Would you look at those?*

Adverbial Forms of the Demonstratives böyle, şöyle, öyle.

There are further derivations of **bu, şu, o** which have produced the words **böyle, şöyle, öyle** the meanings are a follows:

böyle. *In this way/thus.*
Onu böyle yaptım. *I did it like this.*
["böyle" is usually used with the First Person Pronoun.]

şöyle. *like that/in that manner.*
Onu şöyle yapın! *Do it like that!*
["şöyle" is usually used with the imperative.]

öyle. *such as that/like that.*
Onu öyle yaptı. *He did it like that!*
[Past tense is more distant, hence "öyle" is used.]

The **-ce** suffix can also be added to form adverbs:

böylece. *In this way/thus.*
şöylece is not much used.

öylece *such as that/like that.*

The **-ce** suffix give a sense of completion **Böylece iş tamamlandı** *And so the job was done thus.*

Some Examples:

Böyle bir iş yapmayın! *Don't do anything like (this) that!* [in Turkish "bu" and "böyle" are used regarding a specific action, such as "jumping on the bed", whereas English uses the word. "That!" as opposed to the Turkish "This!" for emphasis.] **Böylece onu yapın!** *Do it like that!* [Turkish Lit: "Do it like this!"]

şöyle böyle. *just so-so.* [Lit: "like that, like this", as French "comme ci comme ca".]

When asked *How are you?* then **şöyle böyle** can be given as an answer *"So so, I'm up and down, I'm getting on OK."*

Öyle bir sağanak yağmur yağdı ki. *There was such a downpour that (I can't begin to tell you).*

The "Formula Speak" **Öyle mi?** is used when listening with apparent disbelief to someone describing events, meaning *Well I never!, Go on then!, Really?* This formula is in constant use in normal daily conversation.

Examples of Extended Forms.

Bu ne? *What's this?*
Bu bir büyük kedi. *This is a big cat.*
Bunca kedi uzun kuyruklu(dur). *All these cats are long tailed.*
Bütün bu kediler uzun kuyrukludur. *All these cats are long tailed*

Şu ne? *What is that (just there)?*
O bir gazete *That is a newspaper*
Onca gazete dünkünün. *All those newspapers are yesterday's.*
Bütün o gazeteler dünkünün. *All those newspapers are yesterday's.*

O ne? *What is that over there?*
O bir dergi *That is a magazine.*
Bunlarca dergi *All these are magazines.*

351

Bunlar ne? *What are these?*
Bunlar yeşil elma. *These (ones) are green apples.*

Şunlar ne? *What are those?*
Onlar beyaz evler. *Those are white houses.*

Onlar kim? *Who are those (people) over there?*
Onlar genç kızlar. *Those (people) are young girls.*
Onlarca kızlar genç. *All those girls are young.*

37 SPATIALS

The Basic Spatials.

The suffix **-re-** or **-ra-** means *place* or *place of.*
For instance **nerede?** means *Where?* [Lit: *ne-re-de* what-place-at.]
The demonstratives **bu, şu, o** *this, that, that yonder* are suffixed
with **-ra-** meaning *place of* to form the basic locations:

bura. *here* . [Lit: this place.]
şura. *there* . [Lit: that place.]
ora. *that yonder* [Lit: that place over there.]

There words are not very often used in this pure form but are
extended to show the place *where at, from where, to where* by the
addition of a suitable suffix.

Spatials or "Lost in Space".

Adding the Static Position Suffix (Locative) **-de** or **-da** *in, on,
at* forms the basic locations:

The Singular. Specific Place.

burada. *here.* [Lit: *bu-ra-da* this-place-at.]
şurada. *there*
orada. *over there.*
nerede? *where?*

The Plurals. Spatially More Vague.

buralarda. *hereabouts, around here.* [Lit: *bu-ra-lar-da* these-
places-at.]
şuralarda. *thereabouts, around there.*
oralarda. *thereabouts over there, around about over there.*
nerelerde? *whereabouts?*

353

Extended Spatials.

Adding the Movement Away (Ablative) suffix **-dan** *from* or the Movement Toward (Dative) suffix **-a** *to, towards* then the meanings become:

The Singular.

buradan. *from here.*
buraya. *to here.*
şuradan. *from there.*
şuraya. *to there.*
oradan. *from there.*
oraya. *to there.*
nereden? *where from?*
nereye? *where to?*

And the Plurals Spatially More Vague.

buralardan *from hereabouts, from around here.*
buralara *to hereabouts.*
şuralardan *from thereabouts.*
şuralara *to around there.*
oralardan *from thereabouts (distant).*
oralara *to thereabouts.*
nerelerden? *from whereabouts?*
nerelere? *to whereabouts?*

All the various Noun Conditions can be used to extend the demonstrative pronouns.

bura(sı). *here.*
burayı. *here. (obj.)*
buraya. *to here.*
burada. *at here.*
buradan. *from here.*
buranın. *belonging to here, of here.*
buralar. *hereabouts.*
bura(sı)yla. *with this place here.*

The same is also valid for **şura(sı), ora(sı)** and also interrogative **nere(si)?**

354

Example Basic Spatials.

Buralarda bir güzel restoran var mı? *Is there a good restaurant around here?*
Buraya gel! *Come (to) here!*
Oradan yeşil bir araba geldi. *A green car came from over there.*
Şurada büyük bir otel var. *There is a big hotel there.*

şura has a diminutive form **şuracık** in general use. The meaning becomes *"just here/there, hereabouts"*:
Şuracıkta gazeteyi koyun *Put the newspaper just there/here*
There are similar forms for **bura** becoming **buracık** and **ora** becoming **oracık**. These forms are in use, but not as much as the form **şuracık.**

The suffix -deki/-daki "which is on, in, at."

The suffix of place is **-re** or **-ra** meaning *place/place of.* By suffixing the demonstratives **bu, şu, o** *this, that, that yonder* with **-ra-** place of plus the Static Condition (locative) suffix **-da** *in, on, at* the words *here, there, over there* are formed. These words are used for a general sense of location.

burada. *here.* [Lit: "bu-ra-da" "this-place-at".]
şurada. *there.* [Lit: "şu-ra-da" "that-place nearer-at or in between-at".]
orada *over there.* [Lit: "o-ra-da" "that-place yonder-at".]
nerede? *where?* [Lit: "ne-re-de?" "what-place-at?"]

In conversation and writing these words are often shortened (abraded) to **burda, şurda, orda, nerde?**

In reality there is no such suffix **-daki/-deki** in Turkish. **-deki** is actually two suffixes together, **-de** plus an added **-ki**. *-de* means *on, in, at* while **-ki** means *that which is.*

Most grammar books gloss over this construction although it is in constant daily use to make an **Adjective of Location**. For ease of explanation this book will treat **-daki/-deki** as suffix in its own right. Let us call it a "pseudo" suffix. **Sokaktaki araba** *The car which is in the street* [Lit: 'Sokak-ta-ki street-in-which-is car".] Here **-daki** makes an Adjective of Location "that which is in" This pseudo suffix is very important as it is used a lot in daily conversation and reading.

The suffix **-daki/-deki** is added to words to produce an adjective to describe the location of an object. This is best shown by example. For instance if we say: *The telephone [which is] in my bedroom is broken*, then Turkish trying to turn everything into an adjective will say thus:

Yatak odamdaki telefon bozuktur. [Yatak oda-m-daki telefon bozuk-tu.r] *My bedroom telephone is broken.* [lit: Bedroom-of-me-which-is-in telephone broken-is.] Here **odamdaki telefon** is used as an adjective to describe just where the telephone is! [Room-my-in-which-is telephone.]

This point is a particular difficulty for Turkish learners, as English does not use an adjectival construction. Instead, English uses a Relative Construction *The telephone "which is" in my bedroom is broken.* It is important to understand this adjectival construction of location, as it is in constant daily use in Turkish.

It can also be used as a location in time scale as some of the examples below will show. The vowel of **-ki** is invariable, it does not follow Vowel Harmony Rules, so the full Suffix of Adjectival Location is either **-deki** or **-daki**.

Masadaki kitap *The book (which is) on the table.*
Masadaki kitabı bana verin. *Give me the book (which is) on the table.*
Kilitteki anahtar. *The key (which is) in the lock.*
Kilitteki anahtarı çıkarınız *(Would you) take the key out of the lock.* [Lit: Lock-in-which-is key-the take out!]
Kutudaki kibritler nemlidir. *The matches (which are) in the box are damp.*

The Turkish aspect is different from English and this can only be appreciated by usage and practice, as it is an alien construction for English speakers.

An Example in Time Scale:

Önümüzdeki hafta.[Ön-ümüz-deki hafta] *The week in front of us*
[Lit: Front-of-us-which-is week.]

Önümüzdeki haftanın havası çok güneşli olacak. *The week ahead's weather will be very sunny.*
As already stated, this is a difficult construction but it can be assimilated by reading, listening and using.

Extended Spatials *"to, from, in, at"*.

If we need to show movement from or movement to a place or places then we must use a different suffix such as **-dan** *from* or **-a** *to, towards* in order to modify the meaning:

buradan. [bu -ra -dan.] *(burdan* as spoken.) *from here.*
We also use the same construction in English. If a child strays too near to the fire, then the mother will say: "Get away *from there!*"
şuradan. [şu-ra-dan.] *(şurdan* as spoken.) *from there.*
oradan. [o-ra-dan.] *(ordan* as spoken.) *from over there.*
nereden? [ne-re-den?] *(nerden?* as spoken.) *where from?*

Word Adding **-a** *to, towards*:

buraya. [bu-ra-ya.] *to here.*
şuraya. [şu-ra-ya.] *to there.*
oraya. [o-ra-ya.] *to over there.*
nereye? [ne-re-ye?] *where to?*

We in English do not say "come to here", "go to there", although in Older English we did use these forms "Come hither", "Go hence". However Turkish must use the **-a/-e** and **-den/-dan** suffixes to show movement towards or from a location. Basically Turkish is using "hence", "hither" and even "thence" and "thither". In English these words are no longer used in daily speech. To re-iterate, English would say "hither" and "thither" in the old days, and this is what is happening in Turkish.

Extended Plural Spatial Forms *"hereabouts, thereabouts"*.

The plural forms **buralarda, şuralarda, oralarda, nerelerde** cause the meaning to be:

1. More vague: buralarda. *hereabouts, around here.*
2. More spatial: şuralarda. *thereabouts, around there, over there.*
3. More generalized: oralarda. *thereabouts, over there, around about.*
4. Any mixture of the three: nerelerde? *whereabouts?*

Here we can see then the meanings have become more generalized in both space and location.

We should also remember that the meanings based on **şuralarda** are in the near vicinity whilst the meanings based on **oralarda** are more distant (maybe in another country).

The Plural Forms are also extended with **-dan** *from* and **-a** *to, towards.*

buralardan. (bu-ra-lar-dan.) *from hereabouts.*
şuralardan. (şu-ra-lar-dan.) *from around there.*
oralardan. (o-ra-lar-dan.) *over around there.*
nerelerden? (ne-re-ler-den?) *whereabouts from?*
buralara. (bu-ra-lar-a.) *to around here.*
şuralara. (şu-ra-lar-a.) *to around there.*
oralara. (o-ra-lar-a.) *to those parts.*
nerelere? (ne-re-ler-e?) *whereabouts to?*

The plural forms are vaguer and wider. They are used as in English to make these distinctions in place and space.

Buralarda bir güzel restoran var mı? *Is there a good restaurant around here?*
Buraya gel! *Come (to) here!*
Orada yeşil araba var. *There is a green car over there.*
Şurada büyük otel var. *There is a big hotel there.*
Kredi Bankası nerede? *Where is the Kredi Bank?*
Çarşı nerelerde? *Whereabouts are the shops?*
Buradan saat sekizde çıkalım *Let's leave (from) here at 8 o' clock.*

Particular Locations. *"right here, right there and just where?*

If we need to communicate a more particular place and sense of location then as in English we have to be more precise. This precision in Turkish is achieved by using the suffix **-i** or **-si** meaning *its*. By adding this suffix Turkish makes the place particular:

burası. (bu-ra-sı.) *right here.*[Lit: its place (exactly) here.]
şurası. (şu-ra-sı.) *right there.*
orası. (o-ra-sı.) *right over there.*
neresi? (ne-re-si?) *just where?* [Lit: where exactly?]

The **-si** suffix is the Possessed part of the Possessive Relationship and sometimes the Possessor is "understood". This expression is used to complete the relationship as in: **bankanın burası** or **evin şurası** or **İngiltere'nin orası**, but this is considered to be   pedantic.

More about Exact Locations.

For exact locations the Possessive Adjective suffix **-(s)ı** is added to make the meaning become more exact.

For instance if someone asks you on the telephone:
Neredesin? (ne-re-de-sin?) *Where are you?*
you might answer:
Ankara' dayım. [Ankara'-da-y-ım.] *I 'm in Ankara*
However, if they ask you:
Oranın neresinde? [ne-re-si-n-de?] *Where (of there) exactly?* you might answer:
Banyodayım. [banyo-da-y-ım.] *I am in the bath.*

General and Precise Location.

Here is a little conversation between Ali and his friend Mehmet to explain the above about general and precise location.

Ali: **Neredesin?** [Nerdesin? abraded in conversation] *Where are you?*
Mehmet: **Üsküdar' dayım.** *I am in Üsküdar.*
Ali: **Üsküdar'ın neresinde?** *Whereabouts (of Uskudar)?*
Mehmet: **Ahmet Çeşmesi'nin yanındayım.** *I'm by the Ahmet Fountain.*

The call sign of Ankara Official Radio Station is **Burası Ankara** *This place (exactly) is Ankara.* It is something like British Official

Radio whose call sign is *"London Calling"*.

Some Examples: *right here, just there*. All these mean exactly *right here* or *right there* or *just where?*

Burası soğuk. *It is cold right here.*
Burasına gel! *Come (right to) here.*
Binanın burasından kaçalım! *Let's get away from (of) this building.*

The last two examples are used as a descriptive way when showing a particular location on a map.

In normal conversation we can say:
Buradan kaçalım! *Let's get out of here!*
İzmir? Orası güzel. *Izmir? That very place is beautiful.*

Çantamı, odamın neresine koydum, acaba? *Where exactly did I put my bag in my room I wonder?*
Or more General:
 Çantamı nereye koydum acaba? *Where did I put my bag, I wonder?*

Kitabı dolabın şurasına koyun. *Put the book just over there in(to) the cupboard.*
Or more General: **Kitabı şuraya koyun.** *Put the book just over there.*

Tam saat sekizde burada görüşelim. *Let's meet right here at dead on 8 o' clock.*

Burası, Şurası, Orası. can be only used alone in nominative case:
Burası neresi? *where is this (exactly)?*
Şurası güzelmiş. *Just there is beautiful.*
Orası güzel. *It is nice over there.*

In other cases a possessor is required to possess the "burası surası, orası."

Binanın burasına gel! *Come right here to the building!*
Balkonun şurasında bir kuş vardı. *There was a bird right on the balcony.*
Ormanın orasından ilginç sesler geliyordu. *There are interesting*

sounds coming out of forest ('s place.)

Example of a Particular Location.

Here is a snippet of conversation between Mehmet and Ali to show the difference between the **nereye?** *where to?* [Lit: to where?] as a general location and the **neresine?** *just where to?* [Lit: to the where?] as an exact location type of usage.

Mehmet: **Bu akşam nereye gidiyorsun?** *Where are you going (to) this evening?*
Ali: **Merkeze gidiyorum.** *I'm going to the town centre.*
Mehmet: **Merkezin neresine?** *Where to (exactly) of the town centre?*
Ali: **Büyük Efes Oteline gidiyorum** *I'm going to the Grand Efes Hotel.*

38 SPATIAL RELATIONSHIPS

"Lost in Space".

Some Space Oddities.

As in English spatials may either be adjectives or nouns.
Consider: *The exterior door. The outside wall.* Here the word *exterior* and *outside* are adjectives describing the nouns they possess, *the door* and *the wall*.

As in English these spatials can also be nouns.
Consider: *At the back of the house. From the top of the table.* Here both *back* and *top* are nouns. This is shown by the use of the Definite Article "the back" and "the top."

English method: *At the back of the house.* becomes in Turkish: *At the house's back.* This is exactly the same as the Possessive Relationship in Turkish:

Evin arkası. *The back of the house* [Lit: the house-of the back-its.]
Masanın üstü. *The top of the table* [Lit: the table-of the top-its.]

Spatial Relationships are just another form of the Possessive Relationship in Turkish where one noun owns the second **ev-in arka-sı** *the back of the house.* Further suffixes can be added, "to, from, at etc." to complete the meaning as required.

Masanın üstünden. *From the top of the table.* [uses **-den** suffix.]
Masanın üstünde. *On the top of the table.* [uses **-de** suffix.]
Masanın üstüne. *To the top of the table.* [uses **-e** suffix]

This then is the way that Turkish treats Spatial Relationships and some of the main ones are shown below.

dış / dışı *exterior, outside.*

Used as an Adjective (dış).
dış kapı. *the outside gate.*
dış avlu. *the outside yard.*

Used as a Noun (dışı).
kapının dışı. *the outside of the gate.*
bankanın dışına. *to the outside of the bank.*
evin dışında. *at the outside of the house.*
bahçenin dışından. *from the outside the garden.*

A cafe sign.

"Please do not bring anything to eat and drink from outside."

LÜTFEN DIŞARIDAN YİYECEK VE İÇECEK GETİRMEYİNİZ.

kapının dışından. *from (the) outside (of the) gate.*
bankanın dışından. *from (the) outside (of the) bank.*
peronun dışına. *to (the) outside (of the) railway platform.*
English sometimes drops the little word *of.*
The noun **dışı** *the exterior* takes a buffer letter **-n-** when adding the **-de** and **-dan** suffixes.

A little warning: Do not mix this word with **diş** *tooth* which is spelt with a **Dotted-i.**

dışardan. *from outside.* is used without a preceding noun, because it is a adverb of place.
dışarı gidiyorum. *I'm going out.* (**dışarıya** also could be used.)
dışarıdan geliyorum. *I'm coming from outside.*
dışarıdayım *I am outside.*

(or **dışardayım** like **buradayım** which is spoken **burdayım** the shortened forms being generally used in daily conversation.)

As an Adverb of Place: dışardan *from outside.*

A sign in a park cafe.

"In here which are sold products from outside to bring is prohibited. We thank you."

> # BURDA SATILAN ÜRÜNLERİ DIŞARDAN GETİRMEK YASAKTIR. TEŞEKKÜR EDERİZ.

Some Examples:

Evin dışına çıktı. *He went out of the house.* [to the outside of the house.]

Kapının dışında bir adam bekliyordu. *A man was waiting outside the door.* [at the outside of...]

Evin dışından arabalar geçiyor. *Cars are passing outside the house.* [by way of the outside of the house.]

iç interior, internal.

-(n)in içine. *to the inside of.*
-(n)in içinde. *at the inside of.*
-(n)in içinden. *from the inside of.*

Used as an Adjective.
iç hastalıkları. *internal diseases.*
iç savaş. *civil war.*

Used as a Noun.
odanın içi. *the inside of the room.*
ormanın içinde. *in the depths the forest.*
garın içinden. *from the inside of the railway station.*

Some Further Examples:
Tirenin içinde yer buldu, oturdu. *He found a place in the train and sat down.*

Bu kutuda ne var? Bilmem, içine bakmadım. *What is in this box? I don't know, I haven't looked inside.*

Odanın içinden bir gürültü geliyordu. *A noise was coming from inside the room.*

Bu odanın içindekilerin hepsi kiralıktır. [iç-i-nde-ki-ler-in hep-si.] *The contents of this room are all on hire.*

Eşyalarımı kutu içine koydum. *I put my things into a box/boxes.*

Eşyalarımı kutunun içine koydum. *I put my things into the box.*

Bir hafta içinde kitabını bitirecek. *He will finish his book within a week.*

Bu şehrin içinde çok insan var. *There are many people in this town.*

As an Adverb of Place içeri *inside.*

içeri *inside* is used without a preceding noun, because it is a adverb of place.
içeri *I'm going in(side).* ("içeriye" could also be used.)
içerden geliyorum. *I'm coming from inside.*

Also **içeri** and **dışarı** can be used with nouns.
Lütfen kapıdan içeri giriniz. *Please go (pass) inside through (or from) the door.*
Evimden dışarı çık! *Get out of my house!.*

yan *side, next to.*

-(n)in yanına. *to the side of.*
-(n)in yanında. *at/by the side of.*
-(n)in yanından. *from the side of.*

Used as an Adjective.
yan kapı. *side gate.*
yan sokak. *side road.*

Used as a Noun.
kapının yanında. *right/just next to the gate.*
bankanın yanından. *from next to the bank.*
sol duvarın yanına. *next to the left wall.*
duvarın sol yanına. *next to the left side of the wall.*

Some Further Examples.
Mehmet, Ali'nin yanına oturdu. *Mehmet sat down next to Ali.*

Mehmet, Ali'nin yanında oturdu. *Mehmet sat next to Ali.*

Kitabı, yatağın yanındaki masanın üstüne attı. *He threw the book on top of the table beside the bed.*

taraf *side, side part.*

-(n)in tarafına. *to the side part of.*
-(n)in tarafında. *at/by the side part of.*
-(n)in tarafından. *from the side part of.*

Used as a Noun.
taraf is not an adjective, it is only used as a noun.
kapının tarafında. *at the side of the gate.*

bankanın tarafından. *from the side (of) the bank.*
peronun tarafına. *to the side of the railway platform.*

Some examples with **taraf** *side part.*
Arabanın alt tarafından bir şeyler damlıyor. *Something(s) is dripping from the underside of the car.*

Sen kimin tarafındasın? Benim mi onun mu? *Whose side are you on? Mine or his?*

Dolabın üst tarafına baktın mı? *Have you looked at (to) the topside of the cupboard?*

üst *top, topmost.*

-(n)in üstüne. *to the top of.*
-(n)in üstünde. *at/by the top of.*
-(n)in üstünden. *from the top of.*

Used as an Adjective.
üst tepe. *the top hill.*
en üst pencere. *the uppermost window.* (superlative.)

Used as a Noun.
bardağın üstünde. *on top of the glass.*
ağaçların üstüne. *towards the top of the trees.*
arabamın üstünden. *from the top of the my car*

Some Further Examples.
Kitabı, masanın üstüne koydu. *He put the book on top of the table.*

Kapının üzerinde büyük bir pencere vardı. *There was a big window over (on top of) the door.*

üzeri *over.*

üzeri *over, on top of, in addition to, besides.*
-(n)in üzerine. *over.*
-(n)in üstünde. *at/by the top of, over the top of..*
-(n)in üstünden *from the top of, from over the top of..*

Used in Construction.

üzeri is not an noun or adjective. It is only used in prepositional constructions.
Elma üzerine portakal getir. *In addition to apples get (some) oranges.*

binanın üzerinden. *from over the building.*
masanın üzerindeki fincan. *the cup which is on top of the table.*

Some Further Examples.
Bu sözün üzerine çok kızdım. *Upon these words I became very angry.*

Bunun üzerine çok kızdım. *Upon this I became very angry.*

civar *vicinity, neighbourhood, locality, precincts of.*

-nin civarıda. *close by, hereabouts.*
Sis saat on civarında kaybolmaya başladı. *The fog began to lift around 10 o'clock.*

Saat iki civarı otogarda sizi bekleyeceğiz. *We will wait at the station for you around 2 o'clock.*

Bu civarda bir banka var mı? *Is there a bank nearby?*

Ahmet Beyler Kadıköy'e yeni taşındığı için civarı iyi tanımıyorlar. *Because the Ahmet family have only just (newly) moved to Kadiköy they do not know the neighbourhood well.*

Teknik gezi sırasında Samsun'la birlikte civar köylerde de incelemeler yapıldı. *In the course of the Technical walk-around, Samsun together with the local villages also were examined.*

Cebinde 20 TL civarında para kalmıştı. *He had about 20TL left in his pocket.*

Bu civarların kekliği çok lezzetlidir. *Partridge of this locality is very tasty.*

"Z" partisi Adana ve civar illerden daha çok oy aldı. *The "Z" party polled many more votes from Adana and its environs.*

Acaba bu civarlarda bir hastane var mı? Eğer varsa lütfen bana telefon numarasını verir misiniz? *Is there hospital around here, I wonder? If there is could you give me its telephone number, please?*

50 yaş civarında hastalıklar ardı ardına gelmeye başlar. *At* *around fifty years of age illnesses begin to come one after the other.*

Hırsızlar 17-18 yaş civarında 2 gençti. *The thieves were two youths about seventeen or eighteen years old.*

alt *under.*

alt. *bottom, under, below, underneath.*
-(n)in altına. *under, to the under of.*
-(n)in altında. *under, at/by the under of.*
-(n)in altından. *from underneath.*

Used as an Adjective.
alt kapı. *the bottom gate.*
alt dolap. *the lower cupboard.*

Used as a Noun.
Alt dolabın altına fincanları koyunuz. *Put the cups (to the) underneath the bottom cupboard.*

Masanın altından topu cekin. *Get the ball from under the table.*

Sağ ayağımın altı kaşınıyor. *The underneath of my right foot is itching.*

Some Further Examples.

Köpek dolabın altına girdi, orada yatıyor. *The dog went under the cupboard (entered to the underneath the cupboard) and is lying there.*

Köpek dolabın altında yatıyor. *The dog is lying under the cupboard.*

Köpeğimiz hep ayak altında. *Our dog is always underfoot.*

orta *middle, center.*

-(n)in ortasına. *to the middle of.*
-(n)in ortasında. *at the middle of.*
-(n)in ortasından. *from the middle of.*

Used as an Adjective.
orta kapı. *the middle gate.*
orta oda. *the centre room.*

Used as a Noun.
parkın ortasına. *to the middle of the park.*
bahçenin ortasında. *in the middle of the garden.*
orta odanın ortasından. *from the centre of the middle room.*

Some Further Examples.

Yemeğin ortasında geldi. *He arrived in the middle of the meal.*

Her zaman yemek ortasında gelir. *He always comes in the middle of dinner.*

Sokağın ortasında yürüyor. *He is walking in the middle of the street.*

Tam sokağın ortasında yürüyor. *He is walking right in the middle of the street.*

Tam sokağın ortasından yürüyor. *He is walking exactly down the middle of the street.*

Ahmed'in kitabının ortasına kadar okudum. *I read as far as the middle of Ahmet's book.*

Buraya hafta ortasında vardı. *He arrived here in midweek.*

Buraya haftanın ortasında vardı. *He arrived here in the middle of the week.*

art. *behind.*

art. *behind, rear side, backside.*
-(n)in ardına. *to the behind of.*
-(n)in ardında. *at the rear of.*
-(n)in ardından. *from behind of.*

Used as a Noun.
art is not an adjective. It is only used as a noun.

kapının ardında. *at the rear the door, behind the door.*
bankanın ardından. *from behind the bank.*
mutfağın ardına. *to the rear of the kitchen.*

arka. *back, rear.*

-(n)in arkasına. *to the back of.*
-(n)in arkasında . *at/by back of.*
-(n)in arkasından. *from the back of.*

Used as an Adjective.
arka kapı. *the back gate.*
arka bahçe. *the back garden.*

Used as a Noun.
kapının arkası. *the back of the door.*
garajın arkasından. *from back of the garage.*
kuyruğun arkasına. *to the back of the queue.*

Some Further Examples.

Evimin arkasında büyük bir bahçe var. *There is a big garden behind my house.*

Masanın arkasına baktınız ml? *Did you look behind (to the back) the table?*

ön. *front.*

-(n)in önüne. *to the front of.*
-(n)in önünde. *at/by front of.*
-(n)in önünden. *from the front of.*

Used as an Adjective.
ön kapı. *the front door.*
ön pencereler. *the front windows.*

Used as a Noun.
kapının önünde. *in front of the door.*
manavın önüne. *to the front of the greengrocer's.*

rafların önünden. *from the front of the shelves.*

Some Further Examples.

Otobüs, tam evimizin önünde durur. *The bus stops just in front of our house.*

Bahçemizin önündeki duvarda oturduk. *We sat on the wall which is in front of our garden.*

yakın. *near.*

yakın. *near, nearby, close to, in the vicinity of.*
-(n)in yakınına. *to the nearby of.*
-(n)in yakınında. *nearby.*
-(n)in yakınından. *from near the.*

Used as an Adjective.
yakın kapı. *the nearby gate.*
yakın bir ofis. *an office nearby.*

Used as a Noun.
kapının yakınında. *near the gate.*
kapının yakınlarında. *near by the gate.* (plural is more vague.)
bankanın yakınından. *from close to the bank.* [Lit: from the near of the bank]
otogarın yakınına. *in the vicinity of bus station.*

Used as an Adverb of Place **yakın** *near.*
bankaya yakın. *near to the bank.*

ara. *space between.*

-(n)in arasına. *in between.*
-(n)in arasında. *between.*
-(n)in arasından. *from between.*

Used as an Adjective.
ara kapı. *the door between.* (a connecting door between rooms.)

Used as a Noun.
hafta arası. *mid-week.*

Kapıların arasında bir basamak var. *There is a step in between (of) the doors.*

Masaların arasına iskemleyi koyun. *Put the chair (to the) between (of the) tables.*

Bunların arasından bir tane alın. *Take one from between these.*

This word refers to the space between two or more things. it is used in constructions which mean "between" or "among" and is preceded either by a plural noun or several nouns connected by **ile** *also, and.*

Some Further Examples.

Evlerimizin arasında büyük bir bina var. *There is a big building between our houses.*

O evlerin arasında bir park var. *There is a park amongst those houses.*

Amerika ile Avrupa arasında Atlas Okyanusu var. *The Atlantic Ocean is between America and Europe.*

karşı. *opposite, against.*

-(n)in karşısına. *to the opposite side of, against.*
-(n)in karşısında. *at the opposite side of, against.*
-(n)in karşısından. *from the opposite side of, against.*

Used as an Adjective.
karşı kapı. *the opposite gate.*
karşı kaldırım. *the opposite pavement.* (USA: opposite sidewalk.)

Used as a Noun.
kapının karşısında. *opposite the gate.*
bankanın karşısındaki sokak. *the street opposite the bank.*
Mehmet, kahvenin karşısından çıktı. *Mehmet came out from opposite the cafe.*

Some Further Examples.
Fabrika, evimizin karşısında. *The factory is opposite our house.* (across from our house.)

Mehmet'in karşısına oturdu. *He sat down facing (opposite, across from) Mehmet.*

Bir kedi karşıma çıktı. *A cat appeared in front of me.*

etraf *around.*

Etraf was originally an Arabic Plural of **taraf** *side.*
etraf. *around, environment, surroundings.*
-(n)in etrafına. *to the surrounds of.*
-(n)in etrafında. *around the.*
-(n)in etrafından. *from around the.*

Used as a Noun.
etraf is not an adjective. It is only used as a noun.
Masamızın etrafına bolca çiçek koyuldu. *Flowers galore were put around our table.*

Etrafımda çocuklar oynuyordu. *The children were playing (all) around me.*

Bostanın etrafından. *From around the vegetable garden.*

çevre *around, surrounding.*

A sign in a park *"Let us keep our surroundings clean."*

ÇEVRİMİZE
TEMİZ TUTALIM.

çevre is synonymous with *etraf* shown above, and is gradually replacing the Arabic word.
-(n)in çevresine. *to the surrounds of..*

-(n)in çevresinde. *around the..*
-(n)in çevresinden *from around the..*

Used as an Adjective.
çevre yolu. *circular road.* (bypass road.)

Used as a Noun.
Kentin çevreleri. *The surroundings of the town.*

Bankanın çevresinde bir park bulunur. *There is a park surrounding the bank.*

Fabrikanın çevresine bir engel koydular. *They have put a barrier around the factory.*

In Geometry **Çevre** also means *perimeter.*
Karenin çevresi 24 cm(dir). *The perimeter of the square is 24 cm.*
The other words are **alan** *area* and **hacim** *volume.*

A building site sign **Çevre-miz-e**. An actual example:

İNSAAT SIRASINDA
ÇEVRİMİZE
VERECEĞEMİZ
ZARALARDAN VE
RAHATSIZLIKLARDAN
DOLAYI
ÖZÜR DİLERİZ.

"We apologize on account of the dangers and discomforts that we will give to our surroundings during building works."

Explanation:

çevre-miz-e [surroundings-of-us-to]
inşaat sırasında *during the building (works)*
vereceğimiz zararlardan *from the damages that we will give*
rahat-sız-lık-lar-dan dolayı [lit: discomfortnesses-from because of]
on account of discomfort (the word is just "discomfort" in English
-dan dolayı *because of/on account of.* This construction takes the
"movement away from" (ablative) case.

aşağı *down, downstairs*

-(n)in aşağısı *downwards*
-(n)in aşağısında *below, downstairs*
-(n)in -aşağısından *from below, less than*

Used as an Adjective
aşağı mahalle *a low town district* (Figuratively: slum)
aşağı kat *the floor below*

Used as a Noun
inişin aşağısı *downhill* [Lit: The down of the hill]
Merdivenin aşağısına *To downstairs*

Yolun aşağısından yürüyün. *Walk from the bottom of the road.*

Dağın aşağısı serin. *It is chilly down the mountain.* [Lit: The down
of the mountain is chilly.]

Dağın aşağısındaki ağaçlar çok güzel. *The trees which are at the
lower side of the mountain are very beautiful.*

Dağın aşağısından gelen rüzgar çok soğuk. *The wind which comes
from the lower side of the mountain is so cold.*

Used as an Adverb of Place
aşağı *downstairs*

Aşağı gidiyorum. *I'm going downstairs* or **Aşağıya gidiyorum.** *I'm
going (to) downstairs*

"Aşağı" and "yukarı" are also used for the geographical terms
"upper/lower" in Turkish.

As an example **Yukarı Bavyera** *Upper Bavaria*, **Aşağı Bavyera** *Lower Bavaria.*

Some places in Turkey called "Lower".
Aşağıazaplı, village in Adıyaman Province.
Aşağınasırlı, a village in the District of Gölbaşı.
Aşağı Gökdere, Eğridir, Isparta.
Aşağı Pınar, Neolithic excavation in the outskirts of the town of Kırklareli.
Akbank Aşağıayrancı Şubesi, a local bank in Ankara Çankaya.
Aşağı Dudullu İlköğretim Okulu, Ümraniye, İstanbul.
Aşağı Yuvalı Köyü, a village in Gümüşhane.
Aşağı Hadim Cami, a mosque in Konya.

yukarı. *above, up upstairs.*

-(n)in yukarısına. *upwards.*
-(n)in yukarısında. *up, upstairs.*
-(n)in yukarısından. *from above/more than.*

Used as an Adjective.
yukarı ev. *the house above.*
yukarı dal. *the branch (of a tree) above.*

Used as a Noun.
yokuş yukarı. *uphill.*
merdivenin yukarısı. *upstairs.*
Tepenin yukarısından indik. *We came down from the top of the hill.*

Some places in Turkey called "Upper".
Yukarı Borandere, Kayseri.
Yukarı Düden Şelalesi Antalya.
Yukarı Ağadeve, Hamur, Ağrı Province.
Yukarı Karahayıt Hotels.
Yukarı Norgâh in Erzurum.
Yukarı Pınarca Köyü Trabzon.
Yukarı Nasırlı Turkey.
Yukarı Gökdere, Eğridir, Isparta.

peş. *back, the space behind.*

"Peş" means "the back of a moving object". Usually found in the form "peşinden" which has come to mean "after". Used only of a moving object when something or someone follows after something else that is also in motion.

Taksiyle otobüsün peşinden gittik. *We went after the bus by taxi.* [We followed the bus by taxi.]

Benim peşime düşün! *Follow me!* [LIT: Fall in behind me.]

The word **peşin, peşinat** means *pre-payment, paid in advance, following on.*
peşin para. *cash, ready money, spot cash.*

General Space Examples.

Bir adam, vapurun arkasından suyun içine duştu. *A man fell from the back of the ship into the water.*

Onlarla bizim aramızda, bahçe üzerine kavga çıktı. *A fight arose between them and us over the garden.*

Büyük bir ağacın altında yere yattı. *He lay on the ground under a big tree.*

Her şeyim el altında. *Everything of mine is at hand.*

Dükkanın arkasında büyük elma ağaçları var. *There are big apple trees behind the store.*

Halil her aksam içki içip, gece ortasında eve gelir. *Halil drinks every evening and comes home in the middle of the night.*

Size bir paket getirdim, eşyalarınızın arasına attım. *I brought you a package and threw it among your things.*

Bu kış, sizinkinin karşısındaki evde oturacağız. *This winter we will live in the house which is opposite yours.*

Paketin içindekilerini bize gösterir misiniz? *Will you show us the contents of the package?*

Evin dış kısmına baktık, içine ama girmedik. *We looked at the outside part of the house, but we didn't go inside.*

Askerler, şehrin önüne duvar yaptılar. *The soldiers made a wall in front of the city.*

Ahmet daima o kızın peşinden gider. *Ahmet always follows that girl.*

39 TIME, SEASONS , NUMBERS

About Time and Numbers.

saniye, saniyelik. *second.*
an. *moment.*
dakika, dakikalık. *minute.*
saat, saatlik. *hour.*
[Plural **saatler** does not follow vowel harmony rules.]

gün, günlük. *day.*
hafta, haftalık *week.*
ay, aylık. *month.* [also *moon.*]
yıl, yıllık or **sene senelik.** (Arab.) *year.*

The terms ending in "-lik" refer to a specific noun of an amount: **iki hafta sonra** *two days later* but Turkish says:
İki haftalık bir tatil yapacağım. *I will take a two week (amount) holiday.*
Bir dakikalık saygı duruşu. *A minute's silence (stoppage) of respect.*

The many words for "time".

zaman. *time.*
vakit. (vakti.) *time as a particular occasion.*
defa. *time. (as an event or occasion.)*
kere. *time (as an event, occasion or point in time.)*
kez. *a point in time.*

zaman. *time.*
"zaman" is the main word in use for "time, occasion"
ne zaman? *what time?, when?*
kaç zaman. *how long?, how much time?*
zamandan zamana. [zaman-dan zaman-a] *from time to time.*
her zaman *all the time, every time, always.*

380

her ne zaman. *whenever* [lit: every which/what time]

vakit. (vakti.) *point in time, occasion.*
"vakit" apocoptates loses final vowel when suffixed with a vowel.
Boş, vaktimiz var mı? *Have we got time to spare?*
vaktim yok, vaktim kalmadı *I haven't got time.*
This word is used most for "time to spare".

kere. *times, occasions.*
dört kere. *four times.*
Onu, beş kere yaptım. *I did it five times.*

kez. *time, point in time.*
This is a provincialism, but is also used regularly in modern daily speech.
üç kez. *three times.*
her kez. *always.*
bu kez. *this time.*

Telling the Time.

State the actual time "to o'clock":
It is # min. to # o'clock using **-e var.**
Saat iki'ye on (dakika) var. *It is ten (minutes) to two.*
[There are 10 to hour 2.]

State the actual time "past o'clock":
It is # min. past # o'clock using **-i geçiyor.**
Saat iki'yi on (dakika) geçiyor. *It is ten (minutes) past two.*
[10 are passing the hour 2.]

State at the time "when to 'o'clock":
At # min. to # o'clock using **-e kala.**
Saat iki'ye on (dakika) kala. *At ten to two.*
[To the hour 2 remain 10.]

State at the time "when past 'o'clock":
At #min. past # o'clock using **-i geçe.**
Saat iki'yi on (dakika) geçe. *At ten past two.*
[The hour 2 pass 10.]

Saat kaç acaba? *What time is it please?*
Saatiniz kaç acaba? *Have you got the time please?*
Saat yedi'yi çeyrek geçiyor. *It is a quarter past seven.*
[A quarter is passing seven.]
Saat yedi'ye çeyrek var. *It is a quarter past seven.*
[There is a quarter to seven.]

Sentence structure can only be used with the suffix **-ken** *while*
Ne zaman gelirsin? *When (at what time) will you come?*

Saat 7'yi çeyrek geçerken gelirim. *I will arrive at a quarter past
seven.* [I'll come while a quarter is passing 7 o'clock.]

Saat yedi'yi çeyrek geçiyorken gelirim. *I'll come at quarter past
seven.* [I'll come while a quarter is passing the seven.]

Saat yedi'yi çeyrek geçe gelirim. *I'll come at quarter past seven.*
[I'll come (as) a quarter is passing the seven.]

Saat altı'ya beş varken gelirim. *I'll come at five to six.* [I'll come
while there is 5 to six.]

Saat altı'ya beş kala gelirim. *I'll come at five to six.* [I'll come (as) 5
remain to six.]

Saat 7:15 (yedi on beş'te) gelirim. (Digital)
I'll come at seven-fifteen.

Some times of day.

şafak. *dawn.*
kahvaltı. *breakfast.*
sabah. *morning.*
sabahleyin. *at morning, in the morning.*
gün. *day.*
bütün gün. *all day long.*
her gün. *every day.*
gündüz. *daytime, daylight.*
öğle. *noon.*
öğleden sonra. *afternoon.*
öğle yemeği. *lunch.*

akşam. *evening.*
akşamleyin. *in the evening, at eventide.*
akşam üstü. *teatime, early evening.*
akşam yemeği. *dinner, evening meal.*
dün. *yesterday.*
dün sabah. *yesterday morning.*
dün akşam. *yesterday evening.*
dün gece. *last night.*
evvelki gün. *the day before yesterday.*
alacakaranlık. [alaca-karanlık] *twilight.*
gece. *night.*
geceleyin. *in the night, at night.*
gece yarısı [Lit: night its-half] *midnight.*
geçen gün. *the day past, the other day, yesterday.*
geçen ay. *last month.*
geçen sene/yil. *last year.*
geçen hafta. *last week.*
geçenlerde. *recently (in the past), lately.*
erken. *early.*
geç. *late.*
ne zaman. *when. (what time, the time that.)*
ay *month.*
cumartesi gecesi. *Saturday night.*
ertesi gün. *the following day.*
ertesi hafta. *the following week.*
evvelki/evvelsi gün. *the day before yesterday.*
geceleri. *at nights.*
gelecek hafta. *next week.*
hafta. *week.*
öbür gün. *the day after tomorrow.*
öbür hafta. *the week after next.*
öğleleri. *at noon times.*
öğleyin. *at noon.*
pazar sabahı. *Sunday morning.*
sabahları. *in the mornings.*
son günlerde. *in the last few days.*
son zamanlarda. *recently.*
yarın. *tomorrow.*
yil/sene. *year.*

Saying ?*How long for..*"

Ne iş yaparsınız? *What is your job?* [Lit: "What do you do (generally)?" uses General Simple Tense.]

Öğretmenim. *I am a teacher.*

Dört yıldır öğretmenim. *I have been a teacher for four years.* [Lit: "It is four years I am a teacher."]

İki bin üçten beri öğretmenim. *I have been a teacher since 2003.* [Lit: "I am a teacher since 2003".]

Dünden beri hastayım. *I have been ill since yesterday.*

Pazar Gününden/Pazardan beri evdeyim. *I have been at home since Sunday.*

Saying *"since.."*

This construction is the Short Infinitive [formed by dropping the final -**"k"** **gelme(k)** *the coming*] + Motion Coward Condition and suffixed with -**li** *furnished with*. The verb **olmak** *to be, become* completes this "since" construction.

Ben, Londra'ya gelmeyeli bir hafta oluyor. *It is a week since I am coming to London.* ["It is a week since I came to London.."]

Ben Londra'da kalmayalı üç sene oldu. *It was three years since I stayed in London.* ["I stayed in London 3 years ago.".]

Ben, sinemaya gitmeyeli 3 ay oluyor. *It is three months since I have been to the cinema.*

Birbirimizi görmeyeli beş yıl oldu/oluyor. *It is five years since we have seen/are seeing each other.*

Onlar evleneli sadece/yalnızca 2 ay oldu/oluyor. *It is just two months since they were/are (got) married.*

Timing Events.

çoktan, bile, zaten *already, besides.*

Hâlâ öğle yemeğini yedin mi? *Have you eaten your lunch yet?*

Ooo, çoktan yedim. *Oh, I have already eaten.*

Yedim bile. *I have already eaten.*

Sanırım bir şeyler yemek istiyor musun? *(I suppose) Do you want something to eat?*

Gelecek zaman bana hiç bir şey getirme. *Do not bring me anything next time.*

Ben yedim zaten. *Besides, I have already eaten.*

Yeni, şimdi, henüz. *just..*

Hasan,lütfen banyoya girme, yeni/şimdi/henüz (onu) temizledim. *Hasan, please don't go into the bathroom, I have just cleaned (it).*

Kuruması gerek/lazım. Tamam mı? *It needs to dry. OK?*

Bana 100 lira ödünç verir misin Ayşe? *Can you lend me 100 Tl Ayşe?*

Üzgünüm [or Kusura bakma]**, veremem.** *I am sorry, I can't give (it).*

Daha yeni/şimdi faturaları ödedim. *I have just paid the bills.*

Daha, henüz, hâlâ. *yet.*

Daha/henüz ödevini bitirmedin mi? *Haven't/have you finished your homework yet?*

Hayır, daha bitirmedim. Henüz değil. *No, I haven't finished yet. Not yet.*

Daha gelmediler. *They haven't come yet.*

Şimdiye kadar, şu ana kadar *So far, up to now, until now*

Bu kış şimdiye kadar/şu ana kadar kar yağmadı. [şimdi-y-e, an-a.] *It has not snowed so far this winter.*

Bugün şimdiye kadar/şu ana kadar hiçbir şey yemedik. *We have not eaten anything so far today.*

ilk *the (very) first, the original.*

Bu ilk kez araba sürüşüm/İlk kez araba sürdüm. *This is the very first time I have driven a car.*

ilk means *the very first one*, whereas **birinci** means *the first of a series*:
Dünyanın ilk insan Adam adlı'dı. *The world's first man was called Adam.*

Birinci yarış başlamak üzeredir. *The first race is about to begin.*

son *last, end.*

Bu, son iki saatte içtiğin beşinci kahve. *This is the fifth cup of coffee you have drunk in the last two hours.*

Son beş saatte iki fincan kahve içtin. *You have drunk two cups of coffee in the last five hours.*

hayatımda. *ever in my life.*

hayatında. [informal.] and **hayatınızda.** [formal.] *ever in your life.*
onun hayatında. *ever in his life.* [hayat-ı-n-da in his life.]
hayatımızda. *ever in our life.*
hayatlarında. *ever in their life.*

Bu hayatımda okuduğum en sıkıcı kitap. *This is the most boring book I have ever read (in my life).*

Bu hayatımda içinde bulunduğum en zor durum. *This is the most difficult situation I have ever been in, (in my life).*

Hayatımda tanıştığım en konuşkan/geveze insan. *He is the most talkative person I have met (in my life.)*

Saying *"Have you ever been to?"*.

There are two methods to translate this in Turkish:

(1) Formal Method: using **-de/-te -da/-ta bulunmak** *to be found (in/on/at a place.)*
Hiç Ankara'da bulundun mu? *Have you ever been to Ankara?*

(2) Informal Method: using **-a/-e gitmek** *to go (to a place)*
Hiç Ankara' ya gittin mi? *Have you ever been to Ankara* [Colloquial Speech informal.] The inclusion of **hiç...** signifies *ever...*

Saying *"once, twice, several times."*.

bir kez, bir defa, bir kere. *once.*
iki kez, iki defa, iki kere. *twice.*
birçok kez, defa, kere. *several times.*
hiç. *ever.* [in positive sentences]
hiç. *never.* [in negative sentences.]

Neredeydin? [colloquial Nerdeydin?] *Where have you been?/Where were you?*

Hiç Antalya'da bulundun mu? *Have you ever been to Antalya?*

Hiç Antalya'ya gittin mi? *Have you ever been to Antalya?*

Evet, bir defa/iki defa/ orada bulundum. *Yes, I have been there once/twice.*

Evet, bir çok kere (bir çok kez/ bir çok defa) oraya gittim. *Yes, I have been there many times.*

Yo, Antalya'ya hiç gitmedim. *No, I have not been/never been there.*

Yo, Antalya'da hiç bulunmadım. *No, I have not been/never been there.*

Yo is a gentle conversational way of saying "No". It is not so strong as using **Hayır** *No*. It may be a contraction of "yok" "there is not"

Seasons and the Weather.

Names of the Months.

January. **ocak.**
February. **şubat.**
March. **mart.**
April. **nisan.**
May. **mayıs.**
June. **haziran.**
July. **temmuz.**
August. **ağustos.**
September. **eylül.**
October. **ekim.**
November. **kasım.**
December. **aralık.**

Names of the Months and Days of the Week are usually written without a capital letter in Turkish.

The Weekday Names.

Sunday. **pazar.** (Lit: market.)
Monday **pazartesi.** (Lit: after Sunday.)
Tuesday. **salı.** ("slaughter day".)
Wednesday. **çarşamba** (Lit: 4 days after Sabbath from Persian.)
An idiom:
Bu iş, çarşamba pazar gibi. *This job is a complete mess up.*
[lit: This job is like a Wednesday Market.]
Thursday. **perşembe** (Lit: 5 days after Sabbath from Persian.)

Friday. **cuma** (Lit: reunion related to Persian/Arabic.)
Saturday. **cumartesi** (Lit: after Friday.)

The Seasons of the Year "Yıl Mevsimi".

ilkbahar. [also **bahar** is sometimes used.] *spring.*
yaz. *summer.*
sonbahar. (also **güz.**) *autumn* (or *fall* American Usage.)
kış *winter*

When saying *in the summer* Turkish says **yazın** or *in the winter*
kışın is used. This ending **-in** is an old Instrumental Case which is
no longer used in day to day speaking other than these examples.

For saying *in the spring* and *in the autumn*, the Static Condition
(Locative) Suffix is used **sonbaharda** and **ilkbaharda.** Very often
the simple word **bahar** can supplant either **ilkbahar** or **sonbahar**
depending on the choice of the speaker.

The Cardinal Points "Dört Yön".

Kuzey. *North.*
Güney. *South.*
Doğu. *East.*
Bati. *West.*

A Weather Vocabulary.

berbat. *awful.*
fırtına. *storm.*
soğuk. *cold.*
güneş. *sun.* (n.)
sıcak. *hot.*
güneşli. *sunny.* (adj.)
güzel. *good, nice.*
hava sıcaklığı. *temperature.*
harika. *marvellous.*
sıcaklık. *heat.*

yağmur. *rain.* (noun.)
derece. *degree(s).*
yağmur yağmak. *rain.* (transitive verb.)
şemsiye. *umbrella.*
yağmurlu, yağışlı. *rainy.* (adj.)
ılık. *warm.*
kar, karlı *snow.* (n.), *snowy* (adj.)
hava. *weather.*
kar yağmak. *snow.* (v.)
hava tahmini. *weather forecast*
kar yağışlı, karlı *snowy* (adj.)
hava durumu. weather condition. (forecast)
dolu. *hail*
rüzgar, rüzgarlı . *wind.* (n.), *windy.* (adj.)
hafif. *light.*
yel. *wind.*
sert. *heavy.*
poyraz. *breeze.*
durmak. *stop, cease.* (v.)
rüzgar esmek. *to blow wind* (v.)
yıldırım. *lightning.* (n.)
rüzgarlı. *windy.* (adj.)

Weather Expressions.

Ne güzel bir gün! *What a lovely day!*
Hava yarın nasıl olacak? *What will the weather be like tomorrow?*
Yine güneşli, fakat biraz rüzgarlı. *It's sunny again, but a little windy.*
Kaç derece? *What is the temperature?*
Hava çok sıcak. *The weather is very hot.*
Neredeyse 31 derece. *Nearly 31°C (degree Celsius).*
Erzurum'da kar yağacağını düşünüyor musun? *Do you think it will snow in Erzurum?*

Sanmıyorum. Kar için erken. *I don't think so. It is early to snow.*
Fırtına olacağını düşünüyor musun? *Do you think there will be a storm?*
Sanmıyorum. *I don't think so.*

Ama Ağrı'da kar yağıyor. *But it is snowing in Ağrı.*
Orada kar yağışı ne zaman durur? *When will it stop snowing up there?*
Yakında durur. *It will stop soon.*

Yağmur mu başlayacak? *Will it start to rain?*
Evet, birazdan yağmur başlayacak gibi. *Yes, looks like rain soon.*
Şemsiyeye ihtiyacım olur mu? *Do I need an umbrella?*
Sana şemsiyeni yanına almanı öneririm. *I suggest you to get your umbrella with you.*

Ne berbat hava! Saat başı değişiyor. *What an awful weather! It changes hourly.*
Yağmur mu, kar mı yağıyor? *Is it snowing or raining?*
Yağmur yağıyor. Kar yağıyor. *It is raining. It is snowing*

Weather Forecast "Hava Durumu".

Açık. *Clear.*
Sıcak. *Hot/Heat.*
Soğuk. *Cold/Chill.*
Az bulutlu. *Light cloud.*
Parçalı bulutlu. *Partly cloudy.*
Çok bulutlu. *Very cloudy.*
Duman. *Smoke, muggy.*
Pus. *Mist, haze.*
Sis. *Fog.*
Hafif yağmurlu. *Light Rain.*
Yağmurlu. *Rainy.*
Kuvvetli yağmurlu. *Heavy rain.*
Hafif sağanak yağışlı. *Light downpour.*
Sağanak yağışlı. *Continuous rain.*
Kuvvetli sağanak yağışlı. *Heavy continuous rain.*
Hafif kar yağışlı. *Light snow.*
Kar yağışlı. *Snow.*
Yoğun kar yağışlı. *Dense snow.*
Yer yer sağanak yağışlı. *Outbreaks of snow.*
Dolu. *Frost.*
Gök gürültülü sağanak yağışlı. *Thunderstorms.*

Actual Weather Forecasts.

Türkiye'de yağışlar kesilmiyor, art arda gelmeye devam edecek. Bugün de birçok yerde kar var, soğuk hava Marmara ve Karadeniz'de daha uzun süre kalacak. *In Turkey the rain will not stop, it will continue back to back. Today there will be a little snow, The cold weather will continue in Marmara and Black Sea (areas).*

İstanbul'da hafif karla karışık yağmur var, yarın ise hafif yağmur olacak. Ankara'da kar iki gün daha aralıklarla yağacak. Bursa'da da kar var. İzmir çok soğuk ve bulutlu. Adana üç gün sağanak yağmurlu. *There is mixed rain and snow in Istanbul, as for tomorrow it will be light rain. In Ankara it will snow periodically for a further two days. Izmir, very cold and cloudy. Adana, three days rain showers.*

Marmara soğuklardan en fazla etkilenen bölge. Ayın sonuna kadar sıcaklık fazla yükselmeyecek. Bugün Tekirdağ, Balıkesir, Bilecik ve Bursa'da hafif kar var. Sıcaklık 5 dereceyi geçemiyor. Yarın bölgede yağış çok zayıf. *Marmara is area most affected by the cold. It will not get any warmer up to the month's end. Today there is light snow in Tekirdağ, Balıkesir, Bilecik and Bursa. The temperature will not move from 5 degrees. Tomorrow the rains will be very light in the area.*

İç Anadolu'nun genelinde Pazartesi, Salı ve Perşembe günleri yine aralıklarla kar olacak. Yarın Sivas çevresinde kar yoğunluğunu artıracak. *Throughout central Anatolia it will be snow showers on Monday, Tuesday and Wednesday. Tomorrow the snow will fall more heavily around Sivas.*

Ege bugün de soğuk. Güneyi yağışlı. Afyon, Kütahya-Uşak çevresinde kar olacak. Muğla merkezde de sulu kar görülebilir. Yarın sıcaklık biraz yükseliyor. Çarşamba günü yeni bir yağışlı hava, kuvvetli rüzgarlarla birlikte bölgeye gelecek. *The Aegean is also cold today. The south showery. Around Afyon, Kütahya-Uşak it will snow. In the centre of Muğla watery snow may be seen. Tomorrow the temperature will rise. On Wednesday there will be showery weather together with strong winds.*

Akdeniz'de Güneydoğuda ve Girne'de sağanak yağışlar üç gün devam edecek. Antalya'nın özellikle sahil beldelerinde yağmur

daha kuvvetli. **Lodos sıcaklığı yükseltmeye başlıyor, Antalya 14 derece.** *In the South-east Mediterranean and Girne (Kyrenia Cyprus) the showers will continue for three days. Especially for the beach resorts of Antalya the rain will be heavier. The South-west wind temperature will begin to increase.*

Doğu Anadolu'da köy yollarının çoğu kapandı. Bugün Erzurum-Van arasında kar yağışı zayıflasa da bölgede üç gün daha aralıklarla devam edecek. *Many village roads in Eastern Anatolia have been closed. Today between Erzurum and Van the snow may ease and continue periodically for the next three days.*

Karadeniz'de yağışlar bugün oldukça zayıfladı. Bolu, Giresun ve Gümüşhane'de kar var, Trabzon'da hava kapalı. Yarın yağış Bolu, Kastamonu, Samsun arasında yeniden kuvvetlenecek. *In the Black Sea the showers will ease back today. There is snow in Bolu, Giresun and Gümüşhane, in Trabzon the weather is overcast. Tomorrow snow will increase again between Bolu, Kastamonu, Samsun.*

Numbers.

Cardinal Numbers 0 49.

sıfır-0 bir-1 iki-2 üç-3 dört-4 beş-5 altı-6 yedi-7 sekiz-8 dokuz-9
on-10 on bir-11 on iki-12 on uç-13 on dört-14 on beş-15 on altı-16 on yedi-17 on sekiz-18 on dokuz-19

yirmi-20 yirmi bir-21 yirmi iki-22 yirmi uç-23 yirmi dört-24 yirmi beş-25 yirmi altı-26 yirmi yedi-27 yirmi sekiz-28 yirmi dokuz-29

otuz-30 otuz bir-31 otuz iki-32 otuz uç-33 otuz dört-34 otuz beş-35 otuz altı-36 otuz yedi-37 otuz sekiz-38 otuz dokuz-39

kırk-40 kırk bir-41 kırk iki-42 kırk uç-43 kırk dört-44 kırk

393

beş-45 kırk altı-46 kırk yedi-47 kırk sekiz-48 kırk dokuz-49

Cardinal Numbers 50 99.

elli-50 elli bir-51 elli iki-52 elli uç-53 elli dört-54 elli beş-
55 elli altı-56 elli yedi-57 elli sekiz-58 elli dokuz-59

altmış-60 altmış bir-61 altmış iki-62 altmış uç-63 altmış dört-
64 altmış beş-65 altmış altı-66 altmış yedi-67 altmış sekiz-
68 altmış dokuz-69

yetmiş-70 yetmiş bir-71 yetmiş iki-72 yetmiş uç-73 yetmiş
dört-74 yetmiş beş-75 yetmiş altı-76 yetmiş yedi-77 yetmiş
sekiz-78 yetmiş dokuz-79

seksen-80 seksen bir-81 seksen iki-82 seksen uç-83 seksen
dört-84 seksen beş-85 seksen altı-86 seksen yedi-87 seksen
sekiz-88 seksen dokuz-89

doksan-90 doksan bir-91 doksan iki-92 doksan uç-93 doksan
dört-94 doksan beş-95 doksan altı-96 doksan yedi-97 doksan
sekiz-98 doksan dokuz-99

Cardinal Numbers 100 1,000,000.

yüz-100 iki yüz-200 uç yüz-300 dört yüz-400 beş yüz-500 altı
yüz-600 yedi yüz-700 sekiz yüz-800 dokuz yüz-900

bin-1000 iki bin-2000 uç bin-3000 dört bin-4000 beş bin-
5000 altı bin-6000 yedi bin-7000 sekiz bin-8000 dokuz bin-
9000

on bin-10000 on bir bin-11000 on iki bin-12000 on uç bin-
13000 on dört bin-14000 on beş bin-15000 on altı bin-16000 on
yedi bin-17000 on sekiz bin-18000 on dokuz bin-19000

yirmi bin-20000 yirmi bir bin-21000 yirmi iki bin-22000 yirmi
uç bin-23000 yirmi dört bin-24000 yirmi beş bin-25000 yirmi
altı bin-26000 yirmi yedi bin-27000 yirmi sekiz bin-28000

otuz bin-30000 kırk bin-40000 elli bin-50000 altmış bin-60000 yetmiş bin-70000 seksen bin-80000 doksan bin-90000 bir milyon-1000000

Peculiarities of Numbers.

yüz *100* also means "face" or "reason".
Bu yüzden, O yüzden. *Because of this, For that reason.*
Binanın ön yüzü. *The front face of the building, Facade.*

Cardinal numbers are followed by singular nouns.
iki ev *two houses*
beş yüz araba *five-hundred cars*
kırk ağaç *forty trees*

beş yüz yirmi üç bin yedi yüz elli sekiz *523,758.*
Which may also be written in official papers and banks without any spaces: **beşyüzyirmiüçbinyediyüzellisekiz** *523,758.*

When English states a small general numerical amount it says: "Two or three" Example: "Two or three eggs", "two or three cars." However Turkish will say "üç beş" "three (or) five". Example: **üç beş yumurta** *three (or) five eggs.* [English: "two or three eggs".]

In Turkish the number **kırk** *forty* is used to signify an uncountable amount. **Kırk yılda bir** *Once in forty years* is equivalent to "Once in a blue moon" in English.

Ordinal Numbers *first, second, etc.*

sıfırıncı *zeroth;*
ilk *first; 1st, the original*
birinci *first; 1st of a list*
ikinci *second; 2nd*
üçüncü *third; 3rd*
dördüncü *fourth; 4th*
beşinci *fifth; 5th*
altıncı *sixth; 6th*
yedinci *seventh; 7th*

sekizinci *eighth; 8th*
dokuzuncu *ninth; 9th*
onuncu *tenth; 10th*
on sekizinci *eighteenth; 18th*
yirmi üçüncü *twenty-third; 23rd*
otuz dördüncü *thirty-fourth; 34th*
elli beşinci *fifty-fifth; 55th*
kırk altıncı *forty-sixth; 46th*
altmış yedinci *sixty-seventh; 67th*
seksen sekizinci *eighty-eighth; 88th*
doksan dokuzuncu *ninety-ninth; 99th*
yüzüncü *hundredth; 100th*
bininci *thousandth; 1000th*

Fractions and Percentage.

yarım (noun) *half*
yarım elma *a half an apple*
yarı (adj.) *half*
yarı elma *a half apple*
elmanın yarısı *the apple half*
buçuk *half* [an hour, a kilo, a serving.]
çeyrek *quarter of* [an hour, a kilo, a serving.]
bir *one, #1* [And is also the indefinite article *a* or *an.*]
üçte iki [üç-te iki] *two-thirds* [lit: 3-in 2 written 3/2.]
yüzde yirmi beş *twenty-five percent* [Lit: 100-in 25 written %25.]

Distributive Numbers One each, two each, three each.

yarımşar *half each*
birer *one each*
ikişer *two each*
üçer *three each*
dörder *four each*
beşer *five each*
altışar *six each*
yedişer *seven each*
sekizer *eight each*

dokuzar *nine each*
onar *ten each*
on birer *eleven each*
yirmişer *twenty each*
yirmi beşer *twenty-five each*
otuzar *thirty each*
kırkar *forty each*
ellişer *fifty each*
yüzer *a hundred each*
ikişer yüz (not iki yüzer) *two hundred each*
biner *a thousand each*
ikişer bin (not iki biner) *two thousand each*
birer milyon (not milyonar nor bir milyonar) *a million each*
Kızlara ikişer elma verin. *Give the girls two apples each.*

40 COLOURS

Türk Renkleri Turkish Colours.

The Farsi Word **siyah** *black* is mainly used for **siyah zeytin** *black olives* (for eating), otherwise the word **kara** *black* is always used. **Kara** is also used figuratively as in **kara düşünceleri** *black (dark thoughts.)*

The word **kara** also has separate meaning *land, shore* as in:
karayolları. *land roads (network), main roads.*
kara kuvvetleri. *land forces.*
kara suları. *territorial waters.*
karaburun. [Lit: land-nose.] *peninsular.*

Qualities of Colours.

The suffix **-(i)mtrak** is used with colours to produce adjectives of colour quality:

karamtırak. *blackish, darkish, dusky.*
sarımtırak. *yellowish, sallow.*
mavimtırak. *blueish, blued, steel coloured.*

This suffix always retains the form **-mtırak** and does not follow vowel harmony rules.

The suffix **-(i)msi** is also used with colours to produce adjectives of colour quality:

morumsu. *purplish.*
mavimsi. *bluish.*
This suffix follows vowel harmony rules.

renk *colour*, **rengi** *its colour*, **renkli** *coloured*, **renkler** *colours*

Basic Colours.

siyah (Farsi) *black*
simsiyah *pitch black*
kara *black*
kapkara *pitch black*
beyaz *snow white*
bembeyaz *snow white*
kırmızı *red*
kıpkırmızı *bright red*
mavi *blue*
masmavi *bright blue*
turuncu *orange*
yeşil *green*
yemyeşil *bright green*
mor *purple*
mosmor *deep purple*
pembe *pink*
pespembe *shocking pink*
pembe *pink*
tozpembe *light (dusty) pink*
kahverengi *brown*
sarı *yellow*
sapsarı *bright yellow*
gri *grey*

Extended Colours *" light and dark"*.

ala *variegated*
ala *light brown*
acı renkli *lurid coloured*
alaca *spotted, mottled*
alacalı bulacalı *many coloured*
alaca buluca *spotted*
açık renkli *light coloured*
açık yeşil *light green*
koyu renkli *dark coloured*
koyu gri *dark grey*
koyu yeşil *dark green*

turkuvaz *turquoise*
lacivert *navy blue*
çakır (renkli) *grey-blue*
bej *beige*
eflatun *lilac*
morumsu kırmızı renk *magenta*
galibarda *fuchsia*
menekşe rengi *violet*
bordo [Fr. bordeaux] *claret*
gül rengi *rose colour*
çim rengi *lime colour*
zeytin rengi *olive colour*
haki rengi *khaki, olive drab*
metalik rengi *metallic colour*
altunî *gold coloured*
altın renkli *gold coloured*
gümüş rengi *silver colour*
gümüş renkli *silver coloured*
gök kuşağı *the rainbow*
ak (Old Turkish) *white*
al (Old Turkish) *red*
çim lime colour from *turf, grass, lawn*
zeytin *olive fruit*
altın *gold*
gümüş *silver*
menekşe *violet flower*
gül *rose flower*
alabalık *rainbow trout*
sarımtırak altuni metalik rengi *yellowish golden metallic colour*
kahverengi *brown* [lit: coffee coloured]

About Old Turkish Names for Colours

The Old Turkish Words for *Red* **Al** and *White* **Ak** are mostly used in place names and family names; otherwise the words "beyaz white, kırmızı- red" are used.

Alsancak. (an area of İzmir.) *Red Banner.*
Akhisar. (a town in Turkey.) *Whitefort.*

Bay Alkan. *Mr. Redblood.*
Akdemir Sanayi A. Ş. *The White-Iron Industry Ltd.*

Seeing "red".

The word **kızıl** means *red-coloured* and is used in certain situations
as these examples show:
Kızıldeniz. *the Red Sea.*
Kızılderili. *American Red-Indian.*
kızılötesi. *infra-red.*
kızıl saçlı. *red haired.*
Kızılay. *the Red Crescent.* (same as The Red Cross health service.)
Kızılırmak. *the Red River.* (the longest river in Turkey.)

41 CONVERSATIONAL ITEMS

Common Daily Talk.

How to say *"Thank you"*.

Here we point out the difference in usage of **teşekkür ederim** *thank you* and the more sincere **sağ olun** *stay healthy*.

What are the services being rendered to us?

(1) **sağ olun** *be healthy, be strong* is used as *thank you* for a service which:
(a) Was not necessary.
(b) For someone who has gone out of his way to help you.

(2) While **teşekkür ederim** *thank you* [Lit: "a thanking perform I", from Arabic] is used in normal circumstances and receiving presents.

Scenario (1).

(a) The waiter puts a nice meal in front of you. Your *thank you* is **teşekkür ederim**, it is his job.

(b) The waiter puts a bottle of wine in front of you. Your *thank you* is **teşekkür ederim**, it is his job.

(c) Then the waiter uncorks the bottle of wine and pours it in your glass. Your *thank you* is **sağ olun**, he need not have performed this service.

The recipient of your gratitude will often answer your **sağ olun** with the rejoinder **siz de sağ olun** *health to you also* [this is the Polite Version said to stranger]. Other forms are **sen de sağ ol**, or quite short **siz de** or **sen de** *you too*.

Scenario (2).

You ask someone the time. He looks at his watch and says *"Half past three"*. Your answer is **sağ olun**, you have caused him to perform a service to you.

Scenario (3).

You drop your handkerchief a stranger picks it up and hand it to you. Your answer is **sağ olun**, He need not have done it.

Many tourists use **sağ olun** wrongly instead of using **teşekkür ederim** as they copy the boy waiter's way of thanking as the waiters often use **sağ olun** for misguided effect. The rule is, if in doubt then use **teşekkür ederim.**

How to answer a "thank you".

The answer to **teşekkür ederim** is **bir şey değil** *It is nothing* or **rica ederim** *I request!*, same as "bitte schön" in German.

Also used is **ne demek?** *what does it mean?* This expression **ne demek?** sounds quite comical in English. But it actually means something like: *It doesn't matter at all.* The answer **Rica ederim** is the politest one. The recipient of your gratitude will often answer your **sen sağol** with the rejoinder **sen de sağol** *health to you too.*

Other Versions are:

sağ ol. [familiar.]
sağ olun. [polite and/or singular.]
sağ olunuz. [public and/or plural]

A simple **teşekkürler** also means a very informal *thanks* and is used in shops and for small duties performed.

A little Caveat or "take care" when giving thanks.

Many people when first learning Turkish are tempted to use the Present Continuous Tense form **teşekkür ediyorum.** This form sounds quite comical to the Turkish ear and can also be construed as being sarcastic. One should always use the Present Simple form

teşekkür ederim and you will not go wrong or be misunderstood.

Turkish Modes of Address.

Who are you?

The usual method of address when you do not know the person's name or title is as follows:

For males: **Beyefendi** *Sir.*
Daily pronunciation is truncated to: **Beyfendi**
For females: **Hanımefendi** *Miss* or *Madam.*
Daily pronunciation is truncated to: **Hanfendi.**

These are used in formal situations and to strangers.

Personal Addressing Formal and Informal.

Once names are known then **bey** and **hanım** are used after the first name. This usage is formal and semi-formal. These titles follow the given-name (Christian name) and are written without a capital letter:

Mustafa bey. *Mr. Mustapha.*
Ayşe hanım. *Miss* or *Mrs. Ayshe.*

These are used in formal situations when you know the person's first name but also in informal situations to acquaintances, friends and even to you own family members.

Surnames are not usually used in conversational Turkish, so the **Mustafa bey** can mean *Mr. Mustafa* and **Ayşe hanım** can mean *Mrs.* or *Miss Ayşe* (in a formal situation) or it can mean just a friendly *Mustafa* or *Ayşe* (without the title) between acquaintances.

All About Names and Surnames.

Turkish has two words for the first name of a person **isim** or **ad** and they can both be used at any time as they are interchangeable. The Turkish word for surname is **soyadı**, there is no corresponding word for surname based in the word "isim"

İsminiz ne? *What is your first name?*
İsmim Ayşe. *My name is Ayşe.*

isim *name* becomes **isminiz** *your name* and **ismim** *my name*. This is one of the nouns that "apocopate". (loses an internal vowel.)

Adınız ne? *What is your first name?*
Adım Ali *My name is Ali.*
Soyadınız ne? *What is your surname?*
Soyadım Karaca *My surname is Karaca.*

Finding out about a Third Person.

The third person suffix is **-i** or **-ı** meaning *his, her, its.*

Onun ismi ne? *What is his name?*
Onun ismi Mehmet *His name is Mehmet.*
Onun adı ne? *What is her name?*
Onun adı Deren *Her name is Deren.*
Onun soyadı ne? *What is his surname?*
Onun soyadı Gürses *His surname is Gürses.*

When talking about a third person remote from us we may ask the question: *What is that man's name?* In this case the words "man's name" is translated correctly by using the Possessive Relationship to show that the two words belong to each other.

adamın ismi. *the man's name.* [Lit: the name of the man.]
adamın adı. *the man's name.*
adamın soyadı. *the man's surname.*
O Beyefendinin soyadı ne? *What is that gentleman's surname?* [Lit: the surname of the man.]
O Beyefendinin ismi ne? *What is that gentleman's name?*

To make the sentence more conversational we would normally say: *I wonder what that lady's name is?* "I wonder" is simply translated by adding the word **acaba** at the beginning or end of the Turkish question.

O Hanımefendinin adı ne, acaba? *I wonder what that lady's name is?*

Acaba, Mehmet'in soyadı ne? *I wonder what Mehmet's surname is?*

Kız kardeşinizin ismi ne, acaba? *What is your sister's name, I wonder?*

There is an increasing use of addressing people by their surname, especially used on television in interviews etc.

This method uses the word **Sayın** *esteemed* before the surname directly. If the interviewee's name is **Musafa Kurt**, then he may be addressed as **Mustafa bey** (formal and informal) or directly by his surname as **Sayın Kurt** *Esteemed Kurt* (formal and public) or **Bay Kurt** *Mr. Kurt* (polite and official). **Bay** *Mr.* and **Sayın** *Esteemed* are usually spelt with capital letters, but they can be found without capital letters.

Addressing Letters and Envelopes.

Sayın Mustafa Kurt. *Esteemed Mustafa Kurt.*
Çekmece Mah. *Çekmece District.*
Uzunyol Sok. Nolu:24 D:6. *Uzunyol Street No.24 Apt No. 6.*
Bağarası Köyü. *Bağarası Village.*
02332 İZMİR, TÜRKİYE. *Post Code. Postal County. TURKEY.*

Abbreviations Used in Addresses.

Sok. (Sokak or Sokağı) *Street.*
D. (Daire) *Apartment, Suite.*
Cad. (Cadde or Caddesi) *Road.*
Apt. (Apartman) *Apartment*
Bul. (Bulvar or Bulvarı) *Avenue.*
K. (Kat) *Floor.*
Yol. (Yol or Yolu) *Way, Route.*
No. (Numara) *Number.*

Mah. (Mahalle or Mahallesi) *Local District.*
Nolu. (Numaralı) *Numbered.*

Greetings.

In semi formal situations there is a four stage greeting procedure:

(i) The Welcome: hoş geldiniz or less formal **hoş geldin** *Welcome!*
This is answered by **hoş bulduk** *We found it well!*

(ii) The Greeting: This is an exchange of **merhaba** *Hello.*

(iii) The Asking after Health Stage: nasılsınız? (formal)
or **nasılsın?** (informal) *How are you?*

(iv) The Response: This is answered by **İyiyim, teşekkür ederim** *I am well, thank you.*

This then followed by a question about the other's health: **Siz nasılsınız?** *You, how are you?*

Daily Greetings.

günaydın. *good morning, good day, good afternoon.*
iyi günler. *good day.*
iyi akşamlar. *good evening.* (said on arrival.)
iyi geceler. *good night* .(said on leaving company.)
görüşmek üzere. *see you soon.*
hoşça kal. *so long* [Lit: stay joyful.]

In Turkish the plural is used in "Good day, Good evening, Good night" similar to the Spanish "Buenos Días"

Some Daily Informal Greetings.

For an informal greeting like *Hi!* in English, Turkish uses **Selam!** to which the answer is the same **selam!**

Also one can use *What's up?* **Na'ber? Na'ber?** is commonly used in everyday language. It is actually **Ne haber?** *What news?* The answer is generally **İyidir, senden?** [Lit: It's good, and from you?]

Another informal greeting is **Ne var ne yok?** *What is happening?* [Lit: What is there (going on?) What isn't there (going on?)].

The answer to this one is **İyilik!** *Goodness! Wellness!*

There is also the "Formula speak" **hayrola!** meaning -*What's up!, what's the matter?* [I hope that nothing is wrong!]

A Long Goodbye.

There is a "Formula Speak" that is used quite lot and is very common for saying your "Goodbyes". This is often used when leaving company or on going away to somewhere. The person(s) who are leaving will say **Allaha ısmalardık!** *Goodbye!* [a quasi religious-type formula]. The answer said by those staying behind is **Güle güle!** *Cheerio!* [Lit: Go with a smile!]. If you use this formula after visiting your Turkish friends they will be suitably impressed.

The Muslim Peace Greeting.

Selâmünaleyküm (a Muslim peace greeting) answered by **Aleykümselâm.**

This greeting is mainly used between passing strangers, normally both male, during travel or on entry to a crowded room, such as a tea house, when one cannot address everybody personally.

How to say *"Too much, Too many"*.

The translation of *too, too much* is a common difficulty for the student of Turkish. The dictionary equivalent is **fazla** *in excess* or **lüzumdan fazla** *in excess of its necessity.*

(1) *Too* meaning "very".

However in daily conversational Turkish **çok** *very* is used to convey the meaning *too much, too many.*

In such a sentence as *I didn't buy it, it was too expensive.* the word "too" should simply be translated by **çok** *very.*
Onu almadım, çok pahalıydı *I didn't buy it, it was too expensive.*

(2) *Too* meaning "overly, excessively".

fazla *in excess* should be used where the context does not make sense by using **çok** *very.*
Baban, seninle fazla sabırlıdır *Your father is too patient with you.*

(3) *Too* as "ability to" or "inability to".

For the type of sentence *He was too tired to undress (himself)* where neither **çok** *very* or **fazla** *in excess* is not suitable Turkish uses a special comparative type construction.
Soyunamayacak kadar yorgundu [Lit: He was tired the amount pertaining-to-his-future inability-to-undress.] *He was too tired to get undressed.*

Explanation:

Verb Forms Basic Infinitive (-mek/-mak.)
soymak. *to undress somebody else.*

Reflexive Infinitive.
soyunmak. *to undress oneself.*

Negative Reflexive Infinitive.
soyunmamak. *not to undress oneself.*

Negative Potential Reflexive Infinitive.
soyunamamak. *not to be able to undress oneself.*

Future Relative Reflexive Participle. ("-ecek/-acak")
soyunacak. *a future undressing of oneself.*

Negative Future Relative Reflexive Participle.
soyunmayacak. *a future not undressing oneself.*

Negative Future Potential Relative Reflexive Participle.

soyunamayacak. *a future not being able to undress oneself.*

A further example of this type.

The verb is basically **gitmek** *to go* which in this sentence takes the form of the Negative Potential **gidememek** *not to be able to go.*

Sinemaya gidemeyecek kadar meşgulüm. *I am too busy to go to the cinema.*

The construction for "too" therefore is: Future Potential Relative Participle + **kadar** + comparison verb + person.

Ayşe, bu yıl tatil yapamayacak o kadar hastaydı.
Ayşe, this year her-future-inability-to-make-a- holiday that-amount ill she was. *Ayşe was too ill to go on holiday this year.*

Araba güzel zaman içinde duramayacak kadar çabuk sürüyordu.
[Lit:The car in-good-time its-future-inability-to-stop that-amount quickly was-going.] *The car was going too fast to be able to stop in time.*

Daily Talk.

Günaydın . *Good morning.*
İyi akşamlar. *Good evening.*
İyi geceler. *-Good night.*
In English the expressions *Good evening* and *Good night* are singular. In Turkish they are plural, as is the Spanish "Buenos Dias".

Hello...

Merhaba *Hello!, Hi!* **Merhaba** corresponds to *Hello!, Hi!* in English. Its usage is identical in either language. The reply for **Merhaba** is **Merhaba.** However **Merhaba** is not used for *Hello!* on the telephone. This type of "Hello!" is **Alo! Selam** *Hello!, Hi!* **Selam** is more informal than **Merhaba.**

Selamünaleyküm: literally means *May God's peace be upon you* and is used by Muslims as a greeting. **Aleykümselam**: is said in reply to the greeting **Selamünaleyküm**.

Hoş geldin (familiar/singular) or **Hoş geldiniz** (polite/plural) corresponds *Welcome!* in English. The reply for **Hoş geldin(iz)** is **Hoş bulduk**. *We found it well.*

...and Goodbye.

Allahaısmarladık [Allaha ısmarladık], **Hoşca kalın** *Goodbye* **Hoşça kal** (familiar) or **Hoşça kalın** (polite) corresponds to *Stay well, Keep happy* in English.

Güle güle *Goodbye* [lit: Smiling, smiling.] The person staying behind, says **Güle güle** corresponds *Go well.* in English The person is leaving leaves, says **Allahaısmarladık** or **Hoşça kalın**. **Allahaısmarladık** *Goodbye* [Lit: I leave you to God's care.] Either **Allahaısmarladık** or **Hoşça kalın** is correct in informal situations. But in formal situations **Hoşça kalın** is better.

İyi günler *Good day*. Its usage is almost the same as in English. It is also the formal of **Allahaısmarladık** and **Hoşça kalın**. The reply for **İyi günler** is either **İyi günler** or **Size de** *To you also*.

Görüşürüz *See you later*. [Lit: We will see each other.] The reply for **Görüşürüz** is **Görüşürüz**.

Allah rahatlık versin. This is an informal expression for *Good night*. [Lit: May God give you peace and comfort.] This is generally used by the members of the family at home or friends before going to bed.
The reply for **Allah rahatlık versin** is **Sana da** (singular/informal), or **Size de** (plural/formal) *And to you also*.

Thanks and Be Happy.

Teşekkür ederim *Thank you*. This is used in all normal situations. The reply for **teşekkür ederim** is **Bir şey değil** or **Rica ederim** *You are welcome*.

411

sağol (familiar) or **sağolun** (polite) [Lit: "Health to you"] equates to *thank you* but is more sincere than **Teşekkür ederim.** The reply for **sağ olun** is **sen de sağ olun** *And health to you also.* **Sağ ol** is conjugated for persons. So: **sen de sağ ol** is the response for **sağ ol** and **siz de sağ olun** is the response to **sağ olun.**

Gözün aydın (familiar/singular) or **Gözünüz aydın** (polite/plural) [Lit: "May your eyes shine."] hen something which the speaker longing for comes true, he tells the others about it. Their response is **Gözün(üz) aydın** *Your eyes shine* to the speaker. The expression indicates that the others share the speaker's happiness, and that they are also happy about it. The reply for **Gözünüz aydın** is **Teşekkür ederim.**

Hayırlı olsun *Let it be with goodness.* Used when someone opens a shop or starts a new business, others say **Hayırlı olsun** to him. The expression indicates the speaker's wish that the new business will bring him prosperity, and it will be profitable. The reply for **Hayırlı olsun** is **Teşekkür ederim.**

Güle güle kullan/kullanın. *Use it with a smile.* When someone buys a thing, such as a new clothes, shoes or a car his friends say **Güle güle kullan/kullanın.** This indicates the speaker's wish that use it with joy. **Hayırlı olsun** can also be used in this case. The reply for both expressions is **Teşekkür ederim.**

Have a Good Journey.

İyi yolculuklar/Hayırlı yolculuklar. *Have a nice journey.*
İyi tatiller. *Have a nice holiday.*
İyi şanslar. *Good Luck.*
İyi eğlenceler. *Have a nice time.*
İyi seneler/yıllar, Mutlu seneler/yıllar. *Happy new year.*
Doğum/Yaş günün kutlu olsun! *Happy birthday!*
Afiyet olsun. *Bon appetite, Enjoy your meal.*

Well done and Take It Easy.

Kolay gelsin *May it come easy.* Used when the speaker sees someone working, busy with something. It can be a physical, or mental work. It indicates the speaker's wish that whatever that person is doing at the moment, may be easy for him. The reply for **Kolay gelsin** is **Teşekkür ederim.**

Aferin *Bravo, Well done!* Very often used in competition and especially to congratulate young children.

Sorry About It.

Affedersin (singular/familiar) or **Affedersiniz** (plural/polite): *Excuse me./Pardon me.* **Affedersin(iz)! Merkeze nasıl gidebilirim?** *Excuse me! How can I get to the city centre?*

Özür dilerim: *I am sorry.* Sometimes **Affedersin(iz)** is used instead of **Özür dilerim**. However **Özür dilerim** is more formal. It sounds better in formal situations.

Bir şey değil, Rica ederim: *You are welcome.* Used in reply to **Teşekkür ederim**

Ways of saying "Yes" in Turkish.

Evet. *Yes* in the sense of answering "Yes/No" questions in English.
Tamam. *Yes* in the sense of "O.K."
Peki. *Yes* in the sense of "All right, O.K., If that's so then."
Oldu. *Yes* in the sense of "That's good, agreed."
Evet, efendim. "Yes, Sir or Madam."
Var. *Yes, there is.* Answers questions which contain "var mı?" "Is there?, Are there?"

Ways of saying "No" in Turkish.

Hayır. *No* in the sense of answering yes/no questions in English.
Olmaz *No* in the sense of *That's not possible, I don't agree with you, That won't do.*
Yok, Yo. informal and gentle saying of *No.* [Also answers questions containing **Yok mu?** *Isn't there?*]

Hayır efendim *No sir./No madam.* "Efendim" must be used in this case else this answer could be construed as being curt.

Words of Condolence What a pity.

Geçmiş olsun *May it pass away* This expression is used when a friend is ill or has had an accident, like "Get well soon" in English. The reply for **Geçmiş olsun** is **Teşekkür ederim.**

Başın sağ olsun. (singular/familiar) or **Başınız sağ olsun.** (plural/polite) *Health to your head.* This equates to *My condolences to you, So sorry about it.* in English.
The reply for **Başınız sağ olsun.** is **Siz de sağ olun, Dostlar sağolsun.**

Çok yazık!/Ne yazık! *What a pity!*
Çok üzüldüm! *I'm sorry to hear that!*

Saying "another" and "the other".

When we say "other, another, the other" in English often we make no distinction in the meaning. Turkish, however, does show a difference.

başka means *another.*
diğer ,öbür means *the other* where there is an alternative choice available.

Başka bir kız arkadaşım var. *I have got another girlfriend.*
Diğeri beni terketti. *The other one left me.*

Avustralya'nın Melbourne kentindeki Thomastown banliyösünde, arabasına benzin alırken çakmağıyla oynayan genç sürücü kendini birden alev topunun ortasında buldu Parlayan alevlerin arasında ne yapacağını şaşırdı. Dikkatsiz genç, alevleri söndürme çabası sonuç vermeyince arabasını alevler içinde bırakarak ön kapının üzerinden atlayarak kaçtı. Benzincideki *başka* bir sürücü *diğer* yangın söndürme tüpüyle koşarak alevleri söndürdü ve büyük bir faciayı önledi. *In the city of Melbourne, Australia, in the suburb of Thomastown, a young driver who was playing with his cigarette lighter while filling up*

*his car suddenly found himself in a ball of flame. He was puzzled about what to do in the glowing flames. The reckless youth, giving up his attempt to extinguish the flames and fled by leaving his car and jumping out of the front door. At the gas station **another** driver came running with **the other** fire extinguisher to put out the flames and prevented a major disaster.*
- Sabah Gazetisi.

42 WORD RECOGNITION IN TURKISH

Word Formation in Turkish.

In English we have many little suffixes such as *-ness, -ly, -tion* etc. which we use to form and modify words and meanings from existing nouns and words. The same exists in the Turkish language and here we list some of the main ones.
Sometimes (as in English) the connection of the modified word is not always apparent from the original; however in your studies this list will help you to recognize parts of speech and take an educated guess at the actual meaning of the word in question.
It is all part of the language learning curve. Each word has to be learnt but being able to recognize word endings can often be a help in reading and communicating.

Forming Nouns and Adjectives.

-lık-/lik-/-luk/-lük.

Makes concrete and abstract nouns like *-ness* or *-tion* in English.
iyi *good* forms **iyilik** *goodness.*
göz *eye* forms **gözlük** *spectacles.*
güzel *nice, lovely* forms **güzellik** *beauty.*
Also forms nouns of place and usage.
kömür *coal* forms **kömürlük** *coal cellar.*
elma *apple* forms **elmalik** *apple orchard.*
tuz *salt* forms **tuzluk** *salt cellar.*

-lı-/li-/-lu/-lü.

 Forms adjectives furnished with, containing, emanating from, and nationalities.
şehir *town* forms **şehirli** *a townsman.*

para *money* forms **paralı** *requiring payment in cash.*
ağaç *tree* forms **ağaçlı** *a copse, a glade.*
İngiliz *English* forms **İngilizli** *an Englishman.*

-sız/-siz/-suz/-süz.

Forms adjectives of lacking, lack of, without, -less.
su *water* forms **susuz** *thirsty.*
para *money* forms **parasız** *stony broke.*
zarar *damage, injury* forms **zararsız** *undamaged.*

-ci/-cı/-cu/-cü or -çi/-çı/-çu/-çü.

Forms nouns of occupation, work etc.
taksi *taxi* forms **taksici** *taxi driver.*
kebap *kebab* forms **kebapçı** *kebab seller.*
balık *fish* forms **balıkçı** *fisherman.*
yol *road, way* forms **yolcu** *traveller.*

-ca/-ce/-ça/-çe.

Forms the names of national languages and also adverbs and adjectives.
Türk *Turk, Turkish* forms **Türkçe** *Turkish [as a language.]*
İngiliz *English (as an adjective)* forms **İngilizce** *the English language.*
İspanyol *Spanish (as an adjective)* forms **İspanyolca** *the Spanish language.*
aptal *fool* forms **aptalca** *foolishly.*
yavaş *slow* forms **yavaşça** *slowly.*
sert *hard* forms **sertçe** *hardish.*
giz, gizli *secret* forms **gizlice** *secretly.*

Gives the meaning of likeliness.
Çocukca davranıyorsun. *You are behaving childishly.*
İnsanca yasamalıyız. *We must live humanly.*

Gives the meaning "in terms of, on the point of".
Kiloca senden daha fazla. *He weighs more than you in kilograms.*
Akılca birbirinizden farkınız yok. *There is no difference between*

*you in **terms of intellect**.*

Gives the meaning "according to".
Sence yaptığın doğru mu? *Do **you think** it is right what you have done.*
Bence sana yeşil çok yakışıyor. *I **think** green suits you well.*

Gives the meaning of "muchness, exaggeration".
Yüzlerce kitap okumuş. *He has read hundreds of books.*

Enumerates a time period.
Bu okulda yıllarca çalıştım. *I worked at this school **for years**.*
Seni saatlerce bekledim. *I waited for you for hours.*
Defalarca sana yazmak istedim. *I wanted to write to you **so many times**.*

Gives the meaning "togetherness, unity".
Bu kararı ailece aldık. *We took this decision **as all the family**.*
Sınıfça pikniğe gittik. *We went to picnic **all together with the class**.*

Makes an adverb.
Sessizce beni dinle. *Listen to me **quietly**.*
Onunla gizlice buluştum. *I met him **secretly**.*

Gives the meaning "downsizing, decreasing, restriction"
Yaşlıca bir adam bana seni sordu. *An **oldish** man asked me for you.*
Büyükçe bir taşı fırlattı. *He threw away a **somewhat large** stone.*

-daş .

Basically this suffix means "fellow".
vatan *native country* forms **vatandaş** *fellow countryman; citizen.*
arka *back, behind* forms **arkadaş** *friend.*
yol *road, way* forms **yoldaş** *fellow traveller.*

-inci/-ıncı/-uncu/-üncü.

Used for ordinal numbers.
üç *three* forms **üçüncü** *the third.*
beş *five* forms **beşinci** *the fifth.*

-msı/-msi.

Adds an "-ish" to certain adjectives.
acı *bitter* forms **acımsı** *slightly bitter.*
ekşi *sour* forms **ekşimsi** *sourish.*

-cil/-cıl.

Adds "concern about.." to certain words.
ben *I* forms **bencil** *selfish.*
insan *person* forms **insancıl** *humane; caring.*

-şın.

Used with colour names.
sarı *yellow* forms **sarışın** *blonde.*

-sal.

Adjectivally takes on the noun meaning.
kum *sand* forms **kumsal** *sandy.*
kadın *woman* forms **kadınsal** *feminine.*

-cağız.

A diminutive suffix, for persons and pets.
kız *girl* forms **kızcağız** *poor little girl.*
çocuk *child* forms **çocukcağız** *poor little child.*

-cık/-cik/-cuk/-cük.

A diminutive suffix for size, quantity.
az *little, a bit* forms **azıcık** *just a bit.*
küçük *small* forms **küçücük** *tiny, smallish.*
büyük *big* forms **büyücük** *biggish.*

Note: A final **-k** is dropped when adding this suffix.

-tı/-ti/-tu/-tü.

Forms nouns from certain verbs.

horuldamak *to snore, to gurgle* forms **horultu** *a snore.*
cıvıldamak *to chirp, to twitter* forms **cıvıltı** *a chirping; a twittering.*

Forming Verbs from Nouns or Adjectives.

-lamak/-lemek.

su *water* forms **sulamak** *to water; to irrigate.*
taş *stone* forms **taşlamak** *to pave; to throw stones at.*
uğur *good luck* forms **uğurlamak** *to see somebody off.*
temiz *clean* forms **temizlemek** *to clean something.*

-almak.

az *less* forms **azalmak** *to lessen.*
dar *narrow* forms **daralmak** *to become narrow.*

-l.
doğru *correct, accurate* forms **doğrulamak** *to correct.*
sivri *sharp* forms **sivrilmek** *to become pointed.*

-a/-e.

kan *blood* forms **kanamak** *to bleed.*
yaş *age* forms **yaşamak** *to live; to exist.*
tür *a sort* forms **türemek** *to derive.*

-ar.
mor *purple* forms **morarmak** *to turn purple.*

-damak/-demek.

fısıltı *a mutter* forms **fısıldamak** *to murmur; to whisper.*
horultu *a snore* forms **horuldamak** *to snore.*
gürültü *noise* forms **gürüldemek** *to rumble.*

-atmak/-etmek.

yön *direction* forms **yönetmek** *to direct; to administer.*
göz *eye* forms **gözetmek** *to look after.*

-ıkma/-ikmek.

geç *late* forms **gecikmek** *to be late.*
bir *one* forms **birikmek** *to collect; to assemble.*

-ımsamak/-imsemek.

az *less, small* forms **azımsamak** *to regard as of little value.*
benim *my* forms **benimsemek** *to regard as one's own.*
küçük *small* forms **küçümsemek** *to regard as small; to condescend.*

-kırmak.

fıştı *a squirt* forms **fışkırmak** *to gush.*
haykırış *a squeal* forms **haykırmak** *to scream.*

-lanmak/-lenmek.

ev *house* forms **evlenmek** *to marry.*

-laşmak/-leşmak.

şaka *joke* forms **şakalaşmak** *to joke with each other.*
dar *narrow* forms **darlaşmak** *to narrow down.*
soğuk *cold* forms **soğuklaşmak** *to get cold.*

-samak/-semek.

Very often means "to regard as".
su *water* forms **susamak** *to get thirsty.*
garip *odd, peculiar* forms **garipsemek** *to regard as strange, curious.*
önem *importance* forms **önemsemek** *to regard as important.*

Forming Nouns from Verb Roots.

-ca/-ça -ce/-çe.

düşünmek *to think* forms **düşünce** *thought; opinion.*
eğlenmek *to enjoy oneself* forms **eğlence** *amusement; entertainment.*

-acak/-ecek.

This is a form of the Future Participle used as a noun.
giymek *to dress* forms **giyecek** *clothes; outfit.*
olmak *to become* forms **olacak** *suitable; reasonable.*
açmak *to open* forms **açacak** *can or bottle opener.*

-ak/-ek.

yatmak *to lie down* forms **yatak** *bed.*
kaçmak *to escape* forms **kaçak** *escapee.*
durmak *to halt/stop* forms **durak** *bus stop; a halt.*

-ga/-ge.

bölmek *to divide, partition* forms **bölge** *zone; area.*
süpürmek *to sweep. brush* forms **süpürge** *a broom; a brush; a whisk.*

-gan/-kan/-gen/-ken.

çalışmak *to work* forms **çalışkan** *industrious.*
unutmak *to forget* forms **unutkan** *forgetful.*
kaymak *to slide* forms **kaygan** *slippery.*

-gı/-gi.

sevmek *to love, like* forms **sevgi** *love; affection.*
çalmak *to play (mus.) ; to steal* forms **çalgı** *musical instrument.*
asmak *to hang (up)* forms **askı** *peg; hanger.*

-gıç/-giç.

bilmek *to know* forms **bilgiç** *info; data.*
başlanmak *to begin, to be begun* forms **başlangıç** *initial start up.*

-gın/-kın/-gin/-kin/-gün/-kün/-gun/-kun.

Forms nouns and adjectives of description and result.
bıkmak *to be fed up with.* forms **bıkkın** *bored; fed up.*

yormak *to tire, to become weary* forms **yorgun** *tired.*
solmak *to fade* forms **solgun** *faded.*
şaşmak *to deviate* forms **şaşkın** *bewildered; amazed.*
kızmak *to get angry, to get hot* forms **kızgın** *angry; hot.*

-ı/-i/-u/-ü.

Added to single syllable verb roots ending in a consonant to form a noun.
ölmek *to die* forms **ölü** *a corpse.*
yapmak *to make* forms **yapı** *a construction; a building.*
dolmak *to fill* forms **dolu** *full (adj.)*
kokmak *to smell* forms **koku** *a smell.*
koşmak *to run* forms **koşu** *a race.*

-ıcı/-ici/-ucu/-ücü.

Forms a nouns of profession and "doers".
yapmak *to do* forms **yapıcı** *performer; doer; builder.*
görmek *to see* forms **görücü** *matchmaker (for intended marriage).*
almak *to take* forms **alıcı** *purchaser.*
satmak *to sell* forms **satıcı** *seller; dealer.*

-ık/-ik/-uk/-ük.

Forms nouns and adjectives of result (from which there is no return.)
kesmek *to cut* forms **kesik** *a cut.*
açmak *to open* forms **açık** *open (adj.)*
bozmak *to spoil* forms **bozuk** *ruined; spoiled; out of order.*
çıkmak *to go/come out* forms **çıkık** *dislocated, projecting.*
delmek *to bore, to drill* forms **delik** *hole.*
saçmak *to scatter* forms **saçık** *scattered.*

-ım/-im/-um/-üm.

Forms nouns of a single occasion/happening.
saymak *to count* forms **sayım** *census; count.*
seçmek *to choose* forms **seçim** *choice; election; selection.*
ölmek *to die* forms **ölüm** *death.*

ölçmek *to measure* forms **ölçüm** *measurement.*
satmak *to sell* forms **satım** *a (single) sale.*

-ın/-in/-un/-ün.

yığmak *to heap up* forms **yığın** *heap, stack.*
akmak *to flow, stream out* forms **akın** *raid; rush.*
ekmek *to plant, sow (v.); bread (n.)* forms **ekin** *crop.*

-inç/-inç/-unç/-ünç.

gülmek *to laugh* forms **gülünç** *laughable, ridiculous.*
sevmek *to like, love* forms **sevinç** *mirth, delight.*

-ıntı/-inti/-untu/-üntü.

esmek *to blow* forms **esinti** *breeze.*
çıkmak; *to go out, exit* forms **çıkıntı** *projection, bulge, ledge.*
dökmek *to pour, dump, empty* forms **döküntü** *spillage, debris, waste.*

-ar/-er/-ır/-ir/-ur/-ür and -r.

From the Simple Present Participle Positive.
gelmek *to come* forms **gelir** *income; takings.*
gider *to go, leave* forms **gider** *expenditure.*
okumak *to read* forms **okur** *reader.*

-ış/-iş/-uş/-üş.

The Co-operative (in concert) Verb Mood sign.
oturmak *to sit, to reside* forms **oturuş** *way of sitting.*
yürümek *to walk* forms **yürüyüş** *a walk.*
satmak *to sell* forms **satış** *general sales* as in **satış müdürü** *sales manager.*

-ıt/-it/-ut/-üt.

geçmek *to pass* forms **geçit** *passageway.*
yaş *age* forms **yaşıt** *of the same age.*

yakmak *to burn* forms **yakıt** *fuel.*
ölçmek *to measure* forms **ölçüt** *measure of value.*

-tı/-ti/-tu/-tü.

belirmek *to emerge, appear* forms **belirti** *indication, indicator.*
kızartmak *to redden/chafe; to grill* forms **kızartı** *eruption/glow.*

Forming New Verbs from Existing Verbs.

-ala/-ele.

kovmak *to drive away* forms **kovalamak** *to chase (after).*
silkmek *to shake, toss* forms **silkelemek** *to shake s.o. out.*

-ımsa/-imse.

Forms a verbs "to regard as".
gülmek *to laugh* forms **gülümsemek** *to smile.*
anmak *to mention* forms **anımsamak** *to recollect.*

-ın/-in/-un/-ün.

Forms verbs with a Reciprocal meaning.
gezmek *to wander* forms **gezinmek** *to roam.*
görmek *to see* forms **görünmek** *to seem, appear.*
sevmek *to love, like* forms **sevinmek** *to feel glad.*
taşımak *to move* forms **taşınmak** *to move in/out.*

-r.

Forms a Causative Verb.
kaçmak *to escape* forms **kaçırmak** *to miss; to kidnap.*
batmak *to sink (by itself)* forms **batırmak** *to sink s.o.*
içmek *to drink* forms **içirmek** *to ply dinks.*

-ş.

Forms verbs with a Co-operative meaning.
görmek *to see* forms **görüşmek** *to meet.*
uçmak *to fly* forms **uçuşmak** *to fly away.*
gülmek *to laugh* forms **gülüşmek** *to laugh at each other.*

-t.

Forms verbs with a Causative meaning.
uzamak *to lengthen* forms **uzatmak** *to extend.*
sapmak *to deviate* forms **sapıtmak** *to go crazy.*
korkmak *to fear* forms **korkutmak** *to frighten.*
üşümek *to chill/to cool down* forms **üşütmek** *to get a chill/cold.*

-ıl/-il.

Forms Verbs of the Passive Mood.
sevmek *to like, love* forms **sevilmek** *to be loved/liked.*
kırmak *to fracture* forms **kırılmak** *to break s.o.*
satmak *to sell* forms **satılmak** *to be sold.*

43   THE GLOSSARIES

The following Glossaries are appended in this Chapter.

Apocopating Noun List.
A comprehensive list of nouns which lose their terminal vowel when adding a suffix which itself begins with a vowel. In effect a "buffer letter" is not used with these nouns.

Daily Locutions.
A list regularly used locutions translated into Turkish. We all use these kind of sayings in our daily language to help us think and to emphasize our meaning. Using these locutions will make your conversational language seem more fluid and normal in daily speech.

High Usage Word List.
A list of words constantly used in daily speech in Turkish.

Irregular Simple Tense Verb List.
The Simple Tense is the only one that shows partial irregularity in its formation. There are only thirteen verbs that show this irregularity. This list famous thirteen irregular single syllable verbs in the Simple Present. Twelve of them end their root in **-l** or **-r.** The single exception which root ends in **-n** (of these famous 13 exceptions) is **sanmak** which has the form **sanır** *to suppose.* These verbs are in common daily use.

Single Syllable Verb List.
Turkish has many single syllable verbs simply because they become very lengthy after addition of suffixes indicating mood, tense and person. Here is a comprehensive list of these verbs; knowing then expands your vocabulary enormously.

Intensive Adjective List.
This is a comprehensive list of Intensified Turkish Adjectives and Adverbs. They are commonly used in conversation, newspapers, periodicals and novels. It is a way that language colours itself.

An Apocopating Noun List.

Nouns which lose their final vowel from the root word. These particular nouns are to be shortened before adding any suffixes beginning with a vowel. This list is comprehensive.

As an example the addition of the vowel **-i -ı -u -ü** is the 3rd Person Singular. In the list below **Ağız** *Mouth* becomes **Ağzı** [Ağzı] *his mouth*. The final internal vowel of the original word is 'lost'. This is the same for all the nouns in this Apocopation Noun Listing.

Noun Possessed Noun Meaning.

Aciz Aczi (NOT acizi) *Impotence*
Ağız Ağzı (NOT ağızı) *Mouth*
Ahit Ahdi *Injunction*
Akıl Aklı *Intelligence*
Akit Aktı *Treaty*
Akis Aksi *Reflection*
Alın Alnı *Forehead*
Asıl Aslı *Origin*
Asır Asrı *Century*
Azim Azmi *Determination*
Bağır Bağrı *Bosom*
Bahis Bahsi (girmek) *to bet*
Beyin Beyni *Brain*
Boyun Boynu *Neck*
Burun Burnu *Nose*
Cisim Cismi *Substance*
Cürüm Cürmü *Crime*
Defin Defni *Burial*
Devir Devri *Period*
Ecir Ecri *Wage*
Emir Emri *Command*
Fasıl Faslı *chapter*
Fetih Fethi *Conquest*
Fikir Fikri *Idea*
Geniz Genzi *Nostril*
Göğüs Göğsü *Breast*
Gönül Gönlü *Heart*

Hacim Hacmi *Volume*
Haciz Haczi *Confiscation*
Hapis Hapsi *Prison*
Hasım Hasmı *Enemy*
Hazım Hazmı *Digestion*
Hışım Hışmı *Rage*
Hüzün Hüznü *Grief*
İlim İlmi *Science*
İsim İsmi *Name*
İzin İzni *Leave*
Kadir Kadri *Worth/Value*
Kahır Kahrı *Anxiety*
Karın Karnı *Stomach*
Kasıt Kastı *Intention*
Kayın Kaynı *Brother-in-law*
Kayıp Kaybı *Loss*
Kesir Kesri *Fraction*
Keşif Keşfi *Discovery*
Keyif Keyfi *Pleasure*
Kısım Kısmı *Part (of)*
Metin Metni *Text*
Nabız Nabzı *Pulse*
Nakil Nakli *Transport*
Nakit Nakdi *Cash*
Nazım Nazmı *Verse*
Nefis Nefsi *Personality*
Nesir Nesri *Prose*
Neşir Neşri *Publication*
Nutuk Nutku *Speech*
Oğul Oğlu *Son*
Resim Resmi *Picture*
Sabır Sabrı *Patience*
Satıh Sathı *Plane (area)*
Seyir Seyri *Motion*
Sıkıt Sıktı *Miscarriage*
Şehir Şehri *City*
Şekil Şekli *Form/Shape*
Şükür Şükrü *Gratitude*
Tavır Tavrı *Mode/Manner*
Ufuk Ufku *Horizon*

Vakit Vakti *Time, occasion*
Vasıf Vasfı *Characteristic*
Zehir Zehri *Poison*
Zihin Zihni *Intellect*
Zulüm Zulmü *Tyranny*

Many of these nouns including the parts of the body:
burun *nose* becomes **burnum** *my nose.*
beyin *brain* becomes **beynim** *my brain.*
are in constant daily use.

The noun "şehir city" itself apocopates normally "Şehre'ye gidiyorum." "I'm going to town." However actual city names being Proper Nouns do not apocopate: "Eskişehir", "Nevşehir" (cities in Turkey). "Eskişehir'e gidiyorum" or "Nevşehir'imiz çok güzel" are without any vowel loss.

Daily Turkish Conversational Locutions.

Here are a few regularly used locutions translated into Turkish. We all use these kind of sayings in our daily language to help us think and to emphasize our meaning. Using these locutions will make your conversational language seem more fluid and normal in daily speech.

acele ; ivedili *In a hurry*
açık havada *In the open*
affedesiniz!; üzülüyorum *I am sorry!*
aldırmam! *I don't care*
Allah aşkına! *For God's sake!*
amacıyla *In order to*
amacıyla *With a view to*
anlaştık *Agreed ; OK!*
ara sıra *Once in a while*
aracıyla *By means of*
arada sırada *Now and again ; now and then*
arkada *At the back*
asla *By no means*
aşağı yukarı *More or less*
aynı zamanda *At the same time*
ayrıksız *With no exceptions*
azar azar *Little by little*
bana kalırsa *As for me*
baştan başa *From end to end*
belki ; olabilir *Maybe*
bile bile ; kasten *On purpose*
bir an önce *The soonest possible*
bir çırpıda *In no time*
bir daha *Once again*
bir dakika *Just a moment*
bir parça *A little bit*
bir şey değil *Don't mention it*
biraz *A little*
birdenbire *All of a sudden*
birer birer *One by one*
boşuna *It is of no use*
böylelikle *In this manner*
bravo! *Well done!*

bu andan sonra *From this moment*
bu arada *In the meantime*
bu halde *In this case*
bundan başka *Besides*
bundan dolayı *Consequently*
bundan sonra *From this time on*
buyurun *Help yourself*
buyurun ; giriniz *Come in!*
bütün dünyada *All over the world*
bütün gün *All day long*
çok geçmeden yakında *Before long*
çoktan beri *A long time ago*
daha az *Less*
daha iyi *Better*
darmadağın *Up side down*
değil mi? *Isn't it?*
değmez *It is not worth while*
derhal *At once*
diğer taraftan *On the other hand*
dikkat et! *Look out!*
doğru ; tamam *That right*
dolmuştur *Full up*
durmadan *On and on*
elde *At hand*
elimde değil *I can't help it*
eliyle *Care of*
eminim *I am sure*
en azından *At least*
en çok ; azami *At most*
er geç *Sooner or later*
esasen ; nitekim *In fact*
eyvallah *So long*
ezberden *By heart*
fark etmez *It is all the same*
galiba *I suppose so*
geçenlerde *Of late*
gelecekte *In the future*
gene görüşeli *See you later*
gerekirse *If need be*
gidelim *Let's go*

gidiş-dönüş bileti *Return ticket*
git gide *Gradually*
git işine *Let me alone*
gölgede *In the shade*
haftada bir *Once a week*
hazır konfeksiyon *Ready made*
hemen hemen *Almost*
hepiniz *All of you*
her bakımdan *In every respect*
her gün *Every day*
her halde ; nasılsa *In any case ; somehow*
her zaman *At any rate*
her zamanki gibi *As usual*
hiç de değil *Not at all*
hoş geldiniz *Welcome!*
ısmarlama *Made to order*
ikiniz de *Both of you*
ilişik olarak *Enclosed*
ilk kez olarak *For the first time*
ilk önce *In the first place*
ilkin *At first*
ister istemez *Willy-nilly*
işe yaramaz *Good for nothing*
işte burada *Right here*
işte orada *Right there*
iyi şanslar *Good luck*
izinli *On leave*
izninizle *With your leave*
kabilse *If possible*
kaç tane *How many?*
kaça? ; ne kadar? *How much.*
kapıda *At the door*
kesinlikle *Once and for all*
kısa süre içinde *At short notice*
kiralık *To let ; to rent*
lütfen ; rica ederim *Please*
merak etmeyin *Don't worry*
modern *Up to date*
nasıl isterseniz *As you please*
nasıl olur? *How is that?*

nasılsınız? *How are you?*
ne çıkar? *What's the matter?*
ne oldu? *What happened?*
ne olur ne olmaz *Just in case*
ne oluyor? *What's happening? ; What's up?*
nede olsa *After all*
neden olmasın? *Why not?*
neniz var? *What's wrong with you?*
nihayet ; sonunda *At last*
nitekim *As a matter of fact*
o zaman ; öyleyse *Then*
o zamandan beri *Ever since*
o zamandan beri *Since then*
olabilir *That maybe*
ona göre *According to that*
ona rağmen *In spite of it*
orada *Over there*
ortada *In the middle*
oy birliği ile *With one accord*
önünde ; karşısında *In front of*
örneğin *For instance*
özür dilerim *I beg your pardon*
pek çok *Too many*
pek fazla *Too much*
peki *All right*
rasgele, rast gele *At random*
sabaha kadar *Till morning*
sabahleyin *In the morning*
sağ salim *Safe and sound*
sağda *On the right*
sahi mi? *Is that so?*
sanki ; güya *As if ; as though*
satılık *For sale*
sık sık *Frequently*
sıra ile *By turns*
sıra ile *In turns*
sırası gelmişken *By the way*
solda *On the left*
sonsuzca *For ever*
sonunda *At the end*

sonunda *In the end*
sonunda *In the long run*
sözde ; sanki *So to say*
Suçüstü *In the very act*
şartıyla *On condition that*
şartıyla *Providing that*
şimdiden sonra *From now on*
şimdilik *for the time being*
şimdiye kadar *Up to now*
şöyle böyle *So-so*
şöyle ki *So that*
şüphesiz *No doubt*
tabii *Of course*
tabii *To be sure*
tam vaktinde *Just in time*
tam vaktinde *On time*
tam zamanında *In due time*
tamam mı? *All set?*
tekrar *Over again*
tekrar ; bir daha *Once more*
tepesinde *On top of*
tersine ; aksine *On the contrary*
teşekkürler *Thanks a lot*
uçakla *By airmail*
usulen *As a rule*
uzun zamandan beri *Long ago*
uzun zamandan beri *Since a long time*
ya sonra? *What next?*
yakışıklı *Good looking*
yan yana *Side by side*
yani *That is to say*
yarım yamalak *Rough and ready*
yaşça küçük *Under age*
yürüyerek *On foot*
yüz yüze *Face to face*
zamanında *In due course*
zamansız *Ill-timed*
zararı yok *No harm done*

Daily Words in Constant Use in Turkish.

Acele et. *Hurry up.*
Acıktım. *I'm hungry.*
Affedersiniz. *Excuse me.*
Akşam. *Evening.*
Allahaısmarladık [said by person leaving] *Bye bye.*
Anlamıyorum. *I can't understand.*
Anlıyorum. *I understand.*
Arkada. *At the back.*
Bana söyleyebilir misiniz? *Can you tell me?*
Bana yardım eder misiniz? *Can you help me?*
Bana yardım edin. *Help me.*
Bana postaneyi gösterebilir misiniz? *Can you show me the post office?*
Ben de memnun oldum *Nice to meet you, too.*
Bey. *Mr.*
Biliyorum. *I know.*
Bilmiyorum. *I don't know.*
Bir şey değil. *You're welcome.*
Bugün. *Today.*
Burada. *Here.*
Buyurun ne istemiştiniz? *What would you like?*
Dün. *Yesterday.*
Elimde var. *Yes, on hand.*
Elimde yok. *No, not on hand.*
Eşiniz nasıl? *How is your wife/husband?*
Gece. *Night.*
Güle güle [said by person staying] *Good bye.*
Günaydın *Good morning*
Hangi? *Which?*
Hanım. *Mrs.*
Hoş geldiniz. *Welcome*
İlerde. *Ahead.*
İmdat. *Help!*
İstemiyorum. *I don't want.*
İstiyorum. *I want.*
İtalya'yım. *I'm Italian.*
İyi akşamlar. *Good evening.*

İyi dileklerimle *Best wishes*
İyi geceler. *Good night.*
İyi günler *Good day*
İyi şanslar *Good luck*
İyi yıllar *Happy new year*
İyi yolculuklar *Have a good holiday*
İyi, teşekkürler, ya siz? *Fine, thanks and you?*
Kaç tane? *How many?*
Kayboldum. *I'm lost.*
Kim? *Who?*
Lütfen. *Please.*
Merhaba *Hello/hi*
Mutlu yıllar *Happy birthday*
Nasıl yardımcı olabilirim ? *How can I help you?*
Nasıl? *How?*
Nasılsınız? *How are you?*
Ne istiyorsunuz? *What would you like?*
Ne kadar uzaklıkta? *How far?*
Ne kadar zamandır? *How long?*
Ne kadar? *How much?*
Ne yapmalıyım? *What must I do?*
Ne zaman? *When?*
Ne? *What?*
Neden? *Why?*
Nerede kalıyorsunuz? *Where are you staying?*
Nerede benzin alabilirim? *Where can I get/buy petrol?*
Nerede bir banka bulabilirim? *Where can I find a bank?*
Nerede? *Where?*
Nerelisiniz? *Where are you from?*
Öğle. *Afternoon.*
Önde. *On/At the front.*
Önemli. *That's important*
Orada. *Over there*
Oraya nasıl gidebilirim? *How can I get there?*
Sabah. *Morning.*
Sağda. *On/At the right.*
Sağ olun, iyim. *Thank you. I'm fine.*
Sizde para var mı? *Do you have any money?*
Size yardım edebilir miyim? *Can I help you?*
Solda. *On/At the left.*

Sorun nedir? *What's your question?*
Şurada. *Just there*
Susadım. *I'm thirsty.*
Tam karşıda ; dosdoğru. *Straight ahead.*
Tamam. *Ok.*
Tanıştığımıza memnun oldum *Nice to meet you*
Teşekkür ederim. *Thank you.*
Türkiyeliyim. *I'm from Turkey.*
Türküm. *I'm Turkish.*
Yarın görüşürüz *See you tomorrow*
Yarın. *Tomorrow.*
Yine görüşürüz. *See you later.*

The Irregular Wide Tense Verb List.

The famous thirteen irregular single syllable verbs in the Simple Present. Twelve of them end their root in **-l** or **-r**.
The single exception which root ends in **-n** (of these famous 13 exceptions) is **sanmak** which has the form **sanır** *to suppose*. These verbs are in common daily use.

Undotted Vowel Group A I O U.

Regular verbs use the regular tense sign **-ar**. The Wide Tense Root of the Regular verb **atmak** *to throw* becomes **atar** as in **at-ar-ım** *I throw.*

Infinitive	Wide	Meaning	Causative	Meaning
almak	alır	*to take/get*	aldırmak	*to make*
bulmak	bulur	*to find*	buldurmak	*to make*
durmak	durur	*to stop/to*	durdurmak	*to make*
kalmak	kalır	*to remain,*	kaldırmak	*to take*
olmak	olur	*to be/to*	oldurmak	*to make*
sanmak	sanır	*to suppose*	(lacking)	-
varmak	varır	*to arrive*	vardırmak	*to make*
vurmak	vurur	*to strike*	vurdurmak	*to make*

439

The Iregular Wide Tense Verbs.

Dotted Vowel Group E İ Ö Ü.

Regular verbs use the regular tense sign **-er**. The Wide Tense Root of **geçmek** *to pass* becomes **geçer** as in **geç-er-im** *I pass.*

Infinitive	Wide	Meaning	Causative	Meaning
bilmek	**bilir**	*to know how*	**bildirmek**	*to make know*
gelmek	**gelir**	*to come*	**geldirmek**	*to make come*
görmek	**görür**	*to see*	**gösterme**	*to show*
ölmek	**ölür**	*to die*	**öldürmek**	*to kill, to*
vermek	**verir**	*to give*	**verdirme**	*to make give*

Turkish Single Syllable Verb List.

Turkish has many single syllable verbs simply because they become very lengthy after addition of suffixes indicating mood, tense and person. Simple Tense Verb Root is shown in second column.

The A-Undotted Single Syllable Verbs.

açmak açar *to open*
akmak akar *to flow*
almak alır *to take/get*
anmak anar *to mention*
artmak artar *to increase*
asmak asar *to hang down*
aşmak aşar *to pass over*
atmak atar *to throw*
bakmak bakar *to look*
banmak banar *to dip into*
basmak basar *to tread on*
bıkmak bıkar *to be fed up*
bozmak bozar *to spoil*
bulmak bulur *to find*
caymak cayar *to change one's mind*
coşmak coşar *to enthuse*
çakmak çakar *to strike*
çalmak çalar *to steal/to play a mus. instr.*
çarpmak çarpar *to bump*
çatmak çatar *to bump against*
çıkmak çıkar *to go out*
çırpmak çırpar *to beat*
doğmak doğar *to be born*
donmak donar *to freeze*
doymak doyar *to be filled*
durmak durur *to stop/to halt*
kaçmak kaçar *to escape*
kalmak kalır *to remain/to stay*

kalkmak kalkar *to stand up*
kapmak kapar *to snatch/to get caught up*
katmak katar *to join*
kaymak kayar *to slip/to slide*
kazmak kazar *to dig*
kıpmak kıpar *to wink/to blink*
kırpmak kırpar *to trim/to clip*
kırmak kırar *to break*
kısmak kısar *to reduce*
kıymak kıyar *to chop up*
kızmak kızar *to get angry*
kokmak kokar *to smell of*
konmak konar *to alight on/to camp*
kopmak kopar *to snap*
korkmak korkar *to be afraid*
koşmak koşar *to run*
koymak koyar *to put/to place*
kurmak kurar *to set up/to establish*
kusmak kusar *to vomit*
olmak olur *to be/to become*
onmak onar *to mend/to heal*
ovmak ovar *to rub*
oymak oyar *to carve*
salmak salar *to let go*
sanmak sanır *to suppose*
sapmak sapar *to swerve*
sarmak sarar *to wrap up*
sarkmak sarkar *to hang down*
sarsmak sarsar *to agitate/to upset s.o.*
satmak satar *to sell*
saymak sayar *to count*
sığmak sığar *to fit into*
sıkmak sıkar *to squeeze/to press*
sızmak sızar *to ooze*
sokmak sokar *to insert*
solmak solar *to fade*
sormak sorur *to ask*
soymak soyar *to undress*
sunmak sunar *to offer/to present*
susmak susar *to be silent*

442

şaşmak şaşar *to be surprised*
takmak takar *to fix to*
tartmak tartar *to weigh*
taşmak taşar *to overflow*
tatmak tadar *to taste of*
tıkmak tıkar *to cram in*
tutmak tutar *to hold/to take hold*
uçmak uçar *to fly*
ummak umar *to hope*
uymak uyar *to suit/to fit*
varmak varır *to arrive*
vurmak vurur *to strike/to hit*
yağmak yağar *to rain/to precipitate*
yakmak yakar *to burn*
yanmak yanar *to ignite*
yapmak yapar *to do/to make*
yarmak yarar *to split*
yatmak yatar *to lie down/to go to bed*
yaymak yayar *to spread*
yazmak yazar *to write*
yığmak yığar *to heap up*
yıkmak yıkar *to demolish*
yılmak yılar *to be afraid*
yırtmak yırtar *to tear/to rip*
yolmak yolar *to pluck*
yonmak yonar *to pare/to sharpen*
yontmak yontar *to snip/to chip*
yormak yorar *to tire*
yummak yumar *to close eyes or fist*
yutmak yutar *to swallow*

The E-Dotted Single Syllable Verbs.

biçmek biçer *to reap*
bilmek bilir *to know how to*
binmek biner *to mount/to board*
bitmek biter *to end*
bölmek böler *to separate/to divide*
bükmek büker *to bend*

çekmek çeker *to pull*
çizmek çizer *to draw*
çökmek çöker *to collapse/to kneel*
çözmek çözer *to solve*
demek der *to say*
değmek değer *to touch*
delmek deler *to pierce/to drill through*
dermek derer *to collect*
dikmek diker *to sow/sew/erect/plant*
ditmek dider *to shred*
dizmek dizer *to line up*
dökmek döker *to pour*
dönmek döner *to spin/to turn*
dövmek döver *to beat/to thrash*
dürtmek dürter *to prod*
düşmek düşer *to fall*
düzmek düzer *to arrange in place*
emmek emer *to suck*
ermek erer *to attain/to reach*
esmek eser *to blow (wind)*
etmek eder *to do*
ezmek ezer *to crush*
gelmek gelir *to come*
germek gerer *to stretch*
gezmek gezer *to stroll*
gitmek gider *to go*
girmek girer *to enter*
giymek giyer *to dress*
göçmek göçer *to migrate*
gömmek gömer *to bury*
görmek görür *to see*
gülmek güler *to laugh*
içmek içer *to drink*
iğmek iğer *to bend/to curve*
inmek iner *to dismount/to alight*
itmek iter *to push*
kentmek kenter *to notch*
kesmek keser *to cut*
küsmek küser *to be offended*
ölmek ölür *to die*

ölçmek ölçer *to measure*
öpmek öper *to kiss*
örmek örer *to knit/to plait*
örtmek örter *to cover/to wrap*
ötmek öter *to sing (bird)*
övmek över *to praise*
pişmek pişer *to cook (itself)*
seçmek seçer *to choose*
sekmek seker *to hop*
sevmek sever *to love*
sezmek sezer *to feel/to perceive*
silmek siler *to wipe/t o polish*
silkmek silker *to shake off*
sinmek siner *to crouch*
sökmek söker *to undo/to pull up*
sönmek söner *to be extinguished*
sövmek söver *to swear*
sünmek süner *to be extended*
sürçmek sürçer *to stumble*
sürtmek sürter *to rub with hand*
süzmek süzer *to strain/to filter*
şişmek şişer *to swell up*
tepmek teper *to kick*
tütmek tüter *to emit smoke*
ürkmek ürker *to jump with fright*
üşmek üşer *to flock*
üzmek üzer *to hurt the feelings of*
vermek verir *to give*
yenmek yener *to win (game)/to conquer*
yermek yerer *to blame*
yetmek yeter *to suffice*
yüzmek yüzer *to swim*

List of Turkish Intensified Adjectives.

Here is a comprehensive list of Intensified Turkish Adjectives and Adverbs. They are commonly used in conversation, newspapers, periodicals and novels. It is a way that language colours itself.

acayip *queer* **apacayip** *very strange*
acele *in a hurry* **alelacele** *very hastily*
açık *clear/open* **apaçık** *very clear/open*
ayrı *separate* **apayrı** *quite separate*
bakkal *grocer* **bakkal çakkal** *grocers and the like*
başka *another* **bambaşka** *quite another thing*
bayağı *common* **basbayağı** *very common*
baygın *unconscious* **aygın baygın** *languid*
bedava *gratis* **besbedava** *completely free*
belli *evident* **besbelli** *very clear*
beter *worse* **besbeter** *even worse*
beyaz *white* **bembeyaz** *brilliant white*
bok (noun) *filth* **bombok** (adj.) *utterly spoilt*
bol *full* **bosbol** *filled to the brim*
boş *empty* **bomboş** *quite empty*
burun *nose* **baltaburun** *hook nosed*
buruşuk *creased* **bumburuşuk** *wrinkled all over*
bütün *all* **büsbütün** *wholly*
canlı *alive* **capcanlı** *animate*
çabuk *quickly* **çarçabuk** *very quickly*
çevre *surroundings* **çepeçevre** *all around*
çöp *rubbish* **çerçöp** *sweepings*
çıplak *naked* **çırılçıplak** *stark naked*
dağınık *untidy* **darmadağınık** *really untidy*
dar *narrow* **dapdar** *cramped, tight-fitting*
daracık *pretty narrow* **dapdaracık** *very narrow*
deli *madman* **zıpırdeli** *frantic madman*
deli *crazy* **zırdeli** *raving mad*
delice *crazily* **deldelice** *madly*
dik *perpendicular* **dimdik** *bolt upright*
diri *alive* **dipdiri** *full of life*
dizgin *(stirrup)* **doludizgin** *at full pelt*
dızlak *bald/naked* **dımdızlak** *destitute*
doğru *right/correct* **dosdoğru** *dead right*

dolu *full* **dopdolu** *crammed full*
duru *limpid* **dupduru** *very clear*
düz *flat* **düpedüz** *dead flat*
düz *straight* **dümdüz** *dead straight*
düz *even* **düpedüz** *dead even*
geniş *wide* **gepgeniş** *expansive*
gıcır *brand new* **gıpgıcır** *spanking brand new*
gündüz *daylight* **güpegündüz** *broad daylight*
ince *thin* **ipince** *very thin*
ılık *tepid* **ıpılık** *lukewarm*
ıslak *wet* **ıpıslak** *sopping/all wet*
ıssız *uninhabited* **ıpıssız** *desolate*
iri *big* **ipiri** *very huge*
kara *black* **kapkara** *black as night*
karışık *mixed up* **karmakarışık** *completely mixed up*
kısa *short* **kıpkısa, kısacık** *very short*
koca *large* **koskoca** *huge*
kocaman *huge* **koskocaman** *enormous*
kolay *easy* **kopkolay** *very easily*
koyu *dense dark* **kopkoyu** *really dark*
kör *blind* **köpkör** *absolutely blind*
kötü *bad* **köpkötü** (child talk) *very bad*
kötürüm *paralyzed* **köskötürüm** *completely paralyzed*
kuru *dry* **kupkuru** *bone dry*
kütük (noun) *a log* **küskütük** (adj.) *hopelessly drunk*
kıvrak *tidy* **kıskıvrak** *neat and tidy*
mavi *blue* **masmavi** *bright blue*
mor *purple* **mosmor** *bright purple*
muhteşem *magnificent* **mupmuhteşem** *splendid*
pak *clean* **akpak** *squeaky clean*
pembe *pink* **pespembe** *shocking pink*
perişan *miserable/worried* **perperişan** *very perturbed*
parça *bits* **paramparça** *in smithereens*
pis *dirty* **pimpis** (child talk) *filthy dirty*
sağlam *healthy* **sapsağlam/sapasağlam** *in fine fettle*
sarı *yellow* **sapsarı** *bright yellow*
sefil *miserable/poor* **sersefil** *very miserable/poor*
sıcak *hot* **sımsıcak** *red-hot*
sıklam *soaked* **sırılsıklam** *sopping wet*
sıkı *tight* **sımsıkı** *very tight*

sivri *sharp* **sipsivri** *dead sharp*
siyah *black* **simsiyah** *jet black*
şirin *charming* **şipşirin** *very charming*
talan *pillage* **alantalan** *in utter confusion*
tamam *complete* **tastamam** *perfect*
tatlı *sweet* **taptatlı** *very sweet*
taze *fresh (food)* **terütaze** *blooming/very fresh*
taze *fresh* **taptaze** *very fresh*
temiz *clean* **tertemiz** *squeaky clean*
top *round, ball-like* **tortop** *quite round*
uslu *well behaved* **upuslu** *very well behaved*
uzun *long* **upuzun** *very long*
uygun *suitable* **upuygun** *quite adequate*
yalnız *alone* **yapayalnız** *absolutely alone*
yassı *flat and wide* **yamyassı** *very flat*
yaş *wet* **yamyaş** *all wet*
yeni *new* **yepyeni** *brand new*
yeşil *green* **yemyeşil** *bright green*
yumru *swollen/round* **yusyumru** *very swollen/round*
yumuşak *soft* **yusyumuşak** *very soft*
yuvarlak *globular* **yusyuvarlak** *absolutely spherical*
zayıf *thin/feeble* **zapzayıf** *very thin/feeble*

Reduplicated Words.

abuk sabuk *codswallop, waffle on, tommy-rot*
abur cubur *junk food, to snack, eat on the hoof*
açık seçik (açık saçik) *clean cut, direct, definite, clear*
adım adım *step by step, incrementally*
afal afal *bewildered, stupefied*
ağır ağır *slow and gradual*, **ateşte ağır ağır kaynamak**, *to simmer*
ahım şahım *beautiful, excellent, favourable (of a thing)*
akın akın *rushing, surging*
akça pakça *pretty (white skinned, pale complexion) girl*
alacalı bulacalı (alaca bulaca) *many coloured, spotted*
alet edevat *paraphernalia, gadgets*
alık alık *stupidly*, **alık alık bakmak**, *to gawk, to gorpe at*
allak bullak *shambolic*, **allak bullak etmek**, *to jumble up*
allı pullu *colorful and decked out with spangles, showily dressed*
anlı şanlı *flamboyant, renowned*
apul apul *with waddling steps, toddling*
ardı ardına *back to back*
aval aval *stupidly (slang)*
avuç avuç *lavishly, in handfuls*
bangır bangır *at the top of one's voice*, **bangır bangır bağırmak,** *to shout loudly*
bas bas *at the top of one's voice*, **bas bas bağırmak,** *to shout at the top of one's voice*
başa baş *neck-and-neck, dead equal, par*
başka başka *one by one, separately, different*
başka bırı *someone else*
başlı başına *on one's own, in its own right, independent*
baştan başa *from top to bottom, end to end, through and through*
bata çıka *to come down to, with difficulty, to flounder*
belli belirsiz *uncertain, indistinct*
bıcı bıcı *bıcı bıcı yapmak,* *to take a bath (child language)*
bıngıl bıngıl *fat and bulging, blubbery, quivering like jelly*
bili bili *chuckie, chuckie (a call for chickens)*
bire bir *one to one*
boğum boğum *gnarled*

boşu boşuna *in vain, needlessly, unnecessarily, uselessly*
bön bön *vacantly,* **bön bön bakmak,** *to look vacantly*
buram buram *a lot, in clouds of*
burcu burcu *fragrant smelling*
büklüm büklüm *curly, in curls*
cayır cayır *fiercely, burning furiously*
cazır cazır *burning with a crackly noise*
cır cır *chattering continuously, a* **cırcır** *is a cicada*
cıvık cıvık *see* **yıvış yıvış**
cıvıl cıvıl *alive and kicking, frisky*
cıyak cıyak *with a screech; with a squawk*
cızır cızır *with a sizzling noise*
cik cik *with a sizzling or sputtering sound*
cümbür cemaat *the whole lot, the whole caboodle*
çalı çırpı *sticks and twigs, brushwood*
çangıl çungul *with a clatter or a crash*
çangır çungur *with a clatter or a crash*
çatır çatır *with a crackling noise, with a crunching noise, by force, willy-nilly, easily, with no difficulty*
çatır çutur *breaking with a crack or a crunch*
çeşit çeşit *assorted, varied, all kinds of*
çıldır çıldır *brightly, with a sparkle, brilliantly*
çıngır çıngır *tinkling, with a tinkle or a rattle*
çıpı çıpı *child's language taking a bath*
çıt çıt or çıtçıt *a snap fastener, press-stud, nail-clipper*
çıtı pıtı *petite, dainty*
çıtır çıtır *with a crackling sound, crispy, crunchy*
çoluk çocuk *wife and children, household*
çör çöp or çer çöp *litter, sweepings, trash*
daldan dala *from branch to branch, always on the move*
darı darına or dar darına *narrowly, hardly, barely ,narrowly, hardly, barely*
derin derin *deeply*
dırdır *continuous grumbling, nagging*
dişe diş *tit for tat, retaliation (from* **diş,** *tooth)*
diz dize *with knees together*
doğru düzgün *straight and correct*
düşe kalka *with great difficulty, struggling along/on*
eciş bücüş *shapeless, crooked, distorted*
eğri büğrü *crinkly, contorted, twisted, gnarled*

el ele *hand in hand, hand by hand, hand to hand*
elden ele *from hand to hand*
enine boyuna *in length and breadth, broadly, in length, in depth*
eski püskü *shabby, ragged, worn-out, threadbare, tattered, tatty*
estek köstek *so so, that's the way it is*
ev bark *hose and home, home and family*
falan feşmekan *and so on, etcetera, blah blah*
falan filan *and so on, etcetera, blah blah*
feryat figan *wailing, in squalls*
fıkır fıkır *lively and flirtatious*
fır fır *around and around (from **fırlamak**, to dodge about, pop up)*
fırıl fırıl *whirling around*
fırt fırt *bumpety bump*
fıs fıs *in whispers, whispering*
fısıl fısıl *in whispers, whispering*
fısır fısır *with a sizzle or a hissing*
fış fış *with a swish or a rustle*
fışır fışır *with a swishing or a rustling*
fokur fokur *bubbling hot and noisy, frothing up*
gelişi güzel (gelişigüzel) *haphazard, slapdash*
gani gani *abundantly*
gıcır gıcır *squeaky clean, brand new*
gıdım gıdım *inching along, bit by bit*
gide gide (gitgide) *as it goes, gradually*
göz göze *eye to eye, to eyeball s.o.*
göze göz *an eye for an eye, (a tooth for a tooth)*
güm güm *with loud thumps, bangs, bumps*
gümbür gümbür *thundering, with a thunder, rumbling, with a rumble*
günden güne *from day to day, daily*
günü gününe *to the very day*
gürül gürül *with a gurgling sound, in a loud/rich voice*
güzel güzel *calmly and quietly, peacefully*
haldır haldır *speedily and noisily*
harala gürele *hustle and bustle*
hıpur hupur *scoffing food, guzzling*
harıl harıl *assiduously, diligently, intensely, intensively*
hava cıva *nonsense, stuff and nonsense, bosh, naff*
hırıl hırıl *wheezy, rattling*
hışır hışır *with a rustling sound*

hop hop *stop!, a warning shout*
horul horul *snoring loudly*
hüngür hüngür *crying one's eyes out, sobbing uncontrollably*
ıvır zıvır *bits and pieces, unimportant details, trifling things*
ıvır zıvır abur cubur *this and that, one thing and another*
içten içe *inwardly, secretly*
incik boncuk *cheap and tawdry jewellery, baubles, trinkets*
kapış kapış *greedily, in a mad scramble*
kara kara *brooding(ly)*
karınca kararınca *in a small way*
karış karış *every inch of, inch by inch*
kaşık kaşık *by/in spoonfuls*
kerli ferli *(middle-aged or elderly man) who is dignified and dressed to the nines*
kıkır kıkır *giggling, laughing internally*
kıpır kıpır *fidgety, restless*
kıtır kıtır *crisp, crackly, crunchy*
konu komşu *the neighbours, the whole neighbourhood*
körü körüne *hit or miss, blindly, carelessly*
kös kös *looking neither right nor left*
kucak kucak *by the armloads, by the armfuls, in abundance*
kuçu kuçu *child's language doggie, bow-wow, woof-woof, used to call a dog*
küt küt *pit a pat, a knocking*
lami cimi *There are no "buts" about it!, That's the way it's got to be!, And that's final!*
lapa lapa *(for snow to fall) in big flakes*
mırıl mırıl *with a mutter, in low, mumbling tones; in a grumbling murmur*
mışıl mışıl *(sleeping) soundly*
omuz omuza *shoulder to shoulder, side by side*
paldır güldür *headlong, pell-mell, helter-skelter*
parıl parıl *brilliantly, glitteringly, sparklingly*
pat pat *chug chug*
peşi peşine *One after another*
pılı pırtı *worn-out things, junk, rummage*
pır pır *whirring, Get going!, Make tracks!, Head for the hills*
pırıl pırıl *squeaky clean, gleaming*
pış pış *nasty*
pıt pıt *pit a pat*

pıtır pıtır *pit a pat, clickety click*
pisi pisi *child's language pussycat, pussy, kitty, used in calling cats*
pisi pisine *in vain, uselessly, for nothing*
poh poh *flattery, fulsome praise*
pütür pütür *chapped, cracked, or chilblained*
saati saatine *punctually*
saçma sapan *stuff and nonsense*
salkım saçak *hanging down untidily*
sapır sapır *in great quantities and continuously*
sere serpe *(moving around) freely, comfortably, (stretched out) at full length,*
sıcağı sıcağına *while the iron is hot*
soy sop *family relations, ancestors*
sus pus *silent and cowering*
süklüm püklüm *in a crestfallen manner, in a hangdog manner, sheepish*
sürüm sürüm *to live a life of great misery, be driven from pillar to post*
sütliman *very still and silent, dead calm*
süzüm süzüm *to behave very coquettishly (refers to bodily movements and facial expressions)*
şakır şakır *with a jingle, rattle, or clack.*
şap şap *kissy kissy*
şap şup *lip smacking, noisy eating*
şapır şupur *lip smacking, noisy eating*
şıkır şıkır *with a jingling, clinking, or clicking noise*
şıp şıp *a drip drop sound*
şıpır şıpır *continuous dripping*
şırıl şırıl *(flowing) with a gentle, continuous splashing*
şöyle böyle *so so, indifferent, comme ci comme ca*
tak tak *rat tat tat, knock knock*
takım takım *in groups, in platoons*
takır takır *very stiff and dry, very stale food*
takır tukur *clatter bang wallop, used to indicate a rattling, clattering, or banging noise which is unpleasantly loud*
tamı tamına *exact, exactly, just so*
tangır tangır *clatteringly, with a racket*
tangır tungur *with a rude clatter*
teke tek *one to one*
tık tık *tick tock, rat a tat*

tıkır tıkır *perfectly, without hesitating or faltering, like clockwork, with a regular click*

tıkış tıkış *crowded*

tıklım tıklım *Very crowded, packed, jammed (with people), congested*

tıngır tıngır *with a continual clanging or rattling sound, completely empty*

tir tir *shivering, trembling*

tiril tiril *spotlessly clean, gauzy, gossamer like*

topu topu *all in all, all told, altogether*

ucu ucuna *ent to end, just about, narrowly*

uslu uslu *polite(ly)*

vızır vızır *(working, moving) continually, constantly*

viyak viyak *squawking*

yaka paça *forcibly*

yan yana *alongside, adjacent*

yana yakıla *complaining(ly)*

yarım yamalak *sloppy, slipshod*

yavaş yavaş *slowly, easing*

yıldan yıla *annually, year on year*

zamazingo *thingamabob, thngy, thingamajig, gadget, gubbins*

zangır zangır *shaking violently, rattling*

zehir zemberek *very poisonous and bitter, vitriolic*

zır zır *noisy in an incessant, nerve-racking way*

zırıl zırıl *incessantly and unpleasantly (of a sound)*

zırt fırt *at any time whatsoever, whenever one feels like it*

zırt pırt *at any time whatsoever, whenever one feels like it, every so often*

zırt zırt *at any time whatsoever, whenever one feels like it, every so often*

44 THE VERB "ETMEK" FULLY CONJUGATED

A Full Conjugation Example of Etmek.

Present Continuous Tense (and Future of Intention)			
Positive forms		Negative forms	
Statement	Interrogative	Statement	Interrogative
I am doing.., I am going to do...			
ediyorum	ediyor muyum?	etmiyorum	etmiyor muyum?
ediyorsun	ediyor musun?	etmiyorsun	etmiyor musun?
ediyor	ediyor mu?	etmiyor	etmiyor mu?
ediyoruz	ediyor muyuz?	etmiyoruz	etmiyor muyuz?
ediyorsunuz	ediyor musunuz?	etmiyorsunuz	etmiyor musunuz?
ediyorlar	ediyorlar mı?	etmiyorlar	etmiyorlar mı?
I am doing.. I'm going to do..	Am I doing..? Am I going to do..?	I am not doing.. I am not going to do..	Am I not doing?. Aren't I going to do..?

Simple Present- Wide Tense (Geniş Zaman)			
Positive forms		Negative forms	
Statement	Interrogative	Statement	Interrogative
The Timless Tense , Habitual, Volition and Uncertain Future I generally do..			
ederim	eder miyim?	etmem	etmez miyim?
edersin	eder misin?	etmezsin	etmez misin?
eder	eder mi?	etmez	etmez mi?
ederiz	eder miyiz?	etmeyiz	etmez miyiz?
edersiniz	eder misiniz?	etmezsiniz	etmez misiniz?
ederler	ederler mi?	etmezler	etmezler mi?
I usually do.. I'll be doing..	Did I usually do..? Should I be doing..?	I did not usually do.. I'll not be doing..	Don't I usually do..? Shouldn't I be doing..?

Past Tense Forms Past Definite			
Positive forms		Negative forms	
Statement	Interrogative	Statement	Interrogative
The Eywitness Past It Definitely Happened.. I did.., I have done..			
ettim	ettim mi?	etmedim	etmedim mi?
ettin	ettin mi?	etmedin	etmedin mi??
etti	etti mi?	etmedi	etmedi mi?
ettik	ettik mi?	etmedik	etmedik mi?
ettiniz	ettiniz mi?	etmediniz	etmediniz mi?
ettiler	ettiler mi?	etmediler	etmediler mi?
I did do.. I have done..	Did I do..? Have I done..?	I did not do.. I have not done..	Didn't I do..? Haven't I done..?

Past Progressive, Dubitative			
Positive forms		Negative forms	
Statement	Interrogative	Statement	Interrogative
The Past Tense of Report and Preumption (Not Witnessed) I think I did..			
ediyormuşum	ediyormuş miyim?	etmiyormuşum	etmiyormuş muyum?
ediyormuşsun	ediyormuş misin?	etmiyormuşsun	etmiyormuş musun?
ediyormuş	ediyormuş mi?	etmiyormuş	etmiyormuş mu?
ediyormuşuz	ediyormuş miyiz?	etmiyormuşuz	etmiyormuş muyuz?
ediyormuşsunuz	ediyormuş misiniz?	etmiyormuşsunuz	etmiyormuş musunuz?
ediyormuşlar (ediyorlarmış)	ediyormuşlar mı? (ediyorlarmış mı?)	etmiyormuşlar (etmiyorlarmış)	etmiyormuşlar mı? (etmiyorlarmış mı?)
(It seems) I was doing.. (Presumably) I was doing..	Was I doing.(I wonder)..? Was I doing (or not)..?	(I think) I was not doing.. (Perhaps) I was not doing..	Wasn't I doing (or not)..? Wasn't I doing (I wonder)..?

456

Indefinite Past Indefinite Past Wide Tense (Geniş Zaman)			
Positive forms		Negative forms	
Statement	Interrogative	Statement	Interrogative
The Timeless Indefinite Past I think I used to do..			
edermişim	edermiş miyim?	etmezmişim	etmezmiş miyim?
edermişsin	edermiş misin?	etmezmişsin	etmezmiş misin?
edermiş	edermiş mi?	etmezmiş	etmezmiş mi?
edermişiz	edermiş miyiz?	etmezmişiz	etmezmiş miyiz?
edermişsiniz	edermiş misiniz?	etmezmişsiniz	etmezmiş misiniz?
edermişler (ederlermiş)	edermişler mi? (ederlermiş mi?)	etmezmişler (etmezlermiş)	etmezmişler mi? (etmezlermiş mi?)
(It seems) I used to do.. (Presumably) I used to do..	Did I used to do.(I wonder)..? Did I used to do (or not)..?	(I think) I used to do.. (Perhaps) I used to do..	Didn't I used to o d(or not)..? Didn't I used to do (I wonder)..?

Past Progressive, Narrative			
Positive forms		Negative forms	
Statement	Interrogative	Statement	Interrogative
The Past Imperfect It was definitely happening.. I was doing..			
ediyordum	ediyor muydum?	etmiyordum	etmiyor muydum?
ediyordun	ediyor muydun?	etmiyordun	etmiyor muydun?
ediyordu	ediyor muydu?	etmiyordu	etmiyor muydu?
ediyorduk	ediyor muyduk?	etmiyorduk	etmiyor muyduk?
ediyordunuz	ediyor muydunuz?	etmiyordunuz	etmiyor muydunuz?
ediyordular (ediyorlardı)	ediyorlar mıydı? (ediyordular mı?)	etmiyordular (etmiyorlardı)	etmiyorlar mıydı? (etmiyordular mı?)
I was doing.. I used to be doing..	Was I doing..? Did I used to be doing..?	I was not doing.. I did not used to be doing..	Wasn't I not doing..? Didn't I used to be not doing..?

Past Perfect, Narrative			
Positive forms		Negative forms	
Statement	Interrogative	Statement	Interrogative
The Pluperfect Definite I had done.. (actually)			
etmiştim	etmiş miydim?	etmemiştim	etmemiş miydim?
etmiştin	etmiş miydin?	etmemiştin	etmemiş miydin?
etmişti	etmiş miydi?	etmemişti	etmemiş miydi?
etmiştik	etmiş miydik?	etmemiştik	etmemiş miydik?
etmiştiniz	etmiş miydiniz?	etmemiştiniz	etmemiş miydiniz?
etmiştiler	etmişler miydi?	etmemişlerdi	etmemişler miydi?
I had done..	Had I done..?	I had not done..	Hadn't I not done..?

Doubtful Distant Past			
Positive forms		Negative forms	
Statement	Interrogative	Statement	Interrogative
The Pluperfect Indefinite I had done.. (I think that..)			
etmişmişim	etmişmiş miyim?	etmemişmişim	etmemişmiş miyim?
etmişmişsin	etmişmiş misin?	etmemişmişsin	etmemişmiş misin?
etmişmiş	etmişmiş mi?	etmemişmiş	etmemişmiş mi?
etmişmişiz	etmişmiş miyiz?	etmemişmişiz	etmemişmiş miyiz?
etmişmişsiniz	etmişmiş misiniz?	etmemişmişsiniz	etmemişmiş misiniz?
etmişmişler (etmişlermiş)	etmişmişler mi? (etmişlermiş mi?)	etmemişmişler (etmemişlermiş)	etmemişmişler mi? (etmemişlermiş mi?)
(Preumably) I had done..	(I wonder) Had I done..?	(I think that) I had not done..	Hadn't I not done..? (it at all?)

Past in the Future			
Positive forms		Negative forms	
Statement	Interrogative	Statement	Interrogative
The Future of "will" and the Past Definite Participle "I shall have done.."			
etmiş olacağım	etmiş olacak mıyım?	etmiş olmayacağım	etmiş olmayacak mıyım?
etmiş olacaksın	etmiş olacak mısın?	etmiş olmayacaksın	etmiş olmayacak mısın?
etmiş olacak	etmiş olacak mı?	etmiş olmayacak	etmiş olmayacak mı?
etmiş olacağız	etmiş olacak mıyız?	etmiş olmayacağız	etmiş olmayacak mıyız?
etmiş olacaksınız	etmiş olacak mısınız?	etmiş olmayacaksınız	etmiş olmayacak mısınız?
etmiş olacaklar	etmiş olacaklar mi?	etmiş olmayacaklar	etmiş olmayacaklar mi?
I shall have done...	Will I have done..?	I shall have not done..	Won't I have not done..?

Future Continuous			
Positive forms		Negative forms	
Statement	Interrogative	Statement	Interrogative
The Future of "will" and the Present Definite Participle "I shall be doing.."			
ediyor olacağım	ediyor olacak mıyım?	ediyor olmayacağım	ediyor olmayacak mıyım?
ediyor olacaksın	ediyor olacak mısın?	ediyor olmayacaksın	ediyor olmayacak mısın?
ediyor olacak	ediyor olacak mı?	ediyor olmayacak	ediyor olmayacak mı?
ediyor olacağız	ediyor olacak mıyız?	ediyor olmayacağız	ediyor olmayacak mıyız?
ediyor olacaksınız	ediyor olacak mısınız?	ediyor olmayacaksınız	ediyor olmayacak mısınız?
ediyor olacaklar	ediyor olacaklar mi?	ediyor olmayacaklar	edyor olmayacaklar mi?
I shall be doing...	Will I be doing..?	I shall not be doing..	Won't I be doing..?

Past Conditional, Narrative			
Positive forms		Negative forms	
Statement	Interrogative	Statement	Interrogative
Definite Past Conditional the situation actually took place If I have done			
etseydim	etse miydim?	etmeseydim	etmese miydim?
etseydin	etse miydin?	etmeseydin	etmese miydin?
etseydi	etse miydi?	etmeseydi	etmese miydi?
etseydik	etse miydik?	etmeseydik	etmese miydik?
etseydiniz	etse miydiniz?	etmeseydiniz	etmese miydiniz
etseydiler	etse miydiler?	etmeseydiler	etmese miydiler?
If I have done...	What if I have done..?	If I have not done..	What if I have not done..?

Past Conditional, Dubitative			
Positive forms		Negative forms	
Statement	Interrogative	Statement	Interrogative
Past Conditional of Presumption the situation might have taken place			
etseymişim	etse miymişim?	etmeseymişim	etmese miymişim?
etseymişsin	etse miymişsin?	etmeseymişsin	etmese miymişsin?
etseymiş	etse miymiş?	etmeseymiş	etmese miymiş?
etseymişiz	etse miymişiz?	etmeseymişiz	etmese miymişiz?
etseymişsiniz	etse miymişsiniz?	etmeseymişsiniz	etmese miymişsiniz?
etseymişler	etse miymişler?	etmeseymişler	etmese miymişler?
If I had (only) done...	What if I had (only) done..?	If I had (only) not done..	What if I had (only) not done..?

Future Simple it will happen			
Positive forms		*Negative forms*	
Statement	Interrogative	Statement	Interrogative
edeceğim	edecek miyim?	etmeyeceğim	etmeyecek miyim?
edeceksin	edecek misin?	etmeyeceksin	etmeyecek misin?
edecek	edecek mi?	etmeyecek	etmeyecek mi?
edeceğiz	edecek miyiz?	etmeyeceğiz	etmeyecek miyiz?
edeceksiniz	edecek misiniz?	etmeyeceksiniz	etmeyecek misiniz?
edecekler	edecekler mi?	etmeyecekler	etmeyecekler mi?
I will do.. I'm going to do..	Shall I do..? Am I going to do..?	I will not do.. I'm not going to do..	Won't I not do..? Aren't I going not to do..?

Future and Conditional in the Past			
Positive forms		*Negative forms*	
Statement	Interrogative	Statement	Interrogative
Future in the Past the Future Stem with the Past Tense of "to be."			
edecektim	edecek miydim?	etmeyecektim	etmeyecek miydim?
edecektin	edecek miydin?	etmeyecektin	etmeyecek miydin?
edecekti	edecek miydi?	etmeyecekti	etmeyecek miydi?
edecektik	edecek miydik?	etmeyecektik	etmeyecek miydik?
edecektiniz	edecek miydiniz?	etmeyecektiniz	etmeyecek miydiniz?
edecektiler	edecekler miydi; edecek miydiler	etmeyeceklerdi; etmeyecektiler	etmeyecek miydiniz?
I would have done.. I was going to do..	Should I have done..? Was I going to do..?	I would not have done.. I was not going to do..	Wouldn't I have not done..? Wasn't I going not to do..?

461

Future Indefinite			
Positive forms		Negative forms	
Statement	Interrogative	Statement	Interrogative
Future Dubitative the Future Tense with Presumption			
edecekmişim	edecekmiş miyim?	etmeyecekmişim	etmeyecekmiş miyim?
edecekmişsin	edecekmiş misin?	etmeyecekmişsin	etmeyecekmiş misin?
edecekmiş	edecekmiş mi?	etmeyecekmiş	etmeyecekmiş mi?
edecekmişiz	edecekmiş miyiz?	etmeyecekmişiz	etmeyecekmiş miyiz?
edecekmişsiniz	edecekmiş misiniz?	etmeyecekmişsiniz	etmeyecekmiş misiniz?
edecekmişler; edeceklermiş	edeceklermiş mi? (edecekmişler mi?)	etmeyeceklermiş (etmeyecekmişler)	etmeyeceklermiş mi? (etmeyecekmişler mi?)
(I think that) I will do.. I'm going to do (probably)..	**Shall I do (at all?)..? Am I going to do (doubtful)..?**	**(It seems that) I will not do.. (Probably) I'm not going to do..**	**Will I not d(then).. (Won't I do it?)..? Aren't I going not to do (it then?)..?**

Definite Past Simple Tense			
Positive forms		Negative forms	
Statement	Interrogative	Statement	Interrogative
The Timeless Definite Past I think I used to do..			
ederdim	eder miydim?	etmezdim	etmez miydim?
ederdin	eder miydin?	etmezdin	etmez miydin?
ederdi	eder miydi?	etmezdi	etmez miydi?
ederdik	eder miydik?	etmezdik	etmez miydik?
ederdiniz	eder miydiniz?	etmezdiniz	etmez miydiniz?
ederlerdi	ederler miydi?	etmezlerdi	etmezler miydi?
I used to do.	**Did I used to do?**	**I did not used to to.**	**Didn't I used to do?**

462

Future Conditional			
Positive forms		*Negative forms*	
Statement	**Interrogative**	**Statement**	**Interrogative**
Future Conditional the Future Stem with the Conditional Endings "If I am going to do.."			
edeceksem	edeceksem mi?	etmeyeceksem	etmeyeceksem mi?
edeceksen	edecekmi?	etmeyeceksen	etmeyecekmi?
edecekse	edecekse mi?	etmeyecekse	etmeyecekse mi?
edeceksek	edeceksek mi?	etmeyeceksek	etmeyeceksek mi?
edecekseniz	edecekseniz mi?	etmeyecekseniz	etmeyecekseniz mi
edecekseler (edeceklerse)	edecekseler mi? (edeceklerse mi?	etmeyecekseler (etmeyeceklerse)	Etmeyecekseler mi? (etmeyeceklerse mi?)
If I'm going to do..	**What if I'm going to do..?**	**If I'm going not to do..**	**What if I'm going not to do..?**

Necessitative Mood Tenses			
Positive forms		*Negative forms*	
Statement	**Interrogative**	**Statement**	**Interrogative**
Simple Tense of Obligation I must, I ought to, I should, I have (got) to, dit..			
etmeliyim	etmeli miyim?	etmemeliyim	etmemeli miyim?
etmelisin	etmeli misin?	etmemelisin	etmemeli misin?
etmeli(dir)	etmeli mi?	etmemeli	etmemeli mi?
etmeliyiz	etmeli miyiz?	etmemeliyiz	etmemeli miyiz?
etmelisiniz	etmeli misiniz?	etmemelisiniz	etmemeli misiniz?
etmeli(dir)ler	etmeliler mi?	etmemeliler	etmemeliler mi?
I must do.. **I ought to do..** **I should do..** **I have (got) to do..**	**Must I do..?** **Ought I to do..?** **Should I do..?** **Have I (got) to do..?**	**I must not do..** **I ought not tto..** **I should not do..** **I have not (got) to do..**	**Must I not do..?** **(Mustn't I do..?)** **Ought I not to do..?** **(Oughtn't I to do..?)** **Should I not do..?** **(Shouldn't I do..?)** **Have I not (got) to do..?** **(Haven't I (got) to do..?)**

Necessitative Past Definite			
Positive forms		*Negative forms*	
Statement	Interrogative	Statement	Interrogative
Necessitive Past Definite Relates tan actual situation I must have done.. it.			
etmeliydim	etmeli miydim?	etmemeliydim	etmemeli miydim?
etmeliydin	etmeli miydin?	etmemeliydin	etmemeli miydin?
etmeliydi	etmeli miydi?	etmemeliydi	etmemeli miydi?
etmeliydik	etmeli miydik?	etmemeliydik	etmemeli miydik?
etmeliydiniz	etmeli miydiniz?	etmemeliydiniz	etmemeli miydiniz?
etmeliydiler	etmeliler miydi?	etmemeliydiler	etmemeli miydiler?
I must have done.. I ought thave done.. I should have done.. I had (got) to do..	Must I have done..? Ought I thave done..? Should I have done..? Had I (got) to do (have done)..?	I must not have done.. I ought not thave done.. I should not have done.. I had not (got) to do (have done)..	Must I not have done..? (Mustn't I have done..?) Ought I not thave done..? (Oughtn't I thave done..?) Should I not have done..? (Shouldn't I have done..?) Had I not (got) to do (have done)..? (Hadn't I (got) to do (have done)..?)

Necessitative Past Dubitative			
Positive forms		Negative forms	
Statement	Interrogative	Statement	Interrogative
Nessecitative Past of Presumption with the Dubative endings I suppose that I should have done..it			
etmeliymişim	etmeli miymişim?	etmemeliymişim	etmemeli miymişim?
etmeliymişsin	etmeli miymişsin?	etmemeliymişsin	etmemeli miymişsin?
etmeliymiş	etmeli miymiş?	etmemeliymiş	etmemeli miymiş?
etmeliymişiz	etmeli miymişiz?	etmemeliymişiz	etmemeli miymişiz?
etmeliymişsiniz	etmeli miymişsiniz?	etmemeliymişsiniz	etmemeli miymişsiniz?
etmeliymişler	etmeli miymişler?	etmemeliymişler	etmemeli miymişler?
(I suppose)I must have done.. (I believe that) I ought thave done.. (Presumeably) I should have done.. (In reality) I had (got) to do..	Must I have done..?(it possibly..?) Ought I thave done..? (at all..?) Should I have done..? (or not..?) (I wonder) Had I (got) td(have done)..?	(Surely..?) I must not have done.. (Really..) I ought not thave done.. (Definitely..) I should not have done.. (It seems that..)I had not (got) td(have done)..	(I wonder..?) Must I not have done..? (Mustn't I have done..? (it at all..?) Ought I not thave done..? (perhaps..?) (Oughtn't I thave done..?) (maybe.?) (I think that..)Should I not have done..? (Shouldn't I have done..? (presumably..?)) (I wonder..?) Had I not (got) to do (have done)..? (in reality..?) (Hadn't I (got) to do (have done)..?)

465

Imperative Mood Tenses			
Positive forms		Negative forms	
Statement	Interrogative	Statement	Interrogative
Do it!, Let him do it! Let me do it!			
edeyim (the Wish/Desire is used in 1st person singular)	edeyim mi? (the Wish/Desire is used in 1st person singuler)	Lacking	Lacking
et (Familiar) etsene (more intimate)	Lacking	etme (Familiar)	Lacking
etsin	etsin mi?	etmesin	etmesin mi?
edelim (the Wish/Desire is used in 1st person plural)	edelim mi? (the Wish/Desire is used in 1st person plural)	Lacking	Lacking
etin (Plural and Polite) etiniz (Public and Notices) etsenize (more intimate)	Lacking	etmeyin (Plural and Polite) etmeyiniz (Public and Notices)	Lacking
etsinler	etsinler mi?	etmesinler	etmesinler mi?
Let me do.. Let you do.. Let him do.. Let us do.. Let you do.. Let them do..	**Should I do..? Ought he to do..? Should we do..? Ought they to do..?**	**Don't (you) do.. Let him not do.. Don't (you) do.. Let them not do..**	**Shouldn't he do.. Shouldn't they do..**
Note the the 1st Person Imperative is a psuedo imperative it is actually the Wish/Desire Tense which is used as in English.			

466

Conditional Mood Tenses			
Positive forms		Negative forms	
Statement	Interrogative	Statement	Interrogative
Simple Conditional Tense If I do...			
etsem	etsem mi?	etmesem	etmesem mi?
etsen	etmi?	etmesen	etmemi?
etse	etse mi?	etmese	etmese mi?
etsek	etsek mi?	etmesek	etmesek mi?
etseniz	etseniz mi?	etmeseniz	etmeseniz mi
etseler	etseler mi?	etmeseler	etmeseler mi?
If I do..	What if I do..?	If I don't do..	What if I don't do..?

Conditional Tense Present Continuous (and Future of Intention)			
Positive forms		Negative forms	
Statement	Interrogative	Statement	Interrogative
Present Progressive Conditional If I am doing.. (Future of Intention If I am going to do..)			
ediyorsam	ediyorsam mı?	etmiyorsam	etmiyorsam mı?
ediyorsan	ediyorsan mı?	etmiyorsan	etmiyorsan mı?
ediyorsa	ediyorsa mı?	etmiyorsa	etmiyorsa mı?
ediyorsak	ediyorsak mı?	etmiyorsak	etmiyorsak mı?
ediyorsanız	ediyorsanız mı?	etmiyorsanız	etmiyorsanız mı?
ediyorlarsa	ediyorlarsa mı?	etmiyorlarsa	etmiyorlarsa mı?
If I am doing.. If I'm going to do..	What if I am doing..? What if I am going to do..?	If I am not doing.. If I am not going to do..	What if I am not doing?. What if I am not going to do..?

Timeless Wide Tense (Geniş Zaman) Present and Future Conditional			
Positive forms		Negative forms	
Statement	Interrogative	Statement	Interrogative
Habitual Conditional If I was to do (all the time. Future Uncertain If I were to do...			
edersem	edersem mi?	etmezsem	etmezsem mi?
edersen	edermi?	etmezsen	etmezmi?
ederse	ederse mi?	etmezse	etmezse mi?
edersek	edersek mi?	etmezsek	etmezsek mi?
ederseniz	ederseniz mi?	etmezseniz	etmezseniz mi
ederseler (ederlerse)	ederseler (ederlerse)	etmezseler (etmezlerse)	etmezseler (etmezlerse)
If I was to do.. If I were to do..	What if I was to do..? What if I were td..?	If I was tnot do.. If were not to do..	What if I was tndo..? What if I were not to do..?

Past Definite Conditional			
Positive forms		Negative forms	
Statement	Interrogative	Statement	Interrogative
Definite Past Conditional (it actually happened) If I had done.. If I have done...			
ettiysem	ettiysem mi?	etmediysem	etmediysem mi?
ettiysen	ettiymi?	etmediysen	etmediymi?
ettiyse	ettiyse mi?	etmediyse	etmediyse mi?
ettiysek	ettiysek mi?	etmediysek	etmediysek mi?
ettiyseniz	ettiyseniz mi?	etmediyseniz	etmediyseniz mi?
ettiyseler	ettiyseler mi?	etmediyseler	etmediyseler mi?
If I had done.. If I have done..	What if had done....? What if I have done.. ..?	If I hadn't done.... If I haven't done....	What If I hadn't done..? What if I haven't done..?

Indefinite Past Conditional			
Positive forms		Negative forms	
Statement	Interrogative	Statement	Interrogative
Past Uncertain (It did not really happen) If only I had done...			
etmişsem	etmişsem mi?	etmemişsem	etmemişsem mi?
etmişsen	etmişmi?	etmemişsen	etmemişmi?
etmişse	etmişse mi?	etmemişse	etmemişse mi?
etmişsek	etmişsek mi?	etmemişsek	etmemişsek mi?
etmişseniz	etmişseniz mi?	etmemişseniz	etmemişseniz mi
etmişseler; etmişlerse	etmişseler; etmişlerse	etmemişseler etmemişlerse	etmemişseler etmemişlerse
If only I had done..	What if only I had done...?	If only I hadn't done....	What if only I hadn't done..?

Wish/Desire Mood Tenses			
Positive forms		Negative forms	
Statement	Interrogative	Statement	Interrogative
Simple Tense of Desire and Wish Let me do (it)... Should I do (it)..			
edeyim	edeyim mi?	etmeyeyim	etmeyeyim mi?
edesin	ede misin?	etmeyesin	etmeye misin?
ede	ede mi?	etmeye	etmeye mi?
edelim	edelim mi?	etmeyelim	etmeyelim mi?
edesiniz	ede misiniz?	etmeyesiniz	etmeye misiniz?
edeler	edeler mi?	etmeyeler	etmeyeler mi?
Let me do..	Should I do (or not)...?	I should not do....	Shouldn't I do (or should I)..?

Wish/Desire Past, Narrative			
Positive forms		Negative forms	
Statement	Interrogative	Statement	Interrogative
Past Tense of Desire and Wish Should I have done..			
edeydim	ede miydim?	etmeyeydim	etmeye miydim
edeydin	ede miydin?	etmeyeydin	etmeye miydin
edeydi	ede miydi?	etmeyeydi	etmeye miydi
edeydik	ede miydik?	etmeyeydik	etmeye miydik
edeydiniz	ede miydiniz?	etmeyeydiniz	etmeye miydiniz
edeydiler	ede miydiler?	etmeyeydiler	etmeye miydiler

Wish/Desire Past, Reportative			
Positive		Negative	
Statement	Interrogative	Statement	Interrogative
It seems that I should have done...			
edeymişim	ede miymişim?	etmeyeymişim	etmeye miymişim?
edeymişsin	ede miymişsin?	etmeyeymişsin	etmeye miymişsin?
edeymiş	ede miymiş?	etmeyeymiş	etmeye miymiş?
edeymişiz	ede miymişiz?	etmeyeymişiz	etmeye miymişiz?
edeymişsiniz	ede miymişsiniz?	etmeyeymişsiniz	etmeye miymişsiniz?
edeymişler	ede miymişler?	etmeyeymişler	etmeye miymişler?

Progressive Present Continuous			
Positive forms		Negative forms	
Statement	Interrogative	Statement	Interrogative
I am presently doing...			
etmekteyim	etmekte miyim?	etmemekteyim	etmemekte miyim?
etmektesin	etmekte misin?	etmemektesin	etmemekte misin?
etmektedir	etmekte midir?	etmemektedir	etmemekte midir?
etmekteyiz	etmekte miyiz?	etmemekteyiz	etmemekte miyiz?
etmektesiniz	etmekte misiniz?	etmemektesiniz	etmemekte misiniz?
etmekteldirer	etmekte midirler?	etmemektedirler	etmemekte midirler?

Progressive Past Continuous			
Positive forms		**Negative forms**	
Statement	**Interrogative**	**Statement**	**Interrogative**
I have been doing...			
etmekteydim	etmekte miydim?	etmemekteydim	etmemekte miydim?
etmekteydin	etmekte miydin?	etmemekteydin	etmemekte miydin?
etmekteydi	etmekte miydi?	etmemekteydi	etmemekte miydi?
etmekteydik	etmekte miydik?	etmemekteydik	etmemekte miydik?
etmekteydiniz	etmekte miydiniz?	etmemekteydiniz	etmemekte miydiniz?
etmektelydiler	etmekte miydiler?	etmemekteydiler	etmemekte miydiler?

Past Progressive Future Continuous			
Positive forms		**Negative forms**	
Statement	**Interrogative**	**Statement**	**Interrogative**
I shall have been doing...			
etmekte olacağım	etmekte mi olacağım?	etmekte olmayacağım	etmekte olmayacak mıyım?
etmekte olacaksın	etmekte mi olacaksın?	etmekte olmayacaksın	etmekte olmayacak mısın?
etmekte olacak	etmekte mi olacak?	etmekte olmayacak	etmekte olmayacak mı?
etmekte olacağız	etmekte mi olacağız?	etmekte olmayacağız	etmekte olmayacak mıyız?
etmekte olacaksınız	etmekte mi olacakınız?	etmekte olmayacaksınız	etmekte olmayacak mısınız?
etmekte olacaklar	etmekte mi olacaklar?	etmekte olmayacaklar	etmekte olmayacaklar mı?

Turkish Infinitive **etmek** *to do, make, perform*		
This verb is one of only five verbs in turkish which softens it root when a vowel is added.		
Infinitive	**Present**	**Past**
etmek *to do*	ediyor *he is doing*	etti *he did*
gitmek *to go*	gidiyor *he is going*	gitti *he went*
tatmak *to taste of*	tadıyor *it tastes of*	tattı *It tasted of*
ditmek *to shred*	didiyor *he shreds*	dittit *he shreded*
gütmek *to nourish*	Güdüyor- *it nourishes*	güttü *it nourished*
All other verb stems which end in **-t** such as **bitmek** *to finish* do not soften the vowel stem to a **-d -** (*bidiyor* is wrong it remains as **bitiyor**)		

45 ABOUT THE AUTHOR AND THE BOOK

The Author, the Book and a Final Note.

The Author.

I first went to Turkey in the late seventies to work a Professional Chartered Engineer in the industrial vehicle sector. I worked in a large factory in the Mersinli area of Izmir, and later in a factory in Manisa. I could not speak Turkish at that time and most of the Turkish employees could not speak English to any great extent. So I made an effort to learn their language.

Eventually my contract ended but as I had found the language so fascinating, I continued my studies back home in England. I was able eventually to pass the National Certificate Turkish Examinations and as I neared retirement I became a part-time lecturer in Turkish at my local Technical College in Coventry UK for a number of years. Eventually some years ago I emigrated from England and retired to live in New Zealand.

I set up free Turkish teaching website (Manisa Turkish) as a thank you to my many Turkish friends and acquaintances who had helped me in many ways during my stay in Turkey while I was domiciled there.

The Book.

This book is the result of notes I made while teaching and later from publishing the Manisa Turkish free website. I am not a trained linguist and I have had quite a lot of help along the road of my own Turkish learning curve. However I feel learners of all levels will find that this book will help in their understanding of Turkish for English Speakers, as most language text books do not explain many of the intricacies of the Turkish language adequately.

"The Turkish Language Explained for English Speakers" does not pretend to be a course in Turkish; there are no exercises, drills or sound files as these can be found in many other text book or on the internet. However, it explains and answers some of the difficulties that the learner of Turkish may encounter along their way.

All I can hope is that for those who are interested in the whys and wherefores of Turkish then they may find amongst these pages the key to their particular problem; I had many myself on my own learning curve. The way I have understood may not be the accepted way for the grammarians and linguists, however if it helps anybody to understand then I am happy. Good Luck.

I leave you with these few words...

Learning Turkish- Logic Reigns Supreme or Does It.

They say that Turkish is easy to learn because it is so logical. The grammar is logical and there are very few exceptions to any of its syntax rules. There is no gender, no masculine, feminine and neuter forms to master, so it must be easy. And so they say thus: the Professors, the Teachers, and especially native Turks themselves.

They say it is 'so' easy. "Why?, Doesn't a Turkish child learn to speak its mother tongue at a very early age?". You may have noticed that the professors, the lecturers and the native speakers state that this facility is so; however you may go on to notice that this list does not include Turkish Language Learners. Ask any of them, or should I say 'any of us', and for the most part you will receive an answer quite to the contrary. A resounding "No! Turkish is so difficult, I've learned the rules but I still cannot understand or make myself understood!".

So the learning road is littered with fallers by the wayside, triers to the man, but despite their industry it is all to no avail and so another well intentioned learner disappears into the distance, consumed by disappointment and their lack of success. They took their courses, they went to their classes, they watched their videos, they listened to their sound tapes and at the end of it all your friendly "Merhaba nasılsın" is met with a blank stare of misapprehension and you can see panic setting in their eyes. So why is it so?

Let us try to give an explanation not only to ourselves, the poor misunderstood Turkish Learner but also to the all the Professors and Teachers and Native Turkish Speakers who say that as Turkish is so logical then it is therefore so easy to learn.

An Analogy Explained.

Well, in these days of computing and programming, let us give an analogy, (a similarity between like features of two things, on which a comparison may be based). How many of us in our forays into computer programming, be it

474

Visual Basic, Java Script or any programming language which is built on logic and which has its own syntax rules, have spent more time debugging our efforts to produce a successful result than actually being able to use our programming "skills" naturally and with ease?

Even when we have learned the rules of syntax of any particular computing language we still meet the stumbling block of logic. Consequently, until everything is in its rightful place our program will not flow and run successfully. In our debugging trials we often have to take the way of seeking examples, be it from a book, from the world-wide web or maybe we enroll for some course or other in order to increase our ability in our endeavour.

We know that each computer language has its own dialect. Visual Basic cannot understand a Java Script programme, it does not know what to do as it is unintelligible and gobbledygook. It does not 'compile', it does not 'run'. Similarly we come against a difference in vocabulary in Turkish, we can take an "educated guess" at a word in German and the Romance Languages, but the Turkish vocabulary stumps us; it is completely alien to us and we can gather no clue to the intended meaning. We can learn some of the dialect; and we need to learn this new vocabulary by heart, but even then after applying all the rules and knowledge that we have absorbed about it we find that we still have further problems with the actual logic of the language. We can always find an example that will show us the way to surmount our difficulties, and we can only say to ourselves "I would not have thought of doing or saying it like that, myself!"

The Problems of Learning Turkish.

This was the situation that I found myself in when I went to Turkey to work in the late seventies. I did not know a word of Turkish, and at the age of forty-five I had to start somewhere. I bought a grammar book and tried to learn the rules, Vowel Harmony, Consonant Change, Affixed Post-positions (agglutination), Verbal Nouns etc. We realize that rules can be learned, but as in computer programming it is their application which becomes difficult especially when the logic of the Turkish Language is so different to that of our own mother tongue English. Moreover we are trying to apply these rules and logic to a completely different dialect. This is why Turkish is very difficult for us English Speakers.

Yes, the Professors, Teachers and Turkish Speakers are right; Turkish is an extremely structured and logical language, as proven by the fact that Turkish children learn to speak it very early in life, but it is this internal structure of the language which defeats us foreigners in our learning attempts. We just cannot "think Turkish!". We never learned how to, and probably many of us never will be able to think with Turkish logic. So even after many years of trying to learn Turkish we are labelled as speaking 'Tarzanca' in the manner of the film hero 'Tarzan of the Apes' as only the best we can do is akin to "Me Tarzan!, you Jane!".

After 34 years of learning I can tell you all that Turkish is very difficult.

John Guise *Kawerau, New Zealand October 2013*

Made in the USA
Lexington, KY
24 October 2017